EARLY MODERN SPAIN

In 1500, Spain faced the great challenge of consolidating the foundations of a new nationhood in the Iberian peninsula, following the reconquest of national territory from the Moors in 1492. At the same time, Spain was the bridge between Europe and the New World, with the exploration of the Americas and the expansion of its empire. Early modern Spain itself was relatively underpopulated, with fragmented communications, and faced the challenges of nascent capitalism common to the rest of Europe.

Early Modern Spain: A Social History explores the solidarities which held the Spanish nation together at this time of conflict and change. The book studies the pattern of fellowship and patronage at the local level which contributed to the notable absence of popular revolts characteristic of other European countries at this time. It also analyses the Counter-Reformation, which transformed religious attitudes, and which had a huge impact on family life, social control and popular culture.

Focusing on the main themes of the development of capitalism, the growth of the state and religious upheaval, this comprehensive social history sheds light on changes throughout Europe in the critical early modern period.

James Casey is Senior Lecturer in European History at the University of East Anglia.

A SOCIAL HISTORY OF EUROPE
Series Editor, Richard Evans
Professor of Modern History, University of Cambridge

A SOCIAL HISTORY OF MODERN SPAIN (1990)
Adrian Shubert

EARLY MODERN SPAIN

A social history

James Casey

London and New York

First published 1999
by Routledge
11 New Fetter Lane, London EC4P 4EE

Simultaneously published in the USA and Canada
by Routledge
29 West 35th Street, New York, NY 10001

Typeset in Baskerville by
J&L Composition Ltd, Filey, North Yorkshire
Printed and bound in Great Britain by
Redwood Books, Trowbridge, Wiltshire

British Library Cataloguing in Publication Data
A catalogue record for this book is available
from the British Library

Library of Congress Cataloging in Publication Data
Casey, James, 1944–
Early modern Spain: a social history/James Casey.
p.   cm. – (A social history of Europe)
Includes bibliographical references and index.
1. Spain – Social conditions – To 1800.   2. Spain –
Economic conditions.   3. Spain – Civilization – 1516–1700.
Spain – Civilization – 18th Century.   I. Title.   II. Series:
Social history of Europe (Routledge (Firm))
HN583.C37   1999
306′.0946–dc21   98–31118
CIP

ISBN 0–415–13813–2 (hbk)
ISBN 0–415–20687–1 (pbk)

CONTENTS

ACKNOWLEDGEMENTS

I would like to thank the editor of the series, Richard Evans, for suggesting the idea of this book, and for his helpful comments later on the text. At the publishers, Heather McCallum and Ian Critchley provided the guidance required for its completion.

I owe a debt to the staff of the University of East Anglia library, particularly Barry Taylor, for his imaginative purchase of history books in Spanish, and the excellent team at inter-library loans.

I have benefitted over many years from the encouragement and support of colleagues in Spain. I would like to thank, among many others, Ricardo García Cárcel and Xavier Gil Pujol of Barcelona, Vicent Olmos and Emilia Salvador of Valencia, Francisco Chacón and Juan Romero Díaz of Murcia, and Inmaculada Arias and Juan Luis Castellano of Granada.

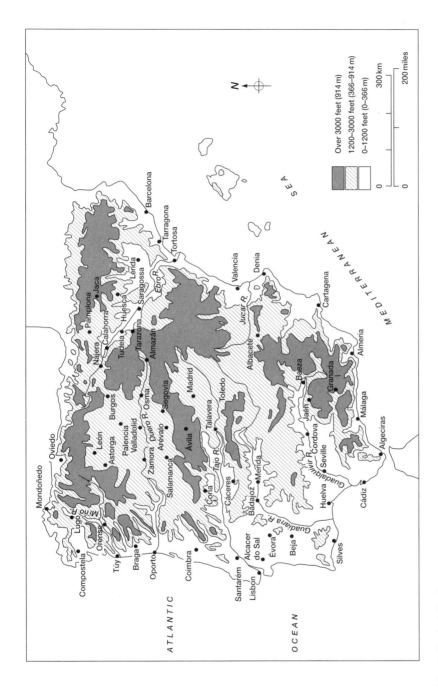

Map 1 Physical Iberia
Source: Bernard Reilly, *The Medieval Spains* (Cambridge 1993).

Map 2 Historic regions of Spain
Source: David Reher, *Town and Country in Pre-industrial Spain* (Cambridge University Press 1970).

Map 3 Places mentioned in the text

INTRODUCTION

The early modern period lacks, almost by definition, the clear features of its predecessor and successor, the medieval and modern worlds. One may say that it is an age of transition, characterised by at least three broad lines of development, in all of which the protagonist of this book, Spain, played a crucial and controversial role. In the first place there was the growth of towns and the market economy, precursor of the Industrial Revolution. One of the turning-points in this process was, of course, the discovery of America and the opening-up of a world economy. Spanish writers – the so-called School of Salamanca – made a significant contribution to our understanding of the changing structure of the market, laying the foundations of the modern science of economics.

Spain was equally involved in that other transformation of the early modern world, the rise of the bureaucratic state. Anthropologists have made us aware of the function of kinship and clientage where the state is weak and where politics cannot be easily separated from the business of everyday life. Spain was one of the pioneers in the creation in the sixteenth century of a modern polity, as the great archives of Simancas still testify, supplemented by a trail of official paper all the way down to the local level. Yet the country remained down to the twentieth century notoriously evasive of control from the centre, as the volume of work done by social anthropologists since the pioneering study of Pitt-Rivers (1954) ably attests. In any case the attempt of a stronger state to assert its authority through its army and bureaucracy is one of the characteristic features of the early modern period in Europe as a whole, and it had enormous consequences for the whole process of social and economic development. Historians sometimes call it the Age of Mercantilism, an alliance of power and profit which laid the basis of capitalism in the seventeenth and eighteenth centuries. Undoubtedly the failure of Spain to protect its own merchants, ships and American treasure helped preserve older forms of social life for longer than in other parts of Western Europe.

Linked to this traditionalism and, as an older Protestant or liberal historiography would have it, partly reinforcing it, was the influence of the Catholic Church. The early modern period had been born, in Spain as in the rest of Europe, under the sign of the Renaissance, that burst of enthusiasm for the humane, memorably summed up by Michelet as the discovery of the world and of man himself. The care for nature, and the careful observation thereof, undoubtedly laid the basis of the scientific revolution which would transform the old world out of all recognition. The writings of the Spanish humanist Luis Vives (1492–1540) are among the most beautiful of the Renaissance world in this respect, pregnant with significance for the future. But his native country was to take another route, becoming the champion of the Counter-Reformation, in a mixture of political and religious commitments which are still controversial, and, it has to be said, not well understood. For Michelet, the Counter-Reformation aborted the work of the Renaissance, condemning much of Europe to absolute monarchy and the tyranny of aristocracy, before the French Revolution took up again the torch of liberation. The link between religion and economic or social forms struck Joseph Townsend, a Wiltshire rector and sharp-eyed, though fair-minded, observer of Spain in the course of his perambulations through the country in 1786–7. The excessive ornamentation of the churches in Barcelona, he thought, was due to the gold and silver of the Indies, which 'came upon them by surprise, and found them unprepared to make a proper use of the abundant treasure'.[1]

Much of the most exciting work in social history nowadays is being done in the realm of popular culture, in the sense of the exploration of the values and solidarities perceived by ordinary people themselves rather than in terms of structures imposed upon them by the historian. There has been a departure from the overarching framework of modernisation which once gave the economist a privileged place as guide to the past. It is certainly a more humane approach to the lives of our ancestors, and its focus is the small-scale community – the family, the neighbourhood, the village. It poses obvious problems for the historian who would attempt to write a social history of the nation-state. No doubt the challenge, in the case of Spain, is that of making sense of the constant interplay between centre and periphery – between the great forces of capitalism sweeping in from America and the 'timeless' life of the peasantry, between the king's judges and tax-collectors and the local elites whose networks of influence constituted an alternative source of power, and finally between the priest or inquisitor and the local wielders of spiritual power, folk-healers and visionaries.

In general, the fascination of pre-industrial Europe lies in understanding ourselves better through the reconstruction of the experiences of those who faced challenges and lived by values other than our own. The struggle of humanity with the environment has now become so specialised and professional that it hardly enters the consciousness of most of us that food, clothing and shelter are something more than items of exchange. Perhaps the first great triumph of social history was in the field of historical geography – the exploration of local communities through a proper understanding of their natural environment and an intuitive sympathy with the material and moral civilisation which they developed in response. This was the memorable achievement of the *Annales* School in the early part of this century. And it was also the French who pioneered the technique of historical demography as a way of getting at the history of the silent majority. It was the social anthropologists who reminded us that economics and demography are, in a sense, dependent on one other factor, sometimes undervalued by the local historian: the creation of viable and stable political entities. Otherwise life is apt to be brutish and short. Hence the preoccupation of the social anthropologist, as we noted, with the exploration of solidarities, and in particular with kinship. That the beliefs of people about what they are doing may be of relevance to the social historian was amply demonstrated by Max Weber in his seminal essay of 1904, *The Protestant Ethic and the Spirit of Capitalism*. Social historians need few promptings nowadays to take this approach.

In the pages that follow, an attempt will be made to explore the character and development of Spanish society between about 1500 and about 1800 from some of these viewpoints. Given the size of the country and the length of the period, the task will not always be easy. Dominating the historiography of Spain has been the phenomenon of economic and military decline from the status of a world power. Attempts to understand and arrest this decline give a certain coherence to the period. The change of dynasty in 1700, from Habsburg to Bourbon, perhaps marked a less radical break than is sometimes imagined, as the government pursued efforts to maintain the American empire and a large fleet in the Atlantic, although the old interference in northern and central Europe, characteristic of the sixteenth and seventeenth centuries, was abandoned. If Spain became a lesser power on the European horizon in the eighteenth century, the long-standing problems of a weak economy and an unbalanced social structure continued to generate political debate, and provide the historian with new insights into the character of Spanish civilisation as a whole.

Thus, Chapters 1 to 4 seek to explore some of the structural constraints on the economy, which kept the country in a 'frontier' situation, as it were – under-populated, ill-integrated – long after the political reconquest from the Moor. Though Spain had major handicaps stemming from the physical environment, the crucial factor in this traditionalism must surely be social and political relation-ships. In a pioneering essay, the philosopher Ortega y Gasset argued that his country – alas for it – had never fully experienced feudalism. A too numerous warrior nobility and fortress towns created a kind of egalitarian and decentralised commonwealth, which the failure of empire tended to reinforce. This is the basic framework of our analysis in Chapters 5 to 7, which look in turn at the nature of late feudalism, the integration of townsmen into a culture of honour and depen-dence, and the difficult equilibrium achieved between the monarchy and its more powerful subjects. Finally, the stability and longevity of that commonwealth depended on a certain culture of civility or good citizenship – on attitudes to law and order, on loyalty to family and clan, on respect for the gods and the precepts of morality – whose transformation in the early modern period laid so many of the foundations of the world in which we still live.

3

1

AN INHOSPITABLE LAND

A country of which 'we had little experience or knowledge in the days of our forefathers': such was the impression which the Venetian Michele Suriano carried home with him at the end of his embassy to the Spanish court in 1559. At the western extremity of the ancient and medieval worlds, cut off from Europe by the Pyrenees (a more impenetrable, if less lofty, barrier than the Alps), Spain had been locked for more than seven centuries in those civil wars known as the Reconquest, which ended with the fall of the last Muslim kingdom of Granada in 1492, and which determined that the country would belong to Christendom rather than to Islam. Stretched out 'like an ox-hide', in the words of the famous classical geographer Strabo, writing in the first century BC, Iberia appeared at the time as a poor, mountainous land, 'whose soil is thin – and even that not uniformly well watered'. With few cities, and few good harbours between Tarragona and the Pillars of Hercules (the western limits of the ancient world), the peninsula nevertheless possessed one navigable river, which fertilised its banks and stimulated trade – the Baetis, or Guadalquivir ('Great River'), as the Moors were to rebaptise it. From these lands of Seville and Cordoba came the grain, wine and olive oil which were exported in quantity to Rome, and here was to be the heart of Muslim power for centuries after the fall of Rome.

Though Spain made a distinctive contribution to classical civilisation, the general impression of later writers, not least Spaniards themselves, was that the country had been somewhat on the margin. In his introduction to one of the early geographies of the peninsula, that of Méndez Silva in 1645, the historiographer Pellicer commented that few classical writers, either Greek or Roman, had left adequate accounts 'of matters affecting us'. Things had got worse as a result of the political chaos caused by the Arab invasions, and he thought that it was only now that a proper inventory of the country, its people, resources and history, could be made.

Pellicer was neglectful, as most of his contemporaries were, of the work of the Arab geographers. The Arab invasion of 711 might be regarded as a continuation of those links with Africa which since prehistoric times and with the Carthaginians had led to the transfer of manpower and culture across the Straits of Gibraltar. But the Spain that we know took shape through a long guerrilla war against Islam,

4

led by Christian chiefs who had taken refuge in the impenetrable Cantabrian and Pyrenean mountain chains. One of these, the king of León, began to reassert old notions of Hispanic unity, under himself as Emperor (Alfonso VI 1065–1109). His control of the increasingly important pilgrimage site of Santiago de Compostela – famed throughout Christendom, along with Rome and Jerusalem – no doubt explains his pre-eminence. The emergence of a more tangible unity among the different Christian kingdoms was a slower process: by the thirteenth century León and Castile had been definitively united, and the Crown was beginning to be looked upon as an inalienable trust rather than a private patrimony which could be divided among several sons. The subsequent dynastic unions of Castile with the Crown of Aragon (marriage of Isabel of Castile with Ferdinand of Aragon in 1469), and then with Portugal (sucession of Philip II to the Portuguese throne in 1580) completed the restoration, as men believed, of that old Roman Iberia, promising a new Augustan age of peace and prosperity.

To say, as did the Venetian ambassador in 1559, that other Europeans had had 'little experience' of the Spaniards before his own day, is somewhat misleading. The Mediterranean coastline had been in continual contact with the south of France since the early Middle Ages. James I of Aragon (1213–76), the famous conqueror of the Balearic Islands and Valencia from the Moors, was the son of the countess of Montpellier, and the culture and language of his new conquests were to be largely that variety of Occitan which obtained in Catalonia. But James's father, Peter II, had been killed in 1213 at the decisive battle of Muret, which gave control of the Languedoc to the king of France, in the name of a crusade against the Albigensian heresy, and ended effectively any Spanish pretensions north of the Pyrenees. However, the expansion of the Crown of Aragon along the Mediterranean coast of Iberia in the following generation opened up new possibilities of trade and naval power. Thanks to the resources of those great emporia, the cities of Barcelona and Valencia, an Aragonese maritime empire began to take shape, with the conquest of the islands of Sicily (1282) and Sardinia (1323–4), and mainland Naples (1435). Castile, high up on the central tableland and turned away from the Mediterranean, was developing significant naval and commercial links through Biscay with the cities of north-west Europe in the later Middle Ages. Its conquest of Granada gave it control of navigation through the Straits of Gibraltar. In the same year (1492), it patronised the voyage of Columbus, which opened up the Atlantic world to commercial activity of a kind which would soon outstrip that of the old inland sea of Europe and North Africa.

One further political event must be considered before we can situate Spain within the early modern world. The succession of the Habsburg Charles V, grandson of the Catholic Kings, Ferdinand and Isabel, to the Spanish Crown in 1516 brought these southern realms right into the heart of European politics at a particularly sensitive time, that of the Reformation and the beginning of the wars of religion. With Charles V, Spain found her destinies yoked to some of the most wealthy, but most fought-over areas of Europe – Flanders, Franche-Comté, eventually Milan (1535–40), not to mention Austria and the German empire, which, after his retirement, was assigned to Charles's brother and not to his son, the Spanish king Philip II (1556–98). Charles V, a Fleming by birth and French by tongue, had no fixed headquarters and spent much of his time outside Spain, though returning there to prepare for death. In the reports of the Venetian ambassadors at this time, Spain tends to figure merely as one part of a federal empire. Antonio Tiepolo (1567) may be the first to signal a new reality. He would pay more attention to Spain than to the other states of the monarchy, he told the senate, because it was 'the most important of all the realms of this most serene king'.

In the history books the period between the treaties of Cateau Cambrésis (1559) and Westphalia (1648) is conventionally known as that of the hegemony of Spain, arbiter of the destinies of Europe. Thereafter a much weakened Spain, stripped of her European possessions in a series of treaties culminating with Utrecht (1713), tends to fade from the textbooks. Yet this state maintained through much of the eighteenth century the third most important fleet in Europe, after that of Britain and France, and, as mistress of much of America, continued to play a significant role in the Atlantic world. It is only with the defeat of the Spanish navy at Trafalgar (1805), and the subsequent loss of control in America, confirmed by the independence of most of the former colonies by 1825, that Spain passed definitively to the second rank of European powers.

In its heyday the empire conferred on this rather poor, once marginal European country, a unique attractiveness. Perhaps the most gifted and certainly the most eloquent of the Venetian ambassadors, Leonardo Donà (1570–3), conveys all the excitement which men of the time felt at the reports of the conquests of Mexico and Peru, and marvelled at a court masque to celebrate the birth of a son to Philip II, in which the portrayal of the submission of two Indian princes 'gave us foreign observers an idea of how great is the power of Castile'. And later ambassadors, like Girolamo Soranzo (1608–11), were dazzled by the silver and gold landed at Seville, the pearls and diamonds at Lisbon. Even the financially exhausted and militarily crippled Spain of 1664–6 could still impress Lady Ann Fanshawe, wife of the British ambassador with the 'curiositys brought from Italy and the Indies', the silver and chocolate (still a novelty) from America, the lacquered or ivory cabinets from India or Japan. The sense of cosmopolitanism, at least in Seville and at court, and of being at the heart of the world was captured in the saying, reported by the French traveller Jouvin in 1672, 'that mass is said at every hour of the day in some part of their empire, that the sun shines there all the time, for when it has set in Spain it is casting its rays in America'.[1]

This imperial radiance was associated with a golden age of Spanish art, literature and learning. Spanish treatises on government, on warfare, on the exploration of the New World became particularly popular in the sixteenth century, followed by an admiration for poetry, plays and novels. Sir Richard Fanshawe, husband of Lady Ann mentioned above, was a gifted translator of Spanish and Portuguese poetry. Inevitably the far-flung nature of the Spanish dominion led to a study of its language and culture, even by its enemies. Queen

Elizabeth may have been the last British monarch to read and speak Spanish, an example imitated by her chief secretary Burghley. The Puritan party at court – men like Sir Philip Sidney and Edmund Spenser – were under the spell of Spanish romances of chivalry. One of Secretary Walsingham's correspondents wrote in 1582 that he was learning the Spanish language, 'which I plainly see that he who would go about in the world ought to know'.[2]

Most people nowadays will think of El Greco, Velázquez, Murillo – and, of course, also of Cervantes – when they evoke the Spanish Golden Age. But Spanish painting – and even more the rich tradition of polychrome sculpture – was less appreciated abroad initially than Spanish books. Some interest was shown by foreign merchants in Murillo, during and soon after his own lifetime; but Spanish art remained to be discovered by the Romantics – like the country itself, which began to attract gentlemen of leisure (as distinct from merchants and ambassadors) during the later eighteenth century. In 1779 Secretary of State Floridablanca deplored the fact that 'some foreigners are buying up in Seville all the canvases that they can acquire of Bartolomé Murillo and other famous painters, and sending them abroad', and he introduced new restrictions.[3] Joseph Townsend's sensitivity to the beauties of the Alhambra palace in Granada in the course of his visit of 1787 is an early symptom of the Romantic appreciation of the exotic, which would heighten sympathy for things Spanish in nineteenth-century Europe.

But for most of the early modern period Spain was trying to live down its Moorish past. The indefatigable traveller and art critic Antonio Ponz, whose journeys across his native land in the 1770s and 1780s are such a mine of information for the social historian, was typical of the classical temper which marked the culmination and waning of early modern civilisation. For him, the Spanish cities, with their narrow, crooked streets and intimate, rambling buildings had to be explained away as an unfortunate legacy of the Islamic period. The Venetian ambassadors shared a similar impression. Federico Badoero in 1557 found most Spanish towns 'neither beautiful nor clean'; and his successor Francesco Soranzo in 1602 commented that, compared with their European counterparts, 'they are remarkable neither for the splendour of their buildings, nor for the beauty of their streets, nor for the grandeur of their public squares'. The qualities which later generations would come to admire, the intimacy of the little squares and labyrinthine neighbourhoods, held little attraction for the classical mind.

The Venetians, and more generally the Italians, were not only the arbiters of good taste in the sixteenth and much of the seventeenth centuries, but also the supreme exponents of political philosophy. They first drew attention to the para-dox of Spain: a great empire which seemed very insecurely balanced on the shoulders of a poor and backward people. Giovanni Botero (1544–1617), one of the pioneers of political economy, helped shape contemporary views of Spain as a giant with feet of clay through his influential writings. He had no first-hand knowledge of the country until a visit he made there in 1603–6, well after he had published his criticism. But from Strabo and from travellers' tales he could find out enough to make some telling points. 'Generally mountainous and lacking in water', Spain had few rivers, therefore few opportunities to build markets and towns, or expand her population. The Spanish temperament, as described in the classical authors and as appeared to be confirmed by the persecutions and wars of Botero's own day, was more attuned to war than to the arts of peace. 'No country is more lacking in crafts and industry,' he thought.

The peninsula lay, in some senses, with its back to Europe. The Pyrenees had few accessible passes. The fertile Mediterranean coastline, the natural gateway to Europe, had few good harbours, and backed on to the high, bare continental plateau of Castile, the meseta. The best harbours, and the easiest communications with the interior, by mule if not by river, faced west, out into the long uncharted waters of the Atlantic. The central tableland had an average altitude of 660 metres (just under 2,200 feet), making the country the most elevated in Europe after Switzerland. A high, squat landmass, Iberia generates a kind of continental climate of its own, with extremes of heat and cold.

Three main features determine the climate of the peninsula. First there is its southerly latitude – considerably to the south of most of Italy, for example. Then one has to take into account the altitude of much of the landmass, which can lead to cold and snow in Old Castile and León, that is those areas to the north of Madrid and the Guadarrama mountains, which bisect the meseta in two. Here the average altitude rises to 1,000 metres above sea level, where, according to a saying related by the Venetian envoy in 1525, there are ten months of *invierno* (winter) and two of *infierno* (hellfire).[4] The third factor shaping the climate of Spain is the westward thrust of the peninsula out into the Atlantic, exposed, therefore, to the cloud, winds and rain from the great ocean. The north-western seaboard, including Galicia and its great pilgrimage centre of Santiago de Compostela, tends to get a lot of rain. Even the south-west, including the fertile valley of the Guadalquivir, is swept generously by the rainclouds in autumn and spring. But the altitudes there are generally low (200 metres on average), and the southerly latitudes lead to rapid evaporation, creating problems of aridity particularly in the summer months. One of the great conditioning influences on the peninsula has been, as Botero put it, the 'lack of water'. In general, as one gets further back from the Atlantic shoreline, rising gradually to altitudes of 800–1,000 metres in the eastern and northern mesetas, the rainclouds peter out. About half of the landmass gets under 500 millimetres (about 20 inches) of rain a year, creating what is known as a semi-arid climate.

Linked to the question of aridity is the lack of tree-cover, commented upon by travellers in the early modern period. A narrow belt – perhaps one-tenth of the surface area – along the Pyrenees, Cantabrian Mountains and Galicia can boast a good natural cover of chestnut, beech and grass. But south of the Cantabrians the landscape is and was steppe-like, on the high Castilian plateau. Antonio Ponz commented on the consequences: the erosion of the soil, the evaporation of what moisture there was, the shortage of firewood and the lack of building materials.[5] The chestnut, needing the rains of north and west Spain, ventured timidly down as far as the Tagus (or beyond, in the west). But the characteristic tree of the Castilian steppe was the stubby, drought-resistant evergreen oak. A kind of climatic frontier was crossed south of the Guadarrama mountains and south of the Tagus River, as one entered New Castile. Here the olive, dreading frosts and happy with little water, came into its own. Further south still, beyond the Sierra Morena, one came to the old Arab heartland of Andalusia, which linked up, via the mountainous kingdom of Granada, with the other Moorish stronghold of south-eastern Spain, Valencia. These areas were famed for their warmth and fertility. The Andalusian Pedro de Medina, in one of the early geographies of Spain (1548), praised Valencia's river banks 'lined with roses and flowers', with 'poplars, pines and other trees'. And that other pioneering geographer, Rodrigo Méndez Silva (1645), found it full of 'gardens, orchards, groves'.

Overall, Méndez Silva's impression of Spain was flattering: a land of 'abundance', blessed with 'the most agreeable, temperate climate in all Europe', halfway between the cold of France and the heat of North Africa. But the future Philip II is found writing to his father in 1545 that the country could never match the subsidies paid by France to its monarch: 'The infertility of these realms is well known to Your Majesty, and one bad year can throw our people into poverty.' And the Jesuit historian Mariana lamented towards the end of the century that lack of rainfall often meant that 'the harvest will not repay the cost of farming'.[6]

The great problem facing most of the peninsula was the thinness of the soil (aggravated by deforestation) and the irregular distribution of water. Much of the northern tableland receives less than 500 millimetres (about 20 inches) of rain a year, much of southern Castile under 400, the higher figure generally being taken as the lower limit for comfortable farming. In the fertile basin of the Guadalquivir, where the Atlantic breezes bring in up to 700 millimetres a year, the supply is concentrated in torrential spring downpours; here the problem is to prevent evaporation during the intense heat of summer.

One of the features of the Iberian landscape which is still marked is the great contrast between regions. Not only is the central plateau difficult of access from the Mediterranean, but it is itself traversed by mountain barriers. We may start with the Cantabrian Mountains to the north, shielding Castile from the Bay of Biscay. Here the Christian armies had taken refuge in the eighth century from the Moorish invaders, and from here had launched the campaigns of Reconquest. The Iberian sierras, sweeping south from there towards the Mediterranean coast, helped foster the separate political identity of the Crown of Aragon, a medieval frontier only partially overcome with the marriage of Ferdinand and Isabel in 1469. Then the Central System, with its centrepiece the Guadarrama mountains to the north of Madrid, separates Old from New Castile. The Christians had built up their towns and settlements behind the Guadarrama, in the land of chestnut, snow and Romanesque churches, before launching the hardest-fought part of the Reconquest, the struggle of the twelfth century for control of New Castile. After New Castile, the Muslims were entrenched behind the Sierra Morena in Andalusia, and beyond and below the Iberian mountains in Valencia. They lost control of these in the thirteenth century. The Sub-Baetic mountains and the desert country of the south-east guaranteed the survival of the last Moorish kingdom, that of Granada, until 1492.

Though the mountains of Spain help to explain some of the human and political development of the peninsula, they were not in themselves great impediments to communication, if the will was there. The Pyrenees and Cantabrians certainly posed formidable problems, with only a limited number of crossings which man or beast could use. The other mountain ranges were more easily passable, at least in the good season. The altitude of the central tableland itself meant, though, that in winter many of the sierras received 20–40 inches of snow, sufficient to block the higher passes for two to three months of the year.[7] The papal nuncio Camillo Borghese was held up on the road from Aragon to Castile by snow in January 1594, as had been the king himself shortly before, travelling in the opposite direction from Castile to Aragon to hold a parliament there at the beginning of February 1585. The Cortes (parliament) of Castile urged in 1588 that 'it would be most useful to erect high stone plinths on the mountain passes to mark out the road, for it happens day after day when the snows fall . . . that travellers lose their way and fall into the ravines'.[8]

In pre-industrial Europe traffic tended to follow the rivers, and here Spain was at a clear disadvantage. As the Venetian ambassador noted in 1602, 'there are few rivers, and none of them can be called really navigable'. Of the five great rivers of the peninsula, four – the Duero, Tagus, Guadiana and Guadalquivir – flowed into the vast emptiness of the Atlantic; only the Ebro linked up with the heart of the classical and medieval world, the Mediterranean. But such discussion is academic, since none of the five was easy to navigate anyway. They carry at times a great volume of water, when the snows melt near their source, or when the autumn rains fall; but then they run very low in the heat of summer. And the steepness of the fall from the central tableland to the coast, particularly on the Mediterranean side, creates rapids – rendering the Ebro, for example, unsafe in places. Plans were afoot in early modern Spain to tame the rivers. The Cortes of 1583–5 held long debates on making the Tagus navigable, from Toledo to Lisbon, according to plans submitted by the great Italian engineer Giovanni Batista Antonelli. The date was significant: the Crown of Portugal had been assumed by Philip II in 1580, and it was hoped that if the Tagus could be made safe for boats, trade between the Portuguese and the Spanish would flourish and 'a good basis would be laid for strengthening that perpetual peace and friendship which it is necessary should exist between us'. Alternatively, any 'stirring or disturbance or hint of such in Portugal' could be the more easily countered by sending troops down by boat. The technical problems – lack of water in summer, rapids – could be mastered 'with weirs and dams'. Hopes were expressed that the Duero and the Guadalquivir (from Seville up to Cordoba) might be made navigable in the same way.[9]

The impressive engineering feat was actually achieved, as regards the Tagus, by 1588. But the cost of maintaining the locks seems to have been too great, and the river reverted to its former state within a few years. Economic factors were clearly more important than engineering. Seville had expressed concern that goods from the New World would now reach the central tableland through Lisbon; León protested that its network of fairs would no longer attract English, Flemish or French goods imported through the Cantabrian ports, since these would now also take the route to Lisbon. In fact, the Tagus was made navigable on the strict condition that only the wares of Portugal and Portuguese Asia should be allowed up the river at all. With such a restriction in force the whole enterprise was surely not cost-efficient, and its abandonment can hardly cause surprise.

It required the more centralist government of the Bourbons after 1700, and particularly the enlightened absolutism of Charles III (1759–88), to take up the challenge anew. Joseph Townsend was able to inspect the herculean enterprise of making the Ebro navigable, with 2,000 soldiers and 1,000 peasants digging away earth for canals. It was the intention to link up these with another big canal traversing Old Castile, so that the Mediterranean could be joined to the Bay of Biscay. The Castilian canal had actually been initiated in 1752 under the marquis of Ensenada. As Townsend noted in 1786, Spain needed long years of peace in order to complete this gargantuan task; but within a few years of his writing the country was swept into the whirlwind of war against the French Revolution and Napoleon, which led to the collapse of the old regime. The canals were never finished.[10]

Unable to be exploited for navigation, the rivers set up obstacles of their own to communication. Though the main ones had long been bridged, the smaller often exercised the ingenuity of the traveller desirous of crossing them. Antonio Ponz was indignant that the main road south-east from Madrid could be cut when the rains came, at a point only five and a half kilometres out of the imperial capital, at the ford of Vallecas. Yet from this village had to come every day 'a great part of the bread which is eaten in Madrid'. Three leagues (16.8 kilometres) further on, one had to cross the Jarama by a small ferry-boat; but if the river was in spate, one had to swing some thirty kilometres south to the nearest bridge, which lay in the vicinity of the royal palace of Aranjuez. On the road south from Madrid to Toledo, commented Ponz at another time, just four small bridges would make all the difference; but the villages along the way preferred to spend their money building church towers – 'a rather mistaken form of piety', when benevolence towards one's fellow man seemed the first duty of religion as the Enlightenment was coming to believe.[11] The need for bridges across the smaller rivers was not really appreciated in an age when travel was so intermittent, and when the expense fell on the locality. A majority of deputies to the Cortes of 1586–8 criticised the government for authorising too many schemes for bridges, without offering any funds of its own to help along the work.

The main rivers had adequate provision anyway since medieval times. There were four bridges across the Tagus, for example, between Toledo and the Portuguese frontier. On the other hand the supply could not be regarded as generous: thus there was no crossing of the Guadalquivir between Seville and Cordoba. And the bridges that did exist were not always reliable. So the Valencian

Cortes of 1563 complained that the crossing of the Xúquer and Corbera, which cut this Mediterranean kingdom in half, was 'very dangerous, because the bridges over these rivers are of wood, and so usually when the floods come they break . . . and persons and animals are occasionally drowned'. But though the local town, Cullera, was authorised at this time to levy a toll in order to build in stone, it had to confess in 1585 that the engineering techniques were beyond it: the river bottom was too sandy, the pillars simply sank, and it returned to a pontoon bridge. Silting was a major problem in the lower reaches of many Spanish rivers, given the steepness of their drop to the coastal plains. This was the reason that there was only a pontoon bridge across the Ebro at Tortosa – an inviting target for incendiaries in 1640 when the Catalan rebels tried to cut the main coastal route south to Valencia. And it proved impossible to build a stone bridge over the river at Seville, for all the wealth and power of that city. By comparison one understands the pride with which the chronicler Escolano could speak in 1610 of the five stone bridges across the Turia at Valencia city, 'each two shots of an arquebus from the next, something which it would be hard to find in any other great city in the world'.[12]

As one accompanies travellers and chroniclers round the peninsula one gets a vivid impression of a vast, underpopulated and uncharted world. Travel was an adventure. You can choose, wrote Ponz, between being scorched on the roads in summer for the lack of trees, or lose your way in winter, with snow, floods and lack of food. On the main highway from Barcelona to court, in the vicinity of Zaragoza, the inns were as bad as the roads, he wrote: short of everything the traveller needed. The count of Gondomar, ambassador to England between 1613 and 1618, got to know the roads well between Madrid, then capital of a world empire, and the Cantabrian ports. His verdict was that 'travelling through (Spain) is more painful and uncomfortable than through any deserted region anywhere in Europe, for there are no beds to be had, no inns, no food'.[13]

In days when horse-power was crucial for getting about, Spain suffered a further disadvantage. The French cleric Barthélemy Joly noted in 1603 that on crossing the Pyrenees one left a land of horses and entered one of mules and ponies. Spain could boast fine Arabian thoroughbreds, but they were scarce, and the smuggling of horses abroad to France was an offence so grave that it came under the jurisdiction of the Inquisition. The problem basically was that 'in almost no part of Spain is there hay or oats, just barley and short straw, as unappetising as one of our mats'. And, Joly went on, it was hard to find horse combs, stable-litter or trained stable-lads in the inns.[14] Don Quixote had, of course, to content himself with a nag, the famous Rocinante. Spain was, above all, the land of the mule. The parliaments of Philip II specified how many leagues a hired mule could be expected to travel in a day, and how much the guide should be paid. Do not pay the muleteer in advance, advised the papal nuncio Borghese in 1594; rather, give him what he needs by the day to buy fodder, and insist that you will not pay for extra days caused by the tiredness or illness of his animals along the way. Here and in Borghese's careful annotations of the amount of money the traveller will need to carry, and the quantity of provisions, there emerges the overwhelming uncertainty of travel in the early modern period. One had to keep a record of the towns where one could hope to find food, lodging, facilities for changing money, before pursuing the next stage of one's journey. Parts of the diary of Borghese's contemporary, Bernardo Catalá de Valeriola (1568–1607), an inveterate traveller between his native Valencia and the court, reflect the informal mapping of routes which the prudent man did for himself in those days.

The routes across the peninsula, in fact, are not always those most familiar to us nowadays. The highway from Valencia to Catalonia did not follow the coast as it does nowadays, but swung inland through the hill country towards the now half-forgotten but then busy staging-post of Sant Mateu. In Sant Mateu the master of the chivalric order of Montesa held his court, and one could therefore be sure of food and protection. Travellers heading north from Madrid towards the Cantabrian ports preferred the easier but longer route via the large town of Valladolid. Urgent dispatches of letters or of fish from the coast might take the modern path over the Somosierra Pass, but there was no proper road here until the 1780s and none suitable for carts until some time after that. Similarly travellers from the court to Valencia would find it easier to take the more circuitous route via the strategic corridor of Almansa (used by the Bourbon armies in 1707 to force their way into the Habsburg-controlled Mediterranean kingdom) rather than risk the direct but dangerous mountain pass which led down from the meseta to the coast. Though a road had been opened here in 1427 to facilitate Valencian access to the wheat-fields of the central tableland, it remained down to the end of the old regime a twisted, uneven track, cut by mountain torrents and infested by bandits.[15]

Perhaps more surprising was the poor state of communications between the political and commercial capitals of empire, Madrid and Seville. The direct road nowadays is through the pass of Despeñaperros ('Dog's Leap'), but work on this was only begun in 1779. There seems always to have been a crossing in this vicinity: the Venetian ambassador Navagero probably used it in 1525 when he referred to the utterly 'depopulated and barren' countryside through which he passed. Building a decent route through Despeñaperros required not only feats of engineering, but also the strengthening of security against bandits, which Charles III tried to achieve by planting colonies of German farmers in the vicinity. Before then the main road lay further to the west, through the now half-forgotten Almodóvar del Campo, which boldly told the king's commissioners in 1575 that it was 'a vital and obligatory stage between the two provinces' (of Castile and Andalusia), having no less than 'twenty public inns' to cater for the traffic.[16] Nearby the 'Royal City' of Ciudad Real was founded by Alfonso the Wise, after the conquest of Andalusia, in much the same spirit as Charles III's colonies near Despeñaperros, with the aim of securing the main road south.

The most frequented route south, since classical times, lay through Extrema-dura, towards the Portuguese frontier. The generally lower altitudes and milder climate of this Atlantic façade of the meseta may have facilitated settlement. The ruins of the famous Roman city of Mérida are in this region, once at the centre of a major network of communications, which led up to Salamanca, the great university town of the later Middle Ages and on to the fairs of León. Down this route came most of the transhumant sheep, which were the wealth of the peninsula, to their winter pastures, and along it went most of the Conquistadors and settlers of the New World. Here the shrine of Guadalupe began to rival Santiago de Compostela from the fourteenth century. But from that time a gradual shift in population, wealth and communication took place towards the east, as the last threat from the Muslim stronghold in Granada receded.

Routes had to be built up in segments, through a proliferation of settlements which conferred security and markets. How else can we explain the importance of a little town like Torre de Juan Abad (300 families), which claimed in 1575 to be 'on the royal highway used by the carts which cross the Sierra Morena coming from Seville and Granada and Andalusia to the court of Madrid and La Mancha'?[17] No doubt the roads here were easier for carts than further west; but perhaps the access to the markets of the flourishing towns of Baeza and Ubeda, gems of the Renaissance but now off the beaten track, had something to do with it as well. The modern period has seen a concentration and simplification of the network of communications as the old pattern of local exchanges ceases to have much meaning.

How big was Spain for the traveller in the days of the mule? Ponz once noted that in Castile men counted by leagues (5.6 kilometres), and in the Crown of Aragon by how far one could travel on foot in an hour – 'which for the traveller comes to the same thing'.[18] The Cortes of 1579–82 expected the hired muleteer to cover nine or ten leagues in a day. Generally, therefore, 50–60 kilometres would seem to constitute a good day's journey at the time. Leaving Valencia on 25 June 1603, the diarist Bernardo Catalá de Valeriola tells us that he reached Madrid, some 350 kilometres away, on 30 June, while his return in winter took slightly longer, from 8 to 14 December. It took the papal nuncio Borghese seven days to get from Madrid to Valencia in the summer of 1594, while Joseph Townsend spent fourteen days in a hired carriage, drawn by seven mules, to cover twice that distance between Barcelona and Madrid in May 1786.[19] On the scale of those days, and with no navigable rivers, Spain constituted a formidable landmass: a fortnight to get from the chief Mediterranean port, Barcelona, inland to the capital, Madrid, and easily another ten days to get from there down to Seville, gateway to the New World.

The mail could achieve faster speeds, it is true. A regular postal service was set up between Valencia and Madrid in the early sixteenth century, with riders guaranteeing to cover a minimum of ten leagues a day, and, if they were paid extra, up to twenty leagues (112 kilometres), which seems to have been regarded as a kind of physical limit. By the early seventeenth century the ordinary mail left Madrid on Sunday and arranged to get to Valencia by Wednesday. The king's business could be dispatched a little faster. The Cortes of 1645 accepted that grievances could be submitted to Madrid, considered, and a reply returned all within ten days. But this was an emergency procedure, and the very length of the interval perhaps suggests some of the limitations to the exercise of political authority from the centre in those days.

Returning to the ordinary traveller, one may note the improvements which were being introduced towards the end of the old regime. After 1763 stage-coaches offered a regular service, once a week, from Madrid to Barcelona or Seville. They promised to cut the old journey time in half, to just six days; but they remained scarce and expensive. No doubt improvements to the roads and the mountain passes under Charles III made such speeds increasingly feasible. But the roads in much of the peninsula remained very uncertain down to the nineteenth century. Théophile Gautier noted how difficult it was to find the road between Malaga and Cordoba in 1840 – 'a fanciful road, hardly even a beaten track, cut by deep ravines at every step'. And George Borrow shortly before lost his way between Salamanca and Valladolid on the Queen's highway, which seemed to him more like 'a medley of bridle-paths and drift ways, where discrimination is very difficult'.[20]

Travellers' tales gradually built up a sense of what Spain was like, but it was a slow process. Maps had been devised first for the seafarer, showing coastlines and havens – the famous portolan charts. The Catalan–Mallorcan school had built up a pioneering reputation for making these, a work ably pursued by the House of Trade in Seville after the discovery of the Indies. But it is somewhat paradoxical that the interior of Spain itself should have been so badly known. The chronicler Escolano complained in 1610 about the inaccuracies in the classical maps of Ptolemy and others, on which much reliance had still to be placed. They gave no latitudes, he commented, or projections from the poles. Because the technical skills of engraving were better there, maps of the peninsula tended to be produced in Flanders; but sheer ignorance of Spain as a country meant that even the famous Ortelius map 'has shuffled the true names and positions of almost all towns', at least in the kingdom of Valencia. Escolano was left to speculate ironically whether future generations would think there had been two Valencias, that of Ortelius and the real one.[21]

The sixteenth century saw heroic attempts to map the peninsula, but in ways which may strike later generations as not fully scientific. What has been called the 'first guide to Imperial Spain' – though perhaps the epithet belongs to Fernando, the son of Christopher Columbus, who attempted a similar task a generation earlier – is that published by Pedro de Medina in 1548. Dedicated to the heir to the throne, the future Philip II, it aimed to teach him about the mighty nation over which he would one day rule. Medina was famous for his cartography of the Atlantic, where Spanish ships ruled the waves, and for his history of the dukes of Medina Sidonia, his fellow Andalusians and patrons. These twin interests, geography and history, are reflected in his 'Great and Memorable Things of Spain' (1548). After a historical introduction, he comes in the twenty-fourth chapter to a 'description' of the country. He admits that he could have followed a division by the great rivers, and, indeed, in Chapter 170 he has some useful things to say about the mountains of the peninsula and the watersheds of the rivers. But he will proceed, he tells us, by kingdoms and historic provinces. His purpose is to describe the 'wealth' of the land in a sense that is no longer current – that is, its grandeur and its cultural patrimony, as well as its material resources. His selection of places for comment is often more informed by their historical associations than by their geographic importance.

Philip II, to whom Medina dedicated the work, was responsible for impressive attempts of his own to map the resources of his realm. One of these was the famous *Relaciones* – questionnaires of 59 and 45 headings sent out in 1575 and 1578 respectively to the local authorities throughout Castile and the Indies. The information was needed, ran the preamble, to promote 'the honour and dignity of these kingdoms', and their 'reputation and grandeur'. As with Pedro de Medina, the object was only partly utilitarian. Thus there were questions about the great men and historical monuments of the locality, as well as about its population and production.

The other great geography of imperial Spain is that of Rodrigo Méndez Silva, published in 1645. Doubly an outsider, as a Portuguese, whose compatriots were just then struggling for independence against the monarchy, and the descendant of converted Jews in trouble with the Inquisition, he threw himself with enthusiasm into a description of Iberia along the familiar lines. There is some geography, with descriptions of the crops, population and industry of the different regions; but fundamentally the country is visualised in moral rather than physical terms, as a federation of communities, whose wealth lies in their patrimony – their historical monuments, in the broad sense, rather than their material resources.

The reader of Medina or Méndez Silva would come away with only a hazy notion of what the country looked like. The best of these cosmographies, in the sense of an inventory of the patrimony, physical and cultural, of a people, were inevitably done at the local level by men who had a deep knowledge of their own surroundings. One of the pioneers was Martín de Viciana, a gentleman somewhat down on his luck, who practised as a notary, and who travelled round the kingdom of Valencia in the 1560s asking the local authorities about the population and production and notable features of their districts. He was followed in 1610 by the priest Gaspar Escolano, more erudite and more classically minded, who never-theless retained a sharp enough eye for the world he saw about him, for numbers of people, distances, types of crop. Both Viciana and Escolano, who are among the outstanding products of a school of historiography which was beginning to flourish in their own day, much as in Elizabethan England, were basically interested in the patrimony of their people in the broad sense. They will situate a town more by reference to its founding myth than to the less exciting criterion of economic significance.

There were attempts made at mapping in the more modern sense. Philip II commissioned Pedro Esquivel, professor of mathematics in the university of Alcalá de Henares, to carry out a survey of the peninsula in 1566. One of those who worked with Esquivel affirmed 'that it is no exaggeration to say that since the creation of the world no region thereof has been described with more care, effort and accuracy'.[22] But the work was probably too great for one team, and was not completed. Some of the maps of seventeenth-century Spain, produced in Flanders and relying on second-hand information, were accurate enough. That of Blaeu, published in Amsterdam in 1672, provided latitudes and gave a scale of Spanish leagues and German miles. The traveller would have a fair idea of the lie of the rivers, but not of mountains or roads.

Certainly the seventeenth century witnessed a stirring of the Spanish authorities in this matter. The Portuguese cartographer João Batista Lavanha was commissioned by the Aragonese to map their kingdom in 1613–4, and Philip III wrote to the Valencian Generalitat (committee of the estates) in 1617 asking them to expedite 'a map or description' of their own province since Aragon and Catalonia were finishing theirs. But it was not until near the end of the century that what has been called the 'first modern map' of Valencia was produced, in 1693. Commissioned by the viceroy and executed by the Jesuit Cassaus, it was designed to show physical relief and main roads, in order to facilitate the movement of the new state militia instituted the year before.[23]

Cassaus only gave the main roads, and was not precise about elevations. There was consequently much left to do in the eighteenth century. The great reforming minister the marquis of Ensenada, in a memorial of about 1748, spoke of the need for a proper mapping of Spain: 'We have no detailed ones . . . There is no one who is able to engrave them, and we have to rely on faulty ones imported from France and Holland.' There was a need to employ more accurate instruments of measurement, such as those being developed in Paris and London, and map design itself would have to be improved, 'either by bringing in foreign craftsmen, or sending our young artists to Paris to learn about maps'.[24] Under Ensenada's inspiration, Tomás López began his mammoth task in the 1760s and 1770s of collecting information from all over Spain for a series of regional maps and descriptions. He produced maps of Granada in 1761 and Valencia in 1762, but was still sending out questionnaires at much later dates. In 1777–8 his list of fifteen questions distributed to the parish priests and local authorities of the kingdom of Valencia included requests for information about shrines and historical monuments, in the spirit of the sixteenth-century cosmographies. But there were five questions about population and economy, and three which could be broadly labelled as topographical. The parish priests were thus invited to submit their own sketch maps of the locality, 'and will give the names of the mountains, where they begin to rise and fall, and a fair estimate of the time it would take to cross them, or of how big they are'. Inevitably such dependence on local informants led to the kind of uncertainties highlighted by one of the priests in his reply – that he could not do the inspection in person, that he would have to rely on 'people who I do not know if they will tell me the truth', and he suggested that López take a horse and go round the places himself.[25]

Eventually it was on foot that the information was gathered for the culminating map of the old regime, that of Antonio Joseph Cavanilles on Valencia (1795). A priest (like Cassaus) and a tutor to aristocratic families, Cavanilles became interested in the work of French naturalists and was appointed professor of botany in Madrid. Entrusted by the Crown with a survey of the vegetation of the peninsula, he decided on his own initiative to add observations on geography and agriculture, 'since we had hardly anything on the situation and character of mountains, and geography in general was very inaccurate'.[26] Beginning with his native Valencia he trekked through this rugged Mediterranean territory for three years, though he was no longer young, at forty-six years of age, when he started. But his efforts resulted in a classic of geographical literature, and a fitting conclusion to the centuries of effort by Spaniards to get to know themselves better. It was left to the military in the nineteenth century to carry this physical inventory of resources to its completion.

2

THE FEWNESS OF PEOPLE

The concern with the mapping of Spain was part of the inventory of resources which marked the growth of the early modern state. One critical aspect of the same process was a new attention to population. Echoing a familiar theme, the Venetian ambassador Mocenigo noted in 1631 that 'the Spains, the states of this king in Italy and all the Spaniards scattered throughout the Indies do not come to two-thirds of the twenty million people' on which the arch-enemy France could count.[1] Since the classical geographer Strabo, whose ideas had been given a new lease of life by Giovanni Botero (1589), the geography (and warlike temper) of Spain was held to be inimical to cities and to a numerous population. In an age when populousness was associated with prosperity and the arts of peace, Spain's lack of people tended to be held up as a reproach. 'All nations marvel at the decline of our population,' wrote the later president of the Council of Castile, the count of Campomanes in 1774 – though, in a change of emphasis which would mark the advent of modern times, he warned that a numerous population by itself was not necessarily a good thing.[2]

At the outset, one may note the impressive range of materials available for a study of demography in Spain, testimony to the pioneering formation there of a modern state and church. There were already good medieval censuses, of a fiscal kind, for the Crown of Aragon. But the first comprehensive survey of Castile was made in 1534, and it excluded nobles and clergy since these did not pay taxes. Additional censuses were made of the royal domain – omitting many seigneurial estates whose owners collected the taxes (*alcabalas*) for themselves – in 1552, 1561, 1585–7 and 1596–7. To crown a century of effort came the universal survey of all households in Castile in 1591, in connection with a new turn of the fiscal screw, the introduction of the *millones*. It was not until the seventeenth century that the Crown of Aragon attracted the attention of the Treasury, with good censuses of Valencia in 1646 or of Aragon in 1642, for example. Valencia, indeed, had already been investigated pretty thoroughly in the sixteenth century, since her Morisco population constituted something of a security risk.

One of the fascinating aspects of this whole process is – as with maps of the terrain – how slowly a reliable picture of the population was built up. The government had taken great pains to find out how many Moriscos were in the kingdom at the time of the expulsion in 1609. Bleda, writing in 1618, must have consulted these state papers when he calculated 340,672 persons expelled; but the Venetian ambassador Gritti at the same time (1619) was putting abroad a much higher figure – 600,000 – which would soon become conventional wisdom as an illustration of the price that Spain paid for her religious fanaticism. The fallibility of memory in an age of essentially oral communication meant that the contours of population may not always have been present in political calculations. Olivares overestimated, with disastrous results, the numbers of Catalans in 1626 when he approached them for military cooperation; and it is puzzling that the government resorted to a hasty count of the Castilian population in 1646 when it already had a more accurate, recent survey of 1631 – which lay forgotten in the state archives until the present day.[3]

Military and fiscal reorganisation under the Bourbons in the eighteenth century created new sources for the demographic historian. Taxes on income led to inventories of the manpower of the Crown of Aragon, listing in some cases individuals and not just households. This was the model which the marquis of Ensenada tried to follow in Castile between 1750 and 1754, listing persons and ages in one of the most complete censuses for any pre-industrial population (though the proposed income tax could not be implemented). The famous Enlightened minister, the count of Aranda, was responsible in 1768 for the first survey of Castile and his native Crown of Aragon together. But the first modern census of Spain as a whole is reckoned to be that of his successor, the count of Floridablanca, in 1787. The latter's motives were avowedly to show the advance of population, and hence of civilisation, under Enlightened Absolutism, 'so that foreigners may see that the kingdom is not quite as deserted as they and their writers believe'. On the eve of the age of Malthus, this optimism may serve as a monument to a more traditional outlook on populousness as a source of wealth.

The Catholic Church had played its part, alongside the state, in making Spaniards aware of their human resources. Its care was to police its flock, and, as elsewhere in early modern Europe, it began to keep records of baptisms, marriages, Easter communions, confirmations and burials. If the individual became aware of himself as a citizen in the early modern period it was surely first as a member of this Christian commonwealth. Biographies of ordinary Spaniards can be reconstructed, particularly from the diocesan archives which record movements from childhood – changes of neighbourhood, the hunt for work – in the effort to counter bigamy among the very mobile population of Spain. The system was only set in place gradually. One of its preconditions was the catholicisation of this frontier society – the forced conversion or expulsion of the large Jewish population in 1492, of the Moors in 1502–25 and the eventual expulsion of the latter in 1609–14. Spain, down to 1609, presents a unique opportunity for a study of the life-cycle of those nominal converts to Christianity, the Moriscos. But it is not until the later seventeenth century, some time after the Moorish expulsion, that parochial and diocesan registers become full enough to permit any very detailed demographic work.

From the Castilian fiscal censuses, supplemented by those of the Crown of Aragon at neighbouring dates, and using a multiplier of four persons per household (now favoured instead of older and higher ratios), historians now estimate the population of Spain as follows:[4]

1534   4,698,000 persons
1591   6,632,000
1787   10,138,000

More work clearly needs to be done on Spanish demography in the seventeenth century. This period of decline has generally been the orphan of historians, its censuses less studied because they seem to lack the rigour of those of the sixteenth and eighteenth centuries. We have to rely at present on regional estimates. Thus, there would have been some 5,240,888 persons in the Spanish heartland, the kingdom of Castile in 1591, and only 4,520,782 in 1631. This sharp downswing in population during the years in which Spain was losing her hegemony as a world power seems to be characteristic of much of the rest of the peninsula as well, and will have to be explained from a variety of perspectives in succeeding chapters. By 1712–17, when the first general count of the Spanish population as a whole was made by the new Bourbon dynasty, the population had probably recovered to its old peak of 1591, in spite of the disasters of the War of the Spanish Succession; but the figures are regarded as uncertain.

The initial expansion of population, visible during the sixteenth century, was probably a continuation of a movement already under way since the later Middle Ages, and was no doubt fostered by the internal peace and economic expansion which followed the unification of the country under the Catholic Kings. But growth seems to have slackened rather early on in Spain's career as an imperial power. The parish registers of Old Castile already record a stagnation of births by about 1570, with a real decline setting in around 1590, particularly in urban areas.[5] To the south, in the emptier lands of New Castile and Murcia, a continuing process of colonisation staved off the fall of baptisms until about 1620. But the middle decades of the seventeenth century witnessed a crisis of natality which seems to have been pretty general throughout the peninsula. The worst-affected areas were probably Old Castile, where population levels were cut by 30 to 40 per cent, and Valencia, where numbers of people by 1646 had fallen to the level of a century before.

Recovery set in during the later seventeenth century, as Spain gradually abandoned what may be regarded as its over-reach for world supremacy. The coastal periphery, Andalusia, Valencia, Catalonia, recovered earliest. In Castile the curve of baptisms generally did not get back to its old height until well into the eighteenth century. It was not until 1787 that Old Castile, León and Extremadura had recovered the manpower of 1591. And even then it figures in the pages of Antonio Ponz as littered with museum towns and abandoned villages. In the more communicable, maritime parts of Spain population expanded fast in the eighteenth century: by as much as 1 per cent per year in Valencia, and by only a little less in Catalonia. But the expansion, in a still essentially agrarian society, was fragile. Droughts and bad harvests after 1762 led to soaring mortality, particularly on the inland meseta of Castile.

In 1591 three-quarters of the Spanish population lived on this central table-land. It had emerged from medieval times, to judge by its profile in 1534, with a heavy concentration of settlement along the milder Atlantic façade, along that famous 'route of silver' which had led, since Roman times, up from Seville through Mérida towards the headquarters of the 'legion', León. To the east, a hotly disputed frontier between Moors and Christians, from Granada up through La Mancha, had kept population to under ten inhabitants per square kilometre. Between 1534 and 1591 there was a filling-up of some of this empty quarter. The average density of Castile and Andalusia rose from 10.70 to 15.85 inhabitants per square kilometre.[6] These figures, however, require to be broken down further by region. Old Castile and Andalusia had between 20 and 30 inhabitants per square kilometre in 1591, as against a figure of under 15 for New Castile, and one of under 8 for the kingdom of Granada, weakened by a recent, bitter civil war and the expulsion of its Moorish people. Whatever the explanation, this was well below the averages for France (34) or Italy (44) at the time, and may explain some of the acerbic comments to be found in the pages of the Venetian ambassadors or of Giovanni Botero. Catalonia, which is now one of the most densely populated parts of Spain, emerges from its census of 1553 with only 10.6 inhabitants per square kilometre, well below the figure for the bleak tableland of Old Castile, which at the time was the political and, thanks to its woollen industry, the economic heart of Spain. Equally the fertile and now densely populated Valencian region had only 13 inhabitants per square kilometre in 1565 (but this is a crude average of the harsh sierras and the prosperous coastal plain, which had between 20 and 50).

By 1787 Spain as a whole had achieved an average density of 20.58 inhabitants, as compared with around 50 in France at the time.[7] At the present day the agrarian heartland of Old Castile and León has still about 27 inhabitants per square kilometre as it had in its sixteenth-century heyday. May one see this as a kind of upper limit for agrarian economies? Average densities in the agricultural regions of Western Europe at the present time are between 25 and 50 – as they were in the more favoured parts of the Continent, like France and Italy, in pre-industrial times. What seems to have characterised early modern Spain was a gradual filling-up of a frontier zone, a rise from around 10 inhabitants per square kilometre in 1500 to double that figure by 1800. In the process the old agrarian heartland of the peninsula was by-passed, as trade and population developed especially on the coastal plains and near the only good communications which Spain had: the sea routes.

Early modern Spain created for the traveller the impression of emptiness. The villagers of Bienservida in New Castile told the king's commissioners in 1575 about their sierras full of 'wild animals like the boar, venison, the doe, mountain goats, hares, rabbits and partridges', while, on the edge of the Sierra Morena, La

Calzada mentioned also the wolf, 'and some bears have been seen in the district'. The grouping of settlements in many parts of the peninsula reinforced the sense of desolation. Joly, travelling in 1603 on the highway which led south-west from Zaragoza towards Madrid, commented: 'The landscape is all so dry that it is almost completely uninhabited, with the settlements grouped near water.'[8] All the greater was the contrast with the oases of cultivation – the coastal plain of Valencia, or the foothills of the Pyrenees from the Basque Country to Catalonia. In 1685 the Jesuit Marcillo commented that the dispersed settlement in well-watered Catalonia meant that 'the whole province looks like one continuous city'.[9]

The country had emerged in 1492 from a long internal war between Christian and Moor, and the process of recolonisation was to continue for some time after that. The first wave of the Reconquest had given the Christians control of the lands north of the Tagus (capture of Toledo 1085) and Ebro (Tortosa 1148). Though most of the Castilian Muslims seem to have fled south, those of Aragon often surrendered on terms which allowed them to hold on to their land, and down to the early seventeenth century their settlements, on the right bank of the Ebro, comprised about a fifth of the population of the kingdom of Aragon. The crusading warfare reached its peak of intensity in the twelfth and thirteenth centuries, with the gradual Christian advance into New Castile and Andalusia (capture of Seville 1248), and by the Aragonese and Catalans into Valencia (1238). As before, those Muslim communities which surrendered were allowed to keep their land, outside the strategic centres. Western Andalusia was quickly emptied of its Muslims, who fell back on the still-independent kingdom of Granada; but their Valencian brothers held their ground, still constituting a third of the population of that kingdom by the time of the definitive expulsion in 1609. The last crusade, the war for the taking of Granada, lasted between 1480 and 1492, and followed the traditional pattern of sieges and negotiations, which left most of the Muslim population in place though under Christian rule. The gradual process of erosion of native rights also followed: the encroachment of settlers, against whom a population without written title-deeds was ill-protected, and the new pressure of the Counter-Reformation church and state, which led to rebellions and persecution, and the eventual expulsion of all the Moriscos from Spain in 1609–14. There were approximately 319,000 of them at the time, a small percentage of the overall population; but their removal from Valencia, and earlier in 1570 from Granada, created much dislocation in those territories.[10] In the long, slow recolonisation which followed, the dispersed hamlets characteristic of the Moors, possibly reflecting original tribal settlement, were regrouped into bigger villages.

Though imperial Spain managed to export warfare abroad for most of the time, the demographic costs of imperialism were high. There were, first, the internal frontiers opened up by rebellions against billeting, conscription or taxation, which acquired particular resonance in the struggles for independence of Catalonia 1640–52 and Portugal 1640–68. And the War of the Spanish

Succession 1700–13 took the form of a major civil war between Castile and the Crown of Aragon.

But it was the continuing burden of providing manpower for the upkeep of empire which represented the really significant drain on the country's resources. The army of Flanders held about 70,000 men at full strength during the monarchy's long struggle to maintain its hegemony in northern Europe between 1567 and 1648.[11] Of these about a tenth were Spaniards, drafted in from the peninsula via Italy, and the rest were mostly Italian, German or Flemish mercenaries. The overall size of the imperial forces – including the Atlantic and Mediterranean fleets, as well as garrisons in Italy and the Caribbean – is hard to estimate exactly, but may not be far off the 140,000 men which Olivares calculated for the Union of Arms in 1625.

Initially the army had relied on volunteers. Philip II was looking for about 9,000 men a year in the later sixteenth century, Philip IV for 12,000, at the peak of conflict between 1635 and 1659.[12] The Venetian ambassador Donà had remarked in 1573, when the peninsular population was buoyant, that 'they can find between 9,000 and 10,000 infantry to serve outside Spain with ease, but they would have some difficulty in getting any more than that'.[13] Philip IV and Olivares were reduced, in fact, to a form of conscription to raise the large contingents they needed.

But conscription was really only systematised under the Bourbons. They needed quite large forces at times, particularly in the War of the Spanish Succession and in the campaigns of Philip V (1700–46) to establish his children on Italian thrones. At the same time the stripping away of the European possessions of the Spanish Crown (especially at the Treaty of Utrecht 1713) made it less easy to recruit foreign mercenaries. Nominally the Bourbons still reckoned on fielding 70,000–80,000 men – a total somewhat, but not drastically inferior to the old imperial army of the Habsburgs. To find these, the *quintas* were introduced in 1702–4, conscripting one out of five young men by a process of lottery. In 1770 the regulations were tightened up, and it was specified that from lists of unmarried men, 17 to 35 years of age, soldiers would be drawn to serve eight years at a time. Skilled workers, professional people and nobles were exempt. There were riots in Catalonia against the new system in 1773, and it proved unworkable in Castile too. Quotas of men were assigned instead to local communities, as they had been on and off since the days of Olivares, leaving them free to decide how to raise the contingents, whether by conscription or offering bounties to volunteers.[14] The peace-time strength of the army seems to have been only about half its nominal tally of 70,000–80,000 men. Half of these were volunteers, often still foreign mercenaries. Many of the rest were 'vagrants', sentenced to the colours by the courts as part of the moral policing so typical of governments in the Age of the Enlightenment.

Of the young men who left Spain for the wars of the Habsburgs, the Valencian writer Escolano and his Italian contemporary Botero concurred for once that barely one in ten would ever return. Whether the loss to the economy was significant was a question posed by some, who regarded the exiles as the dregs of the community. Certainly the army was a real presence in the minds and calcula-tions of young Spaniards of the early modern period. The Valencian chronicler Porcar (1560–1628) refers several times to his page-boy, Pere Pau Lauro, who could not settle down either to study or to follow his father's trade as a tailor, but who took himself off to the wars several times, only to slink home after a few days or weeks. Porcar observed the increasing difficulties which the captains were having in finding volunteers, and he recorded the first whipping of deserters – two sixteen-year-olds – in 1626.[15] The experience of war had social consequences which went beyond the immediate loss of manpower. Cervantes records its potentially disturbing effects on the local community in his account of one young man, who had left his village at twelve and returned at twenty-four years of age, 'dressed as a trooper, ablaze with colour', and who ran off with one of the girls. One of the villagers recalled: 'we would be standing there with our mouths agape, as he told us of all the adventures he had had'.[16]

The Venetian ambassador Navagero did not think that the Christian settlers would put down roots in Granada: 'They go off with a greater will to the wars or to the Indies,' he wrote in 1525. It was, perhaps, unfortunate that vast new frontiers should have opened for Spain, in Africa, in northern Europe and Italy, but, above all, in America just at the time when Iberia itself was settling down to a long internal peace. The chronicler Fernández de Oviedo gives a vivid picture of the colonisation fever which gripped peasants and artisans round Seville in 1513 as Pedrarias Dávila prepared his expedition for Darien: 'there were many who sold the lands and belongings they held from their fathers. Others, less crazy, mortgaged them for a few years, leaving a certain income for one that was less so; while others walked out on their masters, forfeiting their wages.' During Las Casas's recruiting campaign of 1518 the justices and preachers were told to extol the bounty of the Caribbean islands of Hispaniola, San Juan, Cuba and Jamaica. The needy of Castile, 'who live poorly and pay high rents', would come into their own out there.[17]

We cannot know exactly how many people left for the Indies. The Spanish government tried to keep a check on the morals and religion of the fortune-seekers, and its records in the House of Trade in Seville are a monument to the early development of the bureaucratic state. But the task was beyond the resources of the period. The official licences to emigrate, fascinating documents in their own right, average 400 a year when it seems that more than ten times that number of people were sailing with the fleets. The best recent calculations are for 5,274 emigrants a year between 1561 and 1600, falling to 3,869 in the years when the Spanish population was reaching its nadir, 1626–50.[18] If we said that there was an average of 4,000 persons leaving Spain a year to make their home in America over the early modern period as a whole we should not be too far wrong. Given that most of the emigrants were young men, and that there can only have been about 200,000 males in their late teens and early twenties when Spain's population was at its peak in 1591, the drain must have been quite considerable. Emigration tended to proceed by fits and starts, in the kinds of recruiting campaigns of 1513 and 1518 which we mentioned above. It was difficult for the poor to make the trip to the Indies on their own, since the voyage cost some 30 or 40 ducats, a year's wages (or near enough) of a wage labourer around 1600.[19] Nearly two-thirds of a sample of emigrants studied between 1493 and 1559 came from the old 'silver route', stretching up from Seville through Extremadura towards León and Old Castile. Long-established movements of population had built up, no doubt, the traditions and contacts which facilitated emigration from there.

The consequences of this emigration for Spain are hard to estimate exactly. Countering Botero, the Valencian chronicler Escolano in 1610 suggested that the Indies generally appealed to 'turbulent persons without resources, who are attracted by the smell of gold; and we are well rid of them, like an evil humour from the body'. And he pointed to the 'flocks of French' coming into the peninsula to take their place, 'leaving the rigours of their own land for the profound peace and Christian devotion which they know Spain enjoys'. These words were written by a man whose impressions of France were formed by the long nightmare of the Wars of Religion. But the story of French migration across the Pyrenees goes back further – to the thirteenth century when the shepherds of Montaillou brought their flocks down to pasture on the southern slopes, and beyond that to the great pilgrimages starting in Paris or Vézelay towards the shrine of Santiago de Compostela. And it was carried forward in the sixteenth century by the influx of American silver into Spain, which meant, as Barthélemy Joly pointed out in 1603, that a labourer could earn twice what he was getting in France.

Joly found all the servants to be French in the great Catalan convent of Santes Creus, as were most of the bakers and craftsmen at the important shrine of Montserrat. This immigration was at its height in the years between 1540 and 1620 when the Barcelona hospital of the Holy Cross regularly recorded a third of its sick poor as coming from beyond the Pyrenees. Joly was told by his countrymen about their motives for leaving home: taxes (at least in the autonomous kingdom of Catalonia) were lower and life, in general, was better for the common man than in France, 'where the peasant is harshly treated'.[20] The migrants had come mostly from the Massif Central. Rather like the Spanish outflow to the Indies, parties of young peasants were rounded up by entrepreneurs and guided south. The journeys seem to have begun in late spring or early summer, and to have continued even in time of war between Spain and France.[21] Most probably intended to return home after they had made their fortune; a few of those whom death surprised in Granada were in possession of the silver reals which would enable them to move away quickly. But others invested for the future in their adopted environment. Between 10 and 16 per cent of marriages in selected Catalan parishes between 1576 and 1625 involved a bridegroom from north of the Pyrenees.

Ten years' residence and marriage to a Spanish girl conferred citizenship – at least, once cities (like Valencia from the later sixteenth century) ceased to maintain full citizen registers of their own. In fact, it was increasingly the monarchy which began, in the seventeenth century, to arrogate this power to itself. From 1635 there began a newer, harsher kind of warfare between Spain and France, which did not quite seal the frontier but made life increasingly difficult for outsiders. From 1637 the traditional reprisals against an enemy were raised to a new level of bureaucratic efficiency, with a more systematic registration of French nationals and their belongings. Those who had not been resident for ten years or married to a Spaniard were subjected to a tax which seems to have been arbitrary, designed to favour those who were useful to the government and perhaps to encourage others to leave. The Council of Aragon was informed in 1637 that 'more than 8,000 French have gone away, men who were employed in ploughing and other servile occupations'. Though some of the local authorities, like the Valencians, deplored this further blow to population, the outsider could no longer feel so comfortable in the new age of the proto-nation state. Overall the number of French in Spain was calculated at 200,000 by the French ambassador in 1626, falling to around 80,000 in the report of his successor towards the end of the century, at which level it remained in the estimates made for the French Directory in the 1790s.[22]

One of the intriguing features of the mobile, frontier society of early modern Spain was a fairly young age at marriage. Many of the samples from the parish registers of the late sixteenth and seventeenth centuries suggest that men, and particularly women, were marrying rather earlier than their counterparts north of the Pyrenees – women at around twenty years of age in Valladolid, at twenty-one or twenty-two in Cuenca, at twenty to twenty-two in villages which have been studied in the kingdom of Valencia.[23] One might have expected the economic difficulties of the seventeenth century to have modified the pattern in some areas – at least in regions of falling population like Castile. The city of Toledo complained around 1620 that in the old days 'a journeyman or peasant would marry his daughter to a youth who had no money so long as he had a calling', but the decline of manufactures over the last decade had meant 'that there are not now the tenth part of the marriages and baptisms there used to be'.[24] In the provincial capital of Cuenca, where economic opportunity was drastically reduced over the early modern period by the destruction of the woollen manufacture, the age at first marriage of women did tend to creep up, but only slightly: to 22.6 years by the later eighteenth century.

Our first complete picture of the Spanish marriage system comes in the census of Floridablanca (1787). Just over a quarter (27.56 per cent) of women were then married under the age of twenty-five, the watershed from which peasant marriage became frequent in the rest of Western Europe. The figures are somewhat hard to interpret since they suggest a great contrast between average age of women at first marriage of twenty-two or twenty-three years in the south and east – Andalusia, Valencia, New Castile – and twenty-four or twenty-five in the north and west – Old Castile, the Basque Country, Asturias. In Galicia, one of the better-studied areas, the age had been rising over the eighteenth century from twenty-four to about twenty-seven.[25] To complete the picture one may note that celibacy rates – calculated as women over fifty who had never been married at all – were 10.19 per cent of the Spanish female population as a whole in 1787. But the proportions vary from as little as 6.89 per cent in fertile and prosperous Valencia to as much as 15 or 20 per cent in poor, overcrowded Galicia.

It is tempting to see a correlation between these marriage patterns and economic opportunity. But clearly the correspondence is not always exact. Francisco Benlloch, whose description of the Valencian settlement of Llombai in 1756 is a classic of writing on the peasantry, noted that there were no jobs in the village other than in agriculture and little emigration; yet after the father's death his children divided up the inadequate holding, 'to their own impoverishment, which will lead to debt and eventually to misery'. As we have noted, the Valencian region at this time was one of near universal and early marriage. In Asturias, which did have a rather late age at marriage, Jovellanos deplored the excessive subdivision of land which was still going on among the peasantry in 1782: 'I have seen a farm which not many years before was intended for a single peasant split among five.'[26]

Quite a lot of research is now being done on the social and economic context of peasant marriage, which involves attention to household structure and inheritance. In medieval Spain, as one might expect in a frontier society, great emphasis was placed on facilitating population. The custom was that of equal inheritance by all the children, male and female, and marriage seems to have been a partnership between the man and the woman. Thus, though the early laws of Castile limited the amount which a bridegroom could give his wife – the bridewealth or *arras* – to one-tenth of his own estate, in practice land, cattle and clothes were often assigned to the bride amounting to half the property. Customs were similar in the Crown of Aragon; thus, in thirteenth-century Valencia the system of *germanía* (brotherhood, or partnership) meant that a widow would often expect to take half her husband's estate.[27]

As the frontier closed, older laws began to be resurrected, designed to safeguard the integrity of the peasant holding. The dowry began to take on greater importance – the transfer of property from the girl's parents – and this led to a clearer separation between the belongings of the husband and wife. By the fifteenth century in Valencia the peasant widow could no longer take half the holding, but must content herself with the return of her dowry, in addition to the jointure or *creix* (usually one half the dowry) which had been promised her in the original marriage contract.[28] The arrangements certainly left widows with much property. In Castile, by this time, the general rule was that the widow should take back her dowry, together with the *arras* promised by her husband, in addition to one half the acquisitions (*gananciales*) made jointly. These were generally estimated at half the remainder of the estate, since comparatively few husbands entered marriage with an inventory of their own possessions (*capital*).

It was a characteristic of Spanish, and particularly Castilian, law and custom to favour women. The Castilian tradition had been that girls inherited equally with boys. Even in the Crown of Aragon, where Roman law and *patria potestas* had more sway, the medieval system favoured division of at least part of the patrimony. The characteristic feature of the closure of the frontier, and of the consequent concern with protecting the patrimony, was to limit the *legítima*, the legal minimum of the estate which each child must receive at the death of his or her parent. Thus in the kingdom of Valencia the thirteenth-century laws had required a parent to divide at least a third and up to a half of his holding in this way; but fourteenth- and fifteenth-century legislation reduced this to just five shillings to each child. In Catalonia the Cortes of 1585 reduced the *legítima* to one-fourth of the patrimony. Even in Castile, long home to an egalitarian tradition, the major legislation of Toro (1505) revived Visigothic law which permitted a father or mother to leave one child an increment (*mejora*) of one-third of the estate. Finally, laws of 1530, 1574 and 1623 tried – not very successfully – to limit the dowries given to daughters on their marriage to at most five years' income of the parent. All of these measures reflect a closing of the frontier – a concern with protecting the family estate against fragmentation, without, however, endangering the marriages of the next generation.

Along the Pyrenees, from the Basque Country through Aragon to Catalonia the tradition tended to favour a single heir. One can still admire in the solid farm-houses, of mountain stone, the visible link with a fifteenth- and sixteenth-century past. Sometimes the same family is still in possession, with charters going back to that period, and with a burial site within the village church which cements it to its ancestors. This has been the most Catholic part of Spain down to modern times, its religion anchored in a solid material culture. In spite of the concern for keeping the farm together, however, and a fairly marked tendency to place younger children in the ranks of the celibate clergy, Catalonia had a robust demography. There was a relatively young age at first marriage here in the seventeenth century – twenty-two or twenty-three years for women – while in 1787 nearly a third of Catalan women were married by the age of twenty-five as compared with just over a quarter in Spain as a whole.[29]

Much depended here on arrangements for the transmission of accommodation and property to the younger generation. At his marriage the Catalan heir was expected to bring his bride into the parental home, where his father and mother, unmarried brothers and sisters might still be living. Just over a fifth of households in early eighteenth-century Girona seem to have been 'multiple' (consisting of two or more married couples); but the proportion fell to under 10 per cent during the rest of the century. It is still not clear, in fact, just how common the extended household was in Spain as a whole. Studies being conducted in Valencia, where the Pyrenean single heir did not exist, suggest that married children might often enough live with their parents for a time.[30] The pattern was probably common among substantial farmers, who required additional labour. Certainly in a sample of six parishes of the city of Granada in 1752 a good quarter of propertied households – artisans and peasants as well as the bourgeoisie – would have kin of some kind living with them. And, though nuclear families and division of inheritance were clearly the norm, cooperation among families could counter the effects of fragmentation. The censuses require to be studied in depth. Thus in the Granadan village of Orgiva in 1750 the eighteen-year-old María Torralva, 'a maiden and a pauper', living alone with her fifteen-year-old brother Josef, turns out on inspection to be related to another María Torralva, some distance away, a 58-year-old peasant woman who had reared the younger María 'from a very tender age'.

One of the areas where the multiple family household may have been most common was Galicia. The law of inheritance there was that of Castile, specifying equal division of the holding, but a high celibacy rate (as we noted above), delayed marriage and frequent emigration led, in practice, to a system reminiscent of rural Ireland in more modern times where one child, often the youngest, assumed de facto headship of the home while the elder siblings left to make their careers abroad. In the eighteenth-century Tierra de Montes, for example, 9.6 per cent of households contained two or more married couples, and another 15.8 per cent incorporated one or more dependent relatives.[31] The Galician families were large, the land already densely populated; the province lived by exporting its surplus manpower, and restricting the succession to the family farm, in practice if not in law. With a population of 1,400,000 eighteenth-century Galicia sent out every year 25,000–30,000 of its young men – and women – to harvest the wheat in Castile and Portugal. Bands would set out in April or May, walking for between a fortnight and three weeks to reach the grainlands of the south, before returning home with their earnings in the autumn.[32] The end of the wheat harvest in Castile coincided with the feast of Saint James of Compostela (25 July), and the Galician diaspora helped to keep alive devotion to their regional saint, who became the patron of all Spain.

Many of the migrants, in fact, never returned to Galicia: one can find them (like the French) surprised by death along the way, having worked for several years among the widespread little Galician communities of the towns of southern Spain. The Spanish countryside, in general, lived in symbiosis with its towns. Studies of the parish registers of places like Cordoba, Cartagena, Medina del Campo suggest that nearly a third of those marrying in the early modern period had come in from outside; in the case of Madrid the proportion was double that. In one parish of Medina del Campo, then the centre of the great Castilian fairs, over a quarter of the men listed in one census of 1570 subsequently left town. In the regional market town of Cuenca, according to the invaluable mid-nineteenth-century record, the turnover of population was of the order of 10 per cent coming in and 10 per cent going out every year.[33] But immigrants to Cuenca, though they might ease the pressure on the resources of their families back in the countryside of New Castile, had to wait slightly longer before marrying – twenty-four years of age for women, as against twenty-three for their rural cousins in the early modern period. In the city of Valencia, according to the census of 1787, many might never marry at all: 18.10 per cent of women over fifty had never been married, as against only 6.89 per cent in the kingdom of Valencia as a whole.

Marriage was geared to economic opportunity: 'mankind grows and declines in proportion to the supply of food,' wrote Cavanilles in 1795. But the overall reproduction of the Spanish population depended as well on the fertility of these marriages. In Cuenca between 1680 and 1729 a woman, marrying on average at twenty-three years of age, would produce 6.2 offspring if she was still living with her husband at the end of the fertile period – a somewhat lower ratio than that found by Goubert in his classic study of the Beauvaisis. Given that most marriages were interrupted before the end of the wife's fertile period, the actual number of births per couple was always considerably smaller anyway – 5 or 6 in the parishes studied in the kingdom of Valencia in the seventeenth century, and 5.25 in Galicia, but falling to just over 4 as marriage was retarded there in the eighteenth century.[34] One assumes that in many parts of seventeenth-century Spain, with population falling but the age at marriage still relatively young, the ratio of children to married couples must have been low.

There are several factors to be borne in mind in this connection. In the first place many women must have been marrying widowers, given the high mortality of the seventeenth century which we shall explore in a moment; and secondly lack of economic opportunity must have led to many births outside marriage. In the rural areas, it is true, illegitimacy was not particularly high: between 1 and 3.5 per cent of births in Catalonia, around or under (sometimes well under) 1 per cent in the Valencian parishes of the seventeenth century. In Galicia, with high celibacy and delayed marriage, illegitimacy rates reached 5 per cent in the eighteenth century, which may be a maximum for rural Spain under the old regime. But in the towns the numbers of foundlings grew in the bleak seventeenth century – from around 4 to around 8 per cent of births in Seville, with a similar proportion in Madrid.[35] Some of these foundlings were not illegitimate children, and many were brought in from the surrounding countryside as more foundling hospitals were set up in the bigger towns during the sixteenth century. Nevertheless it is significant that around 10 per cent of baptisms in seventeenth- and eighteenth-century Granada, and as many as 15 per cent in Madrid, were the products of unknown parents (counting both foundlings and those formally declared to be illegitimate). Such figures presented a considerable challenge to the society of the time. As the economist Sancho de Moncada wrote in 1619, it was not sufficient just to breed more children in order to restore the population of Spain, and he pointed to North Africa where early marriages and numerous offspring had failed to arrest depopulation. The main thing was 'a well-ordered commonwealth', where children were properly reared and found jobs in order that they themselves should found stable families.[36] Writers of this time, in fact, pointed to the broken homes of Castile, where the father was forced to take to the roads, or emigrate, abandoning his family.

Mortality among foundlings was, as in the rest of Europe, exceptionally high. But even ordinary infant mortality gave no cause for satisfaction. Between 40 and 50 per cent of those born in the Valencian parishes studied in the seventeenth and eighteenth centuries would not survive until adulthood. The situation in eighteenth-century Galicia was a little better: three out of five babies would live to become adults, which may explain some of the demographic pressure experienced by that province. The critical period was the first year of life when between a fifth and a third of the newborn might expect to die. But the sheer hardship of life meant that expectation of life at the higher ages was not very good either. The economist Caxa de Leruela wrote in 1631 of 'so many countrymen who . . . by the time they reach 45 or 50 years of age . . . are aged and broken by the work of ploughing'.[37] In the census of 1787 just over a quarter of the population was aged forty or above, including 14.5 per cent who had survived their fiftieth birthday. In common with the rest of pre-industrial Europe, Spain was predominantly a country of young people: nearly three-quarters of its inhabitants younger than forty, 35.9 per cent younger than sixteen. In conjunction with the considerable number of foundlings in the cities, and the widows and remarried widowers everywhere, this plethora of the young created problems of care. From the studies made of early modern Cuenca, seventeenth-century Granada and selected parishes of Old Castile it would seem that one marriage in five involved a widow or widower. Broken homes no doubt led to the cases of child abandonment to be met with in the records – of the ten-year-old Bernardo Moreno from Galicia, who had come south to Cordoba 'with some men from his homeland' and been taken in by a local farmer, or of the Portuguese Francisco Rodríguez who had found his way to Montilla 'when he was just a child and not capable of reasoning', and who sought to marry in 1640 Antonia María, a waif from Cordoba, who had been taken in by a tailor who had found her 'wandering the streets lost', when she was only six. These cases come from the registers of the bishop of Cordoba, who, like his colleagues, was supposed to keep a check on the movement of those marrying outside the parish in which they were born.

We have to imagine a landscape dotted with small communities – 25,000 of them in the peninsula as a whole, 'including Navarre and Portugal', according to the chronicler Escolano in 1610. There were two great cities – the imperial capital Madrid and its commercial counterpart Seville, which at their peak in the early seventeenth century reached around 130,000–150,000 inhabitants each. Below them came a scattering of regional capitals – Valencia, Granada, Toledo, Valladolid, Barcelona – with at most 50,000 (a kind of upper limit, perhaps, for a pre-industrial administrative and market centre in the Europe of that time). Below these came the market towns, with between 5,000 and 20,000 people – the centre of the Old Castilian fairs, Medina del Campo, would have had just under 15,000 at its peak, and the main port for the export of wool to Italy, Alicante, had 5,000 at most under the Habsburgs.

Concentrations of population in pre-industrial Europe inevitably posed exceptional problems of hygiene. An adequate supply of clean drinking water could not be taken for granted. German and Italian engineers were called upon in 1526 and 1569 to try to pump the waters of the Tagus uphill to the houses of Toledo, without damaging the eight mills and the eight sluice gates (for irrigation) which lay in the vicinity. But down to the early nineteenth century, when George Borrow visited the town, the water from the Tagus was regarded as unsafe for drinking, and the inhabitants preferred to collect rainwater in cisterns of their own. River supply was generally safer, though, than that from wells. Seepage from sewage and parish cemeteries contaminated the wells in Seville. And in Valencia the diarist Porcar tells us that he took advantage of the drought of the winter of 1626–7 to have his well scraped, for the second time in four years.[38]

Great technological skill had to be employed to circumvent these obstacles. Seville relied partly on water brought fifteen miles from Alcalá de Guadaira along an aqueduct built by the Muslims, and on that from Carmona, twenty miles away, running along another Roman aqueduct. A network of underground pipes, made of lead, carried the water to the fountains which stood in every little square and directly to a few of the chief households. Even small towns showed considerable ingenuity: Xàtiva, with about 8,000 inhabitants, had by the middle of the sixteenth century a new aqueduct to add to the old one, both bringing water from a league or so away. At least a quarter of the houses had their own piped supply.[39]

Disposal of sewage was perhaps more of a problem. Valencia had a network of underground sewers inherited from the Romans or Arabs. On Sundays, when the irrigation of the fields outside town was stopped, the full force of the river was allowed to run through them. At periodic intervals – 1614, 1621, 1625 – the diarist Porcar records the opening up of his street to get at the sewers for cleaning. The municipal authorities organised the operation, but local householders paid the bill.[40] In the cities of the central tableland, either because of scarcity of water or, more probably, because of a lack of importance in Roman and Arab times, the disposal of waste was less well organised. The papal envoy Borghese complained in 1594 of the 'insufferable stench' in the streets of Madrid, where urinals had to be emptied directly into the streets; and Joly remarked on a similar phenomenon in Valladolid. It was only in the later eighteenth century that a network of sewers was laid in Madrid.

All towns tended to use the streets as convenient dumping grounds for household rubbish. Despite the sewers, Valencia was not a noticeably clean town, at least in late spring when the silk grubs were removed from the cocoons and thrown out. Since the streets were mostly unpaved, this and other waste was gradually broken down, until the peasants from the surrounding fields came in to scrape it all up for manure. But the *jurats* (municipal magistrates) had to forbid them in 1615 to use spades or other tools of iron in the process, since they carted off too much of the street itself.

The lack of paving turned the streets into mudbaths when the rains fell in autumn and spring, and the first victim was the great religious processions, as the good priest Porcar was careful to note in his diary. Some of the Valencian and the most frequented Sevillian thoroughfares were given a covering of brick or rubble by the early sixteenth century. The Catholic Kings ordered Toledo to be paved in 1502, at the cost of the householders. But travellers tended to comment on the dank, labyrinthine aspect of many Spanish towns, with their twisted streets. The *jurats* of Valencia complained in 1393 that their city had been built by the Moors, 'after their fashion, narrow and cramped'. Despite their efforts at town-planning, and the laying out of avenues like the Alameda in Seville (1574), or the straightening of streets in Valladolid after the great fire of 1561, Antonio Ponz still found the cities of Spain often in conflict with classical standards of beauty at the end of the old regime.

More of a danger to public health was the existence of cemeteries within the built-up area. The middle classes were regularly buried in the body of their local parish church, the less well-off in a yard outside. In the churchyard the corpses were given only a light covering of earth, pending the decomposition of the flesh and the transfer of the bones elsewhere. In sixteenth-century Seville there were complaints of 'dogs often disinterring the bodies and eating at them', and of the dumping of rubbish nearby.[41] Regularly there would be scrapes of the churchyard to remove the bones. Porcar recorded several during his stay as priest in San Martín (Valencia), in 1596, 1615, 1620 and 1628. A dirty operation, it was carried out at night, in winter. In 1787, in answer to increasing concern with public health, Charles III forbade burial in cities, except for those with private chapels. A new cemetery was built outside the walls of Madrid in 1809, but it seems only to have been in regular use from the mid-nineteenth century.

One of the major inconveniences of the Spanish habitat was generally agreed to be the lack of wood in the peninsula – of firewood for boiling water and cooking, of timber for building. In 1786 Antonio Ponz launched a sweeping condemnation: 'The houses of the poor are wretched in the extreme because of the dearth of timber . . . Basic furniture, like chairs and tables, are scarce and meanly fashioned.' Almodóvar del Campo told the king's commissioners in 1575 that it had to bring its timber all the way across La Mancha, from the sierras of Cuenca and Alcaraz, 'and the cost means that there are few good houses or buildings here'. The peasant houses which Jovellanos met with in 1782 on his way from Madrid north to Asturias were made of sun-dried bricks, or of tapia, blocks of clay and pebbles three foot square. Houses like this 'can be easily run up, but just as easily fall to pieces with the action of the sun and rain'. It would be better to bake proper bricks in a kiln – 'if there was any (firewood) to bake them with'.[42]

'The whole house is a single round room,' wrote the magistrate Eugenio de Salazar of one Asturian village he visited in 1560, 'and the humans share it with the pigs and cattle.' Most peasant houses used their upper storey, if they had one, as a store. The Jesuit missionary Pedro de León was accommodated in this kind of loft by the villagers of Extremadura in 1592, so low that he had to squat, and damp. He could see the sky through the rushes which constituted the roof, and 'counted the stars' as he dropped off to sleep.[43] In La Mancha more villages seem to have had tile than thatched roofs, to judge by the Relaciones of 1575; and in the neighbouring kingdom of Valencia the peasants were adamant that they could not live in the thatched houses which the recently expelled Moors (1609) had inhabited. Some indications from the province of Cordoba, bordering on Extremadura, would tend to suggest that thatch was commoner as one moved west.

In the cities artisan dwellings were like 'cages for birds', according to one observer of Toledo in 1576. They were narrow, with only a step ladder to the first floor. Joly found their counterparts in Valencia to consist of a living room downstairs, 'lit only by the light from the front door', leading out to a yard at the back with its well providing water for cooking or washing, and up to a single bedroom on the first floor. The houses of the upper classes were spacious but scarcely comfortable in a modern sense. Joly commented on the absence of privacy, the fact that the rooms led directly one into another, and that the bedrooms were mere 'alcoves' – a word borrowed from the Spanish term *alcoba*.[44] Lack of glass for windows – oiled canvas was used in winter very often, and lattice screens in summer – possibly explains the long, blank walls of streets in Cordoba or Toledo down to the nineteenth century. Houses turned in on themselves, in the Roman and Arab fashion, round the inner patio. The more cosmopolitan centres like Seville, according to its historian Morgado in 1587, were beginning to rebuild 'with plenty of windows giving on to the street'. And in a court town like Valladolid, rebuilt after 1561, Joly could admire the balconies which were an essential part of the spectacle of fiesta.

Lack of wood not only explained, for Jovellanos, the poverty of Castilian dwelling, but also its cooking, with a reliance on stews. The Cortes of 1580 noted how reliant the Old Castilians were on gruel or porridge rather than bread – on boiling rather than baking their rye, millet or barley. The same body emphasised that some form of grain or bread was the bulk of the peasant diet: the shepherd would have his 'bread crumbs fried in suet or milk, or just bread and water', the villager 'bread with some stew of vegetables and a little bacon, or, in Lent, chickpeas instead'.[45] Eight *fanegas* (about four and a half hectolitres) of wheat would be consumed by an individual in a year, thought Sancho de Moncada in 1619; eighteen by the average family, thought another of the economic writers in 1638.[46] It was generally agreed that each of these *fanegas* would produce forty-two standard loaves of one and a half Castilian pounds (690 grams). In other words, something like our modern large supermarket loaf (800 grams) would need to be provided for each adult male every day.

Wheat was the basic ingredient of bread throughout Spain, but the bran was sometimes mixed in to give a cheaper loaf. In bad years round Cordoba barley was baked into bread, according to the Cortes of 1593, and in the wetter lands of the north-west chestnuts might give 'a very savoury flour', according to the agricultural writer Alonso de Herrera. On the drier Mediterrnean coast, the carob might be pressed into service, thought Herrera. A folktale from the Alicante region recounts how a child, seeking carobs in the loft to still his hunger, was frightened by the echo of his voice in the empty room: 'that is the voice of the month of May,' explained his father drily, the phantom of hunger which invaded lofts and stores just before the new harvest.[47]

If bread was the staple, olive oil was its condiment over much of the south and east. Martínez de Mata reckoned around 1650 that an artisan household in Toledo would consume about three *arrobas* (48 litres) of oil a year in lighting but chiefly in cooking. And then there was wine – 'the soul of the worker, the hoer and the reaper', as the deputy for Seville told the Cortes of 1593. The Toledo artisan, thought Martínez de Mata, might drink just over 66 litres of the stuff every year. Meat was consumed in small quantities, averaging out at about 50 grams a day per person according to random calculations for Murcia, Valladolid and Valencia. But it was 350 grams which was being served up to each person every day at the table of the duchess of Gandia in 1676.[48] On Fridays, on vigils of religious feasts and during the forty days of Lent – in all perhaps a third of the year – meat was not permitted anyway, though the special Bull of Crusade allowed its purchasers to consume milk, cheese and lard. Inevitably, therefore, as the jurats of Valencia told the king about 1643, 'the most necessary part of the diet of the inhabitants of this city is fresh and salt fish'. Even in inland La Mancha the peasants mention fish as an important food in the *Relaciones* of 1575.

On the grainlands of the central plateau the real problem was the irregularity of the harvest due to drought. Ponz wrote of the dangers facing the peasantry of La Mancha through their too great a dependence on a single crop. On the northern edge of this great plain the hills of La Alcarria offered a wider variety of foods – not only small flocks of sheep, but 'vegetables, honey, fruit, fish and game', in pursuit of which the peasants of the lowlands would come when famine struck. The year before, 1786, hunger and fever had swept La Mancha. 'Then did I see,' wrote one high-placed observer, 'hundreds of the wretched inhabitants . . . trekking from village to village, trying if they could to beg their way to Madrid, the father and mother covered in rags . . . and the children naked and exhausted.'[49] The Jesuit Luis de Palma recorded the great hunger of 1585 when 'entire villages' from La Mancha had descended on Toledo clamouring for food. 'People are dropping dead by the wayside,' wrote the deputies of Zamora about the great hunger in Galicia in the spring of 1608. Or they reach Zamora 'in such a state that they die soon afterwards'. We fear an outbreak of plague, they went on, 'for this is mostly or always caused by famine'.[50]

Bubonic plague was probably the most feared of the diseases in Spain as in the rest of Europe during the early modern period. In the eighteenth century, certainly, malaria, smallpox and other illnesses were worrying the authorities, and even in the seventeenth century it would seem that typhus and diphtheria were greater killers.[51] Typhus was brought to western Europe in the war for the reconquest of Granada (1480–92), and it seems to have stayed on to do great damage in the Hispanic world throughout the early modern period under the name of *tabardillos*. Characterised by violent, delirious fever and small, purplish eruptions on the skin, it is compatible with some of the symptoms described for the Valencian and Sevillian plagues of 1647–9. The aetiology of typhus, in fact, is much like that of plague. Transmitted by lice or fleas, its favoured habitat is crowded, squalid conditions such as those to be found in many towns. In Cuenca typhus may have been the most frequent single cause of high mortality, with outbreaks in 1606, 1631, 1710, 1735 and 1804, followed by plague in 1599, 1647 and possibly 1684.[52]

Whatever their exact nature in any particular case, epidemics were capable of bringing the life of great cities to a standstill in the seventeenth century. This period witnessed some graphic portrayals of death in art, but its peculiar fascination for the historian of the plague may be that it was then that medics and statesmen really began to combat it in a systematic way. In general, over the sixteenth and seventeenth centuries the plague erupted here and there at intervals, battening on regions or communities before moving on. There was no national epidemic as such – not even the great Castilian plague of 1596–1602, or the Mediterranean outbreak of 1647–52 – but rather a series of localised outbreaks, resembling a kind of war of attrition.

One can get a better idea, perhaps, of the recurring impact of epidemic if one looks at just one community over time. Valencia, with its 50,000 people, was alleged to have lost 11,000 (from the district as well as the city) in 1489–90. Then came the 'many deaths' of March to July 1508, when 300 people a day were dying in the city – fifty times the usual mortality rate for a pre-industrial city, if we can trust the chronicler. There were further outbreaks in July 1519, which contributed to the panic leading up to the revolt of the guilds that year, and again in June 1530, in July 1557 and through to the summer of 1559 when some 30,000 died in the kingdom of Valencia as a whole.[53] Valencia escaped the plague of 1564 in neighbouring Aragon, and that of 1589 in Barcelona. The great Castilian epidemic of 1596–1602 nipped towns like Xàtiva, strategically situated along the main road from the meseta to Valencia, but it failed to penetrate deep into the Mediterranean lands. These were battered soon after, however, by contagion from Italy (the plague of Milan immortalised by Manzoni's novel) in 1630, and from Algiers in 1647. This last of the great Valencian plagues is particularly well documented, thanks to the efforts of a Dominican friar, Francisco Gavaldá, who ran one of the plague hospitals and who was an exceptionally acute observer. He tells us that 16,789 persons died, nearly a third of the city's population. 'I only put down those I could check in the records', he tells us modestly.[54] The epidemic spread through the province and along the Mediterranean coast, down to Andalusia and up to Catalonia. In Seville perhaps 50,000 – again, over a third of the population – were killed. The great plague of 1647–52 was followed by another in 1676–85 with its focus in Andalusia, spreading along the Mediterranean again towards the towns of southern Valencia – Orihuela, Elx, Crevillent. By comparison with these periodic disasters the eighteenth century seems a haven of tranquillity.

Determining when a plague outbreak actually began is not easy. The chronicler of Segovia, Diego de Colmenares, conveys a vivid sense of the apprehension and uncertainty as sickness and rumour of sickness began to mount. Though the great Castilian epidemic only reached Segovia in February 1599, 'from the year 1596 the towns of Vizcaya and some in Castile were infected with a virulent and contagious illness . . . with swellings or tumours and carbuncles in the groin, on the throat and under the arms; the pulse began to race and become irregular, followed by sweating and vomiting'. Ortiz de Zúñiga, chronicler of Seville and eye-witness of the terrible events there in 1649, also conveys the build-up of tension. 'From the year 1646 the plague had been nipping the port towns of Andalusia.' But it was after the floods of 4 April 1649 that people in Seville began complaining of 'dizziness, nausea and upset stomachs'. Then, later in the month, came 'violent fevers, lumps, carbuncles, bubos and other kinds of deadly complications'. When people were dying at the rate of 500 a day – perhaps thirty times as many as would normally have died in a city that size – the authorities declared a state of plague.[55]

There was considerable reluctance, of course, to take such a step because it meant a virtual blockade of the infected city. There had been sickness in Cadiz since the end of 1648, but Seville only closed its gates against this port in February 1649 after the annual fleet for the Indies had cleared harbour. But there was also genuine uncertainty about the symptoms of plague. The panel of doctors assembled by the viceroy in the spring of 1648 could not agree whether the recent epidemic in Valencia had been plague or not. Some of the early symptoms reported in Seville and Valencia – particularly the dizziness and fever – might be typhus. It was only in 1898 that the plague bacillus was identified, and typhus only fully understood in the early twentieth century. The pattern of outbreaks in Spain seems to conform, though, to what we know of plague in the rest of pre-industrial Europe. Generally there had been a bad harvest the year before – in August 1598 round Segovia, according to Colmenares, and in Valencia before 1647, according to Gavaldá. These observers were inclined to blame the weakened physical condition of the poor as an explanation of why the disease took hold; historians nowadays think in terms of the import of grain and of the accompanying rats, though it has to be said that there are few references to rats in the Spanish or European literature of the period. The mixture of humidity and heat, though, seems to have provided ideal conditions for the flea, the real carrier of plague and typhus, to multiply – as in April 1649 after flooding in Seville. And – though the plague erupted in Segovia in February 1599 – the chronicler Colmenares referred darkly to 'the autumn, always an unhealthy time', with its mixture of warmth and rain. And in Valencia the plague of 1647 reached its height in October.

The blockade of infected areas was the first general response to epidemic, as on 21 May 1649 when a government decree forbade the entry to Madrid of people and goods coming from Seville and other Andalusian towns on pain of death. Contemporaries blamed outbreaks on contagion – on the two ships from Flanders which had touched at Santander in 1596, on a ship from Algiers docking in Valencia in 1647. But the decision to interrupt communications was harrowing. What was one to do, for example, with the 114 Christians ransomed from slavery in Algiers, who had landed in Valencia in October 1647? The panel of doctors voted that all their belongings should be destroyed, their bodies shaved and immersed repeatedly in sea-water during a strict quarantine. Enforcing quarantine was not, however, easy: in Valencia in 1647 the nobility fled at an early stage to their country houses, and Gavaldá tells us that the full penalty was never imposed on those who came in from infected areas, while in Barcelona fugitives from the besieging Castilian army seem to have kept the plague going over the winter of 1651–2.[56] Part of the problem was jurisdictional. As early as June 1599 the city of Valencia dispatched commissioners to the frontiers of the kingdom to ward off contagion from Castile; but in January 1600 when the disease took hold in Xàtiva it could only demand that all persons who had come from there since Christmas should leave the capital, and turned to the king's judges to punish those who had broken the quarantine at the frontier.

An interesting feature of the seventeenth century, in fact, is the increasing coordination of quarantine measures at national level. In Segovia in 1599 it was the bishop and aldermen who were in charge. But in Seville and Valencia in 1647–9 the intervention of the Crown is more apparent – in particular through the creation of 'Health Committees', associating royal judges with the municipal magistrates for the first time. Gavaldá notes the reluctance of the Valencian *jurats* to sacrifice their traditional prerogatives in the matter. By the summer of 1649 the Crown had posted guards along the Sierra Morena to seal off Andalusia, and the year before distributed copies of Luis de Mercado's excellent tract on plague (1598) to local authorities. The setting up on a permanent basis of a *Junta de Sanidad* in Madrid in 1720 at least facilitated the coordination of information – which Gavaldá, for one, regarded as vital and its absence a major handicap in 1647.

Within an infected city the burden of administration had to be left, of course, to the local authorities. Gavaldá gives a vivid sense of the early, tentative responses, and the growth of self-confidence by a process of trial and error over the summer and autumn of 1647. The first steps were generally to collect reliable information about the sick, who would be transported to isolation hospitals set up often outside the walls. The dead were supposed to be collected – by slaves and amnestied prisoners – and buried in special lime pits outside the city. In Seville there are reports of corpses being dragged out of houses secretly at night and abandoned in the street, or in the porch of a church, their belongings thrown after them, without waiting for the municipal carts. The plague pits in that city were a horrific spectacle, reports Ortiz de Zúñiga, with the piles of bodies 'barely covered with earth giving off an intolerable stench', and 'corrupting the air', which promoted further infection.

The so-called 'miasma' theory, by which plague was attributed to this kind of putrefaction, gave creditable results in practice. It led the Valencians to send round carts collecting rubbish for the first time, to householders being instructed to clean the fronts of their houses every day, and to the repeated scrubbing of hospital floors. 'Cleanliness is one of the greatest foes of plague,' commented Gavaldá, who had first-hand experience of running a hospital. In Seville there were blazing bonfires of rosemary and thyme, in Segovia of juniper to purify the air; and perhaps the fires kept burning within the hospitals for the same purpose made the environment less hospitable for the flea .

Doctors played a crucial role in all these epidemics. Juan Tomás Porcell, a

Sardinian educated in Salamanca, practised the first systematic (and rare) autopsies on plague victims in the hospitals of Zaragoza in 1564.[57] With an already distinguished school of anatomy, Spain contributed notably to the European literature on this disease. The therapy was, admittedly, experimental. The doctors noted, in Cordoba in 1649 as in Valencia two years before, that bleedings (that universal remedy of early modern medicine) were counterproductive, weakening and killing the patient.[58] All doctors could do was to help the pustules mature, and, for the rest, provide good food and a clean environment in which nature would take its course. The medical authorities in Valencia stressed the importance of food, and parish deputies were instructed to provide each home where a sickness had been reported with 'a quarter of a chicken, a portion of mutton, biscuits and sweets'.

One of the interesting features of the therapy, in fact, was the concern – perhaps attributable to the theory of bodily humours – with keeping the patient in good heart. Segovia, like Seville, forbade bells to be tolled for the dead, 'to alleviate some of the frightful sadness'. And in Seville the magistrates sent musicians through the streets 'so that our humours should not turn to gloom and melancholy'. In Valencia in 1647 the viceroy ordered that business was to proceed as usual; the courts continued to sit, the corn exchange to open its doors, and royal officials were forbidden to leave their posts. But in other cities – where the doctors could agree that they were dealing with plague – there were stricter measures against public assemblies: the closure of schools and theatres in Segovia and Seville, for example.

A dilemma arose with regard to religious processions. Explanations of disease in terms of magic were not much honoured in Spain, where the careful legalism of the Inquisition discounted most reports of witchcraft. Typically it was a doctor attached to the Inquisition of Seville who cast scorn on the idea that pestilential powders (invoked in some parts of Europe) could spread disease.[59] More room was made – as by Ortiz de Zúñiga – for the influence of the stars on the bodily humours. But the more common explanation was in terms of a punishment for sin. Inevitably, therefore, prayers were organised to beg God's mercy. There were big processions in Seville in the early months with statues and relics. In Valencia they walked through the streets, 'some with rough cords bound tightly at the waist, others dragging huge chains, and others carrying heavy crosses', accompanied by 400 girls, 'all barefoot, with their hair hanging down and their faces covered with black veils'. But Gavaldá, Dominican friar though he was, felt that it would be more prudent to stay at home and pray, and his compatriot, the Jesuit Arcayna, referred to the medical opinion that women and children were laying themselves more open to infection by these exhausting penances.[60] Barcelona suspended processions shortly after the outbreak of plague there in 1651. In general, the church seems to have cooperated quite happily with the secular authorities in this matter, and the emphasis was always on the physical rather than metaphysical explanation of disease. Valencia spent 200 pounds in March 1600 on 'good works and masses' against the threat of plague, but 4,000 on checking the health of immigrants at the frontier.

How much damage did plague do? Recovery rates in hospital could be quite high. Several hundred left those of Segovia at the end of the epidemic of 1599, in a joyful procession, accompanied by their priests and doctors on horseback. The unfortunate ones were generally those who had contracted the pneumonic plague or typhus – those in Valencia or Seville who were gripped by sudden delirious fevers and carried off within twenty-four hours. And it was chiefly the lower classes who suffered. No nobleman died in Valencia, Gavaldá tells us, 'because, except for the royal officials and one or two others, all left town'. His own figure of 16,789 dead may be too high; but the best recent estimates still suggest up to a third of the city population died. The tendency in recent demographic study, in Spain as in Europe, is to play down the effect of epidemics. Even the great Castilian plague of 1596–1602 which claimed 600,000 lives – perhaps one in ten of the population – only made its impact felt gradually, in the downswing of marriages and births in the 1620s. But it is hard to decide whether this fall was due to the missing cohort of young victims of the great plague, or to the bleak economic prospects for marriage at the later date.[61]

Though plague could devastate rural districts as well as cities, it was always a relatively localised phenomenon. Thus Ortiz de Zúñiga witnessed the great number of immigrants arriving in Seville after 1649 – not enough, though, to prevent wages shooting up, nor to fill even by his own day (1677) 'the great number of houses left empty, and even entire neighbourhoods'. In Valencia the plague of 1647 could hardly have come at a worse time since the kingdom was in the front line against the Catalan rebels and their French backers. The Valencian garrison in the border fortress of Tortosa had to be reduced to half-strength, and the French stormed in during June 1648. The Valencian guilds refused any men because of the recent plague, but 2,000 were somehow assembled from the hinterland, though the viceroy warned that they would be hard to feed since the ports were closed due to quarantine. When in November 1650 the government launched its big offensive for the recovery of Tortosa, the city of Valencia was able to furnish a contingent of 500 men, and other sources brought the total from the little kingdom to over 4,000 – the biggest army the Valencians had assembled in modern times, and a unique tribute to their demographic resilience after one of their worst plagues.

The cost of plague, though, went well beyond the drop in manpower. The Valencian silk-workers complained about the harm to their trade caused by the closure of the port, only opened in April 1649. Towns had to borrow to meet the costs, not least of the food provided for the poor. A tax of two shillings in the pound on the price of wine was one lasting memorial to the Valencian plague of 1647. In Segovia priests 'went round the houses of the nobles and wealthy citizens, whose servants went back with them carrying blankets, sheets, shirts, suits of clothes and delicacies for the hospitals'.

The psychological aspect of plague has also to be taken into account. The spectacle of so much death seems to form a backdrop to the pessimism of the Baroque – a sense of disillusion with this world, so characteristic of Spanish art and literature of the Golden Age. 'In no time does vice have such a free rein as in time of plague,' wrote Gavaldá, as social order broke down, as neighbours turned from each other in fear, as women were left to fend for themselves and men turned to robbery. Yet one would also have to stress a heightened awareness of divine power, reinforcing the Counter-Reformation message. Segovia voted in 1599 to dedicate a day every year to honour Saint Roque, patron saint of plague victims; and the enduring monument to the plague of 1647 is the basilica of Our Lady of the Forsaken, a masterpiece of the Valencian Baroque. It is hard not to feel that the grimness of seventeenth-century plagues owe something to the greater information we have about them than about their predecessors. The collection of information by authorities is one of their most impressive aspects, part of that inventory of the resources of Spain which was proceeding in the early modern period.

3

THE LIMITS OF A
PEASANT ECONOMY

One of the characteristics of the early modern world was the acceleration of that process conveniently if loosely described as the transition from feudalism to capitalism. It was a complex phenomenon, in which economic, social and political factors interact with each other. We shall focus here on agriculture, though the full story will only gradually unfold in the course of the rest of the book. Traditional interpretations of Spain suggested the survival there into modern times of traditional farming and an impoverished peasantry, whose restlessness contributed powerfully to the collapse of nascent democracy in 1936. More recently, a revisionist view has been put forward, which draws attention to the 'Spanish miracle' of the eighteenth and nineteenth centuries, when production and markets seemed to flourish.[1] Yet, on the eve of the modern age, the survival of peasant farming was perhaps the most characteristic feature of the rural landscape – an empty landscape for the statesmen of the Enlightenment: still not fully settled or properly exploited.

A major challenge facing the Spanish farmer was that of the sheer lack of water for cultivation. 'If we were only to bleed the rivers,' wrote the great Jesuit philosopher-historian Mariana in 1598, 'we would not only get more grain but have a healthier countryside.' Considerable technical ingenuity was, in fact, devoted to this problem. The great dam at Tibi was built between 1580 and 1594, fertilising the dry lands of Alicante. Spanning a gorge 78 metres wide, to a height of 45 metres, it was surely the most impressive engineering feat of its kind in pre-industrial Europe – 'really worthy to rank with the works of the Romans for its grandiose and ingenious construction', wrote Escolano shortly after it was completed. But it never actually delivered as much water as was hoped, and other projects – like the proposal of Toledo in the Cortes of 1583–5 to tap the River Tagus – bore even less fruit.

Part of the problem was the sheer immensity of the technological challenge. The rivers of Spain tend to run through broken terrain mostly unsuitable for agriculture, and their flow is uneven – torrential in winter, sluggish in summer. As Jovellanos noted in 1795, government intervention would be needed on a considerable scale to strengthen the banks, to cut deep canals through the hills and to provide locks to level off the flow. Such coordination of effort only became fully available in the twentieth century. In the early modern period individual towns had to bear the brunt of planning and costs, and their endeavours, though sometimes heroic, were generally insufficient. Vilanova de Castelló (Valencia) borrowed heavily over several generations between 1587 and 1645 to build and maintain an irrigation canal. The interest on the debt amounted to nearly 7,000 Valencian pounds a year, dwarfing a municipal budget of just 1,000.[2]

There was also the problem of getting agreement of towns downstream to the diversion of their water. Plans were drawn up in 1616 to irrigate large tracts of Catalonia through the Urgell canal, but nothing was achieved until the nineteenth century. The government wanted the local proprietors to foot the bill, but they were nervous about an expected fall in wheat prices if production was to soar upwards as anticipated.[3] In fact studies of the main regions of irrigation – Valencia and Murcia – would tend to suggest that comparatively little was achieved in the early modern period to add to the infrastructure set in place by the Romans and Arabs. The huerta of Valencia, one of the marvels of its time, was perpetually short of water until the nineteenth century when the canals were improved and artesian wells dug. Before that the farmer might only be able to irrigate his fields once every three weeks in summer.[4] This was no good for market-gardening, and much of the huerta was used for the standard crops of the arid land: wheat, vine and olive.

Where there was an adequate supply of water, this combined with the warmth of the sun to give some of those oases of cultivation for which Spain was famed. Along the banks of the river of Jaén, known to the Arabs as the Guadalbullón ('the river of silver'), were trees laden with cherries, plums, pomegranates, apricots, pears, apples and walnuts, standing amid the vegetable patches and the fields of flax and hemp, according to the proud listing of the local chronicler. But more generally, perhaps, access to water enabled farmers to ride out the uncertainties of the Spanish climate as they struggled to get in their crops of grain. The great Aragonese geographer Asso noted in 1791 that the Monegros might give fifteen times the wheat seed sown if it rained, but in dry years 'not even the seed can be recovered'.[5] The Monegros is an extreme case of a drought-prone area. But the problem was general enough. In the very dry autumn of 1626 and early spring of 1627 none of the unirrigated lands of Valencia could be ploughed or sown, according to the grim reports of the ministers responsible for introducing the additional taxes demanded by Olivares's government.

Another of Olivares's targets in 1626 was Catalonia, which looked so prosperous that it must have money to spare for the king. The Jesuit Manuel Marcillo was to praise the province in 1685 for its dispersed settlement, which kept the farmer close to his fields and fostered good arable cultivation. The pattern of settlement had many causes, but access to water was surely a factor. Along the banks of rivers, wrote the Valencian chronicler Escolano in 1610, one found 'innumerable settlements'. Navagero, travelling through Spain in 1525, found the Basque Country well-peopled: 'everywhere you see little villages, hamlets and farms, which makes a very pleasant picture'. How different were his comments on the road from

Andalusia north through New Castile, with its 'empty and desolate landscape' and its 'uninhabited and uncultivated countryside'. Such comments were sometimes ill-informed and misleading. But commentators of the early modern period were aware of the benefits to be derived from close attention to digging and weeding by a locally resident farming family.

Agriculture is an art, wrote Jovellanos in 1795, and like other arts 'draws its principles from science'. Early modern Spain produced a number of distinguished writers, whose work is at once a reflection of the scientific orientation of their society and of the practical challenges facing the farmer. The outstanding name is that of Gabriel Alonso de Herrera (1470?–1540?). Son of a rich peasant of Talavera de la Reina, he was attached as a page to Archbishop Talavera (to whom he may have been related) when the latter took charge of the recently conquered see of Granada. There he got to know Moorish writings on agriculture, and had also the opportunity to travel in France and Italy. Through his brother who was professor in the new university of Alcalá de Henares, founded by Archbishop Cisneros, Herrera received the backing of that influential prelate and patron of humanism to publish his treatise of 1513 on agriculture. The book is a monument in its own way to Renaissance learning, collating information from the classical writers like Columella (himself a Spaniard of the first century AD) but subjecting them to the test of personal observation. The author's brother Hernando wrote that the nobles abandoned the fables of chivalry to read this fascinating revelation of the real world, and the peasants themselves 'no longer meet in taverns on holy days but read and learn what they must do when they get back to work'.[6]

Some laughed at this pretention. Various deputies to the Cortes of 1580 opposed a subsidy for the reprinting of yet another treatise on agriculture, that of Juan Valverde de Arrieta (1578), on the grounds that farmers scorned such books, quite rightly, since their prescriptions 'are taken from ancient and foreign authors' who knew little of local conditions. But Arrieta, Lope de Deza (1618) and Fray Miquel Agustín (1617) constitute, along with Herrera, major contributions to our understanding of Iberian farming. Herrera's book became a classic: there were twenty-nine editions over the sixteenth and seventeenth centuries (including several Italian and one French translation), and, though it seems to have declined in popularity during the eighteenth century, it was reissued as a guide to good practice by the Economic Society of Madrid as late as 1818.

A common feature of these works is their reverence for nature. They prefer, certainly, the order imposed by man to the wilderness beloved of the Romantics; but they are acutely sensitive to the unity of natural phenomena – the influence of the stars and the relationship between different kinds of plants and the human organism. Check on the phases of the moon, warned Father Agustín, before killing your animals, shearing your sheep or pruning or grafting your trees; and similar advice was extended by Arrieta to the manuring of the soil. Herrera set out the tasks of the agricultural year 'according to the waxing or waning of the moon', and, like Lope de Deza, was sure that astrology could help forecast the weather.

But he also urged the farmer to look around him, at the colour of the sky at dawn and at the season of migration of swallows and cranes, in a significant step forward in humanity's slow inventory of the physical universe.

The emphasis in these writings is more on fertility than on productivity – on the balance which one can achieve with nature rather than on its transformation. As Herrera pointed out, a year of fallow, perhaps more on poorer soil, was the key to good farming. Continuous rotation, with flax and maize planted after wheat, was only for well-watered and well-manured fields. And neither water nor manure should be applied in excess, since the one tended to leach the soil, the other to burn it and foster weeds. The principal task of the farmer, on the dry lands of the central tableland, was to turn the soil frequently in order to counter the loss of natural moisture through evaporation. Plough the fallow 'to the palm of a hand' (21 centimetres) in autumn, advised Arrieta, and spread manure; then plough again, a bit deeper, before Christmas, so that the rains penetrate. Then turn the soil over the following May, allowing the sun to kill weeds at the root; and, finally, sow your grain that autumn, driving the plough in 42 centimetres. 'The more ploughings the better', thought the Catalan agronomist Father Agustín, though the rhythm would be dictated by the type of soil and the climate. The fallow would have to be well-worked and manured between about All Saints' Day (1 November), when the rains softened the earth, and the beginning of Advent (the four weeks before Christmas) or Saint Andrew's Day (30 November), when the wet and cold made the land inhospitable. In the kingdom of Toledo, thought Lope de Deza, the sun would bake the fallow too hard for ploughing by Saint John's Day (24 June), but the Old Castilian farmer might continue for another month.

The main purpose of ploughing in these southern latitudes was to counter evaporation; hence, as Herera noted, 'you must always plough crosswise, cutting across the furrow you have just made'. This stood in marked contrast to the familiar ridge-and-furrow pattern of fields in northern Europe, where the main concern was drainage. The long fields there had evolved in the Middle Ages in order to facilitate the heavy plough with its team of oxen or horses which were needed in damp clay. But in the Iberian peninsula the fields tended to be squat, reflecting the transversal movement of which Herrera spoke. But did this plough-ing lead to good cultivation? Antonio Ponz believed that it turned the earth too lightly, leaving the seed exposed to winter frosts and to being eaten by birds. Arrieta had suggested that the ploughshare would need to bite to a depth of 42 centimetres at sowing, and Pérez del Barrio (1697) even advocated 63.[7] Often, it seems, Spanish ploughs were not sturdy enough to achieve these depths. The Aragonese economist Asso suggested in 1798 that the farmer had to wait until the autumn rains thoroughly soaked the earth before being able to cut through, thus casting up damp clods instead of finely pulverised soil and creating the right environment only for thistles – a constant plague round Zaragoza.

Contemporaries identified two aspects of the problem. Townsend paid par-ticular attention in the course of his travels to the construction of the ploughs themselves. The typical Roman or swing plough of the peninsula, with an iron share but no coulter or mouldboard, seemed suitable to its task on light soils. Townsend noted that the angle of the share could be adjusted to allow the plough to bite less deeply at the first breaking of the fallow, more deeply when sowing. If there was a problem of dampness, mouldboards could be fitted to allow ridges to be formed. But there seemed to be areas of the peninsula – for example, between Madrid and Toledo – where either the soils were too heavy or the ploughs were too short of wood and iron to bite deeply enough into them.[8] More of a problem was the condition of the draught animals. The traditional plough animal had been the ox. Sometimes badly utilised – Caxa de Leruela in 1631 and Townsend in 1791 noted that the system of traction in parts of the peninsula involved the animal in pushing with its forehead against a cross-beam rather than in pulling with its chest against a yoke – it was nevertheless sturdy and ploughed deep. Townsend observed lots of oxen between Malaga and Granada at the end of the eighteenth century, and they were still about two-thirds of the stock used round Segovia at the time.[9] The ox, indeed, continued to be used down to modern times when heavy land needed to be broken for the first time. But a closure of the frontier and a shrinkage of pasture made it at once less necessary and something of a menace (for example, to vines or market gardens).

Also, it was a lumbering, costly animal. It required an outlay of 20–25 ducats, according to an estimate put before the Cortes of 1593–6, and about double that amount in 1631, according to the economic writer Caxa de Leruela. Meanwhile a horse could be had for 12–14 ducats, according to another report to the Cortes in 1624. But the horses of Spain, as we noted earlier, were generally of poor quality, short of proper fodder, and too reliant on barley in New Castile and Andalusia or on the carob bean in Valencia. Instead, recourse was had to the hybrid of horse and donkey, the resistant and nimble mule. However, mules were not cheap. To draw a plough a farmer would need ideally two of them, costing the princely sum of 200 ducats – several years' wages for an agricultural labourer and accessible to most peasants only on two or three years' credit.[10] The rise of the mule, thought Arrieta, was senseless: it led the peasant into debt and ousted the sturdier ox. But Father Agustín noted that 'a pair of mules can do the work of two yoke of oxen'; and Lope de Deza explained the shift in terms of the mule's adaptibility to a wide variety of carrying tasks. In general, the rise of the mule in the sixteenth and seventeenth centuries surely reflected the greater urbanisation of the Spanish countryside – the shrinkage of pasture at the expense of market gardens and vines which required shallower ploughing.

One of the great conflicts in early modern Spain was, as Caxa de Leruela phrased it vividly, that between Cain and Abel, between pasture and arable.[11] This frontier land seemed to be experiencing something akin to the range war of the American West – the battle between the rancher and the dirt-farmer. At first sight the quarrel seems unnecessary in a country like Spain where so much wilderness still survived. Viciana's chronicle of 1563 describes the empty spaces which characterised particularly the south of the kingdom of Valencia; while around Jaén, in Ximénez Patón's chronicle of 1628, the boar, deer and mountain goats still abound in the well-wooded mountains. As late as 1842 George Borrow wrote of the mountains separating Galicia from Castile, covered with chestnut groves, as 'haunts of the wolf, the wild boar and the corzo or mountain-stag', while in the Guadarrama Mountains separating Old and New Castile 'you may wander days and days . . . without coming to any término (townland)'.[12]

In fact, the waste was integrated into a system of shifting cultivation, adapted to the poor soil and shortage of rain. In the *Relaciones* of 1575–8 the villages of Nava del Pino and Sacaruela refer to the process of clearing scrub through setting fire to it, creating a fertile seedbed from the ashes which would yield richly for a year or two before the site was abandoned again to nature. As late as the middle of the nineteenth century the chronicler Las Casas-Deza described vividly the practice in some parts of his native province of Cordoba. Beyond the circle of well-tilled lands radiating out two or three kilometres from town came the hill country, where 'they cut down the plants in March and April, so as to set fire to it in August; then they cast the seed in due time and cover it over with one cut of the plough'.[13] The damage done to tree cover was extensive. Round Valladolid Ponz noted that such shifting cultivation on poor soil had turned the land into pàramos – windswept steppe, lacking vegetation and subject to erosion, of little use to man or beast. Shortly afterwards Cavanilles was to condemn similar wasteful practices in Valencia.

Such extensive farming was only made possible by the lack of individual title to property. Much of the country was held as common land, which belonged to the townships. If it was valuable it might be leased out (*propios*), but most seems to have been classed as *baldíos*, 'empty land', where even municipal boundaries were not clearly demarcated and possession resided with occupation or with the king. Some 25–30 per cent of the Tierra de Campos (Valladolid) was common land in the sixteenth century, and a quarter of the lands of the province of Segovia still in the middle of the eighteenth century after two centuries of sale of commons by the Crown.[14]

After all, the Castilian tableland had developed as a pastoral region, home of the fine merino wool from the thirteenth century. Intense heat in summer, leading to scarcity of grass, drove sheep throughout the Mediterranean basin up into the hills in search of fresher pastures. Spain developed an 'inverse transhumance': because of the high altitudes in Old Castile, its sheep had to move away from the snow and cold, seeking milder winter pastures in the lowlands of Andalusia and Extremadura. Aragonese herds made a similar trek down to the coastal plain of Valencia. Transhumance was widespread over the peninsula and often small scale, from hill to plain and back again, following the seasons. As a result there tended to be a community of pasture in certain areas – throughout the old Muslim kingdom of Granada, for example, and in the kingdom of Valencia, though not without protests from individual townships, eager to safeguard their own grassland.

The best-known of these transhumant arrangements is that of the Mesta, which grouped (essentially) the herds of Old Castile and León and escorted them south in winter to Extremadura and Andalusia. It was set up in 1273, just after the recovery of Andalusia from the Moors. Anyone with ten sheep could apply to belong to the guild. In practice it was a costly business to transport sheep so far, only justified if one owned merino sheep which produced the fine wool increasingly in demand in the manufacturing towns of Flanders in the late Middle Ages. Almost by definition, one might say, it was an organisation which catered to a minority of landowners. Because the Crown received a considerable portion of its revenue from the duty on the export of merino wool, it surrounded the Mesta with privileges, notably allowing it to have its own magistrates (the *alcaldes entregadores*), who would adjudicate disputes over pasture and keep the range open. Ponz still witnessed, at the end of our period, the millions of sheep on the move south from late September or early October every year, in flocks averaging 10,000 head, each under its mayoral and his fifty assistant shepherds. They would cover 100–160 leagues (550–900 kilometres) in just over a month or so. In the winter pastures of the south the lambs were born, protected by enclosures of brushwood and nets erected by the shepherds. Then, the following spring, came the long trek back, to reach the shearing stations of the Guadarrama Mountains, at the entrance to Old Castile, by the month of May. The shearing would last a month or so, after which the flocks moved on to their summer pastures in the north where the shepherds were kept busy supplying them with salt during the mating season.[15] The whole odyssey was one of the most distinctive features of Castilian rural life.

Much effort has gone into quantifying it. There were nearly 3,000,000 transhumants in the Mesta in the early sixteenth century, falling back to under 2,000,000 by the early seventeenth, then recovering to 3,500,000 by the middle of the eighteenth century – even 5,000,000 by the end of the century, according to Ponz. Despite the reverses suffered in the seventeenth century in harmony with other aspects of the depression of that period, it is clear that transhumance remained a permanent feature of Castilian rural life in the old regime. In order to assess the full importance of pastoralism one has to take into account, in addition, the *estantes*, the non-migrating herds. If the Mesta provided Europe with fine wool, these – as the deputy for León reminded the Cortes of 1587 – kept Spain itself supplied with meat and wool. Four times the number of the transhumants, thought Caxa de Leruela in 1631, they numbered about 15,000,000 head in the great fiscal survey of Castile in 1750–4, though falling to 8,000,000 by the end of that century.[16]

Concern about the shrinkage of herds was most forcibly expressed in the late sixteenth and in the seventeenth century, though one might have thought that the increase of population in the eighteenth represented a greater threat to pasture. Certainly contemporaries were aware of a general fencing-off of the open range. The pastoralists themselves were divided: Xèrica (near Segorbe) asked in the Cortes of 1626 for permission to fence off its own extensive pastures 'since the herds which come down from Aragon to spend the winter in Valencia do great damage'. And the Castilian law of 1602 stripping the *alcaldes entregadores* of jurisdiction over non-Mesta flocks seems to be part of the same trend, towards a desire by local pastoralists to keep more of their district under their own control.

49

Caxa de Leruela noted in 1631 that the law of 1602 simply weakened the pastoral interest as a whole, which was threatened by the advance of arable. The sale of *baldíos* for enclosure was one way in which the Crown had been trying to raise money since the later sixteenth century.[17] As in Tudor England, enclosures aroused much moral anguish. It was only in the later eighteenth century that new currents of economic thought extolled the virtues of private enterprise, and only in 1766–70 that a series of government decrees positively encouraged the break-up of the commons. The earlier sales were almost furtive, and often illegal given that the Cortes regularly attached conditions forbidding sales to its vote of subsidies to the Crown. Nevertheless, there was a gradual shift from public to private ownership: the sale of commons under Philip II affected between 25 and 30 per cent of the surface area of the Tierra de Campos, and by 1751 over a quarter of the arable in the Tierra de Coca (Segovia) had been taken in from the commons since the sixteenth century.[18]

When enclosures were for arable, thought Caxa de Leruela, they ultimately did more harm than good. The cutting down of trees, the setting fire to the undergrowth, the eventual abandonment of marginal land which earlier farmers, with good reason, had refused to plough, all led to a general deterioration of the environment for both peasant and shepherd. Though the Crown supposedly sold only land which had already once been farmed, and though a law of 1501 allowed the Mesta to stop the conversion of any of its pasture to arable, Caxa de Leruela (himself a magistrate of that institution) noted how difficult it was in practice to enforce this ruling since there was no proper inventory of the wastelands. Another decree of 1492 had forbidden owners of land once rented to the Mesta to offer the lease to anyone else at a higher rent; nevertheless the pressure of the market ensured that leases trebled in value in the first half of the sixteenth century.[19]

Caxa de Leruela was aware of the hostility of contemporary society towards the Mesta as a corporation of privileged herd-owners who were holding down land which might be developed for more productive purposes. It was the basic aim of his book to counter these accusations and to demonstrate how vital pastoralism was to the whole 'mechanism of society'. Men need bread, but also clothes, and the procurement of these created the 'trades, exchanges, jobs, callings and manufactures' on which civilisation itself had developed. From wool, therefore, began the division of labour and the building of towns. The alleged selfishness of the big rancher was an illusion: most of the herds of Spain were small and a necessary complement to agriculture, not only for the manure and traction they provided, but, more generally, through their ease of transfer and sale, which enabled the peasant to raise cash to pay taxes, rent and dowries. Just what social class Caxa de Leruela had in mind is not entirely clear. He suggested that 500 sheep and 20 mules or their equivalent might constitute a 'moderate' herd, adapted to the farming which a householder might carry on himself, and too small to be 'coveted by the wealthy'. Compared with the 40,000 sheep owned by the royal monastery of the Escorial, or the 20,000 of the duke of Infantado or the 25,000 of the duke of Béjar, such figures might indeed seem modest. But even 500 sheep seem to have been considerably beyond the resources of most Castilian farmers. Two-thirds of the flocks even of the Mesta consisted of under 100 head in the middle of the sixteenth century.[20]

Caxa de Leruela was, no doubt, right to suggest that a healthy pastoralism was an indispensable complement to a healthy agriculture. The problem was perhaps less one of shrinkage of land for pasture – there still seems to have been enough of that even at the end of the eighteenth century – than of a shortage of capital to buy and maintain sheep. Certainly there was a period of crisis, reflected, for example, in the complaints of Cuenca to the Cortes of 1577 that its herds had fallen by half over the last fifteen years. Like Burgos at this time, it blamed less the advance of arable than the crisis in the wool trade – the blockage of the traditional export market with the war in Flanders since 1567, and the general impoverishment of rural society caused by the increase of taxation to sustain Spanish arms abroad. In other words, the herds of Spain – so enduring an ingredient of its rural prosperity – were not so much in competition with arable as victims of a similar recession.

A paradox, as it might seem, of the enclosure movement was that it occurred at a time when the rural population was in decline. There was a drop from the later sixteenth century not only in the number of sheep but also in the cultivation of the arable. A major index of this phenomenon is the record of the tithes or tenth parts of the harvest collected by the church in Spain as in the rest of Christian Europe. The tithe varied in its incidence, being most carefully assessed on grain but often compounded for a lump sum in the case of secondary crops like vegetables. The mulberry and the carob, so important in the kingdom of Valencia by the seventeenth century, tended to be lightly taxed since they had not been widely grown in the thirteenth century when the rules for tithe were set down – as the clergy complained to the Cortes of 1626. The tithe, therefore, can give us at best only an approximation to the real state of the harvests. This is all the more true since it was generally farmed out for a lump sum to tithe-farmers, whose actual collection can only be checked in a few places by reference to local parish records. More often the historian has to deflate the price paid for the tithe-farm by an index of prices in order to arrive at an idea of the actual fluctuations of the harvest.

Much research has been carried out in Spain in recent years on this subject, and we are beginning to see the profile of agricultural production over the early modern period. There are, perhaps, few surprises, with the curve of grain output corresponding roughly to that of population. Between the 1580s and 1630s there was a fall of about 40 per cent in the harvest of wheat and barley in Castile. Recovery set in during the later seventeenth century – in Castile, perhaps in Andalusia, certainly in Murcia and Valencia.[21] By the middle of the eighteenth century the old peak of 1580 was attained again. Thereafter the bad harvests of the 1760s highlighted some of the underlying problems of a traditional economy geared to the production of grain.

The agricultural revolution of modern times, which would permit population to break through the ceiling of about 40 inhabitants to the square kilometre, depended on a variety of factors. The key was probably less the application of new knowledge than of an intensification of techniques already known. The decline of the fallows allowed a finer, more continuous tillage of the soil, creating better conditions for the germination of grain. But in order to eliminate the fallow – as it had been, for example, in the Valencian huerta since medieval times – one needed a good supply of water and manure, and some guarantee that the crops intercalated between the grain would find a market. The secret was to plant crops which rooted in layers of the soil not touched by wheat – turnips in eighteenth-century England, which served as fodder for the cattle, thereby increasing the supply of manure for next year's grain harvest. In 1513 Herrera noted that the farmer could plant millet in May or June after he had lifted his barley, 'burning the stubble first', or flax in March 'on land which has given turnips for Lent'. And, 'as in Lombardy', one could plant turnips after wheat, using them either as fodder for cattle or as a green manure to be ploughed back into the soil, thereby increasing its fertility. In Catalonia it was this 'robbing of the fallow' – the planting of turnips and vetches between years of wheat – which was giving the province its air of rural prosperity in the eighteenth century.[22]

But Valencia and Catalonia were now some of the more densely populated parts of Spain, with the network of markets which made it possible to dispose of cash-crops. On the central tableland a more scattered population would find it hard to integrate legumes or root-crops into its traditional cycle of grain and fallow. Short of humus, the clay surface bakes hard in the summer and turns water-logged after the autumn rains. It was conventional wisdom that such a surface needed a year of continuous ploughing to make it fit for sowing wheat in the following autumn – 'after the rains and frosts have rotted the earth well (in winter), and the sun in the following months has baked and pierced it', in the words of Lope de Deza.[23] An equally compelling reason for the retention of a fallow one year in two, or even two years in three, as was the practice in parts of early modern Spain, was to assure pasture for the numerous flocks of sheep. The stubble provided an essential supplement to the parched waste which constituted grazing in so much of the central tableland. In Old Castile, particularly, the regulation of the fallow became an integral part of village life from at least the sixteenth century. Grain was cultivated in open fields, split into parcels which had to follow a common rotation, so that the herds could wander freely after harvest.[24] The enclosures of the sixteenth and seventeenth centuries made some inroads, but not as many as might be expected. Vineyards were increasingly fenced off. But perhaps one of the worst effects of enclosures was to aggravate the divorce between pasture and arable which has been a handicap for the rural economy.

In the westerly parts of the Meseta, where the soil is sandy and leached by the Atlantic rains, the tendency has been in modern times for pasture to dominate, and for fields to be ploughed intermittently. Part of this system must have been reinforced by developments in the early modern period. Following the long wars of attrition against Portugal after that country asserted its independence in 1640, the flight of the peasantry along the frontier had led to many *despoblados* (deserted villages) – in one area just 13 were left out of 127. The empty land was turned into an open range for 'powerful herd-owners', to the detriment both of local farmers and local flocks. Further south, in Andalusia, a similar divorce between those who owned big herds and those who had large tracts of arable has also been noted for the middle of the eighteenth century.[25] The problem may be compared to that facing much of Africa today – the separation between the pastoralist who occupies and defends an open range, burning vegetation in his path, and the arable farmer, too poor to secure the flocks which might manure his fields.

A combination of integration of cattle with arable, and of better tillage through the planting of fodder crops on the fallow was the kind of formula which evaded early modern Castile. On the well-ploughed, irrigated *huertas* of the Mediterranean coastline productivity was as high as anywhere in Europe in the old regime: ten or fifteen times the seed in the case of wheat, or twenty hectolitres of grain harvested per hectare.[26] Extensive cultivation in the dry lands – the burning of shrubs and the mixing of the ashes with the virgin soil – could give yields nearly as high as this in years when it rained. But on the typical biennial fallow of the central tableland the farmer could expect to get back just five times the seed he had sown, or just over 600 hectolitres per hectare, according to figures given in the middle of the seventeenth century by Fray Juan Martínez, Dominican confessor to King Philip IV.[27] The yields do not seem to vary much over our period, according to the records of even the bigger farms in the eighteenth century.

Inevitably the bigger population of the eighteenth century had to be maintained – decreasingly well, it would appear – on the product of marginal land brought in from the waste. But a major new factor was the increasing commercialisation of the rural economy. Cavanilles observed of his native Valencia in 1795: 'There is no doubt that twice the amount of land is now being cultivated in this kingdom as at the beginning of the century; but there can be little question either but that the greater part of the new acquisitions are planted with carob, olive, almond, vine and mulberry.'[28] One of the reasons for the supplanting of the ox by the mule, thought Caxa de Leruela in 1631, was the spread of vineyards (for the lumbering ox damaged the vine and ate the leaves). Three-quarters of the vines, he went on, had been planted since the beginning of the century. But already the Cortes of 1579–82 had been concerned that 'the planting of vines is spreading apace, and many idlers live by this business', reducing the amount of land available for wheat. In 1513, in a much less populated country, Herrera had warned that viticulture was very labour-intensive and that the farmer might find employment for his slaves in this way, if he had any. Inevitably, one feels, the increase of population during the rest of that century would find its outlet partly in the tending of vines. The problem was that the wine was often not very good, and local landowners tried to protect their own markets by regulations excluding or delaying the import of other vintages. For the agrarian writers of the time the rise of the vineyard symbolised the breakdown of the moral autonomy of the village. It led to the new popularity of the mule, increasingly necessary not only to plough vineyards but also to cart the wine to town and to bring back the luxuries which were contributing to the moral decline of the peasantry. Some say that wine helps the poor to pass their troubles, wrote Caxa de Leruela. But this is either disingenuous or a remedy for despotic government; for if idleness, to which the multitude is prone, and wine take hold in the villages, 'which are the homes of diligence, care and hard work', then it is all up with the rest of the commonwealth.[29]

Mulberry was another of the growing commercial crops of early modern Spain. So great had been the expansion in the valley of the Xúquer, wrote Escolano in 1610, that 'small villages have been turned into populous towns' – places like Carcaixent and Algemesí, which rose to become royal towns in the later sixteenth century on the profits of silk. Mulberry groves, about 4 per cent of the irrigated land of Alzira in 1580, occupied 7.5 per cent by the middle of the seventeenth century, while another three-quarters of the fields were lined with mulberry trees at the edges. In the marquesate of Llombai mulberry plantations accounted for 11 per cent of the irrigated land in 1581, rising to as much as 36.6 per cent in 1699, not counting the trees scattered here and there in other fields.[30] Curiously, perhaps, Valencian mulberry was always irrigated, which produced an abundant leaf but may have harmed its quality. Nevertheless, it was clear that by the end of the old regime large sections of the Valencian peasantry were being kept alive by the products they sold in the urban market.

Wine and mulberry are two of the more spectacular success stories, but everywhere we can find the penetration of cash-crops into the villages. Elx, short of water for wheat, had an abundance of olive and sodawort which combined to give a good soap much in demand abroad; and her neighbour Crevillent wove the esparto grass of her arid territory into mats and sandals, ancestor of the later shoe industry in that region. The villages of La Mancha also give the impression of being very much in contact with the outside world, according to their replies to the government inquiry – the *Relaciones* – of 1575–8. Generally well supplied with bread and wine of their own, they had often to import their timber, fish, iron, even their olive oil, and sometimes their fruit and vegetables. Manzanares, with its 700 mostly peasant families, 'brings in its olive oil from Andalusia and its fish from Seville, Cartagena and Malaga, and iron for its ploughs . . . from Vizcaya, and wood from Alcaraz and Cuenca and Tierra de Segura and other parts, and its silk and other merchandise from Toledo and elsewhere'.[31] The huge consumption of candles in processions and illuminations of houses during fiestas demanded an abundant supply of wax, and considerable attention is devoted in the pages of Viciana (1563–4) to an inventory of the beehives scattered over the kingdom of Valencia. In many of the highland parts of the same territory there were the caves, eight or nine metres deep, where snow was packed over the winter, from where it was ferried down to the scorched plain in summer to keep food fresh.

But the most important of these now half-forgotten rural exchanges was surely that in salt. Salt was a vital commodity in so many ways: 'The supply of salt is very necessary and important,' affirmed the Valencian Cortes of 1563, 'both for the life

of man and for the preservation of the herds, and [as part of] other kinds of food.'
It had been a monopoly of the Crown in Valencia and the rest of the Crown of
Aragon since the Middle Ages, and it became one in Castile in 1563. Spain had
good salt-pans along its coast and was, indeed, one of the principal sources of
supply for the rest of Europe. But the commodity itself was so basic and yet
located in so few places that its distribution always caused great concern. The
poor functioning of the royal monopoly in the kingdom of Valencia – the scarcity
of supply and high prices in the original nine gabelles or salt depots – called forth
constant complaints in the Cortes of the sixteenth and seventeenth centuries.

Overall, trade seemed vital to the peasantry. Not more than one household in
thirty, claimed the Cortes of Castile in 1579–82, could get by with just what it
grew for itself. Towards the middle of the seventeenth century the economic writer
Francisco Martínez de Mata stressed the value of manufactures to the peasantry.
The land was finite, and peasant fathers needed other resources if they were to
place their children in life. It was from their cottage industries of serge and
worsteds that 'they paid for the cost of ploughing and upkeep of their herds,
and for the furnishing of their houses, and gave work to their poorer neighbours'.
Already the Cortes of 1579–82 had conjured up the image of the hill country
round the great weaving towns of Segovia, Cuenca and Toledo, where the
putting-out industry meant that 'there was no man or woman, however old or
useless they might be, nor boy or girl of whatever age, who would not find a means
of livelihood' – before the rise of taxation had destroyed the manufactures.[32]

No doubt it would be a mistake to generalise from these impressions, which
were often designed to plead a special case. An insight into the real obstacles to
the full integration of the rural economy into the market system comes from the
splendid account of the three villages of the marquesate of Llombai in the
kingdom of Valencia, written by the governor of that estate, Francisco Benlloch,
for his mistress the duchess of Gandia in 1756. The population of 597 families had
excellent raw silk and good wine for sale, and they lay along the main route from
Castile to Valencia, which in those days passed through Almansa and Xàtiva.
They also needed to buy much of their bread, vegetables and clothes. But trade
was sluggish, as the governor noted, depending on the visits of itinerant traders
who would charge a third more for what they had to sell than the goods were
worth. The need was for shops, where goods could be stored all the year round;
but these required capital.[33] Also the local silk was sometimes available for sale
and sometimes not.

Not long after, Jovellanos gives us yet another perspective on the limitations of
the rural economy based on his observations of 1782 in the course of a journey to
his native Asturias. Rural manufactures were everywhere: the villages made their
own 'linen, serge, rough clothes and sackcloth, hides, stockings, and all that goes
to clothe and shoe a person, together with furniture, crockery and rural tools'. Yet
this rural industry could not create enough employment to retain the young
people. The peasants needed to be able to sell more to the urban market, and
for that technology and capital needed to be brought in to show them how to

make good-quality articles out of the wood, iron and flax in which their region was rich.[34]

The more general problem over most of Spain was simply the blockages in the distribution of the basic product: grain. Grain was a crop which often had to be traded like any other. Large amounts accumulated in the barns of the feudal lords, landowners, tithe-farmers and royal bailiffs awaiting a purchaser. The trade in tithes often seemed particularly obnoxious, and there were attempts to limit the right of the clergy to export bread from the local community and sell it where the price was higher. Such a conflict had surfaced already in one petition of the Valencian Cortes of 1533. And it underlay much of the indignation of the great Valencian jurist Tomás Cerdán de Tallada against tithe-farmers, who speculated in a commodity which piety would reserve for the poor. The Valencian peasants were not self-sufficient, he noted in his treatise of 1604. Harvesting their wheat in June, they had to sell it cheap in order to pay rents and debts which were generally due at Saint John's Day (24 June); but then they had to buy it back at an inflated price in the autumn for sowing.[35] It was a similar problem which the deputy for Soria highlighted in the Cortes of Castile in 1623: the peasants 'ordinarily sell the wheat which they harvest in August in order to pay their debts, and during the remainder of the year they buy it again at a dearer price both for seed and to keep themselves fed'.

The grain trade never functioned smoothly. In the first place the transport of such a bulky commodity by land always posed problems. The economic writer Fernández Navarrete noted in 1626 how difficult it was for Andalusia to get supplies from neighbouring La Mancha in time of need, and coastal regions like Andalusia or Valencia looked more to Sicily or North Africa. Even within the same region the situation was little better. The magnificent records of the administration of the royal third of the tithe (*tercio diezmo*) in Valencia show the bailiffs battling to dispose of their stocks. With wheat quoted at 21 shillings per *fanega* in Alcoi in 1625 and 28 shillings in Valencia city about 100 kilometres to the north, the Treasury thought that the transport to the capital would eat up the difference and authorised sale locally. Still in the middle of the nineteenth century the famous political economist Pascual Madoz commented that the poor state of the roads round Baena in the province of Cordoba – mudbaths in winter, narrow mule-tracks in summer – 'explains why prices are so low, particularly of wheat and olive oil, which have to be carried abroad on mule-back at great expense'.[36]

For much of the early modern period there was a moral aversion anyway to free trade in grain. Pedro de Valencia noted in 1605 that bread could not simply be left to the free play of market forces: 'We should consider only how many working days ought in justice to be given for a measure of corn so that the labourer may support himself.'[37] So the government adopted the *tasa*, a maximum price for grain, first in 1502 and then definitively from 1539. It exempted the northern provinces to a depth of ten leagues (about 56 kilometres) inland from the Cantabrian coast, because they were so short of wheat at the best of times. Cold regions of millet and cider, commented Pedro de Medina in 1545, the

Basque Country and Asturias had to import whatever wheat and wine they consumed from overseas. The *tasa* did not operate either in the Mediterranean provinces of Catalonia and Valencia, partly because they were under a different political jurisdiction and partly because of their dependence on the grain markets of Sicily and North Africa. The maximum price which was set for the grain of the central tableland had to be adjusted periodically upwards during the sixteenth century, from its original level of three Castilian *reales* per *fanega* in 1502 to eighteen a century later in 1605. There was a battle raging for much of this period between those who believed that a maximum price was essential for a well-ordered commonwealth and those who feared the damage being done to agriculture.

The debate reached a peak of intensity in the later sixteenth and early seventeenth century. Only the peasant and the poor respect the *tasa*, claimed the deputy for Cordoba in the Cortes of 1593, while his colleague from Murcia informed the session of 1583–5 that priests in his town were advising parishioners that they could sell licitly at whatever the market price was across the border in *tasa*-free Valencia. Already in 1569 the great Dominican economist Tomás de Mercado had urged priests to be more strict with those who came to them in confession and said they could not respect the *tasa* – 'for if I keep the law and offer less, [the other party] will find two thousand people who will give him even more; so I, wishing to be good, find I cannot buy'.[38] Meanwhile the Crown, revising the maximum price in 1571, decreed that those who hoped to escape the pains of the law – strict enough since offenders were to be banished from the kingdom for two years and lose half their property at the third offence – might recall the 'chief penalty' which was 'the threat to their own consciences'.

In fact, under a barrage of criticism, the *tasa* had to be revoked in 1619. Reimposed briefly in 1628, it was finally revised in 1632 to exempt the farmer from any maximum for his own grain, while insisting that middlemen must not sell at above the old ceiling of eighteen *reales* per *fanega*, Estimating the actual impact on agriculture of these measures is not easy. As Fernández Navarrete observed in 1626, 'a man who sells his wheat in Seville at eighteen *reales* is giving it away for less than someone in Tierra de Campos who sells for only twelve'. Tierra de Campos was the granary of Old Castile, where wages and the cost of living were much lower than in Seville. One was allowed to add transport costs on to the price at the point of sale, which eased some of the bottleneck and no doubt made it difficult to enforce the maximum exactly. Perhaps in the end the most damaging aspect of the *tasa* was that it brought law itself into disrepute. The massive study of prices by Hamilton estimated that fewer than half the grain transactions in New Castile and Andalusia were observing the maximum.[39]

Inevitably, though, it was left to the Enlightenment, as in the rest of Europe, to begin the dismantling of controls on trade, with the spread of the opinion that the prosperity of the society as a whole could be best assured by leaving producers free to get the highest profit they could for their goods. The count of Campomanes was the main force behind the government decision to abolish the *tasa* and remove restrictions on the movement of grain in 1765. In spite of food riots in Madrid and other towns in 1766 the government held firm. But the transition to a market economy was not an easy one. Most of the provincial corregidores reported in 1769 that the peasantry were generally too poor to benefit, having to sell their stock cheap, as always, just after the harvest to speculators who cornered the market. The authorities had to intervene periodically to prevent dearth – as in Granada in 1780, in time of drought, when they prudently set a ceiling of 64 *reales* per *fanega* on the wheat which shortly before had been selling for 15.[40] The old moral commonwealth was clearly being disbanded, but perhaps not with such self-assurance as in Hanoverian England.

One of the major symptoms of the disorder in rural society, lamented by early modern observers – at once a feature of urbanisation and a handicap to further progress in that direction – was peasant debt. The villages were short of ready cash. The farmer needed two or three years' credit, estimated the Castilian Cortes of 1623, if he was to buy a yoke of mules for ploughing. In 1626 the Valencian Cortes were deploring the haste with which the collectors of the Bull of Crusade did their work. The Bull had been granted by the popes to the kings of Spain to support the wars against the Moors, and amounted to a concession to eat dairy products in Lent in return for contributions to the crusade. It was one of the few taxes to be collected throughout Spain as a whole, and involved the peasantry digging into their pockets for cash. Sold by the preachers who came round just before Lent, in January and February, the Bull had then to be paid for in August after the harvest; but the peasants had not always their money ready in time. The great memorandum of 4 December 1593 to the Cortes of Castile, denouncing the widespread problem of peasant debt, referred to some of the causes: the traditional need to buy seed and cattle, but a new, more sinister contact with the mores of the town and its luxuries. No one should lend money to the peasants, 'which is the ruin of such an innocent and useful body of people', nor sell them on credit 'gold or silver or copper or sugar or spice, or any other merchandise beyond those which they usually and customarily consume'. Some years later Lope de Deza, in a general tirade against the invasion of the provinces by luxury – 'where once two tailors were enough, now they need twenty' – signalled the imitation of urban dress and the recourse to lawsuits by the peasantry as particular problems.[41]

The author went on to point out one of the traps associated with the rural market: peasants could never guarantee regular payments 'because of the uncertainty of the harvests and the illness or death of their livestock'. The envy traditional in small-scale communities led to the increasing use of lawyers and courts to fight vendettas. And, concluded Lope de Deza, 'the moth and worm which are really eating away at the villages and peasantry are the messengers of the courts and the bailiffs and the investigating officers who day after day descend upon them and out of small quarrels and debts make huge gains'.[42] Concern about the growing army of bailiffs and notaries who were battening upon the peasantry underlay much of the legislation of the Valencian Cortes between 1533 and 1645. Those of 1547 wanted to stop the summoning of people from their own communities to appear before the royal courts in Valencia city for debts in respect of 'wheat, livestock, and other merchandise [like] clothes and hoods'. Those of 1552 and 1563 directed their attention to the tithe-farmers, that new scourge created by the speculation in grain, and tried to stop their recourse to the bishop's court against defaulting peasants. And there was a wave of petitions in the Cortes of 1645 against notaries and bailiffs sent out from the central courts in Valencia city to distrain on local communities, and whose costs were alleged to be greater than the sum of the original debt.

Following the major petition of the Castilian Cortes of 4 December 1593, the peasant was exempted from the seizure of his person during the main harvest and sowing period from July to December, except in respect of money owed to his landlord, the king or the person who had lent money for the sowing in the first place. Also, at no time could ploughs or draught animals be seized for debt. When a law of 1623 extended the protection of the peasant's person to the whole year – following a recommendation of Lope de Deza – the deputy for Toledo warned that this might actually harm agriculture, since fewer people would now risk lending money to farmers. In the kingdom of Valencia there was a similar law but it only applied to the underpopulated frontier of Orihuela (1604). When the Cortes of 1645 tried to extend its provisions to the whole kingdom the government turned down the request on the grounds that money-lenders had already taken enough of a beating themselves in recent years.

In general, the whole saga of rural debt seems to highlight the misery of a peasantry which continued to hold on to its lands while carrying an increasing burden of debt. There was no neat transfer of property from the peasant to the capitalist entrepreneur. Many thousands of acres of very good land lie waste, complained the Valencian Cortes of 1645, and no one will farm them 'for fear of the quantity of debts and mortgages that lie on them'. The *estelionato* – that is, the unregistered or unknown mortgage which is suddenly presented to an unsuspecting purchaser – 'only serves to enrich the notaries and solicitors', thought Fernández Navarrete, and he went on to deplore the investment of so much capital in private or public loans, 'to the neglect of ploughing and the rearing of livestock, which used to be regarded as the only true wealth'.[43] How much better it would be, affirmed Lope de Deza shortly before, if those with capital would buy out the land instead of saddling the peasant farmer with mortgages.

In fact, in the case of those transfers of property which did take place, one may wonder what really changed in terms of peasant farming. The great bugbear of the sixteenth and seventeenth centuries was the *mohatra*, the fraudulent sale. One aspect of the practice was denounced by the Cortes of 1586–8 – the alienation of a field or an animal by a peasant at half the price it was worth on condition he could continue to use it for a few more years. At this point the study of the economy leads the historian into the domain of social structure – the pattern of landholding and the feudal system itself – which we shall examine more fully below. But the misery of the indebted villages cannot be fully understood without reference to the context of the economy as a whole, and it is to this that we must now turn.

4

TREASURE AND THE COST
OF EMPIRE

The search for bread and clothes, thought Caxa de Leruela in 1631, was at the origin of the civilising process, distinguishing men from brute beasts. Particularly in order to keep himself clothed man discovered his need for cooperation with his fellows, 'and thus, divinely inspired, [natural reason] invented commerce and trade between peoples', and out of this had developed the commonwealth itself 'with its division of tasks and its hierarchy of ranks, wonderful to behold'.[1] As one follows the early geographers and travellers round the peninsula one cannot but admire the ingenuity which, before the age of machines, helped to create an urban civilisation. Pedro de Medina lovingly describes the iron-working of the Basque Country, the ore 'smelted with a great quantity of charcoal', then pounded with great hammers driven by water-wheels. Three hundred small foundries, each producing 'at least' 46 tons, worked to equip the ships of nearby Bilbao and the king's army. His contemporary, Viciana, found the 200 families of Calig, a hill town on the road from Valencia to Catalonia, active in making 'arquebuses and shotguns and all kinds of sharp metal tools' – of which not a trace remained two hundred years later when Cavanilles visited the place. And the 1,100 households of Puertollano in New Castile boasted to the king's commissioners in 1575 about their excellent woollens, which had provided Philip II himself with his swaddling clothes when he was a baby.[2]

In a pre-industrial economy most industry consisted of the transformation of the fruits of the earth into food for the table, of the building of houses, castles and churches (the cathedral of Granada was a great work-site for 180 years between its inception in 1523 and its completion in 1704), and of the clothing of people. The great variety of regional dress, commented upon still by Ponz and Jovellanos in the 1780s, reflected the dispersal of the clothing trades. In the little kingdom of Valencia one could recognise the peasant of the lowlands by his canvas breeches, whereas the men of the sierras generally dressed in wool. Some of these manufactures achieved what might be called national importance. Segovia, close to the shearing stations of the Mesta and therefore to the best merino wool, increased its production dramatically over the sixteenth century from around 3,000 to as many as 16,000 cloths a year, each cloth measuring some 33.4 metres in length.[3] These woollens were finely woven, packing 2,200 threads into the warp (as compared with 1,800 or less for common varieties), and won the praise even of Barthélemy Joly (1603–4), who had not much else good to say about Spanish manufacture. At the same time Cordoba was producing some 17,000–18,000 cloths, which would place her, with Segovia and perhaps Cuenca among the great European centres of woollen production in the sixteenth century.

Other cities – Toledo, Granada, Valencia – had developed a speciality in silk. So great is the silk industry in Granada, wrote Pedro de Medina, that 'almost all the common people earn their living from it'. In later seventeenth-century Valencia, a city of 50,000 people, some 4,000 were employed directly in the silk manufacture and another 12,000 – 'including many widows and poor girls' – indirectly through spinning at home, according to the calculations of the silk guild itself. The mulberry leaf was normally picked about Saint Joseph's Day (19 March), which is still a red-letter day in the local calendar because of the celebrated festivity of the Fallas. The grubs fed on the leaves between then and the first week in May when the delicate business of unravelling the cocoons and giving a first twist to the thread could begin. Much of this was done by peasant families, who had to fit it into their own calendar; in particular, they aimed to finish and sell the thread by Saint John's Day (24 June) when they would need cash to pay their landlord.[4] The whole process involved a considerable degree of care and skill. The lofts where the grubs spun their cocoons had to be kept clean and at the right temperature. If the silkworms were packed in too tightly, two or three cocoons might get enmeshed, leading to damaged or poor-quality thread.

Pre-industrial manufacture was built up almost like a house of cards, and liable to collapse if one of its constituent elements was removed. The early modern period echoed to complaints about the decline of Spanish industry. The dire straits of the great old woollen manufactures of Castile seem to be well documented. From 600 looms at its peak around 1580 Segovia dropped to 300 by the middle of the seventeenth century and half that figure by the beginning of the next. There were similar complaints of decline in Cordoba around 1600, and in Cuenca as early as the Cortes of 1577. Ponz found the woollen industry of Baeza just a memory by the end of the old regime, the sleepy little town cluttered with the monuments of past glory, while in Cordoba only common baize survived of the great woollen and silk manufacture of the sixteenth century. In Segovia, once the heartland of Castilian industry, only 5,000 pieces of cloth were still being turned out, barely a third of the old total. 'Perhaps half of Toledo is in ruins,' observed Ponz of the former capital of Castilian silk-weaving, 'with just heaps of bricks and broken tiles where once there were houses.'[5]

Not all was gloom. Valencia had recovered from her seventeenth-century woes and was a major silk manufacturer again. But the industry was still beset by problems of poor-quality thread, which made it uncompetitive with the fashionable silk goods of Lyon. Significantly, almost all of the production was destined for the Spanish market; only a tiny proportion – 50,000 of 2,300,000 yards – could be exported, and that just to the Spanish colonies. Something similar could be said of that other success story of the eighteenth century, the development of a cotton manufacture in Catalonia, whose expansion also depended on a protected market in Spain and America.

What seems to have happened over the early modern period was a significant weakening of the front-line industries – those which had once a national and international market – and a reversion instead to smaller centres. Ponz in the 1780s noted the prosperity of the 1,000 families of Béjar, who exported their woollens throughout Castile and even to the Indies. Shortly afterwards Cavanilles wrote of Alcoi: 'Everywhere you go you hear the continual clicking of the looms, and the streets and squares are half -covered with wool which has just been dyed.' These smaller towns may have been growing in the eighteenth century because they had less rigid guild controls on manufacture than the older centres. On the other hand, it is not clear that they were really able to compensate for the decline of Toledo, Segovia, Cuenca and Granada.

Already in 1557 the Venetian ambassador Badoero commented that the Spaniards were exporting too much of their fine wool abroad in a raw state, 'and then come to fetch from these countries [of Western Europe] cloth to wear and tapestries'. Laws were passed to help the manufacturer, who was allowed in Castile from 1462 to buy back at cost price any wool once sold, and in Valencia from 1571 to have first pick of half the wool clipped anywhere in the kingdom. But it has been shown that the wool-exporters were often the same people as those who invested in the manufacture itself.[6] Castile always remained one of the great suppliers of fine raw wool to the rest of Europe – 3,000 tons a year in the later sixteenth century, with the fall in the Flanders market being compensated by the growing demand of the Italians (reflected in the expansion of the port of Alicante), then a decline to well under 3,000 tons as the Italian industry itself went into recession, before the revival later in the seventeenth century to cater to the broadcloth manufacture of England and Holland. By the eighteenth century Castile was exporting more raw wool than ever before – some 5,000 tons a year, according to the admittedly approximate estimates.[7]

The silk industry had a somewhat similar profile. Here the raw material was derived from the cocoons spun by grubs which fed on the leaf of the mulberry tree. Mulberry had been planted extensively in south-eastern Spain from the later Middle Ages. The Granadans were renowned for the black mulberry (*moral*) grown in the hill country, while the Valencians and Murcians produced the faster-growing white mulberry (*morera*), grown in the lowlands and irrigated, which gave a more abundant but fragile thread. The Granadan industry was the jewel in the crown, being almost as tightly regulated and taxed by the government as the wool of the Mesta. It was doubly unfortunate, therefore, that it depended so heavily on Morisco cultivators and spinners, expelled after the great rebellion of 1568, and that government attempts to maintain quality and quantity of production among the new Christian settlers only led to alienation and evasion. The rearing, unravelling and spinning of cocoons was always a risky process anyway, and it was complicated in the case of Granada by strict rules about planting only black mulberries, about allowing tax inspectors into one's house to check on every stage of production, and about only selling the raw silk through special brokers in the great walled silk-market (*alcaicería*) of the city of Granada.[8]

Even in the freer lands of Murcia and Valencia the supply of raw silk was not easy. Bad harvests and the Morisco rebellion in Granada doubled its price in Valencia between 1570 and 1600, leading to imports from the Indies – the Acapulco route to Manila having just then been opened for the first time. Valencia was torn between a desire to get raw silk for her weavers from whatever source, and the aim of protecting her mulberry plantations. The city negotiated with Murcia an interesting measure of protection, which is one of the earliest expressions of Spanish economic unity, which came into force in 1617 excluding foreign silks, and especially raw silk, from the *tierra firme* (mainland) of Spain. Protesting against this restriction on supply of the raw material, the silk-weaving centre of Toledo reminded the Cortes of 1620 that the kingdom of Valencia 'has no greater right [sc. of privileged access to the Castilian market] than the others we have been talking about, like China, Naples, Sicily or Italy'.[9]

A decree of 1699 forbidding the export of Spanish raw silk took protectionism a stage further, and was reissued several times in the eighteenth century. But it had to be relaxed after 1760, in response to the concerns of mulberry-growers to find a market for their crop. And after 1784 the old restriction on the import of foreign raw silk was also lifted, no doubt in response to the abundant production at home. For the curve of domestic supply seems to have followed a familiar pattern: 400,000 pounds of raw silk produced in Valencia round 1580, falling to 200,000 during the following century of recession (figures from 1721), but reviving to well over 1,000,000 by 1769.[10] As with raw wool, those who exported silk raw were often those who supplied the capital, when the opportunity presented itself, to have the material woven locally.

The growing reluctance to invest in domestic manufacture seems to have much to do with its perceived uncompetitiveness. The level of skill in the Spanish clothing trades called forth some critical comments from foreign observers. Townsend thought that Segovian woollens had gone into decline because 'the thread is not even . . . and there is a lot of grease left on it when they give it to be dyed', while Ponz made a somewhat similar point, blaming the use of cheaper bits of the fleece, where the wool was broken and too full of grease. Cavanilles criticised a certain lack of skill in the way Valencians spun and dyed both wool and silk, and Townsend thought that French silks won out because they had a superior thread and design.[11] It is not easy to be sure. The decline of Segovia was partly due to the shift from expensive broadcloth – her staple industry – to the cheaper New Draperies – serges and worsteds – which dominated early seventeenth-century Europe. A similar crisis perhaps overtook Valencian velvet as the European fashion in the seventeenth century shifted towards lighter taffetas and satin. Valencia recovered quite well, after a series of hiccoughs. But there may have been, as Townsend thought, a certain timidity or backwardness when it came to design. That great statesman of the Enlightenment, the count of Campomanes, paid considerable attention to raising the educational level of the Spanish artisan: 'fine and delicate wares he cannot make . . . which is why all of these, even furnishings and clothes, generally come from outside the kingdom'.[12] The Venetian ambassadors often remarked that while Spain produced some excellent items – the broadcloths of Segovia and the velvets of Valencia – these were exceptions in a country which basically lacked an urban infrastructure.

A fundamental belief in early modern Europe generally was that the quality of the product would ensure its sale. The government laid down the basic norms for the weaving of woollen cloth in Castile in 1511, and deputies from Castile met those of Valencia in 1684 – in another early example of Hispanic economic cooperation – in order to establish rules for the manufacture of silk.[13] From the thirteenth century, especially in the Mediterranean states of Valencia, Catalonia and Mallorca which were more in touch with the towns of Europe, one can see the lineaments of guilds beginning to take shape, from at least two directions. In the first place the local authorities appointed, or asked groups of workers to elect, *veedores* who would check the quality of manufactures coming on to the market. Secondly, from below, charitable brotherhoods (*cofradías*) began to take root among urban workers – a remedy for human weakness and sinfulness, as the Cortes of 1329 put it, legalising those of Valencia.[14] During the fifteenth century these brotherhoods were given more responsibility for the regulation of work. From 1392, for example, no one could become a silversmith in Valencia without belonging to the local guild. Examinations began to be introduced for membership – for the shoemakers, for example, in 1458. There followed piecemeal regulations for apprenticeship (often four years in Valencia, but varying according to the trade and the age of the entrant), and for the passage from apprentice to *oficial* or journeyman (who must be no younger than eighteen, according to some guild regulations). In Castile, which was less urbanised, similar developments were taking place from at least the fifteenth century. In towns like Cuenca where there were important manufactures, the woollen masters elected their own *veedores* from 1421; but in Cordoba and Malaga the town councils seem to have kept greater control over the quality of the product, its price and even the requirements of the master's examination.[15]

'If a shoemaker comes along with new tools,' wrote the fourteenth-century political philosopher Eiximenis, 'and makes 70 shoes in a day where others make 20 . . . that would be the ruin of 100 or 200 shoemakers', and the interest of the commonwealth, would require defence of the 200.[16] In the pursuit of this moral community the carpenters of Valencia ruled that the bigger saws of the wealthier guildsmen must be available for use by the poorer brethren, and quotas of wood were reserved for them. The tanners drew their hides from a guild warehouse, and each was limited to a quota; while the mattress-makers forbade any of their members to put more than three mattresses out for sale at any one time.[17] There were similar limitations in force elsewhere: no silk-spinner in Granada could keep more than two machines with up to 200 spindles on each, and no weaver could have more than four looms. Some guilds also restricted the number of apprentices a master could have at any one time – generally not more than three.

This attempt to preserve a stable local community began to buckle under the pressures of the market. In Segovia a sizeable number of weavers had to lease their looms in the sixteenth century off merchants, and virtually all worked for a few big men who supplied them with the raw wool and saw to the sale of the finished cloth. Recalling the reception for Philip II's bride in Segovia in 1570, the chronicler Colmenares noted that the weavers turned out on foot but the 'dealers in wool and manufacturers of cloth' on horseback, 'men who run a kind of family, giving a livelihood to a large number of people inside and outside their own houses, many of them having 200 or even 300 in their employment, working up a wide variety of very fine cloths'.[18] The *Relaciones* of 1575 speak of the silk merchants of Toledo who sometimes sold silk raw but at other times gave it out to be spun, dyed and woven by the local craftsmen, 'and this work is usually in the charge of a single merchant from start to finish, but sometimes is shared between two, one taking care of the spinning and another the dyeing and weaving'. In Cordoba the merchants controlled the supply of raw silk since it had to be imported from some distance away; but the numerous flocks of the sierra gave the villagers abundant wool to spin and weave, and the merchants were content to buy the cloth off them, taking it to the city to be fulled and dyed. But after 1580 merchants are found advancing money to the peasants, who seem to be falling more into dependence upon them.[19]

In general this kind of mixed system of capital and the household economy seems to have prevailed in the chief manufacturing areas, though there were sometimes attempts, as in the rest of seventeenth-century Europe to bypass the guilds. In Catalonia control of the woollen industry had largely passed into the hands of the *paraires*, originally carders or dressers of raw wool, whose power seems to have arisen from their being the first to buy up the fleeces. They would put out spinning and weaving to the appropriate guilds on piece-rates. But a crisis arose towards 1600 when the weavers demanded higher rates, and the magistrates of Barcelona intervened to allow weaving by non-guild labour, though refusing (1614) to let rural labourers wash and comb the raw wool.[20] The town councils, generally run by patricians, were careful as in other parts of Europe not to upset the social balance by allowing freedom of employment.

Even in the eighteenth century, when the guilds came to be perceived as a drag on economic innovation, statesmen were careful to preserve a role for them. Campomanes saw them as useful educators of the craftsman, and as a rudimentary police force, in his great treatise of 1775. A decree of 1789 freed woollen weavers to adopt whatever technique they chose, but required each to affix his name and town to the piece of cloth, reserving the guild seal for those which conformed in weight and number of threads to the official regulations. Still towards the end of the Old Regime the economy was visualised in conservative terms, as part of the maintenance of the worker's family and of a well-ordered community.

The prevailing localism of the Spanish economy is aptly symbolised by the diversity of weights and measures. The city of Toledo asked for their standardisation in 1758 as the foundation 'of a solid and stable national community'. Castile had indeed started down this path as early as the thirteenth century, after the reconquest of Andalusia, but it was left to Ferdinand and Isabella at the end of the fifteenth century to consolidate the process.[21] But the chief inspector could write in 1731: 'Rare is the city, town or hamlet in which the weights or measures conform to the standards of the kingdom.' It proved to be a considerable technological challenge, in fact, for small towns actually to fabricate accurate instruments for this purpose. Vague units such as 'loads', 'bags' or 'baskets' continued to be employed in the documents, to the frustration of statistically minded historians.

Local communities did come together through fairs – fixed times of the year at which one could be sure of finding the difficult and delicate combination of goods and money, supply and demand, together in one place. In 1693 the viceroy of Valencia described that of the wool town of Ontinyent, 'where they tell me that more than 20,000 people will come together from inside and outside the kingdom, often arriving in throngs from their villages and carrying arms in order to protect the money they take with them'. Fairs were instituted by particular royal privileges, and the government of Valencia seems to have been issuing more licences of this kind than before in the later seventeenth century. In general, travellers would be under safeguard against investigation for petty offences while attending; and they would have some immunity from inspection of their baggage – no mean benefit in an age of venal excise and customs officers, whose jurisdiction ran well inland from the actual border crossings of Castile, Valencia, Portugal or elsewhere. Reduction of the excise duty on sales often accompanied the great Castilian fairs; but the Valencian town of Xixona was only allowed a fair in 1626 on condition that there was no reduction of taxes to the Crown.

The greatest fair of them all was that of Medina del Campo. Recalling in 1606 its origins, the town referred to its strategic situation at the confluence of the routes which led across the mountains from the Basque Country, Asturias and Galicia towards the plateau of Castile (thence to link up with the old Roman road running down the west side of the peninsula towards Seville). And it could guarantee food for the itinerant merchant, and above all 'a plentiful supply of wine from its neighbourhood'.[22] Here the dealers in wool for Flanders met with the importers of goods from the Indies, and hospitals and convents from as far away as Toledo had their agents to make purchases of cloth, groceries and medicine, in Medina del Campo and the neighbouring fair towns of Medina de Ríoseco and Villalón. Medina de Ríoseco now is a small market town, but it carries the marks of those times of the year when it used to come alive with throngs of outsiders, whose transactions provided the money to endow its three grandiose churches.

It was a feature of the successful fair that it gathered into itself many different threads of communication. That of Tendilla, which lasted for a month from Saint Mathias's Day (24 February), served as a kind of equivalent to that of Medina del Campo for the eastern Meseta. According to the *Relaciones* of 1575–8 it was the natural meeting-place of the clothiers of Segovia, Cuenca and Soria who set out, as the snows melted, with the fine woollens which they had woven over the previous winter. A small town of under 3,000 inhabitants and now rather off the beaten track, Tendilla must have benefited from the old Roman road which linked Mérida and Zaragoza via Toledo, which the Visigoths had chosen as their capital. Goods from the Indies – 'much spice, indigo, brasil wood and other novel and costly items' – came up naturally along this route from Mérida and Seville, to meet one of Spain's chief imports from northern Europe, the fine linen of Flanders and France.[23]

Spain became one of the earliest economies to be exposed to the influx of bullion on a scale which seemed to transform market relations. As the New World began to yield up its enormous wealth of gold and especially silver, contemporary observers became appalled at what they regarded as the destabilisation of fair exchange. The clearest symptom of this was the rise in prices of commodities – some fourfold over the sixteenth century. Inflation was associated with profiteering. But in order to understand its impact, one had best start by exploring the role of money in pre-industrial Spain.

In the first place there was no standard, universal currency in the modern sense. As the Cortes of 1579–82 pointed out, copper coins circulated in the countryside, especially in the poorer villages, which could not be exchanged outside the locality except at a premium. And a few years later the papal envoy Borghese noted how almost every village between Lleida and Barcelona had its own fractional coinage, which made life difficult for the traveller. The good coin of Spain was the silver *real* and the gold *escudo*. Minted separately in each of the peninsular kingdoms, with different weights and fineness, they were not easy to transfer. Frontier guards at each of the inland crossings checked – or were supposed to check – the export of more coin than the traveller needed for subsistence. Valencian *reales* were not acceptable in Castile anyway, but their Castilian counterparts were highly valued everywhere else, except in Portugal, an interesting symptom already of that country's economic strength (derived from its own empire), which would enable it to become politically independent after 1640. In general silver and gold coins had some of the features of treasure, and were liable to be hoarded or plundered.

American treasure created new opportunities and challenges, with enough silver coming into Spain at the peak of the flow in the 1590s to pay for three weeks' labour by every worker every year – undreamt of wealth for a pre-industrial society.[24] But according to the Venetian ambassador Vendramin (1595) the Spaniards had a saying about the silver from the Indies, 'that it has just the effect on them that rain does on the roof of a house' – that it quickly runs off.[25] In his classic treatise on the new economy, the Dominican Tomás de Mercado wrote in 1569 that 'in Spain, the very source and fount of escudos and crowns, scarcely a handful can be scraped together, whereas if you go to Genoa, Rome, Antwerp or Venice you will see in the streets of the bankers and money-changers, without exaggeration, as many piles of coins minted in Seville as there are piles of melons in San Salvador or in the Arenal'. And the count of Gondomar, on his embassy to London at the beginning of the seventeenth century, remarked that the only coins circulating in that city were of silver whereas you would be hard-pressed to find any in Spain, with incalculable damage to his country's reputation.[26]

The moral theologians of the University of Salamanca began to analyse this problem as part of their new interest in the corrosive effect of money on human relationships. Some of them – Azpilcueta, Tomás de Mercado – were pioneers of what would later be known as the quantity theory of money – that the more currency there was in circulation, the less it was worth and the higher prices of other commodities would be in relation to it. The traveller Barthélemy Joly put it succinctly in 1603: 'Everything is dear in Spain except money' – including wages, which attracted so many of his French compatriots across the Pyrenees to make a living. In France, noted Azpilcueta, 'where money is scarcer than in Spain, bread, wine, cloth and labour are worth much less', and he decribed vividly the tendency of Spanish coins to flow out to where they could purchase more, in return for manufactures 'worth little there and here much'.

There were voices at the time telling the government to devalue in order to make its currency less attractive to export. But as long as Spain remained an imperial power it is difficult to see what the Crown could do other than maintain the full value of silver coin, so essential to purchase services abroad. In order to remedy the shortage of currency at home there was an increasing resort to *vellón*, an alloy of silver and copper, or just copper alone. Initially its minting seemed a useful way of catering to the increasing volume of domestic trade, and the Cortes of 1559 and 1583–5 approved. But then in 1586–8 one gets the first signals of alarm. The Cortes now protested that there was too much *vellón* in circulation, the copper and silver content of the coins worth only a quarter of their face value, which meant that merchants were simply cutting off trade with communities which could only settle their accounts with this debased currency. After the death of Philip II an increasingly bankrupt monarchy resorted to the minting of pure copper, pouring out great quantities of the stuff in the years 1599–1625. After 1625 the Crown was too poor even to buy copper, and preferred to devalue the existing copper currency. In 1636, for example, it called in coins for restamping upwards to three times the original face value, pocketing the difference for the treasury.

It proved difficult enough to get people to surrender their coins for restamping, especially since there were periodic reversals of policy in order to counter inflation – the reduction of the face value of coins by 50 per cent in 1628, by 25 per cent in 1642. *Vellón* began to circulate by weight rather than by value, and was subject to heavy discounts of around 50 per cent against its equivalent in silver. Not all of Spain suffered by this disorganisation of the currency. Silver *reals* seem to have circulated normally enough in Catalonia and Valencia, though they always carried a premium of about 15 per cent if exchanged for the local *vellón*. As a result of the treaties of 1648 and 1659 scaling down imperial commitments in northern Europe, the Spanish government could afford to devalue slightly its magnificent silver currency (1686). The passing of the imperial age is surely symbolised by the transition from the *peso* – the 'piece of eight' (that is, eight *reals*, or ten after

1728) – to the little *peseta* of two *reals*, a silver coin which could pay a labourer's wages for half a day.[27] That is, silver no longer flowed abroad so much in payments to bankers and soldiers but could be used at home; so *vellón* could be partly phased out, and from 1680 its face value was reduced by three-quarters.

This stabilisation of the currency no doubt fostered the revival of the Spanish economy in the eighteenth century, contributing to a spread of the internal market. Silver coins themselves, of course, were notoriously vulnerable to hoarding and theft, and the growth of the economy also depended on some extension of credit facilities. Establishing the famous *Taula* or deposit bank of Valencia in 1408, King Martin claimed that 'people will relax and sleep who before, desirous of avoiding the traps and tricks of thieves and robbers, would stay up and spend the night wide awake'.[28] The strongbox of the new bank was kept in the sacristy of the cathedral, and when in 1628 the clergy protested against keeping it so close to the relics of the saints it was shifted just a short distance away to a special chamber upstairs. Neither it nor its equivalent of the same name in Barcelona were supposed to do anything with the treasure other than keep it under lock and key, issuing the depositor with an *albarà* – a certificate of his holding. In time the albarans began to circulate as a kind of currency, transferring deposits from one citizen to another to whom he owed money. But this nascent paper currency was largely aborted in the seventeenth century, as the Taula began to spend more money than it had in reserve. The successive bankruptcies of 1614, 1634 and 1649 in Valencia led to the conversion of the promissory notes (the albarans) into non-redeemable bonds on the muncipal treasury.

Castilian towns also had municipal deposits not unlike the Taulas. But the chief instrument of credit in the peninsula was the letter of exchange (*cambio*), which had arisen initially as a way of settling bills outside one's place of residence without the need to transport cash. One transferred a credit against a third party in satisfaction of a debt. In 1594 the papal nuncio, Borghese, left a record of those Spanish towns where one could cash in a letter of exchange before setting out on the next stage of one's journey. However, even at the end of the old regime Cabarrús, founder of the state bank of San Carlos (1782), complained of the poor facilities of exchange in the peninsula: 'how many years would pass before you find one in Cordoba for Zaragoza, or in León for Murcia?'[29] The unfortunate traveller had often no alternative but to carry his own box of coins around with him.

But in the sixteenth century there had been a marked quickening of the current of credit at least along the chief routes of the New World economy. Gone were the days when buyer and seller dealt with each other directly, wrote Tomás de Mercado in 1571. Now men from Burgos handle their dealings with the Flemings through agents in the American trades of Seville, and the threads of exchange criss-crossed on a world scale, accounts having to be settled by the same man 'in Cape Verde for black slaves, in Flanders for linen goods, in Florence for woollens, in Toledo and Segovia for textiles, in Lisbon for the produce of the East'. It was increasingly hard, thought Mercado, to talk in terms of the fair price beloved of theologians, for 93 ducats would purchase in Flanders what you would need 100 to buy in Seville, or perhaps 130 to buy in Peru, the dearest place on earth because it was so near the source of silver.[30] The letter of exchange, therefore, might carry an allowance for these differences. And through this chink a gradual breach was made in the old law of usury which forbade a Christian to profit by the money he advanced to another.

The early modern period witnessed in Spain as in the rest of Europe a new attitude to the creation of wealth. The discovery of America provoked not only a pioneering study of the rights of conquered peoples by theologians of the famous university of Salamanca but also an exploration of the corrosive effects of silver on human relationships in the middle years of the sixteenth century. The traditionalism of many of these writers – Martín de Azpilcueta, Tomás de Mercado – should not make us overlook the acuteness of their vision of the market economy and of the powerful force of money. They were concerned fundamentally with the ethics of human relationships. Their successors, the famous *arbitristas* of the early seventeenth century – who also made a distinguished contribution to the nascent science of economics – had other priorities, being called into existence by the crisis in public finance at the time and the need to invent projects (*arbitrios*) which would stem the apparent decline of taxable resources. Some of them were clergy, like Sancho de Moncada, who explained in 1619 that poverty and idleness did 'infinite harm' to the soul. But others – Ibáñez de Salt in Valencia (1638), Alvarez de Toledo in Castile (1623) – were soldiers, and training in the logistics of warfare seems to have led to a new respect for mathematics, statistics and the inventory of resources in Spain and Europe generally in the seventeenth century. With their advent the art of politics tended to become more secular in tone, and economic well-being rather than morality the touchstone of a state's success.

All of the Spanish economic writers could agree that the market economy was a necessary and natural feature of civilisation. 'If a man wants clothes, shoes, food or drink, if he wants to study, work or relax', wrote Tomás de Mercado, he depends by the law of nature on cooperation and exchange with his fellows. But there was concern that money might create imbalances in the commonwealth, above all through the pursuit of 'luxury'. Fernández Navarrete was concerned about the contrast between the wealth of the court and the poverty of the vagabonds on the streets of Madrid or of the peasantry. Population – following the classical authors – was seen as the real wealth of a kingdom, and the fate of Rome at the hands of the Barbarians seemed an awful warning to Spain.[31]

One way of tackling the imbalance was through legislation, limiting the amounts people could spend on 'luxuries'. The *corregidores* (regional officers of the Crown) had reported in 1583 that there was too much money in circulation, 'and people now want delicacies at table and in their wardrobe, and spend far too much furnishing their houses and carriages'.[32] Sumptuary laws to restrict this unbridled consumption, and to prevent the blurring of the hierarchy of birth by one of wealth, had been advocated by the Cortes periodically since at least the 1570s. The government of Philip IV made one last effort in 1623 to stay the rot, outlawing ruffs and the embroidery of clothes, limiting the numbers of household servants and of grammar schools (which led peasant sons into idleness as practitioners of the law), restricting the size of dowries and closing down brothels. Simplicity of customs would hopefully encourage the foundation of families, thereby promoting both population and the productive activity which seemed to go with the artisan and peasant household. The great enemy was always *carestía* – dearth – a tricky word which reflects the preoccupation of the sixteenth and seventeenth centuries with rising prices. Inflation was seen as corrosive, a symptom or a cause of the dissolution of communities and of the hierarchy of ranks. It was an effect – as Mercado taught – of the new abundance of bullion, but this, if not regulated, simply aggravated the old sins of idleness, luxury and greed. Dearth might not only be tackled by an increase of production but by a reform of manners.

An alternative view of the economy and its working began to surface in the early seventeenth century. Gregorio López Madera, venerable elder statesman and devout Catholic though he was, warned that 'though frugality and temperance are very good for an individual, they are not generally so for the commonwealth itself'. Luxury, after all, created employment. 'What would be the use of growing silk and working it up for sale if it were not to go towards beds, drapes and clothes?' How would the ceremonial processions of the king or the church be celebrated 'if houses no longer had rich hangings'? Trade would fall off, as would the royal excise duties, if there was too much puritanism.[33] These ideas were taken up by the economic writer and political agitator Francisco Martínez de Mata towards the middle of the seventeenth century. But they really came into their own during the secular age of the Enlightenment. The new school of political economy received open support from the government, which in 1788 reprimanded the great popular preacher, Fray Diego de Cádiz, for his 'old-fashioned' equation of economic individualism with greed and selfishness.[34]

Nevertheless, statesmen continued to visualise the family household as the keystone of a properly ordered economy. Echoing contemporary German cameralism, their prime aim was to foster a healthy peasant and artisan population. Campomanes warned that ancient Carthage had accumulated a specious prosperity through overseas trade but failed to endure. By contrast contemporary Holland, England and Switzerland seemed to demonstrate the virtues of a gradual increase of population and trade at the grassroots through the founding of household enterprises by farmers and craftsmen. Andalusia was poor, suggested Campomanes, in spite of its fertility, because it lacked a network of medium family businesses in town and country; Galicia, more infertile, abounded in population and was never in arrears with its taxes because the small peasantry had at least each a cow and some cottage industry of linen.[35]

The Economic Societies of 'Friends of their Country', founded initially in the Basque Country in 1765 and popularised in Campomanes's treatise of 1774, were to group members of the local elites who would foment good farming and handcrafts in their districts by books and example. The market and its demands seem to have been subordinated to that older ideal of establishing solid, moderate household enterprises among the peasantry and artisans. Urging nobles and clergy to take a lead here, Antonio Ponz suggested that economic initiatives were a form of patriotism: 'It would be no small gain just to get rid of the multitude of beggars.' Such men, restoring the moral and physical well-being of their 'patria' were, as one of Ponz's correspondents put it, 'just like the men who had first conquered it' from the Moor. Jovellanos, meanwhile, suggested that governments in the past had been too concerned with the extension of overseas trade, involving their countries in costly warfare, 'that horrible scourge of humanity and particularly of agriculture'.[36]

But Jovellanos was aware of the importance of international trade too as fomenting those luxury industries which would create full employment for a people. Pedro de Medina had described his native country in 1548 as 'the centrepiece of the different areas of the globe', set between Africa, Europe and the New World, whose exploration by Iberian navigators was 'such a marvellous event that since God created the world there has been nothing to equal it'.[37] The Venetian ambassadors were also impressed. For Girolamo Soranzo in 1611 the lengthy coastline and the strategic situation between the Mediterranean and the Atlantic meant that Spain 'can call herself the emporium of the universe'. And Tomás de Mercado described his native Seville as 'the richest city without exaggeration in the entire globe'.[38] With over 130,000 people at its peak in the early seventeenth century it was one of the biggest urban conglomerations of its time.

Every year ships left there for South America in voyages which might take around two months. They were organised increasingly in convoys as a security against pirates, a system which acquired definitive form in 1564 under the supervision of the Casa de Contratación (House of Trade), a government committee based in Seville. The so-called Flota generally set out every April for Mexico and the great fair of Vera Cruz, while the 'Galleons' left in August to pick up the treasure of Peru which had been ferried up to the Isthmus of Panama. Both convoys would winter in the Caribbean, heading home from their rendezvous at Havana the following spring.

Until the 1570s exports to the Indies were dominated by grain, oil and wine, creating some prosperity in the countryside round Seville. But the quantities must have been small: only 10 per cent of the Aljarafe, in the fertile Sevillian hinterland, was olive plantation and another 10 per cent vineyard in the middle of the eighteenth century.[39] As the American colonies settled down and came to grow most of their own food, they looked to Europe for manufactures. Valencian and Granadan silk found an outlet, as did Catalan cotton in the eighteenth century. Indeed towards the end of the eighteenth century Spain was able to supply just over half of the value of exports to the Indies. But Spanish textiles always had a hard time competing against French linen and silk or English and Dutch woollens. Return commodities from the Indies included cochineal and hides, and, after the discovery of the route from Acapulco to the Philippines in 1564, Chinese silks (until these were banned from Spain in 1617). With the opening up of frontier areas of Latin America like Colombia and Venezuela in the eighteenth century, cacao, tobacco and, of course, sugar from the Caribbean islands began to join the list. But the chief export from the Indies to Spain was bullion, particularly silver, which fell, though, from about 80 to about 56 per cent of the value of the cargoes over the eighteenth century.[40]

The mines of the Indies were private enterprises. The crown took a fifth of the production for itself, and had a monopoly of the supply of mercury which the miners needed in order to refine the silver ore. It also controlled, in part, the distribution of labour. The Mexican miners made their own arrangements to hire Indians or buy slaves, but the remote Peruvian workings of Potosí had to be supplied with Indians conscripted under the *mita*, the old state labour of the Incas. The American mines, in other words, were a complex mixture of commercial and non-commercial principles. They required considerable capital and technology to exploit properly, qualities which were perhaps not always forthcoming as the miners fell into debt and subdivided their holdings among their children.[41] After expanding greatly in the sixteenth century to an average of 9,700,000 pesos per year in the 1590s, the dispatch of treasure from America to Seville tended to fall slightly thereafter, before dropping sharply after 1631–5. The nature and extent of the movement has been the subject of considerable controversy. Whereas the House of Trade had been able to keep conscientious records of imports for the first century or more of its existence, the sheer pressure of imperial defence led to a fiscal levy on the convoys which drove much of the trade with America into contraband. There seems to have been a continuing high output from the American mines during much of the seventeenth century. The government was having to spend more of its own share of the treasure on administration and defence in the Indies, but private citizens seem to have been exporting huge quantities back to Europe – only little of this was now entering the record of the House of Trade based in Seville and (after 1717) Cadiz. But the best estimates would suggest that treasure imports from the Indies to Europe had actually risen from their old peak of the 1590s to 14,500,000 pesos a year in 1686–95 before nearly doubling to 25,600,000 by 1786–95.[42]

Silver was merely – at least in the case of private silver – the purchase price for commodities which were coming out to America from Europe. Though Spanish goods had fallen as a percentage of this total during the seventeenth century, Seville and then Cadiz managed to retain an important role as a staple for the transatlantic commerce generally. There was some direct dealing between European privateers and the Spanish Main, but less than one might think. Mostly French, English and Dutch merchants preferred to trade peacefully through their middlemen in the Andalusian ports. There was clearly a hiccough during the terrible years of war of the early seventeenth century. But, after the government made peace on all fronts by 1659 and abandoned its attempt to value cargoes for the escort duty (*avería*), contenting itself from 1660 with selling pardons (*indultos*) to traders instead, the actual navigation between Andalusia and the Indies seems to have become buoyant once again. Overall tonnage of shipping stagnated in the later seventeenth century, though it has been suggested that the value of the cargoes increased; but between 1700 and 1778 the tonnage between Cadiz and the Indies tripled.[43] The latter expansion seems to have been helped by a liberalisation of the rules about navigation. The old convoy system became less appropriate as Spain no longer had to face buccaneers and privateers but increasingly the well-organised navy of Great Britain. After 1740, with the outbreak of the War of Jenkins' Ear, ships from Cadiz had to be allowed singly to run the gauntlet of the English blockades. The system worked well enough, perhaps, for it to be increasingly adopted in peace-time as well, and after 1778 ships were allowed to set out individually from all the major ports of Spain, and not just from Cadiz.

Luis Cabrera de Córdova, in his chronicle of 1599 to 1614, recorded faithfully every autumn the arrival of the great fleets from the Indies. 'Their coming has caused great joy everywhere,' he wrote in 1606, reflecting that their loss in a storm the previous year had 'impoverished many in Peru and Seville'; while in 1613 he noted that they had reached port 'all safe, without damage from enemies or the weather, thanks be to God'.[44] His words remind us of the enormous effort which Spain invested in the Indies trade, but prompt the question as to whether it was all worth it. 'In France, Italy and the Netherlands there are no mines of gold or silver,' wrote the *arbitrista* Fernández Navarrete in 1626, 'but their numerous populations drain all the treasure from Spain through their trade and crafts.'[45] However, the conventional wisdom was that states must play an active role in fostering the wealth of their citizenry through protectionism: prosperity and state power marched hand in hand. 'Warfare nowadays is no longer a matter of brute force like a bull-fight or even a battle,' wrote the count of Gondomar in 1619, but rather of 'seeing to the increase of our shipping and the weakening of the commerce of our enemies.' The English, he reported from his embassy at the court of James I, boasted that, in the years since the peace treaty with Spain in 1604, 'they had transferred Seville, Lisbon and the Indies to London'.[46]

Spain adopted some laws protecting her native manufactures through the exclusion of foreign textiles – notably in 1623. One of the problems about the exclusion of foreign goods was that not all parts of the empire shared the same interests. Toledo was angry about the exclusion of raw silk after 1617, which aimed to protect Valencian and Murcian growers but which threatened to push up prices for her own weavers: why should the kingdom of Valencia have greater rights in the Castilian market, she wanted to know, than those of China or Italy? And when Olivares tried to revive the trade of Catalonia and Valencia with his proposed Levant Company of 1630, he was careful to specify that it should not import pepper, clove or nutmeg 'or other spices' so as not to undermine the trade of Portugal with the East round the Cape of Good Hope. There were similar controversies across the Atlantic as the government tried to cut down on the limited trade between Mexico and the Philippines, particularly trying to stop Asian goods getting to Peru via Mexico (1631). Tariffs remained to cut the empire into a multitude of self-contained regions. Attempts to remove the (very recent) tariff barrier between Portugal and Castile after the union of the two Crowns in

1580 came to grief by 1593, since the Crown was so desperately in need of the customs revenue. In 1717 Philip V removed the customs barriers between Castile and the Aragonese kingdoms after these had been defeated in war; but it was not until 1778 that the *almojarifazgo* dividing Andalusia from Castile was abolished, and not until 1840 that the Basque provinces were brought within a national tariff.

The main concern of the Spanish governments was with interlopers in its protected trade routes. It was hard in the so-called Age of Mercantilism to separate peace from war, since states issued letters of marque to their merchants, authorising reprisals against those of another country with which one was technically not at war. Much of the activity of Drake and Hawkins in the Caribbean was carried on in this twilight zone. Merchantmen had to go well armed and merged easily into the privateer. From the later sixteenth century one can perceive a growing attempt on the part of governments to grapple with this problem. Trade embargoes, tried out in 1585 against the English and Dutch, and sharpened in 1603–4, seem to have come into their own with the wars of Philip IV after 1621. In 1624 the Admiralty of Seville was ordered to fit out ships to seize the carrying trade between Spain and northern Europe from the Dutch. Between 1625 and 1628 this *Almirantazgo* tribunal, now with its headquarters in Madrid, began to assert jurisdiction over all parts of the peninsula, commissioning agents to investigate the export of bullion and illicit trade with enemies of the Crown.

An old law of 1491 had required shippers arriving at the Basque ports to post bail that they would export the equivalent within a year in Spanish products, in order to avoid the drain of bullion abroad. This now became the justification for the Almirantazgo commissioners exacting bail from foreigners in all Spanish ports that they would export no coin and that they would not sail to countries with which Spain was at war. Additionally, of course, all imports from the enemy were banned. There were complaints that this degree of control was unworkable or counterproductive. The Valencians complained that the declaration of war on France in 1635 drove away Italians, English and Flemings at the same time 'since the dealings of merchants are so tied up each with the other'. Seville protested in similar terms about the 200 or more small ships which came to Andalusia every year looking for cargoes; these would not come any more if their captains were asked to post bail. And anyway silver must be allowed out in payment of European imports for the Indies, only half of whose value could possibly be met in equivalent Spanish goods.[47]

The trade embargoes proved very difficult to enforce. The government itself had to issue contraband licences from time to time, allowing in fine linen (of which Spain was so short) from France, or authorising Dutch ships to visit the precious Iberian salt-pans, since the Crown needed the tax revenue.[48] Commissioners in the ports seem occasionally to have turned a blind eye. When the agent in Alicante, Marcos Antonio Bisse, began applying the letter of the law from November 1639 he was suspended after twelve months for acting 'in such an excessive fashion that no man can be found, native or foreigner, willing to do business in that port'. Ultimately the restraining factor was the government's fear of a collapse of its revenues from import and export duties. Bartolomé Morquecho's commission against contraband in Seville in 1649 provoked revolt and was similarly brought to a speedy end when the city offered the Crown 100,000 pesos to be rid of him.

Ultimately, as López Madera pointed out in 1621, it was very difficult for Spain to enforce mercantilist laws because her trade and navigation were in foreign hands. 'Our harbours are full of English and Dutch ships,' wrote Gondomar to Philip III in 1619, 'but in theirs there is not one Spaniard.' There had been important colonies of Spanish merchants in Bruges, Rouen and London in the early sixteenth century, but these disappeared fast by the second half of that century for reasons which merit further exploration. Commenting on this reversal of fortune, the city of Toledo noted in 1620 that Spanish merchants were now too content 'to buy off the foreigner his wares on credit, selling these as middlemen, with Spain just a kind of tavern where the foreigner conducts his business'.[49]

The Spanish coastline had generated an active seafaring tradition from early times. The best natural havens were on the Atlantic side of the peninsula, and the *rías* or fjords of Galicia provided the famed bases of the Spanish fleet in Vigo and Corunna. But the Galician ports had a hinterland which, though rich in timber for the dockyards, was too remote from the rest of Spain for any active trade to develop. Urban Spain had developed naturally from the Mediterranean coastline inland, and here, unfortunately, there were few outstanding harbours. Cartagena was the best deep-water haven, and enjoyed a natural shelter from the wind, the great scourge in those days of ships at anchor. But Cartagena was, like Galicia, something of a finis terrae, with one of the most barren hinterlands in the peninsula. Trade between Castile and Italy tended to use Alicante a little further north, once an agreement of 1550 conceded a rebate of 50 per cent on the customs duty payable at the Valencian border.

The biggest commercial centres along the Mediterranean coast – Barcelona, Valencia, Malaga – could offer little protection to shipping. Boats rode at anchor in an open bay, always on the alert for storms and Barbary corsairs, while their cargoes were ferried to the beach in smaller skiffs. There were valiant attempts to build jetties. Pedro de Medina admired the work underway in Malaga in 1548, 'which when it is finished will be one of the great monuments of the world'. Valencia had a wooden jetty from the later fifteenth century, but it was rotting and unsafe. An effort to build in stone, from 1685, swallowed great sums from the municipal budget and involved Genoese as well as native engineers, but it had to be abandoned by 1698 in view of the persistent breaches made by the sea.[50] Many of the Mediterranean harbours suffered anyway from silting, which meant that stone quays would require constant dredging in their vicinity if they were to be kept open. Bilbao, the staple for the export of wool to Flanders, suffered greatly from a similar problem, and silting eventually put Seville out of action as a port for the Indies, the big ships no longer able to get up the Guadalquivir River and docking instead at Cadiz from the middle of the seventeenth century.

In spite of all the handicaps imposed by nature, the coastal populations of Iberia had used their native resources and talent to create a bustling maritime life, though often on a small scale. Near Alicante there was the little port of Vilajoiosa, which, as it told the Cortes of 1645, lives by 'ploughing, fishing and transporting goods', its skippers touching in at harbours all along the coast as far north as Tarragona, peddling fish, flour, brandy and garlic from one to the other. Nearby Benidorm emerges from the pages of Cavanilles in 1795–7 with a rather similar profile. Out of this grassroots activity had arisen the skill in seafaring which carried Catalan, Mallorcan and Valencian sea-captains to Italy and the Levant in the course of the thirteenth and fourteenth centuries, creating a trading empire which caused their admiral Roger de Lauria to boast that no fish could cross the Mediterranean unless its scales were marked with the four crimson bars of the House of Aragon. On the Atlantic coast, meanwhile, the Cantabrian and Basque ships were fishing for the whale from at least 1200, and carrying the wines of nearby Bordeaux to northern Europe. The Admiralty of Castile was created about this time, and from 1300 the export of wool to Flanders found ready transport in the ships of Bilbao. In the sixteenth century the Basques penetrated deep into the ocean, opening up the cod fishing off Newfoundland.

To sustain this enterprise an important technology had to be mobilised. The Barcelona and Valencia dockyards – the *drassanes* – are some of the finest surviving examples of their kind from the fourteenth century. But all along the coast small dockyards were active. Viciana described those of Vinaròs, whose population numbered about 400 families, and which used 40 cartloads of pine and evergreen oak from the hills behind the town every year for its boats. Though there was only an open beach here, big ships could anchor safely near the shore, attracted by the abundant supplies of local wine and a position from which they could take their bearings for the onward journey up or down the Mediterranean coast. Shipbuilding seems to have developed as part of a complex of activity in Vinaròs as elsewhere: access to timber, a tradition of fishing, a geographical position which marked a place out as a stage on the main sea-lanes. The best boats were, no doubt, built in the Basque Country and Catalonia, both close to the rich timber of the Pyrenees and to supplies of iron. The caravel, that sleek pioneer of oceanic discovery in the sixteenth century, owed something to the blending of solid Basque hulls, capable of withstanding Atlantic storms, and Catalan rigging – the lateen sail, designed to maximise the uncertain power of the Mediterranean breezes.

The astrolabe, developed by the Arabs, and maritime or portolan charts, the speciality of the Jews of Mallorca, were other ingredients of Spain's waxing power at sea. The House of Trade in Seville pioneered the mapping of the Atlantic in the wake of the discovery of the New World through a systematic recording of the reports of its pilots.[51] All the more surprising, therefore, is the decline of Spanish navigation. One symptom was the increasing resort to foreign vessels for the transport between Seville and the Indies: these constituted a little over 5 per cent of the total for much of the sixteenth century, but then in the wake of the disaster of the Armada in 1588, for which so many merchantmen had been commandeered, they rose to just over a fifth, and eventually, by the early seventeenth century, a third, before attaining perhaps a proportion of just under one half by the end of that century.[52] Nearly half of the remainder were being built by this time in America, especially in Havana, the rendezvous for the fleets before their return to Seville. The decline of shipbuilding in the Iberian peninsula seemed to be a symptom of a wider malaise: the retreat of Spanish navigation as a whole. 'The Basques have lost the whale-fishing,' lamented Gondomar in 1616, 'and they, together with the Galicians and Portuguese, are in the process of losing that of herring and cod as well.'[53] The reliance of a great city like Valencia on the cod and stockfish brought by Breton skippers is a marked feature of the seventeenth century. What had gone wrong?

The question of shipbuilding itself has generated much debate. Costs in Spanish dockyards may not have been markedly higher than in other parts of Europe, according to the detailed research on one contract in Bilbao for six galleons in 1625–7.[54] But Spain may have been short of some key resources as naval technology developed. Long timbers for the masts had to be imported from the Baltic, and rigging, above all, was noted as an enduring problem, by the Venetian ambassador Donà in 1573 as regards the Barcelona dockyards and by the great marquis of Ensenada, 'father of the Spanish navy', more generally in 1749. Boats of 200–300 tons could be turned out by the small yards of Vinaròs or Vilajoiosa; but these seem to have been increasingly ill-adapted to the challenges of long-distance navigation. 'Never since the creation of the world have men sailed as far as the Spaniards,' wrote Tomás de Mercado, but the cost was high: 'fearful losses and the shipwreck of people and their fortune.'[55] The rotting of the hulls in the tropics was another problem, and few ships on the trans-Atlantic run seem to have made more than four round trips before they were written off. It was bigger boats of 500–600 tons or above which were favoured by the authorities for security, not least against pirates, but these required more capital, skill and equipment, perhaps, than could be provided by most Iberian dockyards – at least at the rate of replacement which was necessary on the oceanic routes.

There was a wider problem, though. The Spanish coasts had fostered an active maritime tradition, but they were only feebly attached to their hinterland, that square, semi-continental landmass, incommunicable by river, on whose high tableland lived a fundamentally peasant people. Spain was dangerously short of sailors compared with England or Flanders, thought the Venetian ambassador Pietro Contarini in 1621. 'What really drives me to distraction is the fewness of our sailors,' wrote Ensenada in 1749.[56]

These defects became more visible in proportion as Spain aspired to rise above a certain level of seafaring and looked to command of the oceans. Taking a ship to the Indies was of a qualitatively different order from the seamanship involved in the old coasting trades. Pilots for the Indies were trained essentially on the job, through a very long apprenticeship of 15–20 years at sea followed by a cursory glance at cosmography for two months; then, if they could establish Christian ancestry, they were licensed by the House of Trade. But the Council of the Indies was complaining already in 1568 and 1578 that the pilots were not up to their job, that they were slipshod about recording shallows, reefs and currents on their voyages. And anyway there were so few of them that foreigners had to be commissioned.[57] The College of San Telmo, founded in 1681 to train orphans in seamanship, and the introduction around the same time of Mercator's Projection for the use of Spanish navigators, showed a continuing willingness to learn and adapt. But the pace was now being set by the foreigner.

A critical problem for Spanish navigation, thought Ensenada, was the horrendous pressure of piracy, which drove up costs and drove Spanish shipping out of business. What was true in 1749 might appear to be even more so in the days of Drake, Hawkins and the buccaneers on the Spanish Main. The need to have the Indies fleet go in convoy from the middle of the sixteenth century was accompanied by a rise in the duty levied to pay for the warships. This *avería* tax rose from 8 per cent of the value of the cargoes to as much as a quarter after the capture of the treasure fleet by the Dutch in 1628. The loss of Spanish control of the sea was a gradual process. By the later seventeenth century the buccaneers were ensconcing themselves in the islands of the Caribbean, though by this time the better organised navies of the French, Dutch and English states were also containing their activities. For the first time there was a clearer separation between years of peace and years of war. In the eighteenth century the Spanish trade with America prospered in peacetime, though it was more vulnerable now to total interruption in time of war by the powerful navy of England.

Writing in 1677 the chronicler Ortiz de Zúñiga traced the decline of his native Seville to the wars which had begun in 1566 with the revolt of Flanders, 'the sepulchre of our armies, the devourer of our treasure'. In 1747–8, in his great memoranda for the new king Ferdinand VI, Ensenada spoke of the need for a long period of peace to cure 'the wounds of such incessant and cruel wars, hardship and misfortunes as this country has endured since the death of Ferdinand the Catholic' – that is, since 1516.[58] But, if men were coming to recognise that war had imposed terrible burdens on imperial Spain, how can we explain the nature of the conflicts themselves? The king and the President of the Council of Castile, in their requests to the Cortes for new taxes, regularly pointed out – as did Philip II in 1586 – that big armies were needed not only for the defence of the Catholic Faith but for the safeguard of trade with the Indies and Flanders. Even the inland towns, like Zamora in 1586 or Granada in the year after the Armada, showed an awareness of the need to pursue the 'Enterprise of England', 'because this is so important for the honour of the Crown and that of the Spanish nation, and the security of these realms and their inhabitants, and the safeguarding of trade with the Indies'.[59]

But where, in reality, was the money going? The court had expanded considerably as the head of a mighty empire during the early modern period. Expenditure here had increased to 1,300,000 ducats a year by the early seventeenth century, and, despite efforts to contain it in the war-torn reign of Philip IV and Olivares, was still around or over this figure in the later seventeenth century. The Bourbons spent lavishly on art and building in the eighteenth century at a time when there was perhaps a little less pressure on the military budget. But it is hard to delimit exactly the expenditure of the court. Under Philip III and Philip IV plans for retrenchment concentrated above all on restricting the *mercedes* or favours paid to individuals; but outgoings here were not always easy to separate from the general costs of the army and the administration itself. The Venetian ambassador Mocenigo (1626–31) calculated that 1,000,000 ducats a year were needed for the court and another 2,000,000 for administration generally, together with just under 5,000,000 for war. But the crippling burden was really the snowball effect of anticipating revenue year after year, leading to periodic bankruptcies and consolidations of the government debt. These in turn generated inexorable increases in the amounts needed to meet payment of interest. Between 1573 and 1602 interest on the government bonds or *juros* doubled to 4,600,000 ducats a year, and rose to 9,147,341 by 1667.[60]

Comparatively little of this huge sum could be raised from the external trade of Spain or from the treasure of the Indies (the latter contributing about a fifth of the king's revenue at its peak around 1600). The bulk had to come from the excise duty (*alcabala*) on domestic trade, augmented after the disaster of the Armada by the *millones*. The *alcabala*, nominally the king's right to a tenth of the value of goods changing hands within Castile, had been commuted from 1534 to a lump sum – *encabezamiento* – guaranteed by the eighteen royal cities which met in the parliament or Cortes. These cities then distributed quotas to the towns of their respective districts, and each town would try further to divide the quota among its guilds and satellite villages.[61] The basis of the Castilian tax system, then, was this devolution of responsibility on to the provinces and on to corporate groups within these, each of which would generally try to raise its quota by some form of excise but might have to resort, at least in part, to a per capita levy or other expedient.

After the government bankruptcy of 1575 the quotas were trebled, but, in the face of protests, the sum was reduced a couple of years later to a figure which still left it about double its previous size. Bitterly denounced by the Cortes as too high and damaging to the economy, this tax increase was nevertheless accepted as less harmful than if the king sent out his own collectors to exact the full legal rate of 10 per cent of all sales. In fact, the *alcabala* seems to have been kept down to about 5 per cent in many towns, with the deficit being made up by other expedients. The clergy were exempt but the nobles were technically not – one reason, perhaps, why the Cortes were keen to keep rates low and make up the deficit in other ways.[62] There were allegations that the royal towns saddled an unfair proportion of the tax on their satellite villages. But the debates in the later sixteenth-century Cortes would tend to suggest that the burden fell heaviest on centres of trade. Most feudal lords had anyway been granted or usurped the right to collect the levy for themselves on their own estates since the later Middle Ages, and they seem to have kept the rates low in order to attract population.

By contrast the *millones* ('millions of ducats'), voted by the Cortes of 1590 to pursue the 'Enterprise of England' and kept going thereafter as part of general military expenditure, fell on the purchase of basic foodstuffs (wine, vinegar, olive oil and meat) and clearly hit the rural population more. Increased at various stages in the early seventeenth century and brought more closely under the supervision of the treasury in Madrid, they stand out as one of the first examples of a standard, relatively centralised tax throughout Castile.

Both excise duties aroused criticism as opening the door to fraud on a massive scale. In 1655 the king told the Cortes that, though nominally worth 10,000,000 ducats a year, they only yielded 3,500,000 to the treasury.[63] Already from the bankruptcy of 1575 a search had begun for some more streamlined system, which would even out inequalities between town and country, and between one province and another, and which would be simple to administer as well as alleviating the burden on domestic trade. One of the options proposed, as early as the Cortes of 1579–82 and revived by Sancho de Moncada in his influential treatise of 1619, was a single, standard duty on the milling of flour – something which everyone consumed. Arguments that such a tax would hit the poor were taken seriously – not least by Moncada, whose testament indicates a certain personal awareness of the fate of paupers. But would the abolition of the excise not ultimately benefit the poor too? – like a pond full of fish, urged the president of the Council of Castile in 1579, where 'if there is a lot of water, the big and the small both do very well . . . whereas if you take away the water their fate is equally wretched'.[64]

In the end the sheer uncertainty of whether the average person bringing grain to be milled would actually have cash to pay a tax of any sort told against this proposal. It left that other *medio universal*, which was increasingly advocated, of a levy on income or wealth. The president of the Council of Castile pointed out the political advantages in terms of preventing rebellion by the poorer citizens (a dimension of the proposal more fully explored in Chapter 7 below).[65] What was now proposed was that citizens earning over 1,000 ducats a year (roughly the salary of a professional man at the time) should lend the government 200 ducats in each of the next five years. It was not quite an income tax: rather individuals or households (it was not entirely clear which) with above a certain amount of property were to be grouped in cohorts worth 1,000 ducats a year, while those with double that revenue were to pay double tax, as were all foreigners. What one notices here, and in the schemes of Don Fernando Alvarez de Toledo at the same time, is an attempt at fiscal discrimination rather than equality – a targeting of foreigners and courtiers (those who drew income directly from the Crown) for special contributions. In any case the President emphasised that the new levy was not a tax but a loan to the government. The amounts collected would be administered by *erarios* – state treasuries or banks, which would pay the contributor interest at 3 per cent while acquiring a monopoly of lending out money (the rate here being as high as 7 per cent). Since the whole scheme was for the good of the citizen, the investigation of wealth by panels of neighbours 'would give no grounds for vendettas, hatred, fear or favour'. But the whole ingenious arrangement assumed a degree of patriotism and supervision which was way ahead of anything that the fiscal system had yet achieved. Local oligarchies were too used to managing their own finances to welcome this unprecedented uniformity. There was a basic reluctance to trust the state with a large, guaranteed income for which it would not be answerable to anyone, and the proposal had to be dropped.

It was left to the Bourbons to try to grasp the nettle again. The *alcabalas* and *millones* have been a disaster for Castile, commented the marquis of Ensenada at the outset of his great reforming ministry in 1747, 'for the wealthy contribute much less in proportion than the poor, who are reduced to the utmost wretchedness, while our manufactures are ruined'.[66] His name came to be associated with the survey of population and property conducted throughout Castile between 1750 and 1754, one of the most impressive undertakings of its kind for any European country in the pre-modern period. But his own fall from power in 1754 and the eternal reluctance of most of his countrymen to move towards a more centralised tax system meant that the great survey lay gathering dust in the archives, unused except by later generations of social historians. The Bourbons had managed – just as they abolished the customs barrier between the Crown of Aragon and Castile in 1717 – to introduce property taxes into these defeated Aragonese kingdoms. The *catastro* in Catalonia and the *equivalente* in Valencia, introduced after the War of the Spanish Succession, involved surveys of wealth, with income from land taxed at 10 per cent and that from 'industry' (a composite term in that artisanal age, referring indiscriminately to the wages for labour or the profits of a business) at 8 per cent. But in a manner typical of early modern Europe generally, such innovations soon became routine – the cadastral surveys were not kept up to date, arbitrary quotas were assigned to local communities, which were allowed to raise the money by local excise or per capita levies.[67]

One of the reasons for the failure of a thoroughgoing fiscal reform under the Bourbons was probably a certain easing of government finances. The old Habsburg excise duties remained important, but had reached their ceiling by the middle of the seventeenth century. Thereafter the government seems to have derived more of its revenue from the American trades – the levies or *indultos* on shipping suspected of carrying contraband, the monopoly of tobacco and chocolate (testimony by the later seventeenth century to the spread of a consumer economy).[68] The other side of the balance-sheet was expenditure. Though Philip V (1700–46) engaged Spain in dynastic wars to put his children on Italian thrones, the general trend of Spanish policy from the later seventeenth century was to cut her commitments in Europe and concentrate on the defence of the sea-lanes to America. This partial retreat from empire may explain why it was possible to cut down so drastically on the government debt. Already in 1649 Philip IV had begun withholding half the interest on the *juros*, but in 1677 the capital value of these bonds was simply reduced by half and by another three-quarters in 1685–7, while interest on the remainder was lowered to 4 per cent or a little over half what it had been a century before.[69]

The success of these measures is not easy to explain, other than that the government no longer needed to borrow so much for foreign wars. When it did resort again to borrowing on a large scale, the domestic and American trades were healthy enough to take up some of the strain. The war of 1779–83 against England had to be paid for, in time-honoured fashion, by loans. But this time the Crown issued bonds – *vales* – directly to its own citizens and did not have recourse, as the Habsburgs had done, to foreign bankers. Instead the 'Five Great Guilds' of Madrid organised much of the credit which the Bourbons needed. The absolute monarchy still had to pay more for its loans, with interest at 4 per cent, than private citizens who could borrow generally at 3 per cent; but the contrast with the earlier failure of the *erarios* in 1623 is striking. In 1782 the government finally set up its state bank, the Bank of San Carlos, in order to guarantee redemption of its bonds for cash if holders so wished. In fact, it was not until the interruption of trade with the Indies during the Revolutionary and Napoleonic Wars that investors lost confidence, a run began on the exchequer and the *vales* were driven down to a discount of 50 per cent of their face value. This marked the collapse of the old fiscal regime, and the need for the iron surgery of the liberal period.

'Sire, finance is the backbone of the government of a monarchy,' wrote Ensenada to his royal master in 1748, 'and because Spain forgot this principle, it has suffered such a lamentable decline over the last two centuries.'[70] Assessing the actual incidence of taxation is a complex business. One has to bear in mind that much taxation in Spain was indirect – the donatives offered, sometimes with grumbling, by feudal lords and local communities. A draft memorial of 1611 for the Cortes noted that towns were increasingly bankrupt through having to levy and billet troops and pay for the plague of 1596–1602. They seem to have resorted increasingly to loans in order to pay their tax quotas to the king, so that the actual disentangling of royal and local fiscalism is not easy.[71] This kind of pressure got worse in the eighteenth century, with the monarchy expecting local communities to supplement the deficits in the state budget. Thus the war of 1739–48 was paid for partly by the royal seizure of half the revenues of the municipalities rather than by the introduction of any new state taxes, and the ambitious road- and canal-building programme of the later eighteenth century was planned from Madrid but financed by local communities.

The nominally privileged Crown of Aragon was already carrying a great weight of muncipal debt by the outset of the seventeenth century. Though Olivares tried to involve it and the rest of the empire in a grandiose scheme known as 'The Union of Arms', by which provincial quotas of troops would be contributed to a collective defence force of 140,000 men, it began to emerge that so much tax was being paid to the local towns and autonomous regional administrations that little was left for Madrid. When the Bourbons tried to take up the torch of fiscal unification after their victory in the War of the Spanish Succession (1700–14) they met similar problems. So heavy was the excise already in Valencia, warned Melchor de Macanaz, their agent for reform in that kingdom, 'that goods for sale are as dear as in Castile, and foodstuffs cost a lot more'. Much of this burden was what Macanaz called waste: fiestas, maladministration, corruption. The little Valencian town of Beniganim told the Cortes of 1645 that it had spent 14,000

Valencian pounds on war in recent years – but 60,000 (it avowed ingenuously) on building its new church.

The brave words of ministers about the need to protect imperial trade must have rung hollow in the villages from where most of the taxes had to come. The subsidy voted by the Valencian Cortes in 1626 involved a massive police operation to check on fraud – the right to inspect cellars for the wine tax, the closure of all ports except four and the stamping of all imports within twenty-four hours for the new customs duty. One is torn between admiration for the superhuman specifications of how and when the stamp was to be obtained (all customs houses must be open, even on holy days, from sun-up to sundown) and scepticism that they could ever have worked in the days before artificial lighting and the telephone. No wonder that Vilajoiosa begged the king in the Cortes of 1604, 1626 and 1645 to remove his customs post a few miles inland, since it only discouraged ships from taking refuge there, even when pursued by Barbary corsairs. No wonder, either, that Townsend approved of the consolidation of many of these old dues into the property tax, the *equivalente*, under the Bourbons. Though quite high, it gave less opportunity for corruption and harassment than its diverse predecessors: 'To this consolidation into a single duty may be attributed in part the general prosperity enjoyed throughout the kingdom of Valencia.'[72]

The debate on fiscal reform in the Old Regime involved much broader questions about the role of the state. Traditional political philosophy in Spain as in other parts of Europe had visualised the 'state' somewhat in the nature of the patrimony of the king – the bundle of rights and tribute which would enable him to carry on his twin role as defender of the commonwealth against external aggression and the arbiter of its internal conflicts. But the commonwealth was separate from the king. And one senses in the debates of the Cortes of the late sixteenth and early seventeenth centuries a fundamental conflict between those who regarded the recent growth of the state with distaste and those who thought it a positive thing in giving more protection to trade. For the former the traditional rights of the king, including the *alcabalas* originally conceded in 1341, were legitimate, but all the increases in taxation and the government debt since 1575 were damaging. Hence the failure to grasp the nettle of an income tax. Since all taxation was harmful, the main aim must be to reduce the government's commitments. So, a flour tax, though it would hit the poor chiefly, could be justified if it were a stop-gap remedy. Taxation was not conceived of as social engineering: it was dangerous to reduce the income of the nobility and the church since they and not the state provided whatever welfare was available to the ordinary citizen. At most, as in 1623, the Cortes would contemplate a punitive levy on those who had benefited by the largesse of the state (and thereby increased its commitments), taxing the fruits of office, pensions and (eventually) *juros*.

In the event the state was not rolled back. The standing army, developed for the trench warfare in Flanders in the later sixteenth century, was kept going and transferred to the peninsula itself by the Bourbons after the disbandment of the European empire. But the administration of the army – and increasingly in the eighteenth century of the navy – reposed on a shaky financial base. The Venetian ambassador Contarini commented in 1621 on the sheer, frustrating inability of the Spanish state to pay its way: 'even for the payment of small items on the ordinary account, you would not believe how long it takes'. Nevertheless, he noted, the government limped along thanks to the sheer vastness of its potential resources, able to count on the services of a considerable array of people since everyone lived in hope of some titbit falling from the royal table. The problem, thought Soranzo in 1602, was corruption: 'Those who handle (the public purse) grow immensely rich.' And Fernández Navarrete drew a contrast in 1626 between the ordinary taxpayer who was wretched and those who had latched on to the court and the fiscal system, who were prospering.[73]

One of the features of the whole system was a kind of 'bastard feudalism' – the devolution of power in the seventeenth century on to those bodies – regional assemblies in the Crown of Aragon, town councils or feudal lords in Castile – which could provide money and men for the war. The medieval Cortes had developed in all the peninsular kingdoms as a way of allowing the commonwealth – particularly the burgesses of the royal domain – to mobilise their wealth in order to buttress the royal patrimony in time of need. What was now becoming apparent, with the anguished debates in the Cortes on taxation after 1575 and the refusal of the Crown of Aragon to join the Union of Arms in 1626, was that fiscal centralisation had reached its pre-modern limit. If the king needed more income, it would have to be through recourse to the 'benevolence' of the subject – through informal donatives bargained for with nobles and towns on an individual basis. All of this carried a social cost.

5

FEUDAL LORDS AND VILLAGE POTENTATES

In his celebrated essay 'Invertebrate Spain' (1921), Ortega y Gasset lamented the lack of a Spanish feudalism equivalent to that of medieval France or England. Instead of a hierarchy of power and authority, stretching down from the throne to the people, this frontier nation had developed as a cluster of autonomous corporations – military brotherhoods, city states – with strong local roots. Admirably democratic in some ways, this system had generated perpetual tensions between centre and periphery, and left both the society and its culture very fragmented.

The pattern of resettlement in the wake of the Reconquista had been much as Ortega suggested: the distribution of lands to cities and to the Military Orders founded in the twelfth century – Santiago, Calatrava and Alcántara – whose members were co-opted for their own lifetime by their fellows. Both were dedicated to the protection of the frontier. The knights and foot-soldiers who comprised the bulk of the crusading armies were rewarded with variable amounts of land, based on the 'ox-gang' (*yugada*), which was the field that a pair of oxen could plough in a day and which ranged in size from 3 to 22 hectares, according to the lie of the terrain and the depth of the soil. Typically, the knight would get twice the portion of a foot-soldier, which seems to have amounted in practice to nearly 80 hectares round thirteenth-century Seville and up to 100 round Cordoba.[1] The organisation of the resettlements drew to some extent on pre-existing Muslim practice, by which the peasantry and landowners had been grouped under the jurisdiction of cities. Castile under the Christians continued to have a basic framework of towns, from where control over the surrounding countryside was exercised. Thus in the early seventeenth century the magistrates of Seville dispensed justice in some 100 villages round about; and for 15 kilometres round Xàtiva, 62 villages had to refer to the urban magistrates any cases involving sentences of death or the galleys, and had to levy the same taxes as in Xàtiva and contribute to the upkeep of its walls.[2] Even in old-settled Spain north of the Duero River, towns and villages were grouped in extensive federations – nominally more egalitarian, but perhaps not too different from the colonised lands to the south.

In a mainly pastoral society, these regional federations had an important function of policing a rather empty countryside. In the cadastral surveys of sixteenth-century Granada and Valencia the land is often ill-mapped, the non-irrigated hill country apparently being occupied by families on a shifting basis. Control over these *baldíos* was becoming at this time a significant cause of conflict, as population increased and the open range came under pressure. The great jurist, Castillo de Bobadilla, in his treatise of 1597, urged that the royal district officer (*corregidor*) must inspect the townlands of his jurisdiction at least once in his three-year term of office, checking on boundaries and markers. Agreements with neighbouring justices were vital on 'irrigation, pasture, felling of timber, tolls on roads and bridges, fording rivers and other matters'.[3]

Control over jurisdiction, thought Castillo de Bobadilla in 1597 and Caxa de Leruela in 1631, was absolutely vital to the health of the local community. It was a major feature of the whole colonisation of Spain that massive efforts were made during this period to rearrange the pattern of such control. Once a community prospered and grew in population, it would inevitably make a bid for the right to administer its own resources. Speaking of the Xúquer district in the kingdom of Valencia, the chronicler Escolano wrote in 1610: 'It is truly an Indies that they have there . . . The trade in silk is so great that small communities have increased and turned themselves into populous towns.' The latter term is, of course, relative: Algemesí, with 480 families, separated itself from the old regional capital Alzira, in 1574, while its neighbour Carcaixent (420 families), followed suit in 1576. In both cases, the money acquired from silk enabled them to win these charters from the Crown, though Algemesí had to wait until 1608 and pay another subsidy before it achieved the coveted title of 'royal town' (*villa*), with a seat in the Cortes. In the parliament of 1604 Alzira complained about the dismemberment of her jurisdiction in this way, for as a result 'she suffers a great lack of timber and grassland'.[4] It was a similar story in Castile. By 1594 the Andalusian town of Bujalance had become so wealthy through its woollen manufacture that it was able to purchase its separation from the jurisdiction of Cordoba. It has been calculated that whereas in 1500 only about 40 per cent of communities in New Castile were autonomous 'towns', by 1700 this proportion had risen to three-quarters. Already in 1565 Alcalá de Henares pleaded with the Crown not to grant autonomy to any more of her satellite villages, for she was losing access to her traditional supplies of food and timber thereby.[5]

Regulation of markets and pasture was one of the most prized aspects of the right to hold a court in those days. Sometimes agreements were reached to maintain common access to grasslands – as between Bujalance and Cordoba after 1594. But such arrangements were subject to multiple tensions and litigation. The deputy for Seville told the Cortes of 1615 that, whatever was said on paper, 'those who buy jurisdictional rights stop anyone else from coming in to pasture'. And Caxa de Leruela a decade and a half later blamed the decline of the herds on this splitting up of the open range. He went on to say that it was the wealthy minority in each local community who sought autonomy in this way – 'in order to make what they can out of the administration of justice, looking to the interests of their friends and *compadres*, and putting the poor under the thumb of the rich'.[6]

There was, indeed, a tendency for this process to dovetail with the growth of feudal jurisdictions. Spain had not had in the Middle Ages a fully fledged system of fiefs and serfs: the militarisation of all free men and the movement of manpower to the frontier had, with some exceptions, told against these west European developments. But one of the aspects of the early modern period was precisely the rise of some of the symptoms of rural subjugation. The big landowners tended to acquire the trappings of power which had hitherto eluded them. Symptomatic was the failure of the peasants of Tejeda in 1453 to stop their local landowner nominating the justice of the peace, who was technically delegated by the city of Salamanca. The man's influence with the Salamanca councillors was too strong.[7] Such de facto control could become institutionalised in due course through the acquisition of feudal jurisdiction. In the kingdom of Valencia landowners had been allowed automatically to appoint their own justices to regulate civil and petty criminal cases (not involving corporal punishment) if they had three Moorish or fifteen Christian families settled on their estates – the so-called Alfonsine jurisdiction, granted by Alfons II in 1327.

It was often the colonisation of land which led, as by a natural progression, to the exercise of some sort of discipline over the settlers by the chief coloniser. In a dry climate and poor soil such as characterised much of Spain, the ability of peasant farmers to go it alone was problematical. Though land was established to free colonists living around the city states like Cordoba or Seville in the wake of the thirteenth-century reconquest, property drifted inevitably into the hands of those with capital. The process of feudalisation was gradual. The townland of Benamejí had been attracting settlers over the years since the threat of border raids from the Moors of Granada ceased in 1492. By 1547 there were some nineteen families tilling the soil and living in the shadow of the fortress which belonged to the Military Order of Santiago. In 1547 Charles V decided, as Master of the Order, to sell the jurisdiction to a private individual, Diego de Bernuy, a wealthy alderman of Burgos. One of the aspects of the transfer which may have appealed to the peasants was that their new lord had the wherewithal to promise to build a flour mill and an oil press, as well as giving each family 2,000 tiles to roof their house and enough tiles to replace the thatch on the village church. He also offered to build a bridge to improve access to and from the settlement.[8]

The acquisition of private jurisdictions had been proceeding quite fast in medieval Spain – from around 1000 in Catalonia, from about 1100 in Castile. But as a recognised part of the structure of the state itself – as a helpmate of the Crown in defending and governing its territories – it seems to have achieved a new importance under the usurping Trastámara dynasty in Castile from the middle of the fourteenth century onwards. Rewarding his supporter Men Rodríguez de Benavides, the new king Henry II granted him in 1371 the fief of Santisteban del Puerto, near Jaén, on the frontier with the Muslim kingdom of Granada, where Benavides was military commander: 'so that you and the men of your lineage may enjoy an increase of fame and honour, and may have the wherewithal to serve us all the better'.[9] Such fiefs carried no specific obligation to provide a fixed number of troops; but, in alliance with other arrangements with leading families and prelates to come to war when summoned with so many 'lances' (*lanzas*) in return for payment, their creation was part of a general trend. This trend can be interpreted either as a devolution of power on to great aristocrats or, more tellingly perhaps, as a primitive coordination of military and administrative responsibility by kings who were moving from charismatic war leaders to heads of a more permanent hierarchy of command. Through Benavides, Henry II probably exercised more real, or at least more ongoing authority on the Jaén frontier than did any of his predecessors. As the tasks of government multiplied in the late medieval and early modern period, some kind of 'bastard feudalism' may have seemed the only answer.

Certainly the Catholic Kings, Ferdinand and Isabel (1474–1516), appear to have cooperated well with the nobility. Many fiefs were distributed in the conquered kingdom of Granada after 1492 to the great families of Castile who had helped them in the crusade. The burdens of empire led their Habsburg successors into a modified continuation of this policy: large numbers of villages were separated from the jurisdiction of their district capital and sold off to private individuals. Thus Villafranca and Castro near Cordoba went to the marquises of Priego in 1549 and 1565 respectively for a sum which worked out at forty-three times their annual rental; Carrión de los Ajos near Seville was transferred to Gonzalo de Céspedes, who had made a fortune in the Indies trade, for over thirty-seven times the rental value.[10] The bulk of the purchasers seem to have been 'new men': in the kingdom of Granada, for example, about two-thirds of them were aldermen or *regidores* of the royal towns – often of the local royal town from which the new fief was broken off. Whereas just under 20 per cent of the population of this region lived under feudal lords on the eve of the sales in 1558, the proportion was nearly 30 per cent two hundred years later.[11]

Granada, as a newly conquered territory, may have been somewhat late in acquiring a feudal character. In other parts, the great lordships seem to have arisen in the fourteenth and fifteenth centuries. In the kingdom of Valencia, for example, the Borjas obtained their duchy of Gandia in 1485, the Cárdenas got their marquisate of Elx in 1470, the Sandoval received Dénia in 1431, followed by the house of Aragon in the duchy of Segorbe in 1435–8 and the Ruiz de Corella in the county of Cocentaina in 1445. After 1490 the proportion of territory and population held in fief hardly advanced much. In western Andalusia (Seville, Cordoba), where the reconquest from the Moor took place in the thirteenth century, the process of seigneurialisation was mainly a late medieval phenomenon, covering 27 per cent of the territory in the generation after the conquest but 49 per cent by the time Isabel came to the throne in 1474. Finally, in the kingdom of Murcia the families living under feudal lords actually fell from just under a half of the population in 1530 to just over a third by 1787, as the royal towns forged ahead since they had access to the best lands and markets. But by this time perhaps half of the villages and half of the population of Castile overall were parcelled out in fiefs.[12]

The process of feudalisation was, we have suggested, a way of bringing local elites into closer cooperation with the Crown. But the monarchy was careful not to surrender too much authority. John II had given the fine port of Cartagena to the Fajardos in 1442, but his daughter Isabel took it back into royal hands in 1503, compensating the holder with the marquisate of Los Vélez on the frontier with Granada. And she recovered that other great harbour, Cadiz, from the Ponce de León in 1492, with the usual offer of compensation elsewhere. The county of Ribagorza, strategically placed on the Pyrenean frontier with France, was eventually prised from the grasp of the dukes of Villahermosa in 1590, after a bitter struggle. Political disloyalty, of course, could bring worse retribution, and Sanlúcar de Barrameda, at the mouth of the Guadalquivir, was confiscated in 1641 after the suspected treason of its master, the duke of Medina Sidonia, while the duke of Medinaceli lost Puerto de Santa María in 1729 for his conduct towards Philip V. In general, the Bourbons looked askance at any sacrifice of the royal domain. Though Philip V did reward a few of his followers in the War of the Spanish Succession with fiefs, that was the end of the story. Rather, during the eighteenth century a more confident royal administration set its face against such petitions, and even looked more kindly on demands of the peasant population for a return to the royal domain.

'Lords of vassals are like the bones and sinew of the state,' wrote the great jurist Castillo de Bobadilla in 1597. Though, as a royal judge, he disliked feudal jurisdictions, he acknowledged that without them the commonwealth would be 'like a body composed of flesh and feathers, without bones or sinews, so that it would only take a reverse in war or the defeat of an army or the death of a king to bring about its collapse'. In fact, the creation of fiefs often provoked bitter conflicts which brought the state itself to its knees. One of the ingredients in the great revolt of the Comuneros (1520–1) was the resentment of the royal towns at the amputation of their townlands in favour of the great nobility. Isabel had ceded large tracts of the district of Segovia in 1480 to her supporter Andrés Cabrera; it was not until 1592 that the ensuing litigation could be settled, by an agreement whereby the Cabreras, counts of Chinchón, would pay the city of Segovia an annuity of 2,000 ducats.[13]

'The king's vassals and subjects can have no greater sadness and resentment,' wrote the Valencian chronicler Viciana in 1563, 'than when the king separates them from his patrimony and royal estate, almost as if they had been overrun by enemies.'[14] He went on to describe the conflict between the town of Onda and Ferdinand the Catholic in 1512, over the latter's desire to transfer it to his nephew, Don Alonso de Aragón. The men of Onda locked the gates against their new master, and pursued Ferdinand with their clamour for '*justicia! justicia!*', until the king lost his temper and his secretary warned them not to press too hard for fear of the consequences. On the other hand, there were certain advantages in being placed under a feudal lord. The people of Segorbe – 'the greater and sounder part' of them, as the careful legal phrase of those pre-democratic days put it – assembled in their town hall on 2 June 1619 and agreed to drop their lawsuit against the duke, their master. Since 1575 and the death of the last male descendant of the family in the direct line, they had been litigating for a return to the royal domain. Now, aware that the lawsuit was costing 'many thousands of ducats' and that the duke, a major figure at the court of both Philip III and Philip IV, 'by his greatness is likely to favour and protect this city, and his children and progeny are likely to do the same, as true lords and fathers of this community', they decided to accept him as their master.[15] In fact, in the very same year as the Cortes of 1626 ratified the agreement, the town of Segorbe began to change its mind and to allege that the deal of 1619 had been struck by a corrupt minority of the inhabitants. In any case, the substantial inducements on offer from the duke – a reduction of rents, helping with paying off the lawyers' bills, a promise to come and live in Segorbe, creating jobs and opportunities for the local people – all reflect more general pressures which can be detected in the spread of feudal jurisdictions in Castile. The town of Uceda, separated from the diocese of Toledo in 1582, failed to meet the price required by the Crown and within a few years had to sell itself back into subjection, this time to the son of the future duke of Lerma, favourite of Philip III.[16] When one remembers that another royal favourite, Olivares, was one of the most active purchasers of fiefs in the 1620s, one may feel both that his vassals benefited and that the Crown's authority suffered little real loss. But what was actually transferred by these sales, and did the peasants gain or lose?

The great jurist Castillo de Bobadilla suggested in 1597 that, though many lords claimed the empty lands (*baldíos*) lying within their fiefs, yet there needed to be an express grant of these by the Crown for that to take effect. And certainly they could not enclose pasture or woods, but must leave them for common use – unless they themselves were the original owners and colonisers of the area. Hunting, equally, must remain open for the local peasantry – 'unless some privilege, contract, custom or consent of the village awarded it to the lord'. However, he acknowledged that in practice 'some seigneurs usurp this right, because they have the power, and molest their vassals, punishing them with heavy fines'.[17]

The original grant of Oropesa to the Alvarez de Toledo family in 1369 included a typically sweeping reference to 'lands, fisheries and pasture'; yet the seventh count of Oropesa found it prudent in 1636 to pay the Crown 60,000 ducats for authorisation to fence off a quarter of the common lands as private pasture. The sheer uncertainty of title to property in an empty landscape has to be borne in mind throughout. In La Calahorra the Muslims had only title to the irrigated fields down to 1570; the *secano* was 'empty land (*baldío*), and anyone who wished could sow it', sometimes handing parcels of it on to their children, 'but no one saw or heard of anyone selling it'.[18] But as part of the joint process of frontier settlement and seigneurialisation in the early modern period, the feudal lords began to enforce control of the open range more strictly. After the duke of Arcos acquired the county of Arcos in 1491, he began levying dues on the peasants of nearby Marbella who tried to exercise their old rights of pasturing their herds in the area. The royal high court intervened in 1516 and 1567 to stop the duke, but he continued to treat the common land of Arcos as his own domain, parcelling out bits of it from time to time to his vassals for ploughing.[19] Other lords, as in the case of Oropesa, reached agreements with the Crown for cash, allowing them exclusive rights to at least part of the commons within their fiefs. The village of Grazalema protested in 1814 that its lord, the duke of Arcos, had bought from the Crown land which allegedly was not surveyed but which really belonged to the community: 'In times preceding the present age it was not easy to win any victory against grandees and powerful men, for their influence might cause lawsuits to drag on over whole centuries, with the verdict leaving matters open.'[20]

Property censuses were one way by which a feudal lord could determine rights of landownership. In Oliva in 1663 the peasants were interrogated by their master, the duke of Gandia, regarding the fields they cultivated. Some had lost their title deeds, but were allowed to continue farming, on payment of quit-rents to the duke. At the next survey in 1744, the seigneurial agent warned of the danger of land drifting out of the feudal domain through neglect. More likely, it was the other way round – the lord of the fief gradually establishing his right to more and more of the land. Thus, in Andalusia the marquises of Priego built up an impressive estate over the early modern period, first establishing their control of the commons (though contested by the peasants), then buying up or annexing peasant farms themselves. By 1752 they were owners of about a fifth of the surface area in six of the eleven townships comprising the marquisate.[21]

What did the seigneurs do with the land thus acquired? Some of it could be used to expand ranching, as in Tudor England. In 1629 Don Sebastián Suárez bought the fief of Lozoya near Segovia, and went on to appropriate the commons for his herds of sheep. To the protest of the villagers, he is alleged to have retorted: 'that there were four roads out of the village, and they could take the one they liked best . . .'. Though the high court intervened in 1637 to order Don Sebastián out of the village for two years, the peasants eventually took matters into their own hands and killed him in 1646.[22] Round Salamanca the frontier wars with the Portuguese in 1640–68 and 1702–13 led to the abandonment of villages on a considerable scale, and the build-up of the famous ranches for fighting-bulls which characterise the region today.

But the general trend was away from herding towards arable farming in early modern Spain. Not many of the feudal lords participated actively in this process. The sugar plantations in Valencia, which involved perhaps the greatest concentrations of serf labour in sixteenth-century Spain, were exceptional and doomed – doomed because serfdom had never really established itself and costs were too high. There had been attempts in the Middle Ages to restrict the mobility of the rural populations, in order to stop them running off to the frontier. Thus in fourteenth and fifteenth-century Catalonia one finds agreements whereby peasants pledge themselves not to leave the estate in return for the seigneur's guarantee that they can pass the farms on to their own heirs. By 1400 these *remensa* households constituted about a quarter of the Catalan population, and as much as three-quarters of the peasantry in the old-established lands of Girona.[23] But the great rebellion of the *remensas*, coinciding with the civil war of 1462–72, resulted in the charter of liberty – the *Sentència de Guadalupe* – issued by Ferdinand the Catholic in 1486, freeing the peasantry of Catalonia. Meanwhile, similar trends in Castile towards arresting the free flow of population to the frontier were interrupted by Sancho IV's decree of 1285, reaffirmed in 1480, that the peasant could leave his master when he chose.

The sugar mills of Valencia were run for a handful of feudal lords by their Morisco vassals. In principle, the Moors were free men like the Christians. The feudal lords were keen, on the one hand, to attract more of them on to their estates, but, on the other, worried that they might become too free. Thus, after their conversion to Christianity, they were required by the Cortes of 1528 not to leave the villages 'without having first settled their accounts and paid what they owe to the *senyor*'. But the Crown's reply to this petition makes it clear that it was more interested in stopping all movement of Moriscos to the coast, where they presented a security risk, and by 1559 a system of passports was introduced for this people, requiring them to show just cause why they were out of their villages.

Though this tying down facilitated seigneurial control, there were difficulties in exploiting Morisco labour. The duke of Gandia looked back nostalgically to a mythical golden age before the expulsion of the Moriscos in 1609, when this people had been there 'to plough the duke's fields and work on his castles, houses and other buildings, and come with their mules and pack-animals when his luggage had to be carried from place to place, while the women were busy spinning and weaving for the ducal household'. In reality, the Gandia accounts for the late sixteenth century suggest a more limited use of Morisco labour. The duke would recruit specialists on the open market for the pruning of his vines in February, at sixty Valencian pennies a day, while Morisco labour gangs were rounded up to assist the pruners at eight pennies per man. Work on the duke's country house in 1585 involved hiring 'Master Peter and his son' for skilled bricklaying, and unskilled serf labour for hauling limestone and water to the site. Some Morisco names tend to recur, suggesting a kind of proletariat in the villages, chosen by the elders to fill the labour quotas.

No doubt the Morisco labour gangs were most significant in the unpleasant work of the sugar mills. But this industry was always somewhat marginal, especially with the exploitation of new lands in the Tropics. Gandia's neighbour, the Cistercian monastery of Valldigna, has preserved a series of accounts from the 1580s which remind us that Morisco labour in the mills had to be paid and could eat into profits. The monastery was having to revise its labour demands on its Morisco peasants constantly over the fifteenth and sixteenth centuries by a series of *concordias* or agreements. That of 1557 provided, among other things, that the peasants were to be called upon to clean the monastery only on feast-days, and that if the monks needed mattresses stitched they were to pay the Morisco women seven pennies each a day.[24] This world came to an end with the expulsion of the Moriscos in 1609. As in America, the Crown defined labour services as unsuitable for free men, and instructed the feudal lords to commute them for other payments in the resettlements.

The Moriscos were not the only ones owing these. The peasants of Villafranca near Cordoba had to turn in four days' work per year on the marquis of Priego's farms, while those of San Pedro de Cardena near Burgos worked for two days a year on the estate of their master in the sixteenth century. Specific tasks of this kind were, however, marginal to the rural economy, as the feudal lords preferred to lease out their demesne rather than cultivate it directly. The greater burden of service was of a more general kind – the hospitality (sometimes called *cena* or supper) which the vassals must provide when their master visited them, the repair of his castle, the gift of a beast at the marriage of their daughters, and the other customs mentioned in the great survey (*Relaciones*) of New Castile in 1575. The town of Lerma in Old Castile protested in 1502 against having to supply the whole seigneurial household with carts, wood, straw, salt and lodging when it came to visit, and the royal court ruled in 1548 that the visit must not exceed twelve days a year in these conditions.[25]

'This burden of lodging and clothing and suchlike which a seigneur lays on his vassals,' wrote Castillo de Bobadilla in 1597, 'asking them for gifts when they or their children marry or at Christmas, and that they bake their bread in his ovens or grind their flour in his mills, that they plough his fields and give him carts to carry wood and building materials or to move house . . . all these are odious burdens and must be cut back.' As a royal judge, he gave his opinion that the courts would favour peasant demands for their abolition, unless the seigneur could prove that they had been introduced in return for some boon conferred on the village by his ancestors. And he advised nobles to 'put their hand on their heart' and ask themselves whether they were really entitled to these things. Shortly before, the Franciscan moralist Juan de Pineda had addressed a similar message to them: 'In this matter of forcing people to make their flour in your mills, there is an impression at the outset of great tyranny and oppression of free men.' The royal courts, he noted, would assume, without proof to the contrary, that 'such abuses were slipped in by tyrannical lords when the kingdom was disturbed by civil strife and the kings had little power'.[26]

In Benamejí it was the seigneur who built the mill and oven for the peasants of this relatively new settlement in 1549, and who claimed in the foundation charter a monopoly of use. But nearby the village of Aguilar took the marquis of Priego to court in 1582 for trying to enforce similar monopolies – usually known as *regalías*, or 'rights of dominion' – in a community which was already functioning before it was alienated from the royal domain. In 1624 the chancery court finally got round to giving its decision: that the marquis could have the only public flour mill in town, but that the peasants could bake bread freely at home, that the marquis would have the butcher's shop but the peasants could run their own general store and tavern . . . But then in 1630, in return for a huge subsidy of 60,000 ducats, the Crown allowed the marquis to control the sale of wine and olive oil in his fief.[27]

One way round the law was to claim that the seigneur was not providing enough facilities for baking or milling. Thus the Moriscos of Muro obtained the right in 1599 to use other than the two flour mills and one oven which their master, the count of Cocentaina, was prepared to build. Less successfully, they sued the count for breach of the laws of Valencia which allowed its people to press their olives where they chose.[28] The expansion of olive cultivation in the eighteenth century undermined the *regalías* of the marquis of Priego, as he found that his presses in Montilla could no longer keep pace with mounting demand. The development of the market economy, indeed, seems to have spelled the end of these rights some time before they were eventually abolished in the nineteenth century. After successive protests by its peasants, the monastery of Valldigna found it useful to concede in 1700 that farmers with crops to sell could do so outside the seigneurial store, whose prices anyway were to be fixed henceforth by the peasant magistrates and not by the monks. And in 1781 it agreed that the villagers could import freely whatever wine they needed, without passing through the seigneurial tavern.[29]

The nineteenth-century transition, whereby feudal lords became essentially landlords, was well under way in the early modern period. We have already noted the process by which fief-holders used their influence to round out control of the commons and even some of the peasant land on their estates. Large-scale farming by the seigneurs themselves was not practicable, given the lack of a serf labour-force and the underdevelopment of the market economy itself. There are some examples to the contrary, like the duke of Cardona round Cordoba in the middle of the seventeenth century. But Castillo de Bobadilla had given fair warning that, while seigneurs could sell the harvests from their own farms, the royal judges would take a dim view of 'business dealings and buying and selling fleeces, olive oil and that kind of thing', because of the 'intimidation, oppression, violence, cornering of the market and harm done to the peasants living on their estates'.[30] They must remember the original purpose of the fief: a delegation of jurisdiction from the Crown, which must not be abused for profit.

Instead, the pattern was that the feudal lords would lease out their lands to others. The duke of Arcos tended to lease his in the marquisate of Comares, whose jurisdiction had come to him in 1490, for nine years at a time; and the marquis of Priego similarly leased his extensive holdings for between three and six years. There was a tendency for such leases to become nearly hereditary. 'Any landlord who threw a tenant out of the home of his ancestors without an extremely good reason,' wrote Jovellanos of his native Asturias in 1782, 'would be looked upon as a tyrant.' Though one would have to distinguish these small peasants of Asturias or Valencia from the bigger capitalist leaseholders of New Castile or Andalusia, even these tended to be brought within a patron–client system. In 1785 Don Francisco Xavier Pallares, farmer of two big *cortijos* belonging to the count of Villa Amena on the frontier of Murcia and Granada, wrote to his master explaining that, with the bad harvest and the sickness of his wife and daughter, he would not be able to pay his rent. 'I would appeal to Your Lordship's compassion, in my great need and with utmost humility, that . . . you would not drive me to the wall in my broken state of health . . . I am confident that Your Lordship's pious heart will see its way to granting my request.' An extension of time to pay off the arrears was granted, and in 1787, when Pallares had got back on his feet, his lease was renewed.[31]

More generally, the land in Spain was cleared and occupied by small peasant farmers, who might then have to reach some sort of accommodation with the feudal lord. In Valdepusa (Toledo), the seigneur originally established 700 *fanegas* of land to settlers in 1457; by 1526 these had taken in, without authorisation, another 800 from the waste, and their master ratified the 'usurpation' that year. In Valldigna there was a serious conflict between the peasantry and the abbey in 1593 over the status of some recently cleared land in Masalalí: was it peasant land, as the Moriscos claimed, which they could hand on to their children and barter away, or leasehold?[32] This uncertainty surfaced in the eighteenth century in Galicia and Asturias, as some landlords sought to profit by the expansion of the economy, taking back from their tenants the fields established for three lives (*foros*). After intervening to protect sitting tenants in 1759–63, the Crown decreed in 1785 that leaseholders could only be evicted on condition that the owner wanted to farm his property himself.

Though we still know too little about how these laws were actually applied, they seem to be in the spirit of the long process of colonisation of this frontier land since the Middle Ages. In Andalusia the dukes of Arcos created their new settlement of Paradas (1460) out of the townland of Marchena, offering rent exemptions for fifteen years and guarantees of fixed rents thereafter to the settlers. Meanwhile, seigneurs further north had to try to stem the tide of emigration to the frontier by offering equally generous terms: hereditary tenures, and rents equivalent to a tenth of the harvest at most, though often much less.[33] Shortage of manpower in the wake of the Black Death in the fourteenth century seems to have consolidated this movement towards a lowering of feudal rents, and sometimes their commutation for fixed sums in cash. In Castile the rents from land, whether leasehold or quit-rents from hereditary peasant farmers, seem to have constituted only a relatively minor proportion of the income of feudal seigneurs – just under 14 per cent in the case of the count of Benavente, for example. The bulk of their revenue came from the sales tax (*alcabala*), which they had been given or usurped from the Crown, and from the 'third of the tithe' (*tercias*), granted to the kings of this crusading nation by the church and often appropriated by the seigneurs.

Where the seigneurs did depend fundamentally on quit-rents – as in the Crown of Aragon – their situation in the sixteenth century, as the market economy developed and price inflation undermined the value of sums paid in cash, placed considerable strains on their relations with their peasants. In 1457 the abbey of Valldigna agreed to accept a fixed sum, the *magram*, in commutation of shares of the wheat harvest formerly paid by the Moriscos. But faced with the erosion of its income in the sixteenth century, it began to demand a share of the new crops being grown by the wealthier tenants – mulberry leaf to feed the silkworms, carob as fodder for mules, even baskets of grapes. In reply to peasant protest that it had vineyards enough of its own, the abbey retorted that it was driven to such measures because the *magram* was now too low. Archbishop Ribera warned his preachers on the mission of 1599 to the Moriscos not to get involved in disputes about rents, telling their audience 'that they should go before the ministers whom His Majesty appoints to administer justice to Old and New Christian alike'.[34]

The records of litigation in the royal courts about rents are, indeed, an impressive testimony to the stresses of the time. Essentially, the Crown kept a fairly vigilant eye on attempts to rescind old charters. When the Moriscos were expelled from Granada in 1570 and from Valencia in 1609 new opportunities seemed to present themselves. But in Granada the Crown issued instructions 'that the settlers are not to be saddled with terms such as that they set aside more land for the seigneur, nor with new burdens more than the Moriscos were subject to'; and the resettlement, indeed, was kept strictly in royal hands. In Valencia the repopulation after 1609 has generated enormous controversy and a growing literature, exploring the complexities of the quadrille danced by the Crown, the seigneurs, the latters' creditors, and, finally, the new settlers themselves. Here one may say that, whatever the objective conditions of the resettlement (and they were often draconian at the outset, then reduced as the seigneurs found they could not attract sufficient immigrants), the peasant lore guarded a memory of royal intervention and of a basic feeling that, whatever they owed the feudal lords, the old Morisco lands were theirs. This was to figure prominently in the great peasant rebellion of 1693, which we shall examine below.[35] A clear statement of the Crown's position came in its great charter of 1614, the *Asiento General* or 'General Settlement' of the kingdom of Valencia, in which Philip III forbade the feudal lords to saddle the new colonists with the debts of the Moriscos, 'given our obligation to see to the maintenance and increase of the population of the realm, which is so important to the service of God and of our self'. A nation of peasant smallholders was the ideal pursued by statesmen in Spain right down to the end of the Old Regime.

The charters of individual communities often specified that the peasant must not alienate his holding to any powerful man, like a noble or a cleric, who could claim exemption from the manorial court. In the same spirit, those inheriting land in Benamejí were obliged to take up residence in the village within two years or forfeit the inheritance (1549). In the Crown of Aragon the peasant was supposed to seek permission from his lord before alienating any part of his holding and pay around 10 per cent of the price as a fee. The *remensas* in fifteenth-century Catalonia lost four-fifths of their farm to the seigneur if they left no child to succeed, and one-third if they failed to specify which of several children should assume headship of the household. Though these restrictions were abolished in 1486, the idea of the land as a pillar of a stable community rather than as an easily transferable economic asset remained. In Valencia the duke of Infantado would scrutinise the accounts of those tenants in arrears with their rent to decide whether they should be transferred to another holding if their family was too small or too big, or they were good or bad workers.[36]

In practice, these controls seem not to have worked very well in early modern Spain, unlike the situation, for example, in seventeenth-century eastern Europe. Already in 1595 the Crown was having to issue decrees amending its earlier rulings on the *suertes* – 'lots' or portions – distributed to the Christian colonists of Granada after 1570. Each had been designed for the upkeep of one household, but now they were being transferred to non-residents, bartered and sold. So the commissioners agreed that a settler could have more than one *suerte*, if acquired by marriage or inheritance, though trying to insist, still, that any outside the village where he had his main residence should be reassigned to a child or kinsman. In fact, during the seventeenth century control was lost, as the lots were divided up, alienated and bartered. The governor of Llombai (Valencia) admitted that it was difficult to supervise these transfers adequately (1756). The record of the sales tax (*lluisme*) in the seigneurial accounts of Valldigna would indicate a very high turnover of peasant land in the seventeenth century, as fields were reassigned, bartered and sold in order to sort out inheritance arrangements (for in most parts of Spain, except for Catalonia, the custom was subdivision of the farm anyway among male and female offspring). In fifteenth-century Sueca around a half of the fields registered in the cadastral survey of 1453 had changed hands by 1465, and another half between 1494 and 1509.[37] About a half of the families disappeared from the lists altogether over this half century, due either to loss of their holding or to emigration.

In New Castile the possession of a yoke of oxen seems to have been the threshold separating the prosperous peasant farmer (*labrador*) from the rest. In Puebla Nueva (Toledo), according to the *Relaciones* of 1575, there were 350 families, 'and of these about 70 are peasants and the rest are day-labourers and artisans . . . and three or four peasants say they are gentlemen (*hidalgos*), because they have a patent of nobility'.[38] By the eighteenth century many peasant communities were, in fact, exceedingly diverse in social composition – perhaps more diverse than they would ever be again, given the need to provide most services for themselves. Thus Llombai in 1756, with only 209 families, could boast 'three notaries . . . a doctor of medicine, two surgeons . . . a veterinary surgeon, a pharmacist . . . a schoolmaster . . . a constable and town-crier', as well as an impressive range of artisans – bricklayer, carpenter, blacksmith, tailor, cobbler and the like. Despite the original egalitarianism of the resettlements, there was a clear drift over the seventeenth century towards social and economic polarisation. Thus in Muro, a resettlement of 382 households, belonging to the count of Cocentaina, three members of the Alonso lineage, all boasting the status of 'don', accounted for about a twelfth of the quit-rents saddled on property in the village (1759). In Gandia in 1752 some 8 per cent of the landowners, who held over 100 *fanegas* (perhaps eight to ten hectares) each, were in possession of nearly half the surface area registered in the cadastre of 1752 – a percentage close to that recorded in 1768 in the nearby royal town of Alzira.[39]

Who were these rich men? The peasants of Valldigna alleged in 1803: 'Those who are called rich or better off among us are very few, and have to devote themselves to farming their own land . . . They can sink into poverty and even to the level of wage-labourers in a very short space of time.'[40] But in New Castile and western Andalusia the market for grain was creating some very impressive rural entrepreneurs. Don Gonzalo Muñoz (1609–70) of Ciudad Real acquired some 500 hectares of land by the time of his death, part of which he placed under entail for his descendants. The most valuable items in his inventory were his flocks of sheep and the 160 oxen which drew his ploughs. Much of his farming was done on fields not his own, but leased from the nobility, and his herds depended on access to common pasture. Made a knight of Alcántara in 1635, he kept a fine house and a number of slaves; but he hardly ever went to court, busying himself instead with farming for markets in Seville and elsewhere.[41]

Such entrepreneurs were clearly not capable of breaking the mould of the Spanish rural economy, which remained rather self-sufficient and geared fundamentally to the exploitation of the elaborate structure of feudal, ecclesiastical and royal extraction of revenue. Thus the Alonsos of Muro were active in the 1690s as tithe-farmers in their area – that is to say, paying a lump sum to the bishop and chapter of Valencia for the right to collect the tenth of the peasant harvests, which they would then transport to market. The Almunias rose during the seventeenth century as money-lenders and tax-farmers for the duke of Gandia. The Valencian jurist Tomás Cerdán de Tallada denounced in 1604 what he took to be a scandalous commercialisation of the whole feudal regime: the exploitation for profit of the tithe, the coming of middlemen between the seigneur and his vassals, whom he was obliged to succour and protect. 'For, in truth, with the money which they receive in a lump sum from the tax-farmers, [the feudal lords] give themselves over to gambling and other vices . . . and waste their estate, so that they no longer live in their villages.'[42]

Francisco Benlloch pointed out in his treatise on feudal government of 1756 that revenue farmers from outside the village were generally resented as 'tumours', which drained the substance of the community. Acknowledging that a great lord, like his master, the duke of Gandia, could not personally administer local rents, he suggested that these could be handed over to the community itself in return for a fixed sum in cash. And, indeed, there seems often to have been a movement in this direction over the early modern period in Castile.[43] The process was, no doubt, uneven, depending a lot on the ability of a rich knot of local inhabitants to guarantee, come what may in the way of bad harvests, a regular money payment in a cash-poor society. It may have assumed more informal aspects of patronage, in keeping with the character of the age. Thus in 1699 the duke of Gandia was writing from court to his steward that he would need to borrow against the latter's name and would allow him to recoup himself out of the following year's revenue. The whole correspondence reveals a network of gifts and loans between the duke and leading personalities in Gandia, which modified the simple relationship of tenant and feudal lord. It was, ultimately, through control of the levers of power and jurisdiction that rural fortunes were amassed in this period, and not just on feudal estates. The Cortes of 1576–8 complained that 'the wealthiest inhabitants of the villages and towns (*pueblos*), who have lawsuits with the local council and owe it money', were buying up municipal office in order to escape tax assessments and to grab a bigger share of the common lands. 'It could be truly and perhaps better said of them that they purchase a kind of lordship over their neighbours.'[44] But what were the structures of command in these peasant communities?

Throughout Spain there was a long tradition of peasant self-government. Benlloch described in 1756 the town hall of Llombai (209 families), with its ground floor a storehouse for the grain needed for sowing or alms to the poor, its upstairs a council chamber where the records were carefully locked away in two cupboards. Though Benlloch, as the governor appointed by the duke of Gandia, presided over meetings, he had no key to the archive, had to fight to get the duke's coat of arms erected over the front door, and was always ill at ease sitting around a table with rustics who 'even keep their caps on . . . and turn up in their underclothes (*paños menores*)'.[45] The most important of these peasant officers was the *justicia*, or the *alcalde*, as he was more commonly known in Castile. These were selected in a variety of ways by the community, with a list of three names generally being drawn up from which the feudal lord would select one. 'You cannot be aware, Sir, what a rural alcalde is in his own village,' the peasant hero Pedro Crespo tells the army commander in Calderón's great drama *The Mayor of Zalamea* (around 1640), as he has one of his officers executed for rape.

These justices were supposed to act in consultation with trained lawyers, usually the local notary. More delicate was their relationship with the feudal lord's own judge, the *alcalde mayor*. Castillo de Bobadilla tended to stress the limitation of the latter's power. Disputes over pasture or over crimes committed in the open countryside would normally anyway come before the special tribunals of the Mesta and the Hermandad (which we shall examine below in Chapter 8). Otherwise, the peasant alcaldes had equal jurisdiction with their superiors when it came to trying civil or criminal cases. If they heard the case first, then an appeal would lie either to the alcalde mayor or to the royal court, despite the attempt of seigneurs to reserve appeals to their own judges. Practice varied a good deal from this norm. In the Crown of Aragon it was probably always more difficult than in Castile to appeal outside the seigneurial estate. In Valldigna, the justice was often simply one of the monks who held dominion there, and he regulated the multiple petty conflicts of rural life, over trespass and debts and vagrancy. His register is a series of short entries, recording the complaint and the statement of witnesses and the decision. The atmosphere conjured up is that of the peasant court, the 'Tribunal of the Waters', which still meets outside the cathedral of Valencia on a Thursday morning, and from which appeals are unthinkable. Certainly it was one of the aims of local communities to have their own elected justices decide matters in first instance. Still in 1756 the governor of Llombai noted how imprecise were the frontiers between his own court – supposedly in charge of all serious crimes and civil cases on appeal – and that of the peasant magistrates. Let the governor beware 'of falling out with the village administration, but keep on good terms, even if it means nearly letting them do what they like'.[46]

The administration of justice was only one part of a wider organisation of community life. The 300 families of Montiel in New Castile had in 1575, in addition to their two justices, six aldermen (*regidores*), a market inspector, two constables and a clerk of the council. Elsewhere in these *Relaciones*, we meet references to attorneys, militia captains, treasurers or tax collectors. Since these offices were often annually elected, they involved quite a heavy burden at times on small communities. The backbone of the community was the *regidores*, who were chosen much like the justices. In Medina de Ríoseco it was the outgoing aldermen who drew up a list of names, from which the feudal lord, the Admiral of Castile, selected half as their successors for the year ahead. When the Admiral protested in 1538 that it was the same group of forty names which were being rotated and tried to insert his own nominees, a popular outcry forced him to back down.[47] Sale of office by the Crown shortly afterwards began to reinforce this local oligarchy. In the kingdom of Granada during the seventeenth and eighteenth centuries a knot of families tended to dominate the posts of village *regidor*, often going on to get one of their kinsmen, educated in law, appointed *alcalde mayor* through their influence with the seigneur, to whom they rendered services as tax farmers and the like. Thus the Parada and Guzmán clans, whose members were rich farmers and petty gentlemen (*hidalgos*), controlled the village of Gabia la Grande in the later eighteenth century through a decree giving half the posts to the few *hidalgo* families in town, as well as by slipping in their own protégés to other positions. To complete their domination of the area, one of their number was appointed as *alcalde mayor* of the neighbouring village of Alhendín by its feudal lord.[48]

In earlier times there had been 'open assemblies' of the inhabitants which could have acted as a check on this process. They seem to have been most active in the Crown of Aragon, where the heads of households would be called together once or twice a year, often in the town square, to approve any important business. The Moriscos of Valldigna held two sessions in 1607–8, summoning a notary to keep a record of the proceedings. The seigneurs were sometimes nervous of such large gatherings, since it was these which would decide whether to appoint attorneys to carry some complaint before the king's court. The count of Cocentaina began to insist in the later sixteenth century that the Moriscos of his village of Muro seek his prior authorisation before assembling and have some member of the count's household present who could understand Arabic.[49] After the expulsion of the Moriscos, he further required of the new settlers that they submit to him in advance a list of the topics they wanted to discuss and vote on them by an open show of hands. The dukes of Lerma graciously agreed that their vassals of Dénia could discuss complaints against the seigneur without the governor being present, who would in any case leave before votes were taken (1563).

That we know as much as we do about life in these communities is due to the records kept by the local councils. The account books of the Morisco councillors of Valldigna in 1607–8 show the immense task of raising money to satisfy the Crown as well as the seigneur – the payments of the cloth and salt taxes, the 'benevolence' exacted that year by Philip III, the wages of the coastal militia, the gifts or bribes to soldiers in transit 'so that they would not stop in the village', all of this absorbed most disposable funds. But these village magistrates also found money to hire a horse for a woman to visit her husband gaoled by the Inquisition in Valencia, for payments to the midwife, for repairs to the well and even to the council chamber . . . In Christian communities, of course, more was spent on the church. With just under 200 households, the count of Real's village of Catarroja seems to have lived out its own life in the seventeenth century under the guidance of its elected councillors. The council had a budget of about 1,000 Valencian pounds a year, which it spent on a schoolteacher, blacksmith and doctor, on the upkeep of the drainage canals in this marshy area and the decoration of the church, on gifts of mutton to the poor at Christmas and Easter and on the burial of paupers . . . Taxation also, as in Valldigna, ate heavily into income.[50]

One of the features of the early modern period seems to be, in fact, the slippage of responsibility for raising taxes and troops from the feudal lords to the peasant communities themselves. In 1636 the assembly of Muro met in the village church, shortly after its mistress, the countess of Cocentaina, had pleaded poverty and inability to raise any troops for the Crown. Now the peasants themselves set down solemnly in writing their own economic hardship, while offering Philip IV whatever other communities throughout the kingdom of Valencia were prepared to give. In the Andalusian village of Luque the order came from the Crown in 1659 to find 13 soldiers or pay a commutation of 50 ducats per man. The town council decided to raise the levy, seizing 'the persons who are least necessary to this town' in their homes in a series of dawn raids. Again in 1695 the council was faced with an order from Madrid to send 16 soldiers to the front – one for every 100 families. No volunteers were forthcoming, whereupon the magistrates resolved to designate sixteen of the 'less useful', while recognising that 'all the citizens are people who attend to their work and obligations, and there is no vagrant, or scandalous or seditious person among them'. The unfortunate sixteen were rounded up and locked into the butcher's shop as the strongest place in town, since the gaol was in ruins.[51] What is surprising about all this is the direct dealing between the rural magistrates and the Crown, while the feudal lord, the count of Luque, only intervenes peripherally – as in 1683 when he invoked an old privilege which said that while he was in residence, no troops could be quartered in town. With the reform of the tax system in the Crown of Aragon under the Bourbons, the nobles became liable to assessments. In 1736 the count of Carlet objected to the town of Carlet assessing his quota, 'for he would become their vassal rather than their lord'.[52]

The feudal ideal was one of paternalism. A lord was not there just to collect rents from tenants, commented the duke of Sessa in 1620, as he asked the famous

Jesuit philosopher Mariana for advice on how to run his estates. Rent collectors were all that was required 'in the land between Algiers and Constantinople, but the laws of a Christian lord aim to win greater respect among his vassals'.[53] The duke of Gandia's instructions for the newly appointed bailiff of Albalat (1594) bade him write to the duke in person about any vassal who was 'living with a concubine', or about any other 'sin' which came to his notice. Such close control was becoming less easy as seigneurs began to live away from their villages, in the district capital or at court. The leading Valencian jurist Tomás Cerdán de Tallada complained in 1604 of a cooling of relations between lord and vassal as tax-farmers came between them: 'the peasants, seeing the absence of their master, lose respect for his ministers, and get up to all kinds of impudence and nonsense, with a falling away from good customs'. His Castilian contemporary, Castillo de Bobadilla, wrote in 1597 of the change coming over rural society. In the old days seigneurs had been more respected: 'there were not so many of them as nowadays, when you meet them at every turn, merchants and others, who lack the qualities of a proper lord, who can command the respect of his vassals'. Too many were absentees, leaving administration to some servant, who is out to feather his own nest and accepts bribes. But he praised the count of Oropesa, who did live on his estates, and kept a committee of theologians and lawyers before whom the peasants could plead damages inflicted by the hunt or by the activities of the count's officials.[54]

It became part of the conventional wisdom in political circles at this time that a revival of the feudal system would be a good thing, in order to stem the depopulation of the Spanish countryside. The movement coincided with the selling off of many fiefs by a bankrupt monarchy, but the ideology was based on quite other considerations. As the Cortes of 1615 put it: 'With the absence of their lords, vassals lose gifts of alms, subsidies and help in time of need, and have to put up with a thousand and one grievances from the *alcalde mayor*, since their master is not there to defend and restore them.'[55] It is around this time, in fact, that we get the great idealisation of the rural world in various cultural manifestations. Lope de Vega places on the Madrid stage the figure of the heroic peasant standing up for his rights against a tyrannous lord. Since Lope was the protégé of the duke of Sessa and was writing for an urban and courtly audience, we cannot expect his plays simply to justify rural insurrection, as they seem to do. Rather, they seem to develop out of a long period of gestation during the previous century, in which men of letters had cultivated the serenity and sincerity of rural life as contrasted with the bustle and artificiality of the city, and had begun to collect already popular sayings and the simple peasant songs – *villancicos* – which began to be sung at Christmas especially. Though the older tradition of the peasant as a figure of fun survived – and rivals the bucolic idyll in Cervantes's *Don Quixote* (1605–14), for example – nevertheless, the economic decline of Spain at this time gave new urgency to the task of restoring the dignity of the *labrador*, the substantial peasant farmer.[56] An idealised feudal system, of patronage and justice, was one part of the dream of statesmen; but did it work?

There was disquiet in the Cortes that seigneurs often reduced the *alcabalas* on their estates in order to attract trade, and the great fairs of Tendilla might serve as an example of this. The duke of Lerma, as favourite of Philip III, acquired the right to collect the customs duties in his seaport of Dénia. By 1643, thanks to the 'ample courtesy' which the dukes extended to merchants, Dénia was attracting about an eighth of the value of cargoes entering the kingdom of Valencia. Six years later, in response to complaints from the farmers of the royal customs duty, the Crown closed this loophole by taking back the alienated revenues. The people of Dénia benefited in other ways, though, from the largesse of their masters: the poor received gifts of money at Christmas and cheap grain in time of need, and the middle classes could profit by the six bursaries endowed by the great duke of Lerma for girls to enter his new Augustinian convent. Lerma's successor as royal favourite, Olivares, displayed in his will a greater concern for his own vassals than for the people of Spain. His grandfather had already set up an endowment to provide bread for the poor, furnish a dowry for the daughters of his poorer vassals, and help the latter with the payment of their taxes to the king. Now in 1642 the count-duke devoted the immense sum of 50,000 ducats 'to public causes and the increase of my vassals in the first place, and then to that of the other vassals of the king, our lord'.[57]

On the other hand, the difficult economic circumstances of the late sixteenth and seventeenth centuries led many seigneurs to grab money where they could. The general assembly of the village of Muro, meeting in the parish church in 1657, complained, in the measured tones so typical of the bureaucratised world of the Spanish peasantry, that their rents were unpayable and arrears were building up, and the inhabitants 'had barely enough to eat and were in a desperate plight, lacking strength to work'. Their absentee master, the count of Cocentaina, had promised reduction of rents but had done nothing about it.[58] Though many of the seigneurs in Old Castile seem to have commuted the *alcabalas* for a lump sum, as on the royal domain, leaving it up to their vassals to raise the money in their own way, the chronicler Cabrera de Córdova condemned the new lords who were purchasing these revenues off the Crown: 'they were not happy with the old commutation agreed with the treasury, but would increase it by a third or a half, or would revert to collecting it directly themselves at the full rate of ten per cent'.[59]

Castillo de Bobadilla gave his opinion in 1597 that those living on seigneurial estates ultimately lost out. Peasants on the royal domain 'are better protected from warfare, less vexed, and enjoy greater peace and justice'. His views perhaps reflect an older world of private armies and robber barons. But the seventeenth century was to show that the main burden on the citizen would come from the state, against which seigneurial jurisdictions might provide some protection. At least this was the opinion of the deputy of Salamanca to the Cortes of 1625, who pointed out that feudal lords got the tax quotas reduced for their peasants, and shifted the burden of billeting on to the royal towns. And in 1640, in the kingdom of Valencia, the royal town of Callosa was complaining that her inhabitants were leaving for the shelter of the neighbouring seigneurial estates, which were better protected against levies of troops and taxes.[60] The sheer problem of royal fiscalism in its various guises is suggested by the history of peasant revolts in seventeenth-century Catalonia. The revolution of 1640 began as a protest against billeting and threatened to spread into an attack on the nobility, until they managed to divert popular anger against the court. The insurrection of the *Barretines* in 1688 was initially a peasant protest against the burden of troop billets in a period of agricultural hardship, but developed into a challenge to the right of the seigneurs to collect the ecclesiastical tithe for themselves, and to control the baking of bread and the supply of meat.[61]

Studies of the widespread revolts in the French countryside in the seventeenth century have raised the question of how far the feudal lords were indeed able to or disposed to shield their vassals against royal tax demands, since they themselves were often the beneficiaries of the monarchical system. The duke of Gandia, who had received generous treatment from the Crown in the matter of his debts, remarked in 1636 that, though he was too poor to raise troops himself, he had facilitated the activity of recruiting officers on his estates, 'for they could not have raised a man, had I not lent my authority'. And in Castile around the same time, the duke of Béjar, while interceding with the Crown on behalf of his vassals in the matter of tax demands, levies and billets, was forced to admit that it was dangerous to resist too much.[62] We shall explore this topic later in relation to the aristocracy (see below, Chapter 7). Here one may simply note that, given that the Crown was now dealing directly with the peasant communities themselves, through their elected magistrates rather than through the feudal lords, the exemption from state fiscalism looked increasingly problematic. The great peasant revolt of 1693 in Valencia, the Second *Germanía*, revealed one dangerous implication of this process: that the rural communities and the Crown might reach an agreement to provide more taxes, at the expense of the seigneurs. The rebel leader, Francesc Garcia, was alleged to have offered the king, through two Franciscan intermediaries at court, a regiment of volunteers, 'fitted out and paid', for the war then raging against Louis XIV on the Pyrenean frontier.[63]

The question of resistance to the seigneurs was bound up with the whole attitude of the monarchy and its ministers to the feudal hierarchy. For a royal judge like Castillo de Bobadilla disorder in the countryside was of immediate concern to the government, which would intervene to adjudicate disputes. 'Thus I have advised some lords on occasion that, regarding acts of insolence or offences committed against them by their vassals . . . they might draw up heads of indictment and even gaol . . . those at fault, but for redress they should have recourse to the king.' And a few years later Venetian ambassador Soranzo commented that even the grandees commanded little respect from their vassals, 'for they can be summoned to court by any one of these who feels himself aggrieved, and they are obliged to obey the law like the meanest commoner'.[64] No doubt the reality was more complex than the theory, especially in the more remote parts of Spain, which were hard to police. The community of Ariza in Aragon had long been clamouring for its restoration to the royal domain, before matters came to a head in 1556 with the introduction of a new impost by its seigneur, Don Juan de Palafox. Faced with the refusal of the peasants to pay, Palafox brought in a gang of men armed with arquebuses and crossbows, who were quartered on the population and seized the crops. Recourse to the courts got nowhere, and the assassination of Palafox by his vassals in 1561 only entailed further retribution by his enraged kinsmen. Eventually at the Cortes of 1585 Philip II gave way to the noble call for a full acknowledgement of seigneurial authority in Ariza.[65]

The fairly frequent disturbances in the Aragonese – and Valencian – fiefs at this time bring to light several general points. In the first place, there needed to be some perceived sense of injustice – often the setting aside of old charters, or the introduction of new levies – for the peasants to act. Outside encouragement seems to explain one of the most serious revolts: that of Ribagorza against the dukes of Villahermosa between 1578 and 1589. The Crown had been interested in reco-vering this fief, strategically sited in the high Pyrenees along the border with France, as early as 1554. In 1578 the deputies who assembled every January in Benabarre from the various villages on the estate to discuss matters of general concern, withdrew their allegiance to the duke. Their leader, Juan de Ager, claimed to be acting in the king's name, as he 'seized and killed those whom he judged deserving of death', and he would not respect the warrant of either the courts in Zaragoza or of the king himself, apparently on the pretext familiar to rural insurgents that he knew the royal will better than did the authorities. Meanwhile, in the highest part of this mountain territory, the town of Benasque decided to oppose Ager. 'As far as I can tell,' the chronicler Argensola tells us, they did so 'not because they loved the duke, though they did not hate him either, but for their own advantage, since they thought that they could have their own way better under the duke than under the king.' The leaders of Benasque were the Bardaxí, a gentry family which had small lordships of their own in the area and kept bandit gangs in their pay, 'men who turn their hand to whatever is asked of them, without thinking of the danger to their own life or conscience'.[66] Unwisely, the duke of Villahermosa now used these bandits to storm Benabarre, kill Ager and reimpose his authority (1587), whereupon the other side gathered its own outlaws, and an authentic civil war began to rage in and around the disputed county of Ribagorza. The events merged with the general resistance of the Aragonese nobility to Philip II over their laws and privileges in 1590, and was settled when the king's army invaded Aragon the following year and arrested Villahermosa (on rather flimsy grounds), reincorporating Ribagorza into the royal domain.

The Aragonese troubles suggest the influence of factions within the rural community, and the link between these and the outside world, in the development of relationships of confrontation between vassals and seigneur. The question of social divisions may also have to be taken into account. Resolving in 1645 to reopen its lawsuit for restoration to the royal domain, the town of Segorbe accused its duke of having obtained the agreement of 1619 to drop litigation (above, p. 92) by fraud. He had overawed the assembly of inhabitants, 'who are common folk, by gifts, promises, blandishments and threats'. Just what was at stake in any of these encounters has to be the object of specialised research. A difference would have to be drawn between a wealthy, middle-class town like Segorbe and a hill village like Muro, though both were involved in protests against their seigneurs. The economic circumstances of the seventeenth century no doubt led to a general resentment of excessive rents. Franciscan friars and many of the parish priests were to be found in Valencia preaching that these were too high, especially when added to the king's increasing demands for taxes and soldiers. One report spoke of their being motivated by 'compassion', but went on to attack their 'lack of understanding, and a proper religious outlook'.[67] The priests were undoubtedly a force behind the peasant uprising of 1693, though they did not furnish the leaders. If the rebels unfurled banners of Our Lady and Saint Vincent Ferrer, they also brandished their charters. The actual fighting was done by poorer peasants, but behind them one can detect the shadowy figures of the village 'magnates', as the duke of Gandia was to call them – men like the Alonso family of Muro, whom we have met before, who were active in mediating between the insurgents and the Crown. The actual uprising of July 1693 was sparked off by the arrest of four rent-strikers by the duke of Gandia. It was a spontaneous movement of popular anger in the hot harvest months, when rents fell due, and it rather quickly evaporated in the face of the royal militia. But it can only be understood as part of a wider negotiation under way on the estates of the duke of Gandia and others for the commutation of feudal rents by a fixed sum – a sum which would be guaranteed by the wealthier members of the community.[68]

The debate remained to envenom relations on the Gandia estates during the eighteenth century. Though the seigneurs were often now absentees, it is important not to overestimate the relay of power to an elite of peasant farmers. The count of Aranda retired to his fief of Epila near Zaragoza to live out the last three years of his life (1795–8), after a busy career in government. There, in the Aragonese countryside, he took up the reins of local administration again as the undisputed master. Shortly before, Jovellanos had observed that the gentry of Asturias 'live for the most part on their lands and deal at all hours of the day with their peasants'. On New Year's Day they came with their gifts of chickens and fruit to the big house, where a big meal awaited them, presided over by the master and his wife.[69] Antonio Ponz found lots of improving landlords as he travelled round Spain in the 1780s – the marquis of Santa Cruz and his woollen factory in La Mancha, the count of Sástago with his irrigation canals and olive plantations in Aragon. Clearly, some of the feudal lords were beginning to envisage a new role for themselves at this time as *Amigos del País* – 'Friends of their Country', to quote the title of the local improvement clubs of which many were members.

But it is also true that a long tradition of peasant self-government and the growth of a rural middle class continued to pose a challenge to their authority in certain circumstances. The duke of Infantado was warned by his steward in 1796 to keep a particularly vigilant eye on the *hacendados*, the wealthy vassals, 'given the enormous influence they have in the running of the villages, since they are usually the leaders when it comes to resisting the payment of dues to Your Excellency, to which end they stir up unjust lawsuits'. On the other hand, the villages of the duke of Arcos were complaining in 1814 that their wealthier inhabitants were often on the side of the seigneur, 'the only way they can have of turning themselves into *señores* and despots, though on a smaller scale'.[70]

When one looks at the record of usurpation of common land and the farming out of seigneurial mills and the like, one can see their point. As population increased in the eighteenth century, a certain land hunger began to sour relations within the rural communities. The flashpoint was often the common lands, which the Crown ordered in 1766 to be subdivided into small plots and leased cheaply, preferably to labourers and poorer peasants. When it reversed this policy in 1770 and decided that substantial farmers with plough-teams would make a better job of cultivation, it aroused much controversy. It had already, folllowing bread riots of 1766, decreed that the poorer members of a community were to be represented in its government by the election of *diputados* and *personeros del común*. In the Andalusian agro-town of Osuna, the elections were usually conducted on a very low turn-out of 5 per cent or less. The wage-labourers took their case for access to common land through other channels – through a religious confraternity and through a self-taught leader from their own ranks, Antonio Calderón. In a confused struggle, the duke of Osuna seemed to back Calderón against the local oligarchy in 1767–8.[71]

The attitude of small-town elites towards their feudal lord depended on a variety of factors. In many cases they benefited from alliance with him, through control of rents, mills and offices. But there always existed the risk of conflict over where ultimate authority lay. Don Mateo Cebrián, member of the gentry of Gandia and dean of the collegiate church of that town, clashed with the duchess of Gandia over her intervention in the former Jesuit college. This quarrel led to the dismissal of Mateo's cousin, Francisco, from his post of ducal attorney, entrusted with defending the seigneur's privileges (1786). It turned out to be a bad move on the duchess's part, since, within a few years, the Cebrián clan turned from gamekeepers to poachers and threw their great influence behind a popular movement to have the town reincorporated in the royal domain.[72] On another part of the Gandia estates, meanwhile, the village of Catadau was litigating for its restoration to the Crown's jurisdiction. The protagonists seem again to be some of the wealthier members of the community. Their success, though, depended on leading a wider popular movement. Since Catadau had been riven by social divisions increasingly over the later eighteenth century, as population expanded and the wealthier farmers and traders got the poor into their debt, the question has been asked as to how the unity of the village was maintained during the costly lawsuit against the dukes of Gandia.[73]

No doubt, the pattern of resistance to the seigneurs, or cooperation with them, requires a detailed investigation of the social and economic structure of the individual communities. One can, however, draw a few general conclusions. In principle, despite the occasional collaboration between the wealthier local families and the feudal lord, the feudal system was often deeply unpopular with those who had a claim to status in their own right and who could remember a time – usually before the great alienations of the fifteenth century – when their town had belonged to the Crown. In the eighteenth century the changes which were beginning to affect the economy as a whole – growth of population and trade, breakdown of the old autarky of the countryside – exposed some of the contradictions of the seigneurie. Its justification, as set out by Castillo de Bobadilla in 1597, was as an arm of government, a delegation of responsibility for good order on to a family of honour. Towards the end of the Old Regime it was apparent that this ideal was very far from the practice. In Elx, in the kingdom of Valencia, the marquises were increasingly involved in marketing crops and keeping stricter accounts of their revenues, rather abandoning the old ideal of protection of their vassals – though the police power of their court still served them well when it came to collecting rents. The better-off families of Elx shared the new commitment to production for the market, indulging especially in the sale of olive oil and soda-wort (in which the area was rich), and in speculation with grain. Old controls typical of the Christian commonwealth were now seen as an impediment to economic growth and prosperity. Thus, in 1765 the government proclaimed the end of restrictions on the grain trade. The upheaval which followed in Elx in the spring of 1766 was compounded of many factors: resentment by the poor at the abandonment of the 'moral economy' which took their need for bread as its highest priority, resentment by some of the lower middle classes at the continuing monopolisation of mills, ovens and shops by either the seigneur or a handful of privileged families, and, finally, a resurfacing of the old demand of the better-off that their town should be returned to the royal domain (from which it had been alienated in 1470).[74]

The revolts of 1766, here and elsewhere in Spain, resolved very little. They exposed, rather, some of the fundamental dilemmas in the transition from a feudal to a capitalistic economy if that transition did not include some formal recognition of the new political weight exercised by big farmers at the expense of feudal lords. Indeed, it was probably becoming apparent that the crisis of social relations between rulers and ruled could not be resolved without a major refashioning of the structures of power in the nation as a whole.

6

PATRICIANS AND PAUPERS
The urban commonwealth

The early modern city had an identity which its successors lacked. Marked out by walls and privileges, by charters of liberty and separate citizenship rights, it stood as a bastion of freedom in a still feudal countryside. It may be difficult to draw too clear a contrast of this kind in the case of Spain. In the first place, the criterion of size – that a city should have 10,000 or more inhabitants – may not capture the reality of a land of agro-towns. Equally, many small places maintained traditions of political hegemony. Burgos, though it had fallen from about 13,000 to about 3,500 people between 1592 and 1669, still claimed its ancient headship of Castile, contesting the right of Toledo (also on its way to becoming a musuem town) to take precedence in the Cortes or parliament.[1]

About one in ten Spaniards lived in towns which, at one time or another between 1500 and 1800, reached the 10,000 mark.[2] This was slightly higher than the European average. There were two giants: the political capital, Madrid, which reached its maximum of about 150,000 in the middle of the seventeenth century, and the gateway to the New World, Seville, which also had 150,000 people before the plague of 1649 and the fading of its economic hegemony. Then came a scattering of provincial capitals – Granada, Valencia, Barcelona – with around 40,000–50,000 inhabitants each, before one reached the average city, with its bishop and royal judge (*corregidor*), of 10,000–20,000 people. The city was in part a market, but it provided a wider range of services than that. Liñán Verdugo's guide-book to seventeenth-century Madrid depicts the countryman coming to town with his satchels of legal documents slung across his shoulder, and Lope de Vega's eponymous hero, *Peribáñez*, came up to Toledo to have his community's statue of Saint Roque repainted.

The political role of the urban commune has been emphasised by historians of medieval Europe. The acquisition of charters of self-government in Spain might sometimes be accompanied by violence, as in Santiago de Compostela in 1116–17, when the merchants rose up against their bishop. But more usually the Spanish towns, as heirs to a long Roman and Arabic tradition, were regarded by rulers as integral parts of the hierarchy of power, and received their charters in the twelfth and thirteenth centuries in order to attract settlers and provide a nucleus of regional government.[3] The Catholic Kings, granting self-government to Granada in 1500, spoke of their desire to 'ennoble the said city. . . and that the nobles and gentlemen who come to settle and live there may have offices and dignities . . . and that all the citizens and inhabitants . . . may have franchises and liberties, so that the said city may come to be populous and renowned'.[4] It was not only as allies of the Crown in the task of government that the cities had a crucial role to play, but as exemplars of virtue for their own citizens. It was this aspect of things which the Granadan chronicler Bermúdez de Pedraza stressed in 1608: 'in great and populous cities . . . there are many convents of holy friars and nuns, and virtuous clerics and laymen of godly life, for whose sake God forgives the sins of the rest'. And Escolano shortly afterwards wrote of his native Valencia that she had not only access to a wide range of commodities by sea, but 'her citizens, living near the sea, have a sharpness of wit from the diversity of nations with which they deal every day and the knowledge of a variety of things drawn from them'.[5] On the other hand, there were already voices warning against the artificiality and pressure of urban life. The great Renaissance humanist, Fray Antonio de Guevara, penned an eloquent praise of rural existence in 1539: 'in the village there are no windows overlooking your house, there are no people jostling you, there are no horses running you down . . . '. And the figure of the city swindler which he evoked was to be taken up and developed by seventeenth-century writers. The government itself, as part of its measures for arresting the decline of Spain, tried to halt immigration to the really big cities – Madrid, Seville, Granada – employing the language of surgery about the accumulation of 'evil humours' and the need for a 'copious blood-letting'.[6]

But this early concern with economic realities – unemployment, pauperism, disease – could not mask the older pride in the city as a manifestation of virtue. The Spanish cities were sacred spaces, with their great cathedrals and convents, and their protecting shrines. Madrid had her three patrons: Our Lady of Almudena (an image found at the reconquest of the city from the Moor), Our Lady of Atocha (an image carved by Saint Luke, hidden as the Saracens overwhelmed Madrid, then miraculously rediscovered at the Reconquest), and Saint Isidore, a virtuous peasant whose spirit appeared to the king at the decisive battle of Las Navas de Tolosa (1212) which opened the way to the reconquest of Andalusia. Isidore was canonised in 1622 as part of the government campaign to restore the dignity of agriculture, while Our Lady of Atocha was endowed with a sumptuous shrine by Philip II in 1588, being paraded through the streets of Madrid in time of plague or war. The crusading memory seems to have played a decisive role in the sense of identity of many Spanish towns. Thus, Valencia celebrated its birthday every year on 9 October, the day, not on which the city had actually been retaken from the Moors, but on which the mosques had been reconsecrated for Christian worship, and the religious imagery was paramount in the fiestas mounted by the city fathers. No civic guard in the style of Rembrandt graces the town halls of Spain. The one great civic monument in old Granada was the column erected by the aldermen in 1628 to honour the Immaculate Conception, on which were displayed the arms of the city, watched over by Saint Cecil (the town patron), Saint James ('hammer of the Moors') and the Virgin herself. The finest embodiment in art of the great trading city of Seville is perhaps the canvas commissioned in 1615 by the king, commemorating the great procession of men and boys that year in honour of the Immaculate Conception, protector of the urban commonwealth.

Max Weber's suggestion that the urban commune transformed relations between people, cutting across older ties of kinship or feudal dependence, may not be applied wholesale to Spain. Belonging to a town by birth or by formal inscription in a register of citizens certainly conferred privileges – as the aldermen of Valencia (*jurats*) pointed out in 1626, when they tried to stop the king collecting tolls from those who had settled within the walls and opened a shop. Only those born in Valencia were supposed to enjoy such exemptions; but since the 1590s the *jurats* had been neglecting to keep registers of concessions of citizenship, and by 1635, when war broke out with France, the monarchy took control of the issue of residence permits to French nationals. After this, it was either the state or the guilds which determined one's right to work locally.

The walls of a town stood as a material symbol of its identity. At the *humilladeros* – the crosses which marked its frontier – the wary traveller would dismount, kneel and pray before setting off into a still dangerous countryside. Since the great wars of the fourteenth century, when Barcelona and Valencia built the magnificent fortifications which survived down to the nineteenth century, the walls of Spanish towns had generally been allowed to fall into decline. Travellers from the war-torn Europe of the 1500s and 1600s were surprised at how Spain managed to get along with medieval ramparts, and how little was spent on the bastions and counter-scarps of contemporary defence. But the walls were still used as a control on movement in and out, and particularly for the collection of the *sisas* or excise tax, which was the basis of municipal budgets. Faced with bankruptcy in 1647, Valencia put forward proposals to limit the entry of carts to just four main gates, to have all carts and coaches thoroughly inspected, and have men on horseback dismount for examination.

Within the walls a labyrinth of twisted streets greeted the traveller. The narrow, badly paved streets of Seville, commented Antonio Ponz in the 1780s, 'kept the mean, confused character imprinted on them by the boorishness or superstition of the Moors'; while the winding alleys and cul-de-sacs of Toledo reflected 'the fierceness and suspicious temperament' of that people.[7] From the fifteenth century, in Spain as in other parts of Europe, the city became a stage on which was played out the ritual of power needed by Renaissance rulers. Harmony, uniformity, grandeur, these were the messages which urban architecture was meant to convey, while at the same time providing space for great processions and tournaments. In 1502 Toledo sought to lay out a fine square in front of the alcázar or royal fortress, whose surrounding buildings should all be of the same height, while Granada in 1513 laid out its 'Field of the Prince' (*Campo del Príncipe)* 'for fiestas of jousting and bull-fighting'.[8] These efforts were usually only successful, however, where either there was much vacant space (as in Granada), or where fire destroyed buildings

(Valladolid in 1561, Toledo in 1585), and, above all, where the monarchy itself got involved in fomenting the buying up and tearing down of houses. The outstanding examples of the central plaza as a theatre of display – Madrid 1618, Cordoba in the 1680s, Salamanca slightly later – reflect the activity of royal ministers or their delegates, and correspond to the triumph of absolute monarchy in seventeenth-century Spain. The Bourbons took this legacy further, but modifying it according to the dictates of patriotism, dear to the Enlightenment. Ponz urged that the well-ordered city should have 'a competent number of statues and a wealth of inscriptions set up in different places, which should set out how the city was founded, some of its local laws, the glory of its sovereigns and of its more illustrious sons . . . [as] an open book from which all could learn'.[9]

By this time, civil society was also claiming its rights. Many Spanish cities had their *alamedas*, walks lined with poplars or other trees. The famous Paseo del Prado in Madrid was laid out by Charles III (1760–88), landscaping a walk which had been enjoyed by the local citizenry for centuries. It was again in the eighteenth century that Granada laid out its *paseo* towards the River Genil, though there had been a cross there for a long time before, which attracted pilgrims and strollers on Saint Sebastian's Day (20 January). In the seventeenth century it was more likely that Granadans would take their promenade along the banks of the other river, the Darro, below the walls of the Alhambra palace, or head out on a summer's evening 'to take the fresh air and say a prayer' at the monument to the Immaculate Conception, which we mentioned earlier.[10] The secularisation of leisure only began to alter the familiar landmarks of the Spanish city from the eighteenth century onwards.

What gave order to Granada, thought its chronicler Bermúdez de Pedraza (1638), was ultimately the network of markets – the *plazas* or squares, 'the stomach of this commonwealth, from which food is distributed throughout its members'. It was an important task of the *corregidor*, affirmed Castillo de Bobadilla, to regulate these activities – to separate out 'the things which give off an evil odour, from which the air usually grows foul and plague ensues'. So, butchers' shops, tanneries, oil presses, ponds for retting flax, stables, 'even ovens for baking bricks', must all be kept to the edge of town. Even respectable trades, like tailors, shoemakers and blacksmiths, 'who as well as cluttering up the street, foul it with their rags and waste', should not be allowed to set up their stalls at street corners.[11] The petitions of the Cortes of Valencia give a vivid picture of streets encumbered with work benches and awnings (1604), of crowded squares where horses, hauling in carts loaded with grain, could too easily trample on the unwary pedestrian (1585), of carpenters filling the little market-place in front of the convent of Our Lady of Ransom with their planks, forcing the vegetable stalls too close to the entrance to the chapel (1547 and 1604). The meeting of peasant and artisan gave the towns of this period their special character.

Though there was a certain distribution of trades by neighbourhood, the topography of the city was surely marked out first by religious buildings. Antonio Ponz, commenting on the great number of little parish churches, gave his opinion that 'in those turbulent times of conquest and civil strife, each kinship group would found a parish of its own'. Though he gave no evidence for his hypothesis, the 21 parish churches of Toledo, for a population of 11,254 families (1561), were uneven in size and endowment, and seem to respond to social rather than pastoral needs. Adding in convents, it has been calculated that a sixth of the area within the walls of Valencia must have been covered by ecclesiastical buildings.[12] Many of these had ties with particular trades through the chapels where the guilds held their reunions. In Granada guilds and neighbourhoods marked out their space, as the manuscript chronicle (1588–1646) of Henríquez de Jorquera tells us, with images and crosses of alabaster or wood, where groups would gather on a Saturday for prayer. As well as churches, the palaces of the nobility gave a structure to the urban landscape, forming so many nuclei around which clustered the homes of their dependants. Mesonero Romanos described the south-western quarters of Madrid, between the streets of Segovia, Toledo and Atocha, where the dukes of Infantado owned many of the buildings, where their kinsmen occupied different palaces, alongside the offices where the peasants came to pay their rents, the homes of employees and the hospital 'for servants of the estate'. In the disturbances of 1520 in Seville, the parish of San Miguel erected barricades on behalf of the duke of Medina Sidonia, while that of San Marcos did the same for his great rival, the duke of Arcos.[13]

Though older treatises – like that of Fray Luis de León in 1583 – might still look askance at the urban world as less godly than that of the farmer, the trend over the early modern period was to try to fit the craftsman into the divine scheme of things. Work was part of God's plan for the redemption of man, affirmed the jurist Gutiérrez de los Ríos in his important treatise of 1600 (dedicated to, of all people, the indolent duke of Lerma). Though agriculture 'makes the mind good, simple and devout', even trade could be considered as developing the soul, so long as it was conducted 'with moderate gain'. Work sharpened the wits and differentiated men from animals, but above all it uprooted the deadly sin of 'idleness' (*ociosidad*). So, another jurist, López Bravo, believed that 'it does not matter that there is nothing noble in workshops and that the man who is immersed in petty, base affairs has rarely the capacity for lofty and generous thoughts', the artisan should be admitted to honour and even local office (so long as he gave up his business for the time being). 'I believe,' he went on, 'that praise should be given to someone who, from a humble origin, raises himself up by the ladder of thrift to wealth and comfort by means of his honest toil.'[14] It took some time for these ideas to be embodied in law. In 1682 the Crown decreed that those who owned a woollen manufacture, so long as they did not work in it in person, were eligible for nobility; and finally in 1783 it adopted López Bravo's recommendation that artisans were all 'honest and honourable' men and entitled to be elected to municipal office.

This, of course, highlighted two fundamental problems: that honour and social status in old Spain had come from one's position in the local community, and that the community was geared to a higher function than the mere making of money.

The great economic historian Carande, in the title of a famous essay, called Seville 'a fortress and a market', and it is a useful reminder of the twin functions of the Spanish town. Talking of the Andalusian towns of the fifteenth century, the chronicler Argote de Molina noted in 1588 that in them resided 'all the armed might' along the Granadan frontier; and two centuries later the political theorist Madramany compared those of the Crown of Aragon after the Reconquest to 'little republics, responsible for civil and military administration', and their alder-men 'in a sense like those invested with military fiefs'.[15] According to the parish priest and historian of Chelva in 1681, though the king was the supreme governor of the realm of Valencia – 'father, tutor and protector of his subjects' – never-theless, he had delegated most ordinary authority on to the aldermen (*jurats*) of the city of Valencia, among whose onerous responsibilities were those of keeping the population fed. The roll of cloth which the *jurats* wore on their shoulders, topping off their splendid crimson robes, were a reminder, thought Escolano in 1610, of the loaves of bread which it was their sacred function to provide for their charges. Consuls, 'like those of ancient Rome', Escolano called them; and it was the Roman image which Castillo de Bobadilla had in mind when he depicted the responsibilities of Castilian aldermen. Though the 'Roman people' had trans-ferred to the Emperor lawmaking and judicial power, 'nonetheless it kept for itself the administration of many things'; and if, for a royal *corregidor* like Castillo de Bobadilla, the aldermen (*regidores*) were only advisers, yet those of the eighteen cities represented in the Cortes or parliament held the dignity of grandees.[16] When the chief magistrates of the city of Valencia set out for court in October 1598 to convey their condolences to the new king on the death of his father, Philip II, all the knights escorted the procession to the gates, while on their arrival 'all Madrid turned out to see the entry', while all the nobles who had fiefs in Valencia and were then at court came to accompany the aldermen from their lodgings to the palace.

The aldermen were entrusted with a wide variety of responsibilities: the supply of bread, ordinary civil and criminal jurisdiction, the regulation of work and trade, the patronage of education and – through the fiesta – of religion as well. Assisting them was a wide variety of officials – judges, market inspectors, constables, tax-collectors, fiesta commissioners – who were sometimes annually renewable, thus involving many citizens in the government of their local commu-nity. The towns of Castile seem to have divided themselves from an early date into so-called 'lineages' or factions – twelve in Soria, seven in Medina del Campo, two in Segovia, three in Trujillo, two in Avila, eight (finally reducing to two) in Salamanca. These lineages were in the nature of political clubs, which may originally have followed some pattern of kinship or neighbourhood. But in 1601–2 those of Soria agreed that a man might claim entry to his wife's group if he had none of his own; and by 1577 a third faction – the 'neutrals' – had formed in Jerez to dispute office with the two old-established ones of the Villavicencio and Dávila. Still, the pride in belonging to these clubs was very tenacious, and down to the end of the Old Regime those of Salamanca sat on separate benches at meetings of the town council.[17] For it was as electors to municipal office that these groupings acquired their significance.

An important development took place in the middle of the fourteenth century, with the rise of the *regidores*, an inner council of aldermen. In 1345 Alfonso XI nominated sixteen such individuals in Burgos, from among the citizens who served as horse-soldiers, 'for in meetings many individuals turn up who only sow discord and raise obstacles in matters which are of interest to and requisite for our royal service and for the common good of this city and of its vassals'.[18] Thereafter the lineages were often involved, especially in Old Castile, in electing this inner council. In Segovia, for example, the two lineages elected ten *regidores*, with another five being deputies of the ordinary tax-payers and of the peasantry of the district. But there was increasing concern that all such elections pandered to the worst instincts of the citizen and impeded that good government which Renaissance thinkers desired. 'Often in the elections . . . the inhabitants engage in great rivalry and argument, and kill one another,' ran one account of Medina del Campo. In 1621 the *corregidor* of Soria complained to the king about the way in which deputies to the Cortes were chosen by the old lineages, 'for among these is a great number of poor people, of very little intelligence, knowing little beyond work in the fields . . . and selling their votes has become a kind of heirloom for them'.[19]

The civil war of 1474–9 over the succession of Queen Isabel the Catholic led to that monarch's intervention in the municipal government of various towns. Thus, in Cáceres from 1477 the queen ordered that the twelve *regidores* were henceforth to be appointed by the Crown for life, at the same time as she demolished the towers from which the urban lineages had fought their feuds.[20] In the late-conquered territories of Andalusia, it would seem, royal control was established earlier, and the lineages played relatively little part. Thus in Seville from 1351 it was the outgoing magistrates who nominated individuals to the post of *regidor* for life, sending up the names to the king for confirmation. Here the division was not by lineage, rather half the nominees had to be of noble birth.

In the Crown of Aragon municipal government was somewhat differently organised, but one can recognise similar trends towards oligarchy and royal control. In Valencia from the middle of the fourteenth century the king began to nominate his own list of twelve knights and twelve commoners, from which were drawn every year by lot the six *jurats* or aldermen. This system seems to have taken definitive shape during the reign of Alfonso the Magnanimous (1416–58). More generally in these Mediterranean kingdoms at this time fixed lists of citizens were drawn up – usually co-opted by their peers, though the king had variable rights of nominating candidates – from among whom the magistrates for the year ahead were drawn by lot.[21] These so-called *insaculats* – that is, 'those whose names had been placed in a bag' for life – constituted an oligarchy of respectable citizens (rather like the *regidores* of Castilian towns) on whom the Crown could more confidently devolve responsibility for local affairs. The *regidores* themselves were developing into a hereditary elite from the fifteenth century onwards. In Seville and in Jerez from around 1400 various of their number began to petition the

Crown for permission to hand the office on to their children. More surprisingly, the same trend is visible in the lineage-based towns of Old Castile, where the factions were persuaded to agree to individuals, with royal permission, passing on the post of town councillor to their descendants.[22]

Consolidating this process was the sale of these posts by an increasingly bankrupt monarchy from 1543 onwards. The sales were not limited to existing offices; rather, new ones were created. In Valladolid the number of *regidores* doubled to forty-one by the early seventeenth century, in Madrid to thirty-seven over the same period, and in Seville to fifty-two. By 1600 a further concession was granted to individuals in return for cash: that their heirs could succeed automatically to the office without having to renegotiate the privilege with the Crown. These posts began to change hands for enormous sums, generally reaching a peak of around 4,000 ducats by the early seventeenth century (as in the case of Valladolid), though as much as 8,500 ducats – a year's income for one of the lower titled nobility – in the metropolis of Seville.[23] This new life-tenured elite was envisaged as a partner for the monarchy in the maintenance of a hierarchical, ordered society. In Valencia the Crown sold off its rights of selecting the candidates for the annual lottery for positions of *jurat*, by establishing a fixed list of sixty citizens appointed for life, who would share the sweets of power. There was a big debate over the wisdom of this move in 1633. The viceroy protested that it would weaken his authority and increase the irresponsibility of the ruling families, but the Council of Aragon seems to have felt that the king's business could be more satisfactorily conducted through dealing with an oligarchy which owed its very existence to royal favour.[24]

The issue had surfaced shortly before in another Valencian town, Castelló de la Plana, where in 1626 the guilds demanded the right to participate in the annual lottery for aldermen. Despite some support, the majority of the Council of Aragon opposed the petition: 'the towns which placed most difficulty in the way of Your Majesty's service have been those where the ordinary people have a role in government, because, having less experience and talent in public affairs, they do not look to the general good but only to getting out of the obligation of paying taxes'.[25] Castillo de Bobadilla, meanwhile, had assigned only a limited role to the popular voice in Castilian towns. It was true that the 'general will and authority' lay with the population as a whole, but it had effectively delegated responsibility on to the aldermen. On the other hand, it was sensible to consult 'persons of zeal, reflection and experience' in matters of importance, 'for the common people take great satisfaction in seeing that a proper effort is being made to reach a satisfactory decision'.[26]

There was, in fact, quite a lively tradition of popular representation in the Crown of Aragon, in harmony with their stronger guild structures. In Barcelona, for example, the Council of One Hundred included 48 patricians, 32 merchants and 64 artisans. Its counterpart in Valencia, the General Council, was a large body of over 140 individuals, with representatives from the parishes (designated by the aldermen) and from the guilds (elected jointly by the aldermen and a committee of guildsmen). In practice, artisans dominated the body, some of them being clearly men of influence who were returned one year for a guild, another for a parish, and so on. It is perhaps misleading to label such individuals as 'representatives of the people'; many of them must have been like the great city politician of Philip IV's reign, Joan Lluch Ivars, described as a 'silk weaver' at the baptism of his first son in 1599, then as a merchant in 1602, then as a 'citizen' in 1604. This cornering of popular office by powerful men took place in Castile even more blatantly. There was no popular assembly as such in Castilian cities, but the parishes were allowed to elect *jurados*, who would assist the aldermen with their 'voice' or opinion, and in a few places with their vote as well. At the election of 1558 in the parish of San Juan in Murcia, four candidates presented themselves. Ginés Juan Jiménez emphasised first his Old Christian ancestry, then his long residence in the parish, his wealth and his maintenance of a horse: 'I am an honourable person, a good Christian, a man of conscience . . .'[27] But the election of 1558 was the first for some time, provoked by the death of the incumbent. As in all small-scale societies, it would have been regarded as something of an affront to challenge an existing office-holder, and *jurados* were not only allowed to continue until their death but increasingly, with royal permission, to designate their successors. The inevitable outcome was that the office came to be bought and sold, fetching 2,500 ducats in Seville, for example, by the early seventeenth century.

The increasing concern of the early modern period was with creating a stable social hierarchy, which meant that government must be reserved to men of good family. The great fear was that sales of office would open the door to 'new men'. The Council of Finance warned in 1600 of the danger of former merchants rising in this way, 'seeking to increase their business and wealth with the power they get from office, to the harm of the poor'. And Castillo de Bobadilla shortly before asked why men spent so much money on acquiring a post of *regidor*: 'It is easy to find the answer that they do so in order to . . . keep the municipal suppliers as their little Indians . . . to usurp the common lands and the public granary. . . and to get the first seats at public functions.'[28] How wise of the city of Valencia, thought Escolano in 1610, to keep merchants and artisans out of magisterial office for this reason.

Reconquest Valencia had, in fact, allowed such men to be appointed, but by the sixteenth century they were required to abandon their business first and become *ciutadans,* that is 'honoured citizens', able to live off their rents. Laws of 1605, 1624 and 1626 barred from municipal office those who had ever worked with their hands and the children of such. In Barcelona, though merchants and artisans were allowed to contribute one alderman (*conseller*) each, the remaining three were chosen from knights and honoured citizens. This group was partly co-opted by existing members, partly designated by the king and open to university graduates in law and medicine.[29]

There was no exact equivalent to the honoured citizens in the towns of Castile, but 'good families' there certainly were. The chronicler of Seville, Ortiz de Zúñiga, referred in 1677 to that class of people below the nobility, 'half way between it and the plebeians'. These *ciudadanos* – guild masters, merchants and 'those who live off their rents in a modest way' – were the backbone of the commonwealth through their property and their interest in political stability.[30] We are not too far here from the great woollen masters of Segovia, praised by its chronicler, Colmenares, in 1637 as 'real fathers of families' to the numerous, turbulent weavers in their employment. Nevertheless, Segovia was to introduce a law in 1648 'that no woollen manufacturer, merchant or trader, notary or attorney, nor the children of such' could become a *regidor*.[31] Madrid required that its aldermen be of noble ancestry by a law of 1603, and similar requirements were introduced in other cities – Cordoba, for example, in 1568, or in Granada in 1739. The royal privilege for Granada spoke of the 'great satisfaction' felt by towns governed by nobles, who were above the petty self-interest of trade, 'to which has to be added that noble *regidores* are always anxious to serve and to attend to the royal business'.

These laws did not stop social mobility; rather they imposed an aristocratic culture on towns, to which the upwardly mobile had to adapt. The theologian and economist, Tomás de Mercado, noted in 1571 how the merchants of Seville had acquired wealth and honour with the great expansion of commerce. The nobles of Seville 'have stooped . . . to marry into trade, and the merchants, with an appetite for nobility, have striven to rise up, founding substantial entailed estates'. By the later seventeenth century a substantial number of the aldermen of Seville had risen to become titled nobles, with fiefs which they had purchased in the previous generation covering the surrounding countryside.[32] The movement of the nobility from the countryside to residence in the cities during the early modern period has been well documented for the Crown of Aragon. By 1639, for example, a quarter of the Catalan aristocracy was living in Barcelona, and in 1621 the upper nobility – those entitled to use the title *don* before their names – were admitted to municipal office alongside the knights. The same concession was made to their brethren in Valencia in 1652. Since these *dons* were often feudal lords and occasionally counts or marquises, there was some debate about whether their interests were compatible with those of a city state.

'Since it is a particular mark of distinction for cities to have titled and powerful families who have citizenship there,' commented Ortiz de Zúñiga in his chronicle of 1677, he set down those who had cast their mantle over his native Seville. The huge palace of the duke of Medina Sidonia, stretching across the two parishes of San Vicente and San Miguel, 'caused the lord king Philip II to remark when he saw it that it looked like the home of the local feudal lord'. And he recalled the benevolence of the family of the future dukes of Alcalá to the city in the hunger year of 1506: nearly two centuries later 'the memory lives on in a plaque which public gratitude erected in the public granary'.[33] Undoubtedly there was a certain ambiguity in the relationship with such powerful citizens. The city of Valencia wrote congratulating the duke of Gandia in October 1624 on the beatification of his great-grandfather, Francis Borgia; but in February 1624 they had been writing to the king complaining of the damage done to trade by the failure of the local feudal lords to pay their debts after the expulsion of the Moriscos. This, of course, was the problem: that the hegemony of the patricians could only be assured if the interests of the common people were also taken into account.

In his great novel *Arroz y Tartana* Blasco Ibáñez portrayed the hill peasants of nineteenth-century Aragon, huddled round their fires on a winter night and dreaming of the fortunes to be made at the foot of the mountains, in the great city of Valencia, where freshly minted coins 'rolled along the streets'. The late sixteenth-century chronicler Morgado compared the restless ebb and flow of migration through his native Seville to the waves of the sea. Writing of the outburst of popular violence in 1520 in his native Segovia, Colmenares called the perpetrators 'rootless and restless men, drawn in by the ease of finding work in the manufacture of wool'. Studies of the parish registers of Spanish towns are making us aware of how important this mobility was, with up to a half of those marrying in some cases having been born elsewhere.

'When the farmers of nearby villages and even those farther away can no longer live honourably among their neighbours because of poverty, they come to Toledo, to one of these small cellars [*sotanillos*] and live in secret want': so ran the report for the government in 1575–80, when perhaps 1,240 out of a population of 11,000 households were living in this kind of way.[34] Some 2,454 new houses were built in Seville between 1561 and 1588, an addition of about a fifth to the existing stock, to cater to the influx of immigrants into this expanding port. Whole blocks were run up by speculators, like Martin López de Aguilar, leading to complaints by the deputies to the Cortes of 1594 about the poor quality of the building.[35] Seville was seen, along with Madrid and Granada (where the chancery court for southern Spain held its sessions), as presenting particular problems with regard to accommodation because of the sheer size of the transient population. But the comment of one deputy to the Cortes of 1623 that, outside these three cities, most people owned rather than rented their houses, seems optimistic. Studies of Santiago de Compostela (1588) and of Barcelona (1716) give figures of a fifth and a third of the inhabitants respectively owning their own dwellings. In Santiago house rents rose sixfold over the sixteenth century, outstripping the general index of prices and suggesting the growing misery of some.[36] Protesting at the impossibility of monitoring the numbers of the poor, the authorities of a much-shrunken Seville commented in 1766 that they rented rooms by the month from a *casero*, a principal tenant of a building, but then 'very quickly the need to find a livelihood elsewhere or their inability to pay for the room, forces them to leave it'. Up to three-quarters of the inhabitants of the poorer parishes might move out in this way, 'with their few bits of furniture', between one Easter communion and the next, 'sometimes not letting on where they are going', so that the priests had no idea of their subsequent whereabouts.[37]

Towns in Spain at this time are perhaps better seen as refuges for the poor, driven out of their own lands, than as sources of employment. The great authority on the poor, Cristóbal Pérez de Herrera, echoed in 1598 earlier statements in the Cortes when he referred to the particular problems of northern Spain: 'men from the Mountains (of Santander), from Asturias, Galicia, Navarre and other infertile regions . . . are more poverty-stricken than people down here (i.e., south of the Guadarrama mountains)'.[38] The great pilgrimage sites of this old-settled Christian part of Spain acted as a magnet for vagrants: 8,000–10,000 French and other foreigners came through Burgos every year on their way to the shrine of Santiago de Compostela, 'but no one knows by what route they leave, nor indeed what they have come for or whether they go on the pilgrimage at all'. These immigrants gave many Spanish cities of the period a cosmopolitan if unstable character. The economic writer Martínez de Mata denounced them in the 1650s, when Spain was at war with France. Despite the hostilities, they were still coming in, taking over the lowly trades of market porters, water carriers, sellers of wine . . . 'They will sweep your house and doorway, clean the sewers, cart off the rubbish and run errands for you.'[39] Labour shortages were palliated by the use of slaves as well. There were 6,327 slaves listed in Seville in 1565, in a population of 109,015 people. But Seville was somewhat exceptional in this respect, because of its great importance in and access to the Atlantic trades. More usually the labour demands of a pre-industrial economy were met by short-range migration – of the kind which would bring down to Barcelona every June men from the mountains of Catalonia to hire themselves out for reaping. 'Dissolute, bold men, most of them,' commented the historian of the disturbances of June 1640 in Barcelona, 'who most of the year live in a disorderly fashion, without a home of their own, a trade or any fixed dwelling.' And in the tense atmosphere of 1652 in Cordoba, efforts were made to disarm the 4,000 or so reapers expected at Saint John's Day (24 June) to spend their wages in the city, as they did every year.[40]

It was characteristic of the pre-industrial world that labour was required in abundance at certain times of the year – for example, harvest – but otherwise left idle. High mortality also tore families apart and exposed the vulnerable. The mother of the eponymous hero of *Lazarillo de Tormes* (1554) had to leave her village for the nearby town of Salamanca after her husband died, in order to find work as a cook and laundress. Nearly a fifth of the households in Castilian cities at this time might be in the care of widows. Their offspring, like the young Lazarillo, were driven to live off their wits from an early age. Nearly two in five of the population (36 per cent) were under sixteen years of age, according to the census of 1787, while by contrast only 14.5 per cent lived beyond their fiftieth birthday. One begins to understand, in the light of these figures, the heroic work of the charitable brotherhood of the Refugio in seventeenth-century Madrid: in a city of at most 150,000 people, its patrols would take in 300–400 children wandering the streets every year.[41] Some of these youngsters may never have had a home in the first place: some 12–15 per cent of infants baptised in Madrid and Valladolid, for example, were foundlings, abandoned at birth to public charity.

Though there were fewer elderly people then than now, nevertheless the problem of the prematurely aged was a significant one. Pérez de Herrera, in his great treatise on the poor of 1598, noted the havoc which disease could wreak: servants coming out of hospital, 'not quite back on their feet yet . . . sell their clothes in order to make ends meet and end up as beggars'. The point was made again a few years later by the social reformer López Bravo: lacking a roof over their heads, the poor, once discharged from hospital, 'find it hard to shake off their malady completely, and very soon they are in the grip of recurring or aggravated fevers'. Finally, the Dominican friar and writer on the plague, Gavaldá, warned of the fate of young women who survived the Valencian epidemic of 1647. With their parents and former employers often dead, they had little alternative but to take to the streets.[42]

Finding work was, indeed, perceived to be a critical remedy for the swelling underworld of early modern towns. From 1439 Valencia had a magistrate who would go the cathedral square every morning, where the unemployed tended to congregate, and see if he could find them something to do. Local innkeepers were forbidden to give a room for more than one night to anyone who lacked employment, unless they were reapers coming in for the harvest. Meanwhile, Granada ordered her innkeepers in 1552 to provide the magistrates every week with a list of their guests and 'the reason for their being in town'.[43] There were too many persons standing around idle in the market squares, thought Pérez de Herrera. When the constables asked them what they were up to, they would say they were porters, waiting for a job. Some regulation must be introduced, he decided, to make such people take whatever jobs were on offer. But the Cortes of 1579–82 had failed to get adopted a petition that every large town in Castile should set up a special officer – a *padre de mozos* ('father of the young') to do just this (and what the Valencians had been doing since 1439).[44]

The problem, of course, was there was not enough work at most times to go round. The guilds had strict regulations about access to their own trades. Technical skill was one thing, but social acceptability was just as important. Some Valencian guilds demanded high fees of outsiders. Thus the shoemakers in 1618 charged new masters 50 shillings if they were the sons of guildsmen, 200 if they were not but born within the city, 300 if they had come in from other parts of Valencia, and as much as 400 if they were from the rest of Spain. The carpenters in 1466 wanted their masters to be married men or, at least, have a house of their own. Though the statesmen of the Enlightenment reduced restrictive practices where they seemed to get in the way of improvements to the manufacturing process, they were keen to retain the social functions of the guilds. Thus, Campomanes argued, in his famous treatise of 1775, that, as well as apprentices and journeymen being under the tight control of the master, the latter should only qualify as such once he had the means to establish a household of his own.[45]

The guild system, of course, had the prime responsibility of rescuing its members from misfortune. Many of them helped fellow craftsmen over periods of sickness, and a few, like the boatmen of Barcelona, even provided a form of old-age pension. It was especially in respect of the funeral of a colleague that the charitable activity of these corporations became most evident. Widows were sometimes helped with cash, or allowed to continue running their late husband's shop for a period, on condition that they employed a qualified journeyman. Journeymen, indeed, seem to be as much part of the system of welfare – though they were excluded from decision-making – as their master; both had to pay subscriptions.[46] Despite the apparent benefits of all this in terms of social stability, Campomanes was very critical of the diversion of guild funds towards wasteful indulgence. The cult of the saintly patron of the trade and other fiestas throughout the year were a ruinous expense: 'household heads neglect their workshops during the year when they hold office in the confraternity. . . and get used to doing no work'. Instead, guild funds should be used for practical charity, such as the support of the old, the sick and orphans.[47]

Inevitably this precarious state of the urban masses posed great challenges to those who enjoyed wealth and power. It had long been accepted, of course, that the poor were a part of the Christian community and, indeed, a powerful incentive to the exercise of virtue through charity. In Valencia each parish had its two 'fathers of the poor', elected each year. In that of San Martín, it was a merchant and an innkeeper in 1616, and a distinguished citizen and a merchant in 1626. Their task was to collect second-hand clothing, which was then displayed in the parish church at the onset of winter (1 November), before being distributed among the poor. And the noble Catalá de Valeriola recalled in his diary how in the hunger year of 1592 he and the churchwardens of San Lorenzo 'decided to make the rounds of the parish so that householders would promise to give so much every week until the harvest, and I was charged with distributing the alms during the first week' – quite a responsibility for a young man of twenty-three.[48] This personal involvement in poor relief remained a characteristic feature of the activities of urban elites down to the end of the Old Regime. Luis de la Palma described how his father, a merchant of Toledo, went every day to visit the incurably sick in hospital: 'he would help to make their beds and to get them undressed, holding a candle while their hair was cut, slicing up their food for them and feeding them with his own hand'. This description of 1595 is very like that which the noted essayist Blanco White penned of his own father, a merchant of Seville, in the closing decades of the eighteenth century: 'he would allow himself no other distraction, after a tiring day at his desk, than a visit to the hospital . . . where 400 or 500 beggars lay dying of hunger and sickness'.[49]

Though these exercises might be good for the soul, more questions were being asked, as in the rest of early modern Europe at this time, about the effectiveness of spontaneous acts of compassion. Religion forbids us to ask whether a man who asks for our help really deserves it, noted Pérez de Herrera; but the magistrate has a wider responsibility for the proper functioning of society. His interest in the problem came, he tells us, from his work as physician on the royal galleys. From talking to the condemned men at the oars, he became aware that 'there are in this kingdom more people than you can imagine who . . . live like pagans . . . most of them with unmarried partners . . . sleeping in doorways and barns', and ready to fall into crime. A year before (1597), the jurist Castillo de Bobadilla had written his great treatise on the tasks of the *corregidor*, which included helping the poor, but also taking firm measures against vagrants. 'The idler who is healthy and begs from door to door is really a thief of the bread of the poor', he thundered, and must be rounded up by the constables from 'hospitals, taverns, inns, the public thoroughfares and elsewhere'.[50] Already in 1393 the city of Valencia had forbidden anyone to beg without a written licence from the magistrates, carried in a ball of lead or wax hanging from the neck and issued only after a report from the parish priest. The chronicler Escolano, himself a parish priest, defended the restrictions, 'since the filth of the wandering, vagrant poor is a breeding ground for filthy habits'.[51]

One of the early concerns was with the fate of youngsters. Homes of 'Christian Doctrine' were set up from the later Middle Ages and seem to have acquired a considerable extension in the sixteenth century under the inspiration of the saintly Juan de Avila. The Escolapians, founded in 1617 by the Catalan Saint José de Calasanz, brought primary schooling to the poor, but only attained real significance in Spain in the eighteenth century, when Goya was one of their pupils. The *Doctrinas* were, by contrast, a mixture of school and orphanage. That of Granada had endowments from various sources, including wheat from the Royal Hospital and alms from funerals, which the orphans were increasingly invited to attend. Out of these somewhat irregular funds, about 50 children – but more usually half that number in the seventeenth century – were supposed to be taught to read and write and apprenticed to a trade. Pérez de Herrera was pessimistic about the state of these institutions: they generally failed to teach orphans a trade, but rather accustomed their inmates to mendicancy (for example, by ceremonial attendance at funerals).[52]

This led to the problem of adult vagrants. Early measures were taken as in the rest of western Europe in the wake of the Black Death to ensure that people were conscripted for work. But it was really in the early sixteenth century that a set of laws was introduced, which appear to reflect a perceived growth of towns and new Renaissance ideas of good order. The Poor Laws of 1523–58 sum up a century and more of tentative efforts and laid down the basic guidelines for dealing with the poor until the collapse of the Old Regime. To beg, paupers would henceforth require a report from their parish priest and a licence from the justices. They would normally only be allowed to beg in their own locality, and must surrender any children over five years of age for apprenticeship to a trade. A decree of 1565 clarified the point that licences to beg would only be issued for old age or infirmity. Anyway, 'since if it were possible to feed the poor without having them wandering through the streets begging, this would be greatly to the service of God', the justices and prelates were to examine all ways of raising funds to provide 'alternative' relief. Efforts to enforce these provisions were inevitably haphazard, given that the initiative depended on the local authorities. The chronicler Ariño described the rounding-up of the beggars of Seville on 29 April 1597: 2,000 men and an unspecified number of women were examined by doctors over the next three or four days, with licences issued to 'the lame, the one-armed, the palsied and the aged' to continue begging, while the rest were ordered to find a job within three days, on pain of a hundred lashes.[53]

Pérez de Herrera was sure that there were enough jobs to go around. But clearly this analysis took little account of the persistent problem of underemployment and the periodic crises which punctuated a pre-industrial economy. Censuses of the sixteenth century would suggest that around 8 per cent of urban households were exempted from tax because they were too poor to pay. In a manufacturing town like Segovia, dependent on immigrant labour, the proportion could rise to 15 per cent. But then in a famine year like 1558 the proportion of paupers would shoot up: nearly one in five people were classified that year in Toledo (population 56,270) as being in need of relief.[54] There was a further problem about the hordes of starving peasants who would descend on a town in time of hunger. Protesting against special relief for Toledo in the famine of 1585, when thousands of poor from La Mancha were alleged to be converging on the city, León invoked 'the many paupers from Oviedo and Asturias, Galicia and the Mountains of Santander who regularly descend on this city . . . and those of Zamora and Toro'.[55] As other commentators pointed out, the laws requiring vagrants to return home made little sense, since the current of emigration was naturally from the poorer hill country of the north where there were few resources to the more prosperous cities of the south. In 1546 Toledo put the homeless poor, who could not be succoured through the usual system of parish relief, either into the hospital or into the homes of wealthier citizens, while the crisis lasted.[56]

The laws invited local authorities to find some way of channelling relief to such homeless people through institutions. The medieval hospitals had been refuges open to pilgrims, the aged, the insane, cripples, as well as the sick. Spain had a network of such institutions, often small and generally run by a charitable confraternity, which often saw its principal task as that of keeping alive the memory of its founders through masses for their souls. Following the stimulus given by the Council of Trent for a more effective use of charitable endowments, the government initiated a major enquiry into the state of affairs in Spain. Under its pressure, some rationalisation was achieved. Thus in Medina del Campo the sixty confraternities were amalgamated into six by 1587, with funds being released for a new general hospital, which would cater to orphans and pilgrims as well as the sick. But other towns, like Zamora or Toledo, seem to have been much less successful in this effort at consolidation of endowments.[57] The question remained anyway as to whether the placing of the poor in institutions was the right way to tackle the problem of poverty. The problem surfaced acutely in the eighteenth century when a more secular-minded government tried to set up *hospicios* or workhouses for the internment of the able-bodied poor. As the city of Seville pointed out in 1766, casual begging was an inevitable part of the livelihood of the labourer: anyone earning under four *reales* a day, such as bricklayers, might well need 'their wives and children to beg for alms', while even the more prosperous silk workers – at least, the journeymen – could be reduced to temporary mendicancy by a slump.[58]

The most sensitive approach to the problem of institutional poor relief was that of Canon Giginta (1579) and the physician Pérez de Herrera (1598). Essentially they campaigned for a pauper hospice – an *albergue* – to be set up in each large town. Here the crippled, the orphan, the temporarily unemployed could be gathered. Entrance would be voluntary: it 'would not resemble a school or anything like a prison, but rather an orderly home of good Christian handicraft workers', according to Giginta. There those genuinely in need of help would be given a bed, a fire, religious instruction and the chance of apprenticeship to a trade. Some of the inmates would be allowed out during the day to beg for alms, 'because humans need diversion and recreation, especially those who are accustomed to leading a life of complete liberty'. With the assurance that such people were under proper supervision, thought Pérez de Herrera, 'any honourable, Christian citizen will be happy to take some of these genuine indigents back to his house for a meal'.[59] These beggar hospitals, despite much enthusiasm in the Cortes, proved in the end difficult to maintain. That of Toledo was inaugurated in 1581, with Giginta triumphantly proclaiming that of the thousand beggars in town most had chosen to leave, others had found work, and 'those who are confined do not amount to more than 330'. But by the end of the decade the hospital was in severe financial difficulty. More realistically perhaps, Zamora declared flatly in 1597 that 'if we had an almshouse here, such a large quantity of paupers would gather that we would never be able to suuport them'.[60] Instead the city preferred the traditional remedies of driving immigrants out, if the situation became dire, and subsidising the local poor through parish relief.

Only where a confraternity was specially dedicated to the building and maintenance of a refuge for the homeless does it seem to have worked. The Brotherhood of the Holy Charity had been founded in Seville in 1565 in order to give a Christian burial to the 'forsaken' (largely vagrants and criminals) and to carry those lying in the street to hospital. In 1662 Don Miguel Mañara, of an ennobled merchant family, transformed the confraternity by getting it to devote its funds to running a night shelter, which would give the homeless a bowl of soup, a warm fire and a bed. After all, he argued, most of those buried by the Brothers 'die of no other disease than their wretchedness and lack of warmth'. Though the great hospital of the Holy Charity, with its canvases by Murillo, became an important institution in late seventeenth-century Seville, much of its money actually went in providing outdoor relief to householders and in ferrying the sick to other hospitals.[61]

The background to all this was the sheer threat of harvest failure and consequent food scarcities. An unskilled labourer in Andalusia might expect to earn, when in work, four *reales* a day in the early seventeenth century; a three-pound loaf, the basis of the daily diet of his family, might be around one *real*, but could rise to four or even six in bad years, as in Seville in 1652. 'Fear of hunger has always kept princes awake at night,' noted Caxa de Leruela in 1631; bread and bullfights were the way to keep subjects tranquil, as in ancient Rome.[62] The *jurats* of Valencia reported to the Crown in 1610 that they advanced 90,000 pounds every year to those who would guarantee to supply the city with meat, 40,000 to suppliers of firewood and and another 40,000 for olive oil. Castillo de Bobadilla noted shortly before the importance of these 'privileged' contractors' (*obligados*) for the provisioning of Castilian towns with meat, fish and oil, and, though deploring monopolies in general, thought that these essential supplies constituted an exception – that the contracts should, indeed, be extended to cover wine and bread. The system was subject to considerable fraud, though. The large households of aristocrats and prelates were sometimes allowed to slaughter their own cattle, for example, though not to put the excess on sale.

Bread was, of course, the major focus of concern. Cities had privileged areas of purchase, usually lying within their jurisdictions. Thus villages within about a 100–kilometre radius of Madrid were required to supply quotas of grain – though the system seems to have functioned, if at all, only within about half that distance, until it was abolished in 1758.[63] Seville protested to the Crown in 1652 about proposals to sell off its village of Alcalá de Guadaira, where most of the mills grinding flour for the city lay. These expensive pieces of equipment – mills and ovens – were as highly prized as the walls which guarded the town. Viciana described lovingly the forty-three flour mills and twenty bakeries which kept Xàtiva (1,750 families) fed, the ten mills lining the river and the twenty ovens needed by the equally numerous population of Orihuela. Sometimes individual villages specialised in this kind of activity: Alfacar's ready supply of water kept its flour mills turning 'day and night', to supply the ovens from which 'more than 100 batches of bread' were carried into Granada every morning.[64]

It was a prime responsibility of the magistrates to police the markets so that food or merchandise reached the customer directly and did not fall into the hands of speculators. There were laws in medieval Seville excluding dealers from the market-place until after mid-day, and forbidding the resale of food or building materials within the city limits. The authorities in Madrid ruled that no family could buy more than twelve loaves (perhaps equivalent to 24 pounds) of bread a day, reckoned enough to feed the largest household. The Cortes of 1523 and 1528 lamented that speculation in grain had become a profession, pushing up prices, and they ruled that henceforth anyone purchasing grain must either intend to sell it outside the city limits or bake it into bread for local consumption. As their successors in the parliament of 1576–8 commented, the law proved to be counter-productive, driving grain off the market in time of demand. Shortly afterwards, Castillo de Bobadilla noted that years of dearth were becoming more frequent, either 'for our sins, or because of the growth of population'. It was dreadful, he thought, to see the uproar of women, children and the old 'crowding with shouts round the house of the *corregidor*, or going out on the highways and into the villages nearby for bread'.[65]

'Many times I had excess wheat removed from the houses not only of lay people but even of canons and wealthy clergy,' Castillo de Bobadilla tells us, to prevent hoarding and dearth. The crown should support *corregidores* in this task a little more effectively, he argued; he himself had been excommunicated for such actions once for eighty days, before Madrid intervened to get the prelate to lift the sentence.

There was, of course, the *tasa*, the fixed price for grain, introduced in 1503 as the problem of dearth became increasingly apparent in Castile. But the devout Antonio de Tapia, bishop of Cordoba, wrote to the government in 1652 that the poor themselves would lose out if he sold off the tithes of his diocese at the official price. In the first place, the revenue of the bishopric would fall, diminishing the funds available for charity, and secondly the wheat would simply find its way into the hands of hoarders and speculators. 'The causes, Sire, of the dearth of wheat in this region are the maladministration and greed of the powerful, who hoard it . . . and with this commerce found their entailed estates.'[66] Anyway, as the *corregidor* of Murcia reported in 1576, money was so scarce that many people might not be able to afford grain when it came on the market at reasonable prices.

Generally households seem to have done little baking on their own. Convents may have baked their own bread, but even the nobility seem to have used public ovens. Bakers were a crucial element in the whole network of supply. We still know too little about how they operated, whether they worked up their own flour or that provided by customers, how many bakeries were owned by the church and the aristocracy (the existence of slaves in some Valencian establishments would suggest fairly large-scale enterprises). The size and price of the loaf were fixed often by the magistrates. Even when the government removed controls on wheat prices in 1765, it still set upper limits for bread – much to the despair of the bakers in Madrid, who claimed that they could not cover their costs.[67] In Valencia from 1630 and down to the early eighteenth century the city council was allowed by the Crown to appoint all the bakers.

But ultimately the critical factor was the supply of grain to the city. It was accepted that the coastal regions, other than the fertile valley of the Guadalquivir, needed to import from abroad. Towards the end of the fifteenth century Valencia appointed a representative to negotiate wheat purchases on its behalf in Sicily. Seville set up a public granary in 1476 and offered a bounty for imports, but does not seem to have intervened directly in purchases.[68] During the sixteenth century these municipal granaries (*pósitos*) began to spread throughout Castile and Valencia. Viciana praised that of Villarreal as a pioneering effort in 1564, for example, and Castillo de Bobadilla in 1597 was urging Castilian towns to adopt them: 'although in these kingdoms they have only been used for a few years past, they are very ancient throughout the world'. By stocking grain in time of plenty, the magistrate could avoid confrontation with the tithe-farmers and hoarders in time of scarcity, he thought. Describing apparently his own experiences, he noted how the parish priests would be asked for lists of needy households, with the number of loaves they might consume; then a *regidor* would be appointed for one week in turn, outside whose house the poor would congregate to get their daily ration. Also 'bakers are to be nominated who will bring to the market-place for sale or to the grilles [sc. from where paupers' loaves were handed out], a certain quantity of bread for travellers and outsiders and poor peasants from the region', who should not simply be expelled from town in hunger years.[69] The provisioning of a great city was a major test of government – a recurrent financial and political challenge for the ruling elites. The local chronicler describes the sheer joy in Granada in April 1636 when the mule trains entered the city carrying enough grain to keep the population fed for the next two months, until the harvest. The purchase had been arranged by the city council, and was proudly paraded along the main street and in front of the royal lawcourts, to the blast of trumpets. But the cost of this municipal welfare – subsidised bread prices and even free distribution of bread in crises – was high. The agricultural writer Lope de Deza noted that the *pósitos* tended, if anything, to push up prices by competing for grain, that their reserves might often not be needed for years, going bad meanwhile, and that the purchasing led to corrupt deals between aldermen and merchants. The great Valencian politician Francisco March had received 88,589 Valencian pounds from the city in 1610–11 to buy wheat, of which he only disbursed 83,402. His heir only managed to pay back the difference to the treasury by 1634, after a hard struggle to sell the wheat itself. The statesmen of the Enlightenment, as part of their drive to liberalise trade, insisted that the municipal granaries must sell at market prices and not subsidise bread; but they found the institution useful enough as an agent of supply to allow it to continue alongside private contractors, down to the middle of the nineteenth century.

Initially towns catered to their obligations by drawing on their *propios* – common lands, mills, houses – which brought in a rental every year. But from the later Middle Ages they were having to introduce permanent excise duties on commodities being traded in the local market. The first such taxes in Valencia, the chronicler Escolano recalled, came in 1334, and they had to be increased thereafter as the monarchy turned to the city for help with its wars. But what really began to cripple Valencia during the sixteenth and seventeenth centuries was the administration of the food supply. Bonds were issued, eventually eating up 147,000 of the 200,000 pounds municipal revenue in interest payments by 1649. This situation provoked a series of political crises, as the magistrates sought to increase taxes – quadrupling the excise on some basic foodstuffs in 1634, for example, and doubling that on textiles in 1649 (when the duty on bread, wine and meat had already reached a ceiling of 33 per cent of value).

Castilian cities were facing similar problems. A turning-point in Seville was the introduction in 1515 of the small impost of two *maravedís* on a pound of meat, from which nobles and clergy were theoretically exempt. Thereafter, mainly thanks to impressive gifts to the monarchy, the city fell heavily into debt, declaring itself officially bankrupt in 1601.[70] Given that the cities generally administered the royal taxes, the *alcabalas*, themselves, it is hard to know what percentage of the excise was eaten up by national compared with local needs. After the Bourbon suppression of the liberties of the Crown of Aragon (1707–16), a consolidated tax was introduced there, of which towns like Barcelona and Valencia could claim a certain percentage for their municipal budgets. In Castile, meanwhile, the Bourbons depended very heavily on the old municipal excises, seizing about half these, for example, to pay for the war of 1739–48.

What was tending to happen over the early modern period as a whole was a loss of financial autonomy by the town councils as the monarchy sought to keep a closer watch on the budget. Castillo de Bobadilla urged the *corregidor* to supervise the use made by the aldermen of funds from municipal lands; some, he suggested, were interested in feathering their own nests. Town councillors are like judicial minors, he affirmed, and require a tutor: the king and the king's representative. Above all, taxation was a royal prerogative. In non-urgent cases towns must get the consent of the Crown for new impositions (not least because of the complexity of deciding whether nobles and non-resident property-holders could be compelled to pay).[71]

Financial considerations had drawn the Spanish city into an expanding political role from the later Middle Ages, through its representatives in the parliament or Cortes. After the incorporation of Granada, there were eighteen Castilian cities represented, to which the Habsburgs resorted increasingly in their attempt to shift the collection of the royal excise (*alcabalas*) into quotas (*encabezamientos*), apportioned to each of them through parliament. Traditionally the cities had been partners of the monarchy – the nucleus of the resettlement of the Moorish frontier and, in the civil wars of the fifteenth century, a bulwark against a plundering baronage through their armed 'brotherhoods' (*hermandades*).

But the restoration of government under Ferdinand and Isabella initiated an uneasy sense that power and influence were passing from the local communities to the court, where aristocratic voices were more likely to find a hearing. The feudal lords began to exempt, often with royal permission, their villages from the jurisdiction of the cities and to reduce the *alcabalas* there, diverting trade from the urban market. There was increasing disenchantment with the *corregidor*, the representative of the Crown in each city, who, far from protecting it against such usurpations, seemed to be part of the problem: that growing network of mafia influence spreading from the court to locally powerful individuals, who were feathering their own nests.

Gathering stormclouds finally broke in 1520, when Charles V, unpopular anyway because of his Flemish favourites, extorted a large subsidy from the Cortes which was to be spent abroad. After the king's departure for Germany, representatives of some of the cities, meeting first in Avila in August and then moving their headquarters shortly afterwards to Tordesillas, hammered out a programme of reform. Basically this required the Cortes to meet henceforward every two or three years, whether summoned by the king or not, in order to discuss the grievances of the people. The latter were to be represented by one of their own number, specially elected in each town, to accompany the existing parliamentary representatives, designated by the aldermen. For the rest, though the king would continue to govern, his officials – and, in particular, the *corregidor* – must be subject to regular investigation of their conduct.[72]

The demands have been seen as a last, brave attempt at giving the towns a voice in the running of the country, and their protagonists – the *Comuneros* – served as an inspiration to nineteenth-century liberals. At its height, in the autumn of 1520, fourteen of the eighteen cities represented in the Cortes had sent representatives to the 'Holy Junta' in Tordesillas, which was trying to coordinate the rebellion. But the movement soon manifested divisions of interest which would spell its undoing. In the first place, the chief town of all, Burgos, anxious about its wool trade to Flanders – found it useful to make its peace with Charles V. The Andalusian cities did not join at all. In Seville, the younger brother of the duke of Arcos stormed the royal alcázar on 16 September 1520 at the head of a crowd of 700, demanding better justice and lower taxes; but the rival house of Medina Sidonia – in the persons of the wife and the mother of the ailing duke – gathered their own clients to recover the fortress, of which they were hereditary wardens. In a tense situation, where ideologies were hopelessly confused with the politics of power, the bishop managed to arrange an uneasy truce. Though the great nobles had their own grievances against Charles V and his Flemish court, they were increasingly nervous at the attempt of some cities to reassert jurisdiction over fiefs recently acquired from the Crown, and at the uprising of peasants on their own estates. Towards the end of 1520 the Comuneros rejected the mediation of the grandees, 'because it is likely that they will look to their own interests and try to aggrandise their houses, to the great damage and hurt of the towns and communities, as they and their ancestors have done all along'.[73] Their further demands that the nobility contribute equally in taxation completed the rift.

The 'juntas' which formed in each city between May and July 1520 were composed of a minority of activists: some *regidores*, including nobles like Juan de Padilla, the leader in Toledo, and clergy, but perhaps above all a 'middle class' of merchants and artisans, who now found themselves leading the debates for the first time, in the crowded churches where these illegal, self-constituted bodies tended to meet. The aldermen in the council chambers bided their time. An eyewitness, the humanist writer Fray Antonio de Guevara, conveys vividly the confusion and fear during the summer of 1520: the murder by the mob of the deputy from Segovia who had voted the taxes for Charles V, the proclamation of the *Comunidad* in the great financial capital, Medina del Campo, 'when the wool shearer Bobadilla rose up with others like himself, and threw the *regidor* Nieto out of the windows of the council chamber', the flight of the Regent and the high court from Valladolid as the mob 'rose up in arms, roaming the streets that night knocking down houses, under their captain, the harness-maker Vera . . .'.[74] For Guevara, the rebels had legitimate grievances, but the uprising itself was plunging Castile back into that state of anarchy from which the Catholic Kings had so recently rescued her: 'there is no safe highway any more . . . no one can plough his land, no one can bring in supplies, no one can administer justice, no one is safe in his own house'. It was probably this war-weariness which told in the end against the success of the revolt, as the respectable classes began to withdraw their support, leaving the hardliners to be crushed at the battle of Villalar on 23 April 1521. Though the monarchy had reasserted its control, it had done so only thanks to the active cooperation of the nobility, whose cavalry carried the day at Villalar, and to the passive support of the urban elites, who now distanced themselves as much as they could from the whole episode. It was mostly members of the lower classes who paid the ultimate price on the scaffold, and city chronicles thereafter tried to emphasise the loyalty of the *regidores* to the Crown.

The social divisions in the Comunero movement were even more apparent in its Valencian counterpart, the revolt of the 'Brotherhoods' or *Germanías* (1519–22). Plague in the great Mediterranean city led in July 1519 to the exodus of many nobles and patricians and to the hunt for public sinners, a campaign fired by preachers and focusing on sodomites and Moors, and eventually on the protectors of the latter, the nobility, who were also accused of not paying their debts. A 'brotherhood' of thirteen guildsmen, in memory of Christ and the twelve apostles, was set up to enforce a godly commonwealth, and in particular the payment of debts (according to the chronicler Escolano). It went on to demand that two guildsmen should be represented on the council of six *jurats* or aldermen, and eventually – to the cry of 'Long live the king, and death to taxes' – mounted an attack on the fiscal offices of both the city and the Crown (21 February 1521). The disturbances were spreading, meanwhile, to other towns, often taking the form of attacks on neighbouring seigneurs. A long-running boundary dispute between the city of Alpuente and the lord of Chelva now came to a head, for example, with armed guildsmen from Valencia joining their 'brothers' in Alpuente in an attack on this hated feudal neighbour (1520).

There was much temporising by the Crown and the nobility at this time, in view of the uncertainties of the situation in Castile. But the viceroy had already withdrawn from the city of Valencia in June 1520, and a year later – after the crushing of the Comuneros at Villalar – the dukes of Gandia and Segorbe summoned their vassals. The participation of the Moors in the feudal levies envenomed old hatreds and led to the pogroms and mass baptisms which characterised the response of the *Agermanats*. The lords, indeed, were not immediately victorious. The silk-weaver Vicent Peris defeated the army of the south at Gandia (25 July 1521). However, the duke of Segorbe was victorious in the north at this time (battle of Sagunto), and the Castilian nobles under the marquis of Los Vélez came to the help of their Valencian brethren, capturing Orihuela (29 August 1521). A ring of steel began to encircle the heartland of the rebellion, the cities of Valencia, Xàtiva and Alzira. Riots in the capital on 4 October 1521 broke the Germanía in two, with merchants and notaries (as Escolano notes) worried about the disruption to trade and the food supply and now seeking an accommodation with the viceroy. Eventually on 18 October a compromise was hammered out, by which an amnesty would be accorded if the rebels laid down their arms and dissolved the junta of thirteen and restored the patrician monopoly of city office. The uneasy truce was broken on 3 March 1522, on the eve of carnival when spirits always ran high. The journeymen wool dressers, after a riot against their masters, were joined by their fellows in the silk trade, in a procession to the house of Vicent Peris, the retired radical leader of the *Agermanat* army, calling out: 'Long live King Charles and death to the masked traitors in our midst!' The latter – 'the honourable, householding wool dressers' – got the viceroy to sound the cathedral bell, which summoned a guild militia to disperse the hotheads and lynch Peris. The

Germanía was over in Valencia city; but Xàtiva held out until 2 December 1522, inspired by a strange visionary, L'Encobert ('The Hidden One'), who claimed to be the son of Prince Juan (himself the only son of Ferdinand and Isabella, who had died tragically young in 1499). He was the instrument chosen by God, he told his followers, to install a reign of justice, the first since the Flood and the last before the recovery of Jerusalem. He would convert the Jews and the Moors in these Last Days – as well as lowering taxes.[75]

The Germanías collapsed, like their counterpart in Castile, largely through internal divisions. Yet the ferocity of the punishment subsequently meted out gives some idea of the fear inspired in the ruling classes. In Valencia, the amnesty of October 1521 was forgotten after the disturbances of March 1522, and those who paid the penalty in executions and confiscations of property seem to have been mostly humble men. The chronicler Viciana in 1563–4 was at pains to distance the patrician elites in the towns from any hint of sympathy for the rebels. With shame he had to acknowledge the 'very evil and scandalous conspiracy in Xàtiva, which most of the common people joined'; but he could point out with relief that the knights and honoured citizens, 'and many respectable householders [*hombres buenos*], who are those who make up the corporation' had to flee for their lives, and joined the royalist army. It was a similar attitude to that taken by the chronicler Colmenares with regard to his beloved city of Segovia, one of the ringleaders in the Comunero movement: the magistrates had been forced to temporise with the common people, who had lost all respect for law and hierarchy in an act of collective madness.

And yet the *jurats* and *regidores* had generally continued in office throughout the disturbances. There was no radical overhaul of the structures of municipal government. What had emerged, though, was the power of the crowd. The parade of the guilds in Valencia before the Regent, Adrian of Utrecht, on 19 February 1520, 'dressed in all their finery, with jackets of brocade and silk, under their forty banners and to the number of 8,000 men' (as Escolano later described them), must have been an awe-inspiring sight. The drums which summoned the guildsmen remind us of the role which the government itself expected them to play as an urban militia, and they proved able to give a good account of themselves in field engagements with the nobility (as at Gandia in 1521). By contrast the Royalists found it difficult to gather their forces: reluctant Moorish peasants living on seigneurial estates, some Castilian mercenaries who deserted when pay was late . . . The forces on each side seem rarely to have exceeded 4,000 men in any encounter, and knives, clubs and swords were still the chief weapons, conferring little advantage, therefore, on the aristocratic side. Towns proved able to hold out behind their medieval walls against royalist cannon (Alzira, for example – though not Villarreal), church towers were still invaluable places of refuge (Olleria, Quart, Torrent), and manor houses (Albatera) could present formidable obstacles to an opponent. It was a very fragmented world, where the great political issues tended to wither away in a morass of local, often ineffectual struggles.

Certainly the result of the great wave of revolts of 1519–22 was to reinforce social hierarchy in Spain. The original grievance in Castile over high taxes was resolved in part by leaving the cities free to administer their own quotas, the *encabezamientos*, and keeping these, for a time, relatively low. But inevitably it was a truce rather than a solution. The bankruptcy of the monarchy by the time of the accession of Philip II (1556–98) raised the old problems of municipal finance, with its implications for the government of towns. When Philip II tried to increase the *alcabalas* threefold in 1575, he unleashed a small storm of protest. The efforts of the Crown to use its intermediaries – the *corregidores* in the first place, but also the bishop in Salamanca and the duke of Infantado in Guadalajara – met with only limited success. As Diego de Abalos, *regidor* of the wool-manufacturing town of Cuenca, put it in 1577, he and his patrician colleagues would not bear the brunt of the excise duties, 'but rather the traders and tax-payers of this city, and it is other people's property that we have to talk about' – which led to efforts to consult the community more widely. A few years later Castillo de Bobadilla would warn the *corregidor* of the danger of pushing through the royal business too eagerly: town councillors needed time to reflect, and the wider community must not be alienated.[76] It was, in fact, by a mixture of threats and promises – of rewards for loyal supporters – that the Crown got at least part of the tax increases it was seeking in 1575–77. But the prolonged negotiations during these two or three years demonstrated the continuing delicacy of the political equilibrium.

Events would show that as long as the patrician elites could guarantee an adequate supply of 'bread and circuses' for their communities, the populace would not repeat the rebellions of 1519–22. But the great food riots of 1648–52 in Andalusia served as a reminder of how insecure this compromise might be. As the price of bread tripled in Granada in the spring of 1648, crowds gathered at various points. While the *corregidor* took to his heels, they advanced on the high court, to the cry 'Long live the king and down with bad government!', and forced the court president to inspect a 'wheaten loaf mixed with millet and ashes'. To the president's promise to have cheap bread provided, the crowd demanded that he appoint the popular Don Luis de Paz, who had been active in charity some time before, as interim *corregidor* in the king's name. The fears of Don Luis that he would look like the leader of an insurrection were calmed by the president: 'Good Don Luis, this is God's business, which we must carry out for his holy service and for the peace of this commonwealth.' Led on horseback by the crowd, Don Luis held aloft a crucifix: 'My children, this is your *corregidor*, not me.' On the following day, 19 May 1648, as the old *corregidor* came out of hiding, the crowd rioted again, and the patricians too closely associated with him had to seek sanctuary in the archbishop's palace. Don Luis had to parade through the streets again in order to restore calm, accompanied by a Capuchin friar, one of the high court judges and two of the titled nobility, holding the reins of his horse. The storm was allowed to blow itself out: a general pardon and a fresh supply of grain enabled the authorities gradually to recover control of the situation.[77]

Fundamentally the tranquillity of the population depended on keeping the 3-pound loaf of bread, reckoned necessary to feed the average household for a day, at two *reales* or thereabouts – approximately half the daily income of a working man at the time. When the loaf reached six *reales* in Seville in the spring of 1652 trouble was bound to follow. The price rises of that year seem to have been provoked less by actual shortages than by the devaluation of the currency decreed by the Crown the previous November in the desperate hunt for revenue to pursue its wars. Lack of business confidence led to the interruption of silk manufacture in Granada and the threat of renewed unrest there, while in Seville the failure of the Crown to pay its bond-holders led the nobility to dismiss some of their servants. The tense situation was contained in Granada, but erupted in rioting in Cordoba on 6 May and particularly in Seville on 22 May 1652, where a mob from the artisan districts of Omnium Sanctorum and the Feria converged on the municipal granary, and isolated groups attacked the houses of individual merchants. As the Regent of the high court (*Audiencia*) of Seville reported to the king on 23 May, a decree reducing the family loaf to one and a half *reales* did not immediately calm the situation. The mob invaded the Audiencia building, threatening the Regent and the archbishop, and eventually forcing these dignitaries to ride round town proclaiming the restoration of the coinage to its old value and the suppression of the excises on food (the *millones*). They then headed for the gaol, where they released the prisoners, and came back to the Audiencia to seize and destroy criminal records. As in Granada in 1648 and in Cordoba earlier in May 1652, tranquillity was only restored by changing the *corregidor* (or *asistente*, as he was known in Seville). A knight of Calatrava, Don Juan de Villasis, was installed as the people's choice in Seville. But the patricians made use of the interval, when the artisans dispersed to their homes, to recruit a mob of their own among the smugglers and ruffians of the San Marcos district, leading a violent assault on the working-class districts on the night of 26–27 May. A hundred were killed and fifty-seven others arraigned for rebellion. The insurrection was effectively over, though tranquillity was only restored to Andalusia that July when the Crown announced a restoration of the currency to its old value.[78]

These disturbances throw light on the fragile compromise on which public order ultimately rested, in particular on the commitment of local elites to providing bread for the population at an affordable price. The social and political hierarchy itself was not called into question: rather, the populace demonstrated its confidence time and again in leading members of the patriciate, chosen as popular *corregidores*. But the eighteenth-century transition to freedom of the grain trade – solemnly proclaimed by the Crown on 11 July 1765 – led to some of the most severe popular rioting in the Old Regime, starting in Madrid on Palm Sunday 1766 and spreading to many of the other provincial cities thereafter.[79] At this stage, and in view of the increasing withdrawal of the patricians into private life – or at least a civic life orientated more to promotion at court than within the local community – it became evident that the structure of local government itself would have to be reformed.

Already in 1652 the popular *corregidor* of Cordoba had warned the Crown about the alienation of the 'middling sort' from the ruling elites and their tendency to do little to counter the fury of the mob. In Seville, the parish clergy of the artisan parishes were rumoured to be encouraging artisan unrest. As the Bourbon government accentuated the trend away from the idea of a 'moral community', buttressed by the guilds and the charitable confraternities and the public granaries, towards a concept of 'enlightened self-interest', the old hierarchy of patricians and paupers became increasingly unstable. Instead, a search began for some way of broadening the basis of municipal government so that it would include the respectable middle classes. As one of its responses to the popular riots of 1766, the Crown decreed that 'deputies of the commons' would henceforth be elected by householders to sit with the hereditary *regidores* and vote on taxes and supply. It was a small step, which was combined with an effort, after the law of 1783 declaring trade to be honourable, to have former shopkeepers or their sons accepted as aldermen – if they had the money to purchase the office in the first place, of course. Further developments would have to await the collapse of the Old Regime in 1808. But one cannot help feeling that for some time before the commonwealth was being redefined as a national rather than a local forum – with enormous implications for the whole self-image and function of ruling elites.

7

THE CONSOLIDATION OF
AN ARISTOCRACY

Onofre Esquerdo, son of a merchant and himself an 'honoured citizen' of Valencia, set out his ideas of nobility in an important manuscript work of about 1686. Early civilised man, he tells us, 'for the benefit of the commonwealth, divided the population of which it was composed into three orders or classes'. These were the tillers of the soil, the handcraft workers and 'those who would govern the others in peace and justice . . . and defend them by force of arms'. Those who aspired to govern, by the pen and the sword, 'must cast off any tie of kinship or friendship' and purge the impurity of the soul, like silver tempered by fire, 'through the hardship, sleepless nights, discomforts and dangers which are experienced on campaign, and have to be put up with at university and when one is sitting examinations'. It was a similar picture which the Castilian authority, Guardiola, painted in 1591. The original equality of man gave way as a grateful citizenry paid tribute to the 'virtue' of those who governed it by the pen and the sword.[1] Men of this period were still close enough to the memory of civil war to recall how fragile was the veneer of civilisation. 'Tell me,' wrote the Valencian chronicler Viciana in 1564 – himself a notary but sprung of a gentry family – 'if we had no knights in the land, how many virgins would be abducted, how many married women and widows put to shame, how many churches desecrated?' The cult of chivalry had its legitimate recompense in the honour paid to the good man: 'for where there is no honour, the spirit weakens, and a society which does not respect its sage and powerful members will not be short of tyrants to crush it'.[2]

Ideas of a ruling elite changed gradually over the early modern period. Antonio Ponz signalled the change of mood, common to the rest of Europe, when he spoke of the improving landlords as 'true conquistadors' towards the end of the Old Regime. This idea that the nobility must become leaders in the material betterment of their country was taken up by Xavier Pérez y López, lawyer and representative of Seville at court, and by the Valencian jurist Mariano Madramany (1750–1822), who embody some of the key ideas of the Enlightenment. For Madramany, 'letters' and 'industry' were necessary for the running of a modern country, whose elites must demonstrate their utility to the *patria* in that way. What the role of a nobility would be in all this was beginning to be questioned: 'some think that . . . it would be useful to the state to have a nobility composed only of individuals' – who had earned their status, that is, through service to the fatherland.[3]

This was to substitute an aristocracy – 'government by the best' – for a nobility – 'men of known families'. In fact, the early modern period had seen much debate already on the values of ancestry. The Renaissance humanist, Fernando del Pulgar, pointed to the varying abilities of children in the same family: can one be surprised if nature itself wills that some rise to eminence through talent at war or letters, while the offspring of the great fall into obscurity, 'since they lack ability and are of weak character'? His conclusion was that 'everything leads us to believe that God made men, not lineages', and that human society can no more be still and motionless than can the heavens.[4] Yet there was still a place for hereditary nobility, as Madramany pointed out right at the end of our period. 'The upbringing which a noble father may perhaps give his children, the care and concern to instil in them lofty aspirations, are almost always lacking in those who have to earn their own nobility.' New men, as magistrates and army officers, may well find it difficult to command respect; and certainly it was useful to have a class of eminent families which 'with their authority and example . . . can uphold in the populace a due reverence for the sovereign'. Haunted still by a sense of how fragile the veneer of public order actually was, the men of the Enlightenment still clung to some idea of hierarchy. Though eager to see nobles get down to work and accept newcomers in their ranks, Pérez y López praised still 'those inhabitants who from time immemorial have kept a tradition of honour in the town where they were born', who have 'fostered and maintained . . . their local *patria*'.[5]

If anything, it would seem that the early modern period saw a strengthening of this idea of ancestry, as part of a growing concern with establishing a settled society and a stable polity. The nascent state of the absolute monarchs and their ally, the Counter-Reformation church, depended upon a clear idea of hierarchy. There is an impression left by writings of the time – by Viciana in Valencia (1564) or Argote de Molina in Andalusia (1588) – that now that the reconquest of Spain has been completed, it was time for the elites to put down roots as well. Viciana set out the genealogies of the Valencian nobles, he tells us, 'so that all may know where they come from, so that by this description each may strive in virtuous rivalry with others, in virtue, diligence, courage and skill'. And Argote affirmed a similar desire to clarify ancestry, 'for our fathers were extremely negligent in these matters'. But it was precisely the passion for genealogy in this period which generated new sources of conflict. Viciana's research stirred bitter controversy, and he confessed his hesitations about how to list noble families, whether by antiquity or by prestige, eventually settling for a simple alphabetical order.[6]

In the proliferating lawsuits of the sixteenth century over noble ancestry (*hidalguía*), one theme emerges strongly: that nobility was equivalent to that more intangible quality of trustworthiness, which would also include being sprung of a pure Christian line. When Luis Ruiz de Arriola tried to prove his *hidalguía* before the courts in 1611, he recalled how his grandfather, a notary of the village of

Colomera near Granada, had always been entrusted with Inquisition business in preference to the other notary in town 'because he was a gentleman from the Basque Country' (where no Moors or Jews had been allowed to live). In another case from Granada, the alderman Guillén de Contreras appealed that his brother should be decapitated as a noble, not hanged as a commoner for fraud (1640). One aged priest who acted as witness to the reputation of the family, recalled how he had listened as a child to his elders discussing family backgrounds: 'In those days most of the citizens who had come to Granada recently would frequent each other and talk about their origins, since the upheavals and rebellions in this kingdom were so fresh in people's minds and there were so many Moors, so that everyone was keen to say who he was and where he came from.' The opening of the Indies kept alive this frontier mentality. Thus, Juan de Córdova, the fourteen-year-old son of a silk merchant in Granada, set out to prove his *hidalguía* in 1625, for 'I am intending to go to the kingdoms of the Indies, so that if I enter religion or marry out there, there may be a record of where I come from and whose son and grandson I am, and that I am a pure-blooded Old Christian.'[7]

It was never suggested, of course, that good lineage on its own should be a passport to elite status. The chronicler of the Andalusian nobility, Argote de Molina, himself of somewhat uncertain gentry background, wrote in 1588 of the famous Stephen Bathory, who had died shortly before, that he had risen from being a 'simple knight' to become king of Poland, while the 'one time schoolmaster', Xarife, had taken command of Morocco. 'This was and is a very common phenomenon in every age, so that with these examples each man may persevere in virtue, for it leads to great things, when allied with diligence and perseverance.' Shortly afterwards, the Cortes of 1593 warned the king against tightening up on the requirements for *hidalguía*: 'If you look at all the histories of old, you will see that no better means was ever found of strengthening the disposition to serve the commonwealth than to allow its members entry into the ruling councils and offices, whereby nobility was acquired.'[8]

But that, perhaps, was the essence of the problem in the early modern period: the rise of too many new men, with the consequent risk of subverting the social hierarchy. Privileges of nobility, but without noble status, had been allowed to those who were regarded as in some way benefiting the commonwealth. Thus, graduates of the principal universities of Salamanca, Valladolid, Alcalá and Bologna enjoyed exemption from taxation, from being gaoled for debt or from being tortured if accused of a crime. Those who had over 1,000 ducats of property in Andalusia were expected to maintain a horse and weapons and were known as 'commoner knights' (*caballeros villanos* or *cuantiosos*), and enjoyed similar privileges. But the question of whether one could go on from there to become a full noble was more delicate. Guardiola noted in 1591 that a brave commoner might be knighted on the field of battle, but only a *hidalgo*, of known ancestry, should be admitted to that vanguard of chivalry, the Military Orders. As in other European countries, the monarchy began to put noble status up for sale in the sixteenth century, though the response seems to have been more disappointing in Castile than elsewhere. The reasons were expressed forcefully enough by Pedro Crespo, the peasant hero of Calderón's drama *The Mayor of Zalamea*, in answer to his son's suggestion that he should buy nobility in order to exempt his household from the billeting of soldiers. 'Is there anyone who is not aware that I, though of pure Christian blood, am a plain man?' People would say 'that I am noble for 5,000 or 6,000 *reales*, and that is money, not honour, for no man can purchase honour'. Yet the father goes on, later in the play, to advise his son, who is setting off to serve the king, to 'aspire, in a prudent way, to better yourself'.

And it is this gradual acceptance by one's fellows and superiors which is a marked feature of the frontier society that was Spain. The family of Saint Teresa of Avila managed in this way to cover their origin as converted Jews and traders, and acquire *hidalguía*, within a couple of generations. The saint's grandfather, Juan Sánchez, had been penanced by the Inquisition for practising Judaic rites in 1485. Ten years later he had moved from Toledo across the Guadarrama mountains to Avila, where he continued his woollen and silk business. His sons branched out into the more respectable world of tax-farming and finance. The eldest son, father of Saint Teresa, married a patrician lady, and in 1522 he and his brothers gathered their aristocratic friends to testify before the courts to the *hidalguía* of the family. Though the case was contested and though Teresa's brothers found it prudent to emigrate to the Indies, where fewer questions were asked, the grandchildren managed to climb a step higher into the Orders of Chivalry.[9] Purity of Blood (*limpieza de sangre*) was an added, complicating factor in the whole story of hierarchy in Spain. One could be a noble and of non-Christian ancestry, and therefore something less than a true noble – ineligible, in theory, for the Orders of Chivalry. Hence the joy which the Valencian noble Bernardo Catalá de Valeriola felt in 1601 when his brother, a Dominican friar, was promoted as assessor (*calificador*) of the Inquisition, for 'they went over again our four quarterings, which pleased me, especially for the Valeriola line' – where there was suspicion of Jewish ancestry.[10]

The sheer proliferation of these investigations of ancestry, covering both *hidalguía* and *limpieza*, gave a new twist to the old concern with establishing one's background in a racially mixed society. From the middle of the sixteenth century, monasteries, cathedral chapters, university colleges and the chancery courts began to pile up archives on this business. The Cortes of 1593 suggested that the great expansion of warrants of nobility being issued by the courts over the previous twenty years had something to do with the need to prove exemptions from the levies of troops and billeting which were becoming an increasing nuisance. But more likely the development of the bureaucratic state itself fostered the need and the ability to set down in writing what had previously been the gossip of a mobile, frontier land. One may note that as well as the formal attempt to prove *hidalguía* in the king's high court, there were many more interim *informaciones de testigos* (affidavits) sworn out by parties seeking release from gaol for debt and the like. These documents had only a doubtful legal status, but they could be a demonstration that a family did indeed enjoy a superior status in the eyes of its neighbours.

Before the diffusion of registers of baptism and marriage in the later sixteenth century, it was actually rather hard to document ancestry, other than by common repute. The witnesses to the investigation of the Granadan merchant's son, Juan de Córdova, spoke of his relationship to the counts of Alcaudete. A sixty-year-old illiterate weaver's wife, presented by the Córdovas, recalled a conversation with a man from Alcaudete, who had told her that Juan's great-great-grandfather 'had been a brother or a first cousin of the count of Alcaudete, but she does not remember for sure if he said brother [*hermano*] or first cousin [*primo hermano*]'.[11] Bernardo Catalá de Valeriola recorded in his diary his anger at the 'boldness' of Doctor Jeroni Valeriola, armed as a knight in the Cortes of 1604 for his services to the Crown, going on to claim that he was of the same Valeriola line as himself. 'Since he and his relatives are wealthy, they are making good matches.' So, to nip this usurpation of status in the bud, Bernardo summoned twenty-six of his friends to testify before the governor of Valencia – *ad perpetuam rei memoriam* – that this new lawyer-knight had no blood ties with himself. The governor rubricked the testimony on 14 March 1605, 'and in case any register of this tribunal goes missing', he had the declarations recorded as well before the chancery court and that of the archbishop.[12]

The sheer impreciseness and confusion of status, therefore, has always to be borne in mind. In the Crown of Aragon it was, indeed, easier to tell who was or was not a noble because of the existence of flourishing estates of the realm, which met in regular session and kept lists of members. In Castile, not paying direct taxes might be one sign of noble status, and there were towns where certain offices were reserved for *hidalgos*. But the Cortes of 1593 pointed out how uncertain and non-universal such indicators were, and that the basic test was common fame, as established by witnesses. As one witness for Jacinto de Fuentes, alderman of Granada, put it in 1625, a *hidalgo* went around with his fellows, 'showing off, and turning up for fiestas and tournaments with many servants and horses . . .'. The more wealth one had, suggested one writer in 1629, the easier it was to rise into this charmed circle: 'for we see time and again that common folk, if they are rich and powerful and show themselves generous to their neighbours who might speak against them . . . not only win a reputation for nobility but for distinction'.[13] The peasant girl Dorotea told Don Quijote in the same vein about her parents, 'plain folk . . . pure Old Christians, but so pure that their wealth and fine life-style are winning them little by little the title of *hidalgos*'.

There was another way of rising in the world, at least in the bad old days of civil war in late medieval Castile: intimidation. In 1550 the town council of Salvatierra, near Cáceres, denounced twenty-five named individuals who had usurped *hidalguía* – 'wealthy men, well connected and well supported by their friends . . . We are afraid that for challenging their status they will wound or kill or dishonour us, as they killed others in this region who stood up to them in the same way.' It was one of the standard questions posed by the courts investigating nobility, whether the family had been exempted from taxes 'because they were men of power, or allied to great men who held castles or fortresses . . . or because they were so wealthy and powerful that no one would have dared include them in a tax list'.[14] Even as the threat of violence receded after the early sixteenth century, money continued to play a key role in the usurpation of noble status. Speaking of *limpieza de sangre* a century later, the Inquisitor General Andrés Pacheco noted: 'great offences are committed in the sight of God in the enquiries . . . and most often those who have most to hide get a declaration of purity of blood, while those who are of Old Christian stock cannot, because they have not intrigued enough or have too many enemies'.[15]

There was increasing concern, therefore, with the disorderliness of social mobility in early modern Spain. The main issue, as regards *hidalguía*, was probably not government fear of losing tax revenue, since the direct taxes paid by commoners were a relatively small and shrinking part of the budget. Rather, it was the tidiness of the bureaucratic mind which led the strengthened monarchy to regulate social hierarchy. Hence in a sweeping decree of 1592 Philip II ruled that witnesses to nobility must be interrogated directly by a high court judge, rather than allowing their statements to be taken down by a clerk, with all the risk that entailed of laxity or fraud. In a major statement on the subject the following year, the Cortes argued that this would damage poor rural *hidalgos*, especially from that seedbed of the medieval Reconquest, the mountains of the north stretching from the Basque Country to Galicia, who had no money to pay for a judge to visit their villages. The new law would only encourage commoners on the town councils, 'with the natural hatred which they bear towards the *hidalgos*, to hound any of that number who lacks means'. And the Cortes went on, as we mentioned above, to point out the inconvenience of too strict a standard of proof for nobility. It was a similar point which some town councillors of Toledo made in 1586 about Philip II's attempt to reserve noble office there for genuine 'old nobles': 'there is no more hateful thing, nor anything which generates more rancour and vendettas or is more likely to upset the peace of a group of citizens than to examine their status and lineages'.[16]

In practice, the law of 1592, as amended in 1594, seems to have been a dead letter for much of the seventeenth century, during which the only curtailment of social mobility may have been the decline of wealth within Spanish society. In any case, a fresh attempt was made to stabilise the social hierarchy with the advent of the new Bourbon dynasty in 1703. The law of that year complained of the continued growth by stealth of the numbers of the nobility. No one henceforth was to be accorded that status unless he had furnished explicit proof to his local town council, which was to forward all documents to the high courts. The law tightened up an older provision of Henry IV (1454–74), never properly enforced. What had changed in the interval was really the institution of parish registers of vital events, so that claimants were now expected regularly to furnish a good run of baptismal certificates going back at least three or four generations.

Overall, the number of *hidalgos* must have risen to a peak some time in the early seventeenth century – though this may be an optical illusion, created by the increasing bureaucratisation of the concept. In Cartagena, for example, a clear list of who was noble only began to be kept from the later sixteenth century, as fiscal pressure grew and tax exemption became an issue. In Castile as a whole, nobles were one in ten of the population in the census of 1591, with great contrasts between the Basque Country, where virtually everyone was an *hidalgo*, and León, where a quarter were, and Andalusia, with only one in twenty.[17] But the following century marked a dramatic reversal of the trend, and by the end of the Old Regime, following the tighter criteria for establishing *hidalguía*, only about 5 per cent of the population were accorded this status in the censuses.

In a sense, what one witnesses is the passing of the age of Don Quixote, of the rustic knight whose ideology of chivalry and lack of means were both an embarrassment in the modern age. The Cortes of 1585 investigated the popularisation of the title 'don', quietly usurped – 'over the last fifty years' – by the upwardly mobile, tax farmers and ministers of the Crown, when in times past it had been reserved for the titled nobility. The complaints about the spread of luxury at this time and the attempt to introduce sumptuary legislation restricting the use of coaches and fine clothes were all tribute to a similar phenomenon, of the rise of an aristocracy of power and wealth, whose lineage and knightly valour might be suspect, but whose role within the body politic had to be recognised by the grant of honours. As well as the creation of the 'dons' from below, there was the explicit conferment of titles by the Crown, corresponding to that fear of Castillo de Bobadilla in 1597 that feudal lords were often just the newly rich. Philip III created 51 marquises and 62 counts in all Spain between 1598 and 1621, while Charles II (1665–1700) made 236 and 80 respectively. There were 60 titled nobles in Spain in 1520, 124 in 1597, 241 in 1631 and 533 by 1700.[18] What we seem to be witnessing here is the harnessing of the idea of nobility more explicitly to the service of the state, through the conferment of public recognition on the wealthy and powerful.

'Nobility is kept alive and strong when it is attached to wealth,' wrote one commentator in 1629, 'and without money it is like a dead thing, for those who are in need have often to turn their hands to vile things.' Viciana advised his readers that, while all nobles were in a sense equals, 'titled lords and wealthy knights' would provide the framework of his study for obvious reasons. And he dedicated the third book of his chronicle to Don Giner Rabaça de Perellós, who 'keeps a household richly adorned, wherein you will find well appointed officers and servants, and many horses and mules in his stables, and in his chamber many rich jewels and ornaments and silverware and tapestries'. Nobility was, of course, character, but 'God has compensated the virtue and honour of these good men with temporal possessions'.[19] Honour led to honours. The king 'is obliged to give alms for the love of God', ran a typical chancery formula of the fifteenth century, setting up lordships in Andalusia; 'it behoves the estate of monarchs and of nobles to ennoble, honour and privilege those vassals who give him loyal and good service'.[20]

It was, as we suggested in Chapter 5, in the later Middle Ages that a feudal aristocracy began to take shape in Castile. As well as the natural trend in this direction prompted by the colonisation of a frontier land, there was a change in the relationship of the nobility with the cities, within whose walls the gestation of their power began, and with the Crown. Feudal lords had come and gone in earlier centuries of Spanish history, but it was from the fourteenth century – as the humanist Antonio de Guevara was one of the first to remark in an essay of 1526 – that a modern aristocratic hierarchy really began to take shape. While the usurping Trastámara dynasty proved remarkably generous after 1369 in rewarding its supporters and courting their continued favours, the new families which rose at this time and which would constitute the political elite of early modern Spain (Velasco, Manrique, Enríquez, Pimentel, Mendoza, Pacheco, Córdoba . . .), managed to perpetuate their power by a new inheritance strategy: the *mayorazgo* or perpetual entail of their estates. 'It is clear that by the division of inheritance patrimonies are weakened and undermined,' wrote the Valencian jurist Cerdán de Tallada. That had been the lesson of the great families of the Middle Ages, with their numerous offspring and clan-like structure, in which a clear line of descent in a particular fief seemed often to be lacking. When the count of Tendilla created his entail in 1478, he said that it was 'to increase our house and make it greater and leave behind a memory of ourselves, and also so that the descendant who is to be lord of all should have more patrimony and power to gather to himself and shelter all our other descendants'.[21]

The trend was not all one way. Successful families liked to split off new acquisitions and create a second patrimony for a younger son. Thus, the Constable of Castile, Juan Fernández de Velasco, duke of Frías, set up a substantial new *mayorazgo* for this purpose in 1612. But his idea was still that the brothers should cooperate for the good of the family as whole: 'In great houses we do not talk or think so much about the law of *legítimas* (guaranteed portions of the inheritance reserved for each child), for the first law is by custom, as it ought to be, that younger brothers depend on the elder and look to enhancing his authority and the grandeur of his house, so that the elder, in return for so much respect, should always look out for his brothers, always helping and favouring them.'[22] The social reformer Mateo López Bravo wrote in 1616 that entails were useful in a monarchy, creating a wealthy elite which had a stake in upholding the political order and which could attach their networks of clients and dependants to the Crown. It was a similar point that the Valencian jurist Cerdán de Tallada made in 1604, that the great estates might provide a framework for the body politic, defending the throne against its enemies both at home and abroad.[23] Yet both writers soon revised their opinion, pointing out the damaging consequences, social and economic, of the institution.

The aim of the *mayorazgo* was to confer stability on the aristocracy, but it is not clear that it was wholly successful in doing so. One problem which became acute was that of succession, where there were no male offspring of the previous holder. In the demographic circumstances of the pre-industrial period, it may come as little surprise to find, for example, that barely 3 per cent of the patricians of Madrid managed to hand on their entails in the direct male line to their great-grandchildren.[24] Females were encouraged to marry cousins in order to preserve the name, and daughters normally took precedence over more distant male kin after the law of 1615 – unless there was a specific intention in the original foundation to exclude them. A more serious problem than the shortage of male heirs, at least in the short term, was the too great numbers of offspring born to many noble houses. Gerbet's systematic study of the nobility of Extremadura under Ferdinand and Isabel indicates that titled families had to provide for five or six surviving children at the death of the holder, whereas the knights and the gentry had four or five. These averages tend to iron out the differences between those who had few and those who were at their wits' end in providing for a numerous progeny. The third duke of Gandia (1495–1543), father of Saint Francis Borgia, had nineteen legitimate children, as well as one illegitimate, whom he recommended to the care of his heir; and the genealogy of the dukes of Infantado in the sixteenth century is replete with successive generations of a dozen or more offspring.[25]

In the Extremadura of Ferdinand and Isabel younger children seem to have found little difficulty in marrying and establishing themselves in life. But as the frontier closed and the entail became more general, the situation became more grim. Already in 1510 and 1542 the Valencian Cortes referred to the plight of younger sons, who were now demanding subsistence payments as a matter of humanity if not of law from their elder brother in order to prevent themselves falling into 'poverty and distress'. The Valencians threw their support, though, behind the elder brother – as did the Catalan gentry in 1585, who strengthened an earlier measure of the fourteenth century that a father did not have to leave more than a quarter of his estate for division among his younger offspring.[26] The Venetian ambassador Soranzo (1597–1602) discussed the options open to these unfortunates: 'either to receive as favour whatever their elder brother is pleased to give them, or to obtain ecclesiastical benefices, or to serve the king in war, or to marry some woman who has means' (taking her surname as a result). In theory the heir was supposed to look after his siblings and see to their placement in life. But was this really the case? 'Ask what has happened to so many sons and daughters and their descendants who have come to grief,' wrote Cerdán de Tallada, 'some falling by the wayside or dying in hospitals, and others . . . taking shelter in convents.' As a judge himself – and a noble, whose relations with all his sons seem to have been particularly close – he bewailed the proliferation of lawsuits over alimony between elder brothers and their cadets. Two centuries later, towards the end of the Old Regime, another member of the gentry class, the reforming statesmen Jovellanos, was still denouncing the mistreatment of *segundones* (younger sons) under the laws of entail. 'Nothing is more repugnant than to see individuals from noble families, whose first-born hold fat *mayorazgos*, lacking a career or a position, condemned to poverty, celibacy and idleness.'[27]

A pious father like Don Luis de Requesens was genuinely troubled by the lack of resources for his younger children, when he came to draw up his will in 1573, shortly before leaving for Flanders as governor of that insurgent province. If he had more than one son, his trustees were 'to try and direct one into the church, and another into the Order of Saint John . . . or into the service of the lord king, each one according to the inclinations he shows'. As regards daughters, if he were to have more than the one whom he had recently married to the marquis of Los Vélez, he could only afford a dowry for a nunnery, not for a marriage. If these girls showed no inclination to become nuns, they were to have a small annuity and go to live with 'some lady who is a kinswoman of our house'.[28]

Undoubtedly mobilising cash for dowries was the single biggest headache in the lives of most aristocrats of the early modern period. The size of the dowry had been tending to grow in the Renaissance period, in Spain as elsewhere in Europe – testimony, some thought, to the materialism of the age and the growth of a money economy, perhaps equally a reflection of the need to mobilise liquid funds somehow when so much land was being tied down by entail. Marriage negotiations among the nobility came to resemble a game of 'beggar my neighbour', or a version of the dog chasing its own tail, with some families scoring a coup at one generation and falling back into debt at the next as they saw their daughters come of age to marry. From the later sixteenth century the dowries of the house of Gandia had reached their peak of 100,000 ducats, virtually twice the annual revenue of the estate. Lesser Valencian aristocrats might be content with about a tenth of this sum on average, often more than what they collected in rent in a year.[29] Since each duke of Gandia regularly married off two of his daughters over the sixteenth and seventeenth centuries, he faced a herculean task in actually funding this strategy – which, of course, brought valuable connections and influence of an indirect kind. The bulk of the dowry would often be settled as an annuity on the entail – easier to do in Valencia than in Castile, where such settlements would require specific royal authorisation.

The success or failure of a particular generation of a noble house might be measured in terms of its ability to settle its daughters in life. But the care for daughters could also be reflected in a concentration of resources upon them at the expense of younger male siblings, who were expected to make their own way in the world. Hence, the Portuguese aristocrat Mello, writing in 1651, noted that a father might well 'recruit' a son-in-law through marriage to his daughter from a slightly lower social category than his own. A saving could be made on the dowry in such a case. If the suitor were not quite of impeccable lineage, yet 'if he stood well at court or were very wealthy or was eminent in arms or letters', he might be an acceptable match. Among the nobles of Extremadura, one suspects that many of the cases of young *hidalgos* leaving home to settle down in their bride's town of residence reflect this pattern, as do the examples of restricted dowry paid out by the members of the Council of Castile to their sons-in-law between 1621 and 1746.[30]

The question of how the great families were to settle their daughters depended, therefore, on the pool of upwardly mobile suitors from the gentry. The younger son had typically to fend for himself – in service to the church or the king or in 'trade overseas', as the refrain cited by Cervantes put it. The Catalan gentleman

Perot de Vilanova tells us in his autobiography how he set out in 1561 to visit his younger brother Gaspar, whom he had not seen for ten years. Educated together at the university of Lleida, Perot had gone on to inherit the family estate, while Gaspar had been placed as a clerk in the Council of Castile. Fitted out with a suit of clothes at the start of his new job in 1552, Gaspar 'since then did not ask or spend a penny from our patrimony'. The two brothers hardly recognised each other, but great joy followed the reunion. Since Gaspar had acquired a position of receiver general of the Council, 'he did a lot for me with his money', commented Perot. 'May God grant him a long life,' he concluded piously, 'for the good of His service, and may he rise to become a great man so that he may do good to Him and to everyone else.'[31] One recalls the words of the Franciscan moralist Juan de Pineda, who wrote scathingly of the imbalance in career prospects between the heir to the *mayorazgo* and his younger brothers. 'The heir is not allowed to study . . . and the other sons who have nothing to inherit are put to school . . . But the schoolmen . . . win honour and wealth, and protect their ignorant, wealthy brothers and run their affairs.'[32]

More often, though, the younger brother remained like a millstone around the neck of the heir. The first count of Carlet provided an annuity of 300 Valencian pounds a year for his younger son, Felipe. After his father's death in 1617, Felipe went off to Flanders to serve as a private soldier. By 1622 he had risen to the rank of captain, whereupon his brother, the second count of Carlet, decided to cut off his annuity, alleging that the estate was so encumbered with debt that he and his wife had barely 2,100 pounds clear between them. A bitter lawsuit followed, which envenomed relations between the two for years thereafter. In a twist to a familiar story, the count of Real managed to offload the alimony he was paying his younger brother, Alfonso de Calatayud, by appointing him to command the company which he had been asked to raise in 1630 for the campaign in Italy. What the count had to pay in bounties and equipment for the soldiers was compensated for by placing Alfonso on the royal payroll. But another brother, the priest Francisco, was at daggers drawn with the count over his annuity, and furious when his request to the Crown to be appointed archdeacon of Alicante in 1643 was countered by his elder brother's desire to obtain the post for one of his own eleven offspring.[33] The sheer volume of petitions for favours coming from the gentry of Castile or Aragon cast light on the tensions within families created by the problem of younger sons, but also suggest the enormous resilience of the system – not a neat pyramid of deference and obligation as envisaged by theorists of the entail, perhaps, but a struggling throng of candidates from which a ruling elite could be recruited.

Before we explore that point in a little more detail, it might be useful to say something about the economic situation of the great families, since on the deepening sense of crisis here so much else was to turn. In general, the rents of the feudal lords were fairly buoyant over the early modern period, with the notable exception of the seventeenth century, an interval of recession. In Old Castile, where seigneurs owned little land directly and relied mainly on fixed dues from copyholders or on alienated royal excise taxes, incomes were probably less dynamic in the sixteenth century than in Andalusia, where many of the lords farmed for the market; but the difference was probably narrowing by the eighteenth century, as a market economy penetrated the countryside of Spain as a whole. In Catalonia and Valencia a more typically feudal system placed some restraints on seigneurial enterprise in this respect, but in Valencia the eighteenth century also saw great expansion: thus, the rents in many parts of the Gandia estates tripled between 1710 and 1790.[34] In other words, it is difficult to see the early modern period as a whole as representing any real crisis for the seigneurial class. Certainly, a sufficient number of the nobility kept a watchful eye on the administration of their rents. Books for the running of seigneurial households became popular from the sixteenth century onwards, setting out the duties of stewards and accountants. One of the letters of Don Diego de Vargas (1643–1704), governor of New Mexico, from El Paso in 1691 to his son-in-law advises him of the arrangements in hand to increase rentals from the family estates round Granada by providing more irrigation. If the grain can be stored after the harvest until the following March or April, then it 'will sell at the best price'.[35]

Yet, despite the large rents of many nobles, 'you will find very few who know how to run their houses properly and who do not have huge debts', as the Venetian ambassador Tiepolo reported already in 1563. He blamed their lavish expenditure on 'liveries, gambling, benevolences, mistresses and jesters'. And his successor, ambassador Soranzo, painted much the same picture in 1602, though adding now that they could no longer get by: 'they do not pay what they owe and they are coming to be hated'.[36] What had gone wrong? There was, in the first place, the sheer difficulty of adjusting agrarian rents – often scattered in remote areas, always liable to be undermined by bad harvests or the poor state of the roads – to the relentless rhythm of an urban economy. Don Luis de Requesens, in his testament of 1573, alluded to the confusion built up in his accounts by the fact that his steward paid the bills which fell due with whatever money he had to hand, either his own or that of his master. In a chivalrous society, one expected to be repaid as much in favours as in cash, and questions only arose when the personal relationship between two men ended.

There was, in other words, an inherent tendency towards indebtedness in the structure of a pre-industrial economy, and the bigger the enterprise, the more sizeable its debt burden was liable to be. At the beginning of our period the count of Tendilla was complaining constantly about his lack of means and his need to sell off part of his large patrimony; yet he was at the same time acquiring other estates and engaging in their colonisation, as was the count of Benavente around the same time. But the process could not go on indefinitely. By 1580 the Cortes of Castile were considering the damage inflicted on society at large by the bankruptcy of so many great families, who had got others to stand surety for their obligations – 'and these cannot refuse to help them out, since they are their vassals or servants or so dependent on them that they cannot turn their backs'. Requesens in 1573 had engaged in a variety of expedients: letters of exchange on the

European fairs, which left him with an uneasy conscience in spite of the reassurance of his confessors ('for I am not a merchant'), mortgages on the estates of 'gentlemen who are friends of mine', and money borrowed on his behalf by his peasantry. Holders of an entail were not legally allowed to mortgage it without special royal dispensation, which created some uncertainty when a nobleman died. Thus, when the duke of Sessa passed away in 1606, of an illness brought on mainly (according to the chronicler Cabrera de Córdova) by 'a great melancholy, to which his many debts and lack of means contributed', his son and heir refused to take responsibility for 80,000 ducats worth of obligations left behind.[37]

The elaborate manoeuvring by the aristocracy and its creditors has to be viewed within a framework of constant renewal of resources within the ruling class. Most wealthy people in the Old Regime were or became nobles, and much of the borrowing was actually the reallocation of resources within this group. This is evidently true when one considers that the biggest cause of debt was likely to be the establishment of dowries. So, when the count of Buñol married his son and heir to the daughter of his creditor, Don Giner Rabaça de Perellós, in August 1609, the dowry of 15,000 Valencian pounds was partly paid in the cancellation of debts on the Buñol estate; and the count of Real's biggest creditors at this time included his own wife, his son-in-law and, indeed, the heiress Ana María Mateu, to whom he married his grandson and heir.[38]

But undoubtedly some great houses got themselves into such a muddle with their accounts that more drastic measures were needed. In 1594 the government had to take over the administration of the estates of the duke of Osuna, assigning him an allowance of 24,000 ducats, while devoting the rest of his rent-roll of 138,062 ducats to administration and the payment of his creditors.[39] These so-called 'sequestrations' became common in the early seventeenth century, but were far from satisfying the creditors. They represented how difficult it was to keep a check on what the seigneur was actually up to among his own vassals, and allegations of massive fraud usually led to some kind of *concordia* or 'agreement' between the two parties. Thus in 1633 the duke of Osuna recovered control of the administration of his estates, with a guarantee of retrenchment on his part and reimbursement of outstanding sums.

The assistance which the Crown gave to the great families in order to persuade the creditors to accept limitations on their demands became particularly evident in Valencia. There the premier nobleman, the duke of Gandia had gone bankrupt in 1604. He nevertheless proved able, in a last exercise of feudal power, to round up his Morisco peasants in the autumn of 1609, following royal orders for the expulsion of this people. His letter to the king of 9 October betrayed his sadness at 'the ruin of this land', but also affirmed: 'I am quite happy about all these losses, since I have been of service to Your Majesty, for it was for this that my house was founded. But I am confident that Your Majesty will be pleased to set it on its feet again, so that you may call on it again in time of need.' A major political battle developed, in fact, between the duke's creditors – well ensconced in the noble estate and led by the count of Buñol's brother – and the embattled grandee, who was a kinsman of the royal favourite, the duke of Lerma. Eventually, in 1621, the Council of Aragon resolved against following the plea of the creditors for the break-up and sale of the Gandia estates – a momentous political decision, which committed the monarchy to a campaign of persuasion among the disgruntled creditors, that they should reach a *concordia* with the duke, limiting their claims. The duke would recover control of his shrunken rent-roll of 28,810 Valencian pounds, out of which he would guarantee, as a first claim on the budget, an annual deposit of 10,000 pounds – a reduction of some two-thirds on the old interest payments. Probably no more than 133 of the 500 creditors ever formally accepted this agreement of 1622, but it was solemnly ratified by the Crown. Commenting on the decree publishing it on 26 February 1622, the priest Joan Porcar confided to his diary that the king had invoked 'all his supreme power and majesty and absolute lordship . . . in order to bail out the duke of Gandia, so that he will never have to pay what he owes to his creditors'.[40] One begins to understand what ambassador Soranzo was referring to when he spoke of the debt-ridden aristocracy becoming 'hateful' to the people; the risk was that they might drag the monarchy down with them.

The Venetian ambassadors had commented on the link between aristocratic indebtedness and the growing power of the monarchy, in the sense that those who were in debt could no longer cause trouble to the Crown. But the economic writers of the seventeenth century were beginning to see things in rather different terms, emphasising the harm done to society as a whole by this phenomenon. Deploring the concentration of nobles in wasteful idleness at court, Fernández Navarrete wrote in 1626 that 'if they would only reside on their estates, they would save money, they would not destroy their vassals, they would have funds with which to serve the king, they would look after their subjects like fathers . . .'. If the great aristocracy only destroyed itself, the situation might be tolerable: 'but, just as great trees, when they crash, bring down all that lives in their shade, so the bankruptcies of these lords ruin a countless number of vassals, servants and friends'.[41]

What seemed to be at stake here was the collapse of a traditional feudal hierarchy. The Venetian ambassadors commented on the loss of the military vocation of the nobility after the conquest of Granada in 1492. 'Young knights and gentlemen,' complained the Cortes in 1590, 'although they have the duty and inclination to ride on horseback, lack anyone to teach them, so that they spend their time idly strutting around, instead of learning skill and dexterity.' And their predecessors had attempted to revive the martial arts by spending public funds on tournaments, providing 'lances for the knights to exercise with, and music for their fiestas'.[42] It was a similar story in the Crown of Aragon. The Cortes of Valencia in 1537, and then again in 1552, arranged for subsidies to mount tournaments, 'for the good of the common weal, and for the better safeguarding and defence of the city and kingdom of Valencia'. In Catalonia, meanwhile, the medieval jousting fraternity of Saint George was revived in 1565 in order to arrest the perceived decline in the military vocation of noble youths. But the decline of the martial spirit seems to have gone on relentlessly. In 1626 Fernández Navarrete could write: 'Not so many years ago in all the noble houses you could find a stock of armour, pikes and arquebuses, which kept alive in the owner and his children the ardour for combat inherited from his ancestors' – but not any more.[43]

In 1604 Barthélemy Joly noted the contrast with France: 'Our gentlemen live in the country and practise soldiery since they are always on horseback, riding to the hunt . . . living in towns undermines the valour of the Spaniards.' But there was, perhaps, a more general problem: that war itself was becoming increasingly professionalised, and no longer open to the casual gentleman adventurer. The Granadan aristocrat, Pérez de Herrasti, could look back in the history of his family which he published in 1750 on the exploits of his ancestor, the second lord of Domingo Pérez, who had served Charles V in Flanders and Tunis. On his father's death in 1538, he had returned to take up his inheritance in Granada, taking with him 'a splendid baggage train of packmules, all well laden and decked out with his coat of arms, and the memoirs of that period assure us that he was carrying more than 20,000 ducats in gold and silver. Weren't those happy times in which a soldier could do so well for himself!'[44] From then on, a mixture of city politics and estate administration had kept the family in Granada, only torn from its roots by the turmoil of civil conflict in the War of the Spanish Succession (1702–13).

For many of the Spanish aristocracy life must have been one of rustic mediocrity. The humanist writer Antonio de Guevara, himself sprung of this milieu, in his attack on the lure of the court (1539), sketched a portrait of the type. The country gentleman should look after his household, 'visit the hospitals, succour the poor, be kind to orphans, give money to the less well-off', as well as 'frequenting monasteries, hearing many masses and listening to the sermons'; after which he could go off 'to prune his vines, see his farm, inspect his livestock and have a word with the ploughman', without losing 'a jot of his honour'.[45] A couple of generations later Cervantes left a memorable portrait of the genre, in the Knight of the Green Coat and, of course, in Don Quixote himself. The fifty-year-old knight of La Mancha, 'in the times when he had nothing to do (which was most of the year), gave himself over to reading about knights errant', forgetting his other occupations, the hunt and the running of his farm, which was tended for him by a lad who doubled up as a lackey when required. The dreadful problem for such men was idleness – the vice of *ocio*, against which preachers of the time were beginning to thunder. Esteban de Garibay, the historian of Philip II's reign, tells us in his memoirs of the pointlessness of his own existence as the eldest son and heir of a small Basque gentleman. After leaving university, he had little to do but mount fiestas and strut around town in fine clothes.

Though Guevara praised the quiet life of the village as truly Christian, he admitted that it was a hard option for a man of spirit to follow: 'Every time a post of bishop or an encomienda or a lieutenancy fall vacant, wild and pointless thoughts assail him, telling him that if he had not gone into retirement, he would surely have been promoted.' So, Cervantes describes the three brothers, *hidalgos* of

León, who were told by their father of the old Spanish proverb, that they must better themselves by service in the church, on the high seas (trade) or at the king's court. The eldest went abroad as a soldier, the second made a fortune in Peru, paying for the law studies of the youngest, who rose eventually to an appointment as judge in the high court of Mexico. It is a fictional portrait of a class to which Cervantes himself belonged and whose aspirations he knew well. As one reads the chronicles of the Spanish regions at this time, one comes across similar experiences. Cristóbal de Espinosa de Monteros figures in the chronicle of Jaén, for example, as a local gentleman who had left to join the army at twelve years of age, 'when a captain passed through this city enlisting people'. After five years at sea, he ended up in Mexico, calling on a wealthy uncle who was a merchant out there and who recommended him to a captain who was organising an expedition against the Indians. By 1608 he was in the Philippines, 'from where his parents in Jaén got a letter, telling them about a great battle which he had had with some pirates'. But since then, silence: 'We have heard nothing further from him.'[46]

Service to the king had been a traditional feature of the age of chivalry, now much augmented by the sheer growth of the Spanish empire. The expansion of the state, with all the opportunities it offered for careers in the army and the bureaucracy, was one of the signal features of the early modern period, and it was symbolised in Spain by the growing importance of the court. Medieval Castile had lacked a fixed capital, even a fixed 'national shrine', like the great mausolea of Westminster Abbey or the Abbey of Saint Denis near Paris, where the rulers of England and France were interred. Instead, the bones of Spanish kings lay scattered in half a dozen locations, following the pattern of the Reconquista. It was one of the achievements of Philip II to give his country a new political and cultural centre – a national pantheon in the Escorial (built between 1562 and 1585), where the rulers, starting with Charles V, came to be buried, and a capital in Madrid. Already in the fifteenth century the high court had been settled in Valladolid, and government papers were becoming so voluminous that it was decided to find them a fixed home too, near Valladolid, in the great castle of Simancas, in 1547. But it was not until 1561 that Philip II chose Madrid as a seat of administration for the empire. It had already been growing in popularity from some time before – the geographer Pedro de Medina refers already in 1548 to the great building work being carried out on the royal residence there. It had advantages over its nearest rivals – better drinking water than nearby Toledo, the old imperial capital of the Visigoths and the seat of the ecclesiastical primate of Spain, and better access to timber and firewood than Valladolid, which was also regarded as damp and unhealthy, though better supplied with bread. Ultimately, though, the decision finally to abandon Valladolid in 1606 (after the capital had been temporarily shifted there in 1601), may have depended, as the chronicler Cabrera de Córdova tells us, on the complaints of other cities – and some of the most important, like Seville – that it was just too remote, too far north.

In any case, the mushroom growth of Madrid – from a city of perhaps 20,000 people in 1561 to one of 45,000 by 1597, then a maximum of 150,000 by the middle of the seventeenth century – caused some soul-searching. Joly pointed out in 1604 the difficulty of keeping this land-locked city supplied with food, while Sancho de Moncada in 1619 noted that Madrid, not being a trading city like Paris or London, was attracting this huge population for all the wrong reasons, as parasites on the court. The Cortes began to complain in the early 1600s that, whereas Philip II had only been spending 400,000 ducats a year on his court, Philip III was managing to get through 1,300,000. There were 1,700 or so posts in the royal households in 1623 – including those of the queen and the king's brothers – as compared with 762 in that of Charles V.[47] However, if the court was beginning to assume a new importance, it was far from satisfying the aspirations of all who sought its favour. The Sevillian nobleman, Alonso Enríquez de Guzmán, who set out, armed with a letter of introduction to a remote kinsman, the Admiral of Castile, to claim a position in Charles V's household in 1518, was rebuffed by the royal secretary, Los Cobos. 'Do not think that you will get what you are seeking just by showing us your family tree,' he was told, for others with as long a lineage and more distinguished service 'cannot get what they ask'. The humanist writer Eugenio de Salazar (c.1530–1601) was pretty scathing about 'men whose rents and fortune are not sufficient for them to have at their beck and call a lackey or a page-boy', but who want command over a city and its region. Since there were so many claimants, 'if God does not work with these offices a miracle like that of the five loaves and two fishes, not one in a hundred of the mouths now gaping open at court will get a bite'.[48]

Talent rather than lineage must be the first rule for appointment to office, affirmed that testy Valencian humanist Fadrique Furió Ceriol in his famous essay on statesmanship of 1559. 'Some will say that knights and lords have to be rewarded according to the authority of their houses and the services of their persons. I would answer to this that I say no different; but that it is not the same thing to reward a man and appoint him to the government.'[49] What, indeed, was happening in Renaissance Spain, as in the rest of Europe at the time, was the formation of a new elite, based on the expanding competence of the state. The chronicler Lorenzo Galíndez de Carvajal (1472–1532) echoed a conventional wisdom when he wrote that the Catholic Kings, Ferdinand and Isabel, 'paid more attention to placing men who were prudent and had talent, though they were of middling background, than men who were high-placed and from the principal families'. And it was the same point which Don Diego Hurtado de Mendoza, himself a younger son of the count of Tendilla, made in his great history of the Morisco uprising of 1568. Recalling how his own family had been edged out of power in Granada, he referred to their rivals, the judges and ministers of the Crown, promoted since the days of Ferdinand and Isabel, as 'a middle class (*gente media*), half-way between the great and the small, men given over to the profession of law'.[50]

In practice, this bureaucratic elite was often drawn from the ranks of the gentry, often from among the small noble families which served as *regidores* in the royal towns of Old Castile. Of those appointed to the chief governing body, the Council of Castile, between 1621 and 1746, 90 per cent could trace their noble ancestry back beyond their great-grandparents, though there was usually a tradition of university study and legal careers in the family.[51] A system of patronage and clientage within the university colleges ensured that the relatives or dependants of existing members of the bureaucracy stood a better chance than outsiders of being considered for promotion. Attempts to open up this *cursus honorum* in the later eighteenth century did not, perhaps, markedly change its basic character. The leading minister of the Enlightenment, Campomanes (1723–1802), was born into a petty *hidalgo* family of Asturias. After learning Latin with an uncle who was a canon, then studying for a while at the university of Seville, he moved to Madrid in 1742 as a clerk in a lawyer's office. He married his employer's daughter, set up his own legal practice in 1749, from where he made useful contacts with the great – the counts of Benavente and Miranda, the archbishop of Toledo – and eventually was promoted as fiscal of the Council of Castile in 1762. His lively, enquiring mind, his range of personal contacts, and his key role in preparing the case for the expulsion of the Jesuits in 1767, gained him the promotions which culminated with his tenure of president of the Council, and effective prime minister of Spain between 1783 and 1791.[52] It is often difficult, at this distance in time, to recapture the personality and charisma of such men that must have recommended them to their superiors. Of some, like the first minister Ensenada (1743–54), the son of a notary with pretensions to *hidalguía*, we are told (by the man himself in his later reminiscences) that he got his start in life as a clerk in various legal offices and commercial companies because of his good handwriting (then a prized asset like command of information technology today). He had the good luck to be noticed by the naval minister Patiño and brought to Madrid as his assistant (1720), from where he climbed to royal favour.[53] From an earlier period, the careers of the great secretaries of the Catholic Kings, of Charles V and of Philip II, suggest broadly similar lines of ascent. Fernando del Pulgar's intelligence shines through in his letters; the more discreet Francisco de los Cobos was a skilled manipulator of patronage. Discretion, charm, a good memory, a knack of pleasing the right people: all of these were ingredients in the making of the perfect bureaucrat.

But the ability of the state to command obedience depended on wider social ties – in spite of Furió Ceriol's warning that 'the good councillor must rid himself of any ties of friendship, kinship, partiality or faction'. In practice, one feels, the stability of the early modern polity depended rather on the contrary phenomenon, of a network of favours which linked the bureaucrat in with the older social elites. Thus, 40 per cent of the Councillors of Castile married women from their province of origin, rather than choosing them randomly at court, and most chose to found their *mayorazgos* not in Madrid but at home. The career of one of the most influential Andalusian families of the seventeenth century, the Bohorques, may serve as an illustration. Alonso Núñez de Bohorques, from the small Sevillian town of Villamartín and claiming descent from a man knighted after a victory over the Moors in 1340, rose through the law to become judge of the high court of

Granada. A strategic marriage to a Girón girl, daughter of another Granadan magistrate and a remote kinswoman of the duke of Osuna, helped his ascent into the Council of Castile by 1588, while he began to purchase lands and jurisdiction round Granada, laying the foundations for a new noble dynasty. His son Antonio Alvarez de Bohorques (1575–1640) obtained a post of gentleman in the royal household and married a cousin of the Ximénez de Góngora clan, who were patricians of Cordoba and members of the Council of Finance, to which Antonio himself was appointed in turn. His interests and connections ranged, thus, from Madrid to Cordoba (which city he represented in the Cortes) and Granada, where he and his mother built a splendid mausoleum for their dynasty (the monastery of Saint Basil). Created marquis of Los Trujillos in 1632, he was in a good position to act as a power-broker between the government and regional elites in Andalusia. The career of Francisco de los Cobos (1482–1547) illustrated much the same phenomenon. Of a petty gentry family of Ubeda (Andalusia), he became by the time of his death a powerful aristocrat as well as a minister of the Crown, lord of several fiefs in Andalusia as well as near the court in Valladolid, and an in-law of the Zafras, who had risen under the Catholic Kings, through ministerial office and a post of town councillor in recently conquered Granada, to lordship in that province.

Service to the Crown, thus, involved a restructuring of the old balance of power between centre and periphery, between bureaucratic and feudal elites. The Venetian ambassador Soranzo (1597–1602) noted an apparent change which was taking place in his own time. Under the late king, Philip II, the great families had been 'without authority, kept down by his majesty, and not employed by him in important positions'; whereas the new monarch 'makes use of them and pays them compliments', appointing great numbers to the Council of State in particular. It has often been suggested that the aristocracy staged a political comeback in the seventeenth century, but it has never been clear whether this was a genuine recovery of power by the old families, or merely an optical illusion, caused by the aristocratisation of the ministerial elite, like the Cobos and the Bohorques.

Service to the Crown had been the origin of the fortune of most of the grandees, and the continuation of that tradition was evident throughout the early modern period. Removed from the governorship of Granada for his lack of success against the Moorish rebels in 1570, the marquis of Mondéjar protested to the low-born chief minister, Cardinal Espinosa, against the damage done to his reputation. The king was obliged in conscience and honour to find him a new job, 'so that my honour, reputation and income do not suffer more than they already have for no good cause, for, given the services of my ancestors, of my father and myself, I deserve much favour and indulgence from His Majesty'.[54] The running of the empire depended in great measure on the willingness of those with resources to deploy their best efforts. The third duke of Alcalá had begun to serve the Crown as viceroy of Catalonia in 1618, then ambassador to Rome in 1625, from where he moved to the viceroyalty of Naples in 1629, then to Sicily in 1632, before dying at the age of fifty-three on his way to the Congress of Cologne

(1637). The duke of Frías, in his testament of 1612, listed his long record of service, including the governorship of Milan, membership of the Council of State and participation in the peace talks with England (1604). 'I have served in this and all other business which has come my way with great love and fidelity to my king and great peril to my own life, including the loss of my health . . . not to mention the heavy expenses and losses to my estate which I have incurred.'[55]

Part of the obligations of service was the looking after hordes of dependants. Employment under the Crown enormously increased one's own patronage and hence influence in the wider world, but equally it could be very costly. When the duke of Alcalá left for his Roman embassy in 1625, he was accompanied by 32 pages from 'illustrious Sevillian families'; and when the duke of Alba passed through Valencia in 1622 on his way to the viceroyalty of Naples, his magnificent suite of 100 men on horseback and 81 on foot, all in livery of bright velvet, caught the eye of the local chronicler. There were official salaries, of course, but they were generally too small. The writer Diego Hurtado de Mendoza, ambassador to Rome, complained in 1552 that the 5,000 escudos assigned to him every year went on feeding his household of 120. He had had to borrow 9,000 more on his own account, especially for repairs to the fortress of Siena through which Spanish troops passed north. Without funds, he could not maintain the authority of his office: 'I would not mention all this, if it did not involve a certain question of honour.' After the fall of Siena to the French later that year, Mendoza was relieved of his post. In a stormy interview with Charles V, he protested that the dismissal had called his honour into question, that he was the victim of slander at court, 'and thus I begged His Majesty to put a stop to the murmuring by giving me new honours and promotion'.[56] Service to the Crown was a delicate business, which, if it could enhance the prestige of a nobleman, could also bring him low if royal favour was withdrawn or deemed inadequate.

Above all, there was the problem of whether the costs of service might outweigh any political gain. The duke of Arcos left at his death in 1573 debts which could be traced back, for the most part, to his campaigns with Philip II in Flanders and subsequent sojourn at court (1558–61). The rewards of office were often substantial – over 700,000 ducats for the count of Benavente, not counting his salary as viceroy of Valencia and Naples; but he managed in this period (1580–1624) to run up debts of over 400,000 ducats, and by 1624 he was officially bankrupt, his estates sequestrated and his family put on an allowance by the courts.[57] But this situation gradually became a vicious circle: without royal favour, earned by unremitting service, one could never hope for relief from debt. The duke of Osuna, bankrupt since 1594, was allowed to divert some of the payments owing to his creditors in order to subsidise further activity on the Crown's behalf. The duke of Medina Sidonia was allowed in 1629 to suspend for six years the reimbursement of the capital on his mortgages, because of 'the diligence with which he attends to his obligations', in the words of the government committee, 'and it is only fair that he should have some relief so that he has the wherewithal to come to Your Majesty's aid when needed'.[58]

However, this alliance with the monarchy posed wider social and political problems, threatening to open a gulf between those who enjoyed the fruits of power and those who had to foot the bill. The Cortes of 1615 had placed among their first demands the need to limit the immigration of the feudal lords to court, since it only encouraged wasteful expenditure and deprived the peasantry of succour. The Junta of Reform, set up in the last years of Philip III's reign to stem the perceived decline of the economy and the finances of the state, returned to the problem, though without coming up with any viable solution. 'If it was once a good policy to keep the nobles near the king's person in order to make sure of them, to get them to spend and waste their substance so that they would no longer have the resources to engage in upheavals,' wrote Fernández Navarrete in 1626, that age was past. Now the danger was rather that lack of means, 'like a bad counsellor, would lead a man to seek, in the revolutions of the commonwealth, what he threw away so prodigally on vice'.[59] The problem was one addressed by the great reforming minister Olivares, albeit from a slightly different perspective. Founding his great new *mayorazgo* of Sanlúcar (1642), he aimed to have his successors enjoy a rent-roll of 100,000 ducats a year. It was potentially 'very dangerous' for the security of the state for a noble to have more; but equally it was desirable that he should have no less, so that he would not have to 'bother and pester (the king) for subsidies . . . which all fall in the end on the shoulders of the people of these realms'.[60]

This was the great issue which the early seventeenth-century monarchy was having to address, of how to settle the fiscal and military burden so that it did not imperil the stability of the social hierarchy. The president of the Council of Castile warned the Cortes of 1623 that taxation would have to be shifted from excises on the food of the poor towards a direct impost on the rich: 'with this [other governments] achieved the tranquillity and security of their commonwealths, for from the extreme poverty of some and the excessive wealth of others, riots, turbulence and civil wars usually follow'. The debates tended to reveal a fundamental disquiet, though, on the part of the provincial oligarchies represented in the Cortes, about the whole growth of the state. A strong state, affirmed the president, would protect Spanish trade as well as religion. But the deputies looked rather to the fortunes made by a new political elite on the back of the tax-payer. Don Fernando Alvarez de Toledo suggested that if the king needed more money, the fairest way would be to tax those who had profited from the growth of the state in recent times. 'If His Majesty who is in heaven granted me an annuity of 3,000 ducats, and now the king our lord, his son, finds himself left with no option but to make the poor even poorer . . . it is incumbent upon me as a gentleman (*hidalgo*) to succour His Majesty with half of the amount of the favour which I so graciously received from his father.'[61]

One of the classic statements of this position came from the pen of Mateo Lisón y Biedma, deputy for Granada in the Cortes of 1621. The growth of court favours 'is one of the main reasons why Your Majesty is short of money and something which your vassals feel most deeply about, seeing that the taxes which they pay in with so much effort, which is to say with the blood and sweat of so many poor people, are turned to the profit, benefit and increase of favourites'. Olivares's planned replacement of the excise on food with forced loans from the wealthy to a state bank (*erario*) was no solution to the real problem, which was the irresponsible growth of a state bureaucracy, misusing tax-payers' money. 'Wealth does not consist of collecting and gathering in a lot, but of holding on to what one has got and spending little.' Lisón needled Olivares by his opposition to fiscal reform. After distributing printed copies of his pamphlets to the members of the Cortes of 1627 – at which time he was no longer deputy for Granada but represented the interests of his city as *procurador mayor* at court – he was ordered out of Madrid by the great minister, who told him that 'the enemy could not do as much damage if they entered these kingdoms with an army'. This was surely to overstate the case, and to ignore the very real ties which, in spite of appearances to the contrary, bound the provincial elites ever more tightly with the court. After all, Lisón had asked for a post in the king's household at the conclusion of the Cortes of 1621, and was to offer the Crown money in 1634 for the sale of positions of familiar of the Inquisition – a way of consolidating his own influence in the kingdom of Granada and, as the royal commissioner in charge of the negotiations pointed out, removing the suspicion of Jewish ancestry attaching to his second wife, Baltasara Madera.[62]

Baltasara was the daughter of the royal minister Gregorio López Madera, member of the Council of Castile since 1619 and purchaser of a small lordship, Cozvíjar, near Granada, through whose chancery court this able lawyer (son of a physician to Philip II) had risen to power. Lisón himself, though a member of the town council of Granada, was laying the foundations of a noble dynasty through strategic marriages like that to Madera, through the accumulation of offices in various towns of the Granadan kingdom, and through building up his own little estate of Algarinejo into a feudal lordship. Though he opposed the sale of feudal jurisdictions in 1626 as undermining the good administration of justice and the authority of cities like Granada, he had already obtained in 1614 a grant of jurisdiction over Algarinejo, 'if people come to settle there'. Indeed, in 1621 he advocated such private enterprise as a way of encouraging the repopulation of rural Spain. His politics, he told Olivares in a stormy interview on 1 June 1627, came from 'grandparents and ancestors who won many lands and cities for their liege lords' – that vivid memory of the Reconquista, still alive among the petty gentry, which might inspire occasional flashes of insubordination towards the king, but ultimately through its very individualism would guard against any wider solidarity at the regional level. From the ideal of chivalry the path led not towards republicanism based on Granada, but towards a refashioned feudal axis linking Algarinejo and the court. Lisón's daughter married an illegitimate son of the great aristocratic house of Fernández de Córdoba, and their heir became first marquis of Algarinejo in 1689, gentleman-in-waiting at the courts of Philip IV and Charles II. It was perhaps typical of the ultimate solidarity of the political elites that the man who represented more than any other the interests of Olivares and the government in Andalusia in the 1620s, Antonio Alvarez de Bohorques, should have stood up in the Cortes of 1623 and asked his colleagues to support a petition for royal favour for the natural rebel, Lisón y Biedma.

The bridge between the court and the country was kept open by what one might call the rambling network of kinship, friendship and patronage among the aristocracy. But there was always the danger that some of the grandees might seek to preserve as much as they could of the old feudal order by challenging the fiscalism of the modern state – that is, by setting themselves up as protectors of their vassals against levies of troops, billets and taxes. 'The landowner serves the king most by the extent to which he defrauds the government rather than by what he pays in taxes,' protested the duke of Medinaceli in 1655, 'because the latter is of value for only one year, but the former ensures the preservation of his goods, lands and capital.' However, as in France at this time, the great families tended in the end to buckle under the pressure of the court, abandoning their local allies. 'The greatest risk which we run,' the duke of Béjar recognised, 'is to think that we can avoid the numerous quarrels and dangers which would inevitably arise from not doing what His Majesty asks.'[63] An illustration of the point came in the failure of the conspiracy of the duke of Medina Sidonia, so immensely powerful in the hinterland of Cadiz, who was at daggers drawn with his kinsman Olivares and minded to follow the example of his brother-in-law, the duke of Braganza, who proclaimed himself king of an independent Portugal in 1640. But Medina Sidonia was less resolute and was arrested, forfeiting his ducal capital, Sanlúcar de Barrameda to the Crown (1645) and losing his near-hereditary post of Captain General of Andalusia. The Venetian ambassador Soranzo had already reached the conclusion in 1602 that, in spite of heavy taxes and unrest in the provinces, general revolt in Spain was unlikely. The grandees would have had to lead any such movement, but 'they have no authority with the people, no fortresses to which to retire, no following, no obedience from their vassals, no good understanding within their own ranks . . .'.[64]

The military power of the aristocracy does, indeed, seem to be in considerable decline at the time Soranzo penned his comment. True, the seigneurial fortresses still dotted the landscape of Castile, 'land of the castles'. These could be grouped into at least two types. First, there were the medieval towers, often situated on a hill overlooking the town beneath and serving as a refuge for the population in time of danger: the hill tower of Cocentaina might serve as an example. But the actual residence of the count of Cocentaina by the fifteenth century was a fortified town house, partly incorporated into the walls of the Old Christian quarter and dominating the Moorish ghetto and the market square nearby. The old castle of Lerma, standing on its hill, would give way to the new palace in town built by the duke, favourite of Philip III, in the early seventeenth century. The counts of Oropesa developed their hilltop fortress in the Toledo region into a fine Renaissance palace, extending downhill from the old fortifications. The old legend about the tearing down of towers by the Catholic Kings, as part of the pacification of the country in the wake of their triumph in the civil war of 1474–9, seems to have some basis in fact. The fine castle of Montilla was dismantled in 1508 as a punishment for its lord's insubordination, and nearby Valenzuela was also demolished after a vaguely similar incident. But those nobles who kept out of trouble were allowed to go quietly on fortifying their residences. The palaces of Los Vélez and of Calahorra, on the dangerous Granadan frontier, are examples of Renaissance comfort combined with military security. Not perhaps until the construction of El Viso by the marquis of Santa Cruz around 1564 do we get a clear statement of aristocratic confidence in public order – that private fortifications are no longer necessary, even in this rather exposed wilderness of La Mancha. Nor should we forget the urban towers – the great palace of the Constable, the duke of Frías, in Burgos (1483), which was part fortress, or the palace which the count of Benavente wanted to build in Valladolid (1518). The day that the work was allowed to proceed, warned the council, 'on that day Your Highness will make him absolute master of Valladolid'. But by this time the urban palaces of the aristocracy – that of the duke of Infantado in Guadalajara or of the duke of Alcalá in Seville (1520) – increasingly lacked fortifications.[65]

Some of these houses still bristled with arms. Viciana in 1564 described the palace of Gandia, with its 'armoury from which fifty men at arms and 600 arquebusiers can quickly be fitted out', while Enrique Cock admired the duke of Infantado's arsenal in Guadalajara in 1585, with its 126 harnesses and goodly supply of arquebuses. Seigneurial levies, as we noted in the last chapter, had been the first real response to the revolt of the Germanías in 1519–22, as indeed to that of the Comuneros. But at the same time that war illustrated some of the weaknesses of the feudal levy, its tendency to disintegrate for lack of pay or food, especially given the interruption to seigneurial rents during the revolt. The same impression is left by its activity in the struggle against the rebellious Moriscos of the Alpujarra (1568–70). Here the great fortresses of Vélez Blanco, of the Alhambra (where the marquis of Mondéjar held nearly independent sway as the king's Captain General of Granada), of Calahorra, and others, were supposed to provide a ring of steel to hold down a recently conquered kingdom. In fact, the marquises of Mondéjar and Los Vélez – quite apart from the rivalry between themselves – found it difficult to get troops of the right calibre to master the insurrection. Discipline in these seigneurial forces proved a headache, and eventually it was the royal army of Italy, commanded by the king's half-brother, Don John of Austria, which carried the day.

One notes from around the time of the Revolt of the Alpujarra an increasing preoccupation with military security. The Venetian ambassador Donà commented in 1573 that Spain, since the closure of the frontier with Granada, had allowed her defences to fall into decay, since she was not directly threatened by any European power. And it was a similar observation which the soldier-historian Francisco Manuel de Mello made about the difficulty of mastering the revolt of the Catalans in 1640: 'there were no carts . . . there were no horses . . . we were short of every kind of ammunition, of planking, pontoon bridges, scouts, tar, pitch, saltpetre, sulphur'.[66] Great efforts had been made, nevertheless, in the interval since 1568 to improve state defences. Under Philip II a major fortification of the Mediterranean coastline was undertaken with a view to preventing the incursion of corsairs from the Berber states. Though some of this work was undertaken by the feudal lords – like the strong tower at Santa Pola run up by the duke of Maqueda in 1557 – it was mainly subsidised by public taxes and administered by public bodies (in the case of Valencia, a committee of the viceroy and representatives of the three estates of the realm). From the time of the sack of Cadiz by the English in 1596, serious efforts were made to institute trained bands of militia throughout the various kingdoms of the peninsula, instead of relying on the ad hoc levies raised by towns or feudal lords. The change may not have been immediately apparent. The trained bands of Sanlúcar de Barrameda in 1609 comprised 1,612 men under officers wholly or partly nominated by the local seigneur, the duke of Medina Sidonia. And in Valencia as late as 1648 the forces sent to defend the frontier against the French and Catalans could only be mobilised through the personal influence of the militia officers with their 'friends, vassals and dependants'.[67]

If the Crown was in some ways assuming more control of the military situation, by instituting militias and establishing publicly funded coastal fortifications, it continued to depend for the operation of the system on the goodwill of the local elites. Olivares found it convenient, as Francisco de Mello tells us, to appoint the marquis of Los Vélez to command the army against rebellious Catalonia in 1640, for he was 'the descendant and heir of the house of . . . Don Luis de Requesens, much esteemed as a son of Catalonia, and he kept up ties of kinship, friendship and marriage with many illustrious houses in that province'.[68] Los Vélez had been viceroy of Valencia shortly before and his subsequent military career was followed with interest by the natives of that kingdom, who often converted their ex-viceroys into protectors at court.

Cementing the institution of patronage was the shared culture of chivalry and religious devotion, explored by Amelang for the Catalan gentry of the seventeenth century.[69] In Valencia the household of Juan de Ribera, the great Counter-Reformation archbishop of the diocese (1569–1611), grouped a score of young nobles at any one time, serving him as pages and learning the rudiments of Latin through a study of the classics (Caesar, Cicero), as well as acquiring a rudimentary acquaintance with Renaissance humanism (Vives, Nebrija). Here the sons of the old Valencian families rubbed shoulders with kinsmen of the Castilian nobility from whose ranks Ribera himself was sprung.[70] But it was above all within their own informal meetings that the nobility was beginning to acquire a new outlook on life, for few were formally educated beyond the basic instruction in Latin grammar. The *Academia de los Nocturnos* ('the academy of those who met at nightfall'), meeting in Valencia between 1591 and 1594, brought together men of letters, like the priest-historian Escolano, jurists (including the austere Tomás Cerdán de Tallada), and cavaliers, like the dashing and undisciplined Don Gaspar Mercader, later first count of Buñol. Its purpose was that of the 'poetic joust' – to familiarise a ruling elite with the peaceful competition of the wit rather than the violent feud of the sword. As its founder, Bernardo Catalá de Valeriola (1568–1607) explained in another context: 'Every kind of emulation is allowed and indulged in in all well-ordered commonwealths, in order that men inclined to virtue should practise and get better at the things which they do best.'[71]

The culture of the class to which Catalá belonged was that of chivalry in a broad sense. These men had mostly ceased receiving formal tuition at fourteen or fifteen years of age. But the Count of Buñol, for example, could read Italian and translated a sonnet of Petrarch. And the great Duke of Alba once recited fifty lines of Virgil 'from memory' to the Master of the Military Order of Montesa, Don Pedro Luis Galcerán de Borja, who 'being so well read, took particular note of it'. The story comes to us from the jurist Tomás Cerdán de Tallada (1604), a keen advocate of learning for the nobility. Yet the aristocratic experience of life was mostly of jousting and bullfighting, of courtship and fiesta, and it was this which found its way into their chief medium of literary expression – the poem. The poems which they wrote for each other, in the *Nocturnos* and elsewhere, were rather artificial constructions, celebrating the hollow victory of the expulsion of the Moriscos (1609), which left so many of them economically ruined, or the virtues of the saints (the count of Buñol was particularly active in the cult of the Immaculate Conception, as well as of the folk saint Mossèn Simó, whom we shall discuss in Chapter 10). But above all it was the vein of amorous gallantry which attracted them. One of the most famous members of the *Nocturnos* was Guillén de Castro (1569–1631), whose play 'The Youth of the Cid' transformed the medieval epic into an affair of love and honour, which served as the basis for Corneille's well-known drama. Castro was a member of the Valencian gentry, serving as a captain in the coastguards before becoming steward to the duke of Gandia around 1600. By 1619 he moved to Madrid, under the patronage of the duke of Osuna (who, in spite of his own bankruptcy, set a small estate at his disposal). The life and culture of the court represented little interruption to the poet, who participated in the literary 'jousts' for the canonisation of Saint Ignatius Loyola in 1621 and for Saint Isidore (patron of Madrid) in 1622.[72] Castro embodied that cosmopolitan culture of chivalry, now shading off into gallantry and the fantastic, which served to bind the elites of Habsburg Spain together.

The Orders of chivalry – Santiago, Calatrava, Alcántara – served also to create a Hispanic elite of specially favoured nobles. Bernardo Catalá de Valeriola tells us in his diary how he received his knighthood of Calatrava in January 1605, in the great convent of the order in Castile – a solemn occasion: 'May God allow me to carry out the good intentions I that day set forth.'[73] Regional patriotism, it is true, could prove stronger than all these ties. Don Diego de Vich (1584–1657), knight of Alcántara, has left a splendid diary and other writings through which we can glimpse the tension between the Valencian elite and the court. A cultivated man, he pleaded his infirmities and that he was 'over sixty years of age' (he was actually fifty-six) – when the king asked him to help defend Catalonia against the French in the spring of 1640. Nor could he send a substitute, he said, for his house had been ruined by the expulsion of its Moorish vassals in 1609 and – another jibe at mistaken royal policy – he had never been paid the allowance owed to him as a knight of Alcántara. In fact, at this time he was spending quite impressive sums on the decoration of his tomb in the convent of Murta. Nor was he reconciled to the monarchy when the royal aesthete, Philip IV, visiting Valencia in 1645, agreed to accept a 'gift' of one of the Vich family heirlooms, a painting by the great Sebastián del Piombo, in settlement of the arrears of one of Don Diego's ancestors who had administered the royal treasury in Valencia.[74]

Not everyone, then, sought the honours of the court. The capital itself was, after all, still so remote. The diary of Bernardo Catalá conveys all the hardship and peril of a journey which, from Valencia, could take five or six days, with bad weather and uncertain communications. Once one had got there, the pressure of business was intense. In 1599, when his fellow Valencian the duke of Lerma had come to power, Catalá resolved to press on this high-placed patron his claim to office; but, to make doubly sure, he insisted on his 'great friend', Don Martín de Idiáquez, secretary of state, talking to Lerma, 'so that it does not slip his mind with the infinite amount of business which they place on his shoulders'. And, finally, there was a certain cultural barrier to be overcome. Catalá's diary was kept in the Catalan language – until he began to frequent the court and to move his household to Castile in 1605, after his appointment as *corregidor* of León. At this stage, the diary, to all appearances spontaneously and unconsciously, lapses into Castilian. This cultural transition was symptomatic of a wider process of integration of provincial elites with the monarchy.

For, in spite of all the differences between court and country, there was an undeniable attraction exerted upon the minds of the provincial elite by the growing concentration of literary and artistic talent around the court. Catalá records his admiration of the great 'convent of the Jerónimos', as he called the royal palace of the Escorial then recently completed (1585), and of the Alcázar of Madrid, 'with its very fine paintings'.[75] The development of the theatre in the early seventeenth century would confirm this cultural hegemony of the capital and of the Castilian language. In the reign of Philip III – particularly after the definitive return of the court from Valladolid to Madrid in 1606 – and then more markedly in that of his successor, Philip IV (1621–65), the artistic patronage of the monarchy began to give Spain for the first time a real cultural centre. But if this formation of a new 'national' commonwealth depended on the integration of its provincial elites, its stability required other forms of social and cultural change among the population at large, which we must now seek to explore.

8

OBEDIENCE TO THE LAW

'Now that the advance of civilisation has made apparent the rights conferred on all men by nature and civil society, and the authority of monarchs is sufficiently powerful to have these respected,' wrote the Granadan magistrate Sempere y Guarinos in 1805, 'we can hardly appreciate the cost and true worth of protection of life and property.' In the days of the overmighty subject, 'no one could live at peace without a godfather'.[1] The contrast could hardly be greater between the time when he wrote and those far-off days in the fifteenth century when the chronicler Pulgar could describe the state of Castile thus: 'Justice was toppled and force reigned supreme, while more room was found for the harsh temptation of arrogance than for the humble promptings of obedience.'[2] But the accession of Isabel (1474) seemed to mark a turning-point. She was 'the most feared and respected queen that ever was in the world', wrote her chronicler Bernáldez, 'for all the dukes, masters (of the Military Orders), counts, marquises and great lords feared her and stood in awe . . . so that throughout the realm there was peace and justice'. Her work was consolidated by her successors, notably Philip II, whose achievement attracted the praise of the moral philosopher Pineda in 1589: 'a stable lad can ask for his eight *reales* wages from the count and a judge will have them paid, and the lad has no cause to fear, whereas a hundred years ago it would not have been worth his while to go on living on the face of the earth'.[3]

Foreign visitors echoed this praise. Barthélemy Joly noted that the law in Castile 'does not spare the great ones as it does in France'. The Venetian ambassadors, meanwhile, quite regularly drew attention to the phenomenon in their reports. Despite their discontent with high taxes, wrote Tiepolo in 1567, the common people of Castile were not likely to revolt because, among other things, 'justice was meted out with equal rigour to the grandees as to any one of themselves'.[4] There was one blemish on the picture, though: the increasing problem of banditry in the Mediterranean provinces – Catalonia, Valencia, Aragon. The scourge was becoming a general one throughout the Mediterranean world at the time, as Braudel once made plain. Its existence, and indeed the shaky nature of law enforcement in Castile itself, throws up the question of how far the state was really able to acquire a monopoly of dispute settlement in the early modern period.

Anthropologists have made us aware of the difficulty of settling disputes in small-scale societies, where the subject of the disagreement – the boundary of a field, perhaps – is either not the real cause of the tension between two parties or will merely serve to envenom relations between them, passing on a sense of injury to the next generation. 'Men may engage in litigation over property without losing goodwill and becoming alienated from each other,' wrote the moral philosopher Camos; but he thought it unlikely. Judges should try to reconcile parties to a dispute rather than adjudicating, urged Castillo de Bobadilla; lawsuits were 'abhorrent', even though one party might lose its rights.[5] The memoir of the Catalan peasant Sebastià Casanovas (1700–56) gives a fascinating insight into a world where much property was tied down by commitments to family and neighbours by agreements which might not be written down, or, if they were, might be undermined by informal understandings. Sebastià's father came back after fighting for the losing side in the War of the Spanish Succession and sued the local bailiff for the income from his farm during his years of exile (1716–23). The governor's court in Girona awarded him 560 Catalan pounds after a confused hearing, in which the sheer lack of written receipts led to a reliance on neighbours' memory of who had paid what to whom. Getting the award enforced presented other difficulties, as the authorities were reluctant to indispose the bailiff, and Casanovas himself, with a wary eye on his own creditors, considered leaving the money with the official as a way of securing the latter's benevolence in other matters.[6]

Law in traditional societies was part of an ongoing regulation of relationships between individuals, in an age when the anonymous exchange of services through the market, satisfied by money or credit, did not yet apply. Cerdán de Tallada noted that law was instituted in order to help men become good. The instructions for the new viceroy of Valencia in 1566 bade him remember that the administration of justice was 'the principal business to which kings and princes and their ministers ought to pay attention'. His task, therefore, was to see that the citizens 'enjoy in peace and quiet their property, and that no one make bold to harm another, rather that they should treat one another with the love and harmony of Christian people'.[7] Like the viceroy, the Castilian *corregidor* was both a law officer and a general administrator. Castillo de Bobadilla's treatise sets out a wide variety of tasks: feeding the poor, maintaining public works, fixing prices on the market, checking on the quality of goods. It was all part of the ideal of a Christian commonwealth, regulated by laws, which were themselves only statements of broader moral principles. The great law code of Castile, the *Nueva Recopilación*, published originally in 1567 and reissued in 1640, reflects the all-embracing nature of law, in which administration, morality and adjudication seem to be gathered together in a way which leaves little room for that separation between public and private space characteristic of a modern society.

At the base of the pyramid stood the elected village or town justices – the *alcaldes*, as they were known in Castile – a mixture of mayor and justice of the peace. Above them were the district governors, the *corregidores* of Castile, from whom appeals lay to the high courts – the Chancillerías of Valladolid and Granada, and the more localised Audiencia of Seville. The autonomous kingdoms of the Crown of Aragon had each their separate Audiencia – in Zaragoza, Barcelona, Valencia – whose magistrates had to be native sons. Adjudication was basically 'popular', or at least assumed to be so. Calderón's great drama *The Mayor of Zalamea* portrays the elected justice, a wealthy peasant, in all his dignity. And Castillo de Bobadilla suggested that even the *corregidor* – not necessarily a trained lawyer – might give judgement without a qualified assessor, at least in smaller towns: 'For the fairness of his proceeding may make up for any defect of formality in a judgement made without consultation with a lawyer.' Peasant *alcaldes*, though often 'unlettered men', judging by 'natural reason', were capable of giving 'just decisions'. However, the *corregidor* would be well-advised to consult as widely as possible before making up his own mind – among the 'senior and most level-headed aldermen', or 'some friar of good life and learning'.[8]

The description of court-rooms of old by Castillo de Bobadilla – 'as much confusion and shouting as you would find in the shambles' – tends to emphasise the impression of informality. But the great jurist noted in his own day (1597) that the imposition of attorneys (*procuradores*) on the parties to litigation before the *corregidor* or audiencias had calmed matters, for they had to submit allegations in writing. One notes an increasing concern with the formalisation of procedures. The royal visitor or inspector of the government of Valencia expressed his disquiet in 1635 with the referral of cases by the local justices to the assembly of heads of household for decision: 'a collection of peasants, who must inevitably be kinsmen or friends of the accused in smaller communities, have absolute discretion, and no one can ask them to explain their judgement'. He affirmed that he could now understand why banditry was so prevalent in Valencia. Though the assessors of the municipal courts – usually notaries – were supposed to appeal against unjust acquittals, there were never enough of them, or they were themselves barely qualified in the law.[9]

There was increasing concern in some quarters during the sixteenth century that adjudication was becoming excessively professionalised – removed from the hands of village authorities who alone knew the real circumstances of the case and taken on appeal to remote, costly and oppressive tribunals. The instructions for the Valencian viceroy in 1566 bade him stop the trend, which was becoming a matter of concern to the parliaments. And the Cortes of Castile were trying to prevent disputes over property worth less than a certain sum being taken on appeal from the locality: the old threshold of 10,000 *maravedís* – equivalent to perhaps a year's wages for an unskilled labourer – was pushed up to 20,000 in 1604 and then 30,000 in 1632. This was part of the general move at this time to restore the rural economy – to prevent what the reforming writer Lope de Deza denounced in 1618 as the wastage of peasant resources on lawsuits. 'Fearful and envious of their neighbours', rustics were being induced by lawyers to pursue their vendettas through the courts. Let them at least accept the arbitration of their elected *alcalde*, if possible without paperwork and on rainy days only, when work was impossible in the fields.[10]

Paradoxically, the sale of jurisdictional autonomy, to small towns as well as to feudal lords, so characteristic of the later sixteenth and seventeenth centuries, was making this informal arbitration less possible. As a memorial to the Junta of Reform explained around 1623, in the old days the village *alcaldes* had been able to 'reconcile neighbours and nip litigation in the bud', because it was so easy to refer troublesome parties, blinded by 'prejudice or hatred', for a definitive ruling to the *corregidor* in the next big town. But now, 'with any and every lawsuit they go on appeal to the chancillerías'. Liberty was a good thing, affirmed Castillo de Bobadilla, and the autonomy of villages had sometimes been justified by their remoteness from the nearest *corregidor*. However, 'I am of the opinion,' he was forced to conclude, that 'the abuse of exempting villages is one of the things that most requires reform in these kingdoms', for it led to more litigation, not less, and, rather than helping the citizen, the main reason for the concessions 'has been and is that the kings need money'. There was a particular problem with seigneurial immunities. Absentee lords were leaving their authority in the hands of 'their household retainers, men who manage business in a very devious fashion, so that they can get money from the public purse, and gifts and presents from litigants'.[11]

In spite of the concerns of Lope de Deza and others, it seems clear that the bulk of litigation had to be settled locally in the seventeenth and eighteenth centuries, with the audiencias exercising only a very loose kind of supervision. Cases taken on appeal rarely received a definitive judgement in these superior tribunals, bogged down as they were by an excess of paperwork and a paucity of magistrates – 'the cemetery of the living', as the chronicler Escolano called them in 1610. 'The proverb says, "let my friend draw up the documents, then it hardly matters who the judge is".' Castillo de Bobadilla was referring here to the rambling network of attorneys and notaries who were actually responsible for assembling the pieces which might be used in litigation, including the *información de testigos*, the 'statements of witnesses', which were used fundamentally as moves in a game of nerves designed to reduce the other side to desist or compromise. There were five notaries in the peasant community of Llombai, with its 600 households, noted the steward of the estate in 1756: 'rather a lot for such a small place, and since they have no other means of subsistence, they get people to sign agreements' – depriving him, as chief magistrate, of the responsibility of adjudication.[12] The feudal lords should not auction off the post of notary on their estates, commented Castillo de Bobadilla, for these men are driven to fraud and extortion in order to get by. No theme was perhaps more common in the centuries of the early modern period than the complaint about the poor quality and excessive powers of the notary. Like pharmacists dealing in poison, thought Castillo de Bobadilla, they needed to be men of breeding and confidence. But now, complained the Cortes of 1579–82, they have become so numerous that they are of suspect lineage, 'and many have been traders and worked with their hands'.[13]

One might conclude, from this brief survey, that the formal process of law in

Spain was much less impressive in practice than the ordered hierarchy of tribunals might lead one to think. The role of written documentation in a pre-industrial society is somewhat problematic anyway, as the letter of the contract is liable to be modified by tacit arrangements between the parties, who typically know each other through ongoing relationships as members of the same small group of friends, kin, neighbours or clients. This consideration is what lies behind the denunciations of *mohatras* – fictitious sales – in early modern Spain. Thus, the Cortes of 1586–8 complained that peasants were being persuaded to sell land or cattle to powerful people for only half what the goods were worth, on the understanding that they would be allowed to continue using them for a certain period.[14] Such agreements may lead to extortion and misunderstandings later, as anthropologists point out, if the original patron–client relationship sours, and moral and legal ownership come into conflict. This ambiguity was, indeed, one of the causes of the latent violence which was never far below the surface in pre-industrial communities. The problem was compounded by the loss of memory typical of an age which relied so much on oral tradition. There were, indeed, written records. But, as the Cortes of Castile and Valencia reiterated time and again, the archiving of court and notarial records was very imperfect. The Castilian parliament of 1579–82, for example, wanted the papers of notaries who had died to be placed with the local justices for safeguard and ease of reference. But tracking down documentation remained an adventure – a costly, time-consuming business of going from place to place in person, and then copying out laboriously by hand the precious icon (whose authenticity and relevance to the dispute in question were sometimes questionable). The faith in the document – any document – seems to increase the more illiterate the society.

Castillo de Bobadilla referred to the great risk of dispute over boundaries of fields, in an age when so much land was ill-surveyed and often given over to rough pasture. Litigation on this subject was possibly the main source of tension in pre-industrial Spain. As one year follows the next, wrote the great jurist, one forgets 'how one of the villagers ploughed up part of the common lands, how an outsider got hold of a piece of the royal demesne, and how a *regidor* . . . took bits for himself'. In the less-policed areas conflicts of memory were liable to take violent forms. It had been 162 years, complained the Valencian hill town of Alpuente in 1645, that she had been contesting her boundary with the lordship of Chelva. 'Every day' the field guards from Chelva confiscated her cattle pasturing on the disputed range, forcing her to take matters into her own hands 'and make good the annoyance'. Not too far away there was a similar, long-running feud between Carlet and Alcudia over pasture rights. When the count of Carlet seized cattle which had come into his territory around 1618, the lord of Alcudia impounded some horses belonging to the count's peasants. Thereupon the latter gathered a gang of a dozen masked men who attacked the hostelry in Alcudia, freed the horses and wounded one of the inhabitants in the process.[15]

The most spectacular example of this kind of range war was the conflict between the so-called 'mountain men' and the Moriscos in the Aragon of the

1580s. The peasants of the Pyrenees had traditionally taken their flocks to winter in the lowlands, along the banks of the River Ebro, where the converted Muslims formed a large part of the farming population. No love was lost between the two communities anyway, but with population rising in the region by about 50 per cent over the sixteenth century, pressure on the available land must have become acute. In any case, when a Morisco killed one of the mountain transhumants in 1585, the latter sacked one village (Codo), from which most of the inhabitants had fled, and massacred between 300 and 400 men, women and children in another (Pina). The fighting coincided with the struggle for possession of the Pyrenean county of Ribagorza between the duke of Villahermosa and his peasants, to which we alluded briefly in Chapter 5. Men of violence were used (or it was hoped they could be used) on one side or the other – the Catalan bandit El Minyó ('The Kid'), fresh from his capture of the king's treasure on its way to Barcelona in 1587, on behalf of the rebels, while the mountain men, after their exploits against the Moriscos, were invited to help the duke. The lawlessness became so worrying that Philip II sought to impose a non-native viceroy on Aragon, setting in train a complex series of confrontations with the Aragonese elites which ended with the sending in of a small royal army in 1591.[16]

Ribagorza was not particularly valuable to the duke in economic terms, but it was a mainstay of his prestige. One of the difficulties in adjudicating disputes in the Old Regime was the loss of face, the dishonour, of having to concede ground to an adversary. The separation between private and public life which has taken place in modern times was something foreign to the outlook of our ancestors. The diary of the vice-chancellor of the Council of Aragon, Don Cristóbal Crespí de Valldaura (1599–1672), gives a vivid insight into the 'theatre of power' – the aura of magnificence and prestige which leaders needed to maintain if they were to get obedience. On a week's retreat around Christmas 1653 in the quiet of the Carthusian monastery of Segovia, Crespí felt the need to justify to his diary his decision to take a back seat in the choir and refectory: 'It seemed to me that it inferred no slight on my office, since I was there as a private individual.' But otherwise his relentless inventory of who sat where and who accompanied whom to the door at audiences occupied much of his time and energy, in spite of his own manifest piety: 'God free our hearts from these vanities,' he wrote, 'so that this maintenance of the authority of office may be only what is necessary for the good administration of justice.'[17] Meanwhile, when the marquis of Almenara had gone to Zaragoza as Philip II's envoy in 1588 to seek a change of the rule against non-native viceroys, the splendour of his household advertised his authority – 'many servants well fitted out', as the chronicler Argensola noted, 'his halls adorned with very rich tapestries, keeping open house for anyone who wished to eat at his table'. Correspondingly, his enemies made it 'a point of honour not to visit him'.[18]

If 'honour' – visible, publicly acknowledged respect – was one weapon in the arsenal of authority in the Old Regime, it was also peculiarly unstable and likely to disturb the hierarchy it was meant to uphold. 'There is no thing more esteemed than good reputation and honour,' affirmed Castillo de Bobadilla, 'for men hold it higher than life and wealth.' And he went on to warn the *corregidor* that much would be pardoned him in the exercise of power if he acted with courtesy, whereas he would never be forgiven for harsh language and insult. 'If some of the *regidores* begin to contradict each other with insulting language and are in open conflict, let the *corregidor* immediately intervene . . . ordering them to hold their peace on penalty of grave sanctions.' Indeed, he may well suspend the session there and then: 'for failure to put out a spark, a city has been known to burn down'.[19]

In small-scale communities disagreements over one issue were liable to generate wider resentment over an implied attack on one's good faith, and this public loss of face would require reparation. The cloth-merchant Jeroni Soria recorded in his diary in 1529 how the attorney handling his mother-in-law's estate had demanded to meet him 'with a cape and a sword', just outside the gates of Valencia, in order to settle a dispute over the inheritance. Though Soria wrote back that he was surprised at a man of law challenging anyone to a duel, he was forced to demonstrate his courage by turning up at the rendezvous, where the two men slashed at each other for half an hour, until the wounds were judged sufficient to establish the honour of both sides. The nobility, of course, had fewer scruples about taking to the sword. Joanot Martorell (1413–68), author of the classic novel of chivalry *Tirant lo Blanc*, would issue challenges of this kind to opponents, damning resort to law as 'not something for knights and gentlemen, but only for women and men of the robe, whose whole defence lies in the pen and in their tongue'.[20]

This attitude was sometimes condemned as hubris – the prompting of the Devil, 'the enemy of human kind', as the *jurats* of Valencia described one vendetta of 1381. A magistrate like Castillo de Bobadilla took up the theme in his work of 1597: feuds were the work of the Devil, fostering an arrogance which would brook no impediment.[21] But the violence of everyday life perhaps assisted the powers of darkness. The Jesuit missionary Pedro de León noted how in the Seville of the 1600s 'it was the custom on Sundays and holidays for crowds of youths to gather outside the Macarena and Cordoba gates and, divided into two gangs, to stone each other'. Ruffians would bring along swords in order to settle scores in the general mêlée. Around the same time in Valencia Escolano was describing the pastimes of the youth, who 'have barely learnt to swing their arms when they head for the river on a summer's day and, split into rival gangs . . . give battle with slings and stones'. Sometimes the high spirits got out of hand – especially since 'youngsters of fifteen or sixteen may be wearing a sword and can shoot' – so that the *jurats* might have to intervene and stop the contest.[22] One of the most famous examples of these rough games concerns the nobility of the capital of the sherry country, Jerez de la Frontera. They would form into two *bandos*, the Villavicencio resplendent in red and white, the Dávila in purple and yellow, and charge on horseback from opposite ends of the main square, hurling reed lances or *cañas* at each other. A fatality in 1597 led to an investigation which condemned the irresponsibility of manoeuvring on horseback in such a confined space, with so few rules.[23]

'Being brought up in isolated farmsteads set among woodland and scrub . . . produces a fierceness of temperament,' wrote Gilabert in 1616 of his fellow Catalans, which made them 'impatient when thwarted.' A century before, the famous Guicciardini, travelling through Catalonia in the winter of 1512, remarked how bandit-ridden this part of the peninsula was: one factor was 'the lie of the land, for the region is . . . mountainous, savage and underpopulated'.[24] In Castile too at this time it was the open, empty steppe of La Mancha, together with the mountain passes from Castile to Andalusia, which tended to be the hardest to police. 'The mountain people are like the land where they are reared,' wrote Argensola in 1608 of the outlaws of his native Aragon, 'tough men, used to hard work, but prone to disturbances and rebellions, implacable in their outbursts of anger and feuding.'[25]

But it was the old customs of the nobility which posed the greatest threat. The early modern state needed the feudal warrior less and the improving landlord more. Urging that the violent marquis of Guadalest be not allowed to return to his native Valencia, the Council of Aragon suggested in 1641 that 'since this gentleman shows spirit and daring' he should be employed abroad, preferably as a soldier. One cannot help feeling that the great duke of Osuna (1579–1624), a pugnacious defender of Spanish interests as viceroy of Naples, presented similar problems when a young man. In 1602 he escaped from house arrest, along with 'the good-for-nothings with whom he usually consorted'.[26]

Gilabert believed that the Catalan nobility presented more of a challenge to public order than the Castilian because they had not yet learned to study law and compete for bureaucratic office to the same extent. A memorial of 1632 denounced their idleness in a changing world: 'they are brought up without religious instruction or letters . . . learning only how to use a pistol'. But there was a further problem, to which Gilabert drew attention: the sheer lack of offices at the Crown's disposal in Catalonia suitable for a gentleman, especially since the king lived in Castile and appointed mainly Castilians to his own household.[27] It was, indeed, not just a Catalan problem. Power in the Old Regime resided in magnificence and in patronage – in the ability to command resources and influence out of which one could build up and reward a following. All men need friends, proclaimed Castillo de Bobadilla, 'for they are the sturdiest pillars and supports for the maintenance and increase [of authority]'. The *corregidor* had to be very careful to keep an even hand in supervising elections to local office and in the distribution of seating and processional rank in public celebrations. There was no town or village, he noted, 'which is not divided into factions and parties (*bandos*) and opposing leagues', and the *corregidor* would need all his wits in order to manouevre between them and prevent violence.[28]

The danger of confrontation between such groups motivated the intervention of the Crown, especially in the aftermath of the civil wars of the fifteenth century. Ferdinand and Isabel wrote to the town councillors of Jerez in 1492, expressing their displeasure that 'you have built up a following among officials and citizens, who come to your door on holidays and take your side in disputes'. These clients were abandoning 'jobs and farms' and living at their patron's expense, giving rise to 'disturbances and scandals'. A law of 1493, repeated in the codes of 1567 and 1640, forbade throughout Castile such men living 'in a permanent way with *regidores* and knights as their familiars or men who share their table', or 'accompanying them when they have a quarrel and escorting them with arms'. A further decree of 1500 prohibited members of a particular faction or *bando* in the Basque Country, Galicia or Asturias from assembling in strength at weddings or funerals.[29] At first sight these factions seem so vaguely defined that the laws must have been difficult to enforce. Certainly the reformer López Bravo was still complaining in 1616 about the problem of wastrels – badly brought up nobles who were poor but yet too proud to work, who found refuge in the houses of the powerful 'as pimps and bullies'.[30] These were the kind of men with whom the great duke of Osuna had allegedly been surrounding himself not long before.

But it was, inevitably, in the mountainous and less-policed territories of the Crown of Aragon that the problem was by then worst. 'Most of the knights live in their villages, which are so small and badly walled that four ruffians can easily break in,' commented Gilabert of his fellow Catalans in 1616, 'and they need to keep armed men in order to defend themselves.'[31] But this was a vicious circle, as the author tacitly acknowledged: so many gangsters roaming around made self-defence imperative. Guicciardini, commenting on the insecurity of the roads in the region in 1512, noted that 'the cause of this disorder lies in the fact that many knights and gentlemen of Catalonia are at daggers drawn and keep up continual wars with one another'. According to a long-established privilege a noble could attack his enemy after five days' warning. 'It is customary also . . . that all the kin take part in the quarrels, and . . . when they exhaust their strength, they turn to the local ruffians.' An Andalusian noble like the essayist Luis Zapata (1532–98?) found it bizarre, as he surveyed the feuds of Catalonia, Valencia and Aragon, 'that if they cannot avenge themselves on the one who caused the offence, they will kill his kinsman, his son, his wife, even his dog or horse'.[32] In these small-scale communities, rather locked in on themselves and lacking the Castilian ease of access to an imperial world, the memory of a wrong was carefully nourished and passed on from generation to generation. The Valencian diarist and later *corregidor* of León, Don Bernardo Catalá de Valeriola, was thus heir to an old memorandum drawn up by his grandfather of those who had fought for his family against the Peñarroja. Imposing the norms of ordered government on such a society was likely to be particularly troublesome.

It was, in fact, the rambling network of obligations to friends and family – part of the maintenance of one's own honour – which made quarrels often intractable. The career of the noble bandit Lupercio de Latrás may illustrate the way violence was liable to spread, moving in the process from feuding to robbery. Latrás was born around 1550/1560, the younger son of the lord of Latrás, a hamlet of the high Pyrenees near Jaca in Aragon. An obscure affray between two factions in the local market town of Hecho left a man dead and Lupercio a refugee in France with a price on his head (1579). The young man now gathered a gang together to force the Hecho authorities to 'come to terms' (*dar paz*), as he put it, only to be confronted by a posse from the royal town of Jaca. The latter took advantage of the situation to lay waste the lordship of Latrás, with which it had had boundary disputes in the past, despite the protests of Lupercio's elder brother, who was not directly involved in the dispute. From his hideout in the impenetrable Pyrenees, Lupercio waylaid traders and travellers to Jaca, using the proceeds to keep his ten to twenty followers happy, until the Crown was forced to offer him an amnesty on condition he enlist in the army of Italy (1582). But following an affair of honour with a brother officer, he was transferred to the army of Flanders, only to be shipwrecked in transit off the Spanish coast in the fateful year of 1588. Taking advantage of the disturbances then raging in Aragon between the duke of Villahermosa and his vassals of Ribagorza (see above, p. 107), Latrás offered his services to the former, but was then captured and executed after the duke surrendered the fief to the Crown.[33]

Violence was intermittent; but contemporaries noted that the threat was never far away, because so many gentlemen kept armed followers, particularly in the Crown of Aragon, hoping to intimidate their opponents. While they lived with their patron the gangsters were under some sort of control, commented Gilabert, but when they left, 'used to a life of ease, they take to the gun rather than the spade in order to make a living'.[34] The power struggles in Catalonia, like those in Aragon, gave them their opportunity. There was a running feud between the bishops of Vic and their undisciplined cathedral chapter, with armed men breaking into the episcopal palace on the eve of Palm Sunday 1580, forcing the government to transfer the prelate to another see shortly afterwards. But his successor had no better luck. The assassination of the archdeacon (1600) sparked a wave of retaliatory killings. We begin to get increasing reference about this time to the two great factions, the *Nyerros* and the *Cadells*, which appear to dominate much of the history of Catalonia for the next couple of generations. Judges, nobles, peasants, clerics were all accused of belonging to one or other of these nebulous groupings. Whether they existed in any concrete form seems doubtful, but they provided a brush with which to smear one's opponent and to justify hatreds, on the assumption that one could never obtain justice through the ordinary channels. The peasants of Ripoll, demanding restoration to the royal domain in 1609–11, accused the abbot, their feudal lord, of keeping a band of *Nyerros* to overawe them. This was the faction associated with the canons of the cathedral chapter of Vic, so that the bishop was alleged to be sheltering *Cadells* in his palace.[35]

It was in this feud that one of the most famous Catalan bandits, Rocaguinarda, won his spurs, as a *Nyerro*, implicated in attacks on the bishop. Born the younger son of wealthy peasants in Vic in 1582, Perot Rocaguinarda was forced to take to his heels after the killings which followed the assassination of the archdeacon in 1600. Cervantes left an endearing portrait of the young rebel, who encountered Don Quixote on his way to Barcelona (1614). 'I am by nature compassionate and well-intentioned, but . . . in seeking to avenge a wrong done to me, I saw all my good intentions fall away . . . One false step leads to the next, one sin to another; just so, one act of revenge feeds into another, and I find myself now fighting other people's battles as well as my own.' In order to subsist in the hills he must steal – as little as possible, of course, and only in order 'to satisfy this gang which follows me'.[36]

The link between economic conditions and banditry was complex. Macanaz, the commissioner charged with the reform of the government of Valencia after 1707, was one who saw a connection. 'The lords in this province levy such exorbitant taxes and tribute from many of their vassals,' he wrote, 'that they reduce them from free men to slaves or make it so hopeless for them to farm the land that they drive them to rob on the highways.' In Castile as well growing poverty during the seventeenth century was blamed by the chronicler Barrionuevo in the 1650s for outbreaks of thieving; and he pointed to the main road to Andalusia where gangs of over twenty waylaid travellers. Travelling from Ecija to Cordoba in 1687 the merchant Lantery thought it best to join a party of nine armed with shotguns, given the risk of banditry.[37]

In a sense it was not simply poverty but the opportunities of preying on increased trade which fostered highway robbery in this period. The transfer of the king's silver to the Genoese bankers for the war in Flanders had to be effected from the 1570s, given the dangers of the Atlantic, via the port of Barcelona. But the mule trains had to cross the ill-policed territory of Catalonia, where they were ambushed on at least two occasions, in 1587 and 1613. The viceroy reported on the parallel growth of counterfeiting – a scourge since copper coins had been introduced in 1587 to cater to the needs of petty trade. Valencia was suffering from a similar growth of counterfeiting at this time. But the more serious problem there was an epidemic of smuggling, of raw silk across the customs frontier with Castile. The towns of Alzira, Carcaixent, Algemesí and others, in the valley of the Xúquer, where most of the mulberry was grown, were full of armed men anyway, engaged in bitter feuds. Robbery of the leaf and the export of raw silk to Toledo were undertaken by gangs 'armed with shotguns, crossbows and the like, riding by night or at other unwonted times along unfrequented paths'.[38] Lack of respect for the law was perhaps as important an ingredient in all this as the use of physical force itself. The royal commissioner in Alicante around 1640 found it impossible to enforce the contraband regulations against those countries like The Netherlands and France with which Spain was then at war, and he denounced the complicity of merchants with native-born ministers of the Crown. Lantery, merchant of Cadiz, recalled in his memoirs of 1673–1700 with what great reluctance the governor, Don Diego Caballero de Yllescas, would apply the law against smugglers. Give 'this wretched tell-tale' his share of the condemned cargo, he would bellow in open court, 'pointing him out with his baton so that everybody would know who it was'. Informers had a short life, 'if they did not get out of Cadiz quickly'.[39]

The enforcement of law, then, had to take account of a culture where the sense of honour and friendship might dictate a line of conduct at variance with that of the public weal. The long survival of the idea of a crime as being fundamentally a hurt inflicted on another party rather than a challenge to good order reflects another aspect of the same phenomenon. The great Castilian law code of the thirteenth century, the *Siete Partidas*, retained the idea of the duel as a useful deterrent to underhand conduct by the nobility, though in other respects it was seeking to impose the rational adjudication of disputes by a qualified judge. Its Valencian counterpart, the Furs, though heavily influenced by the Roman idea of the lawgiver and peacemaker, maintained the right of the nobles 'and other honoured persons who do not work with their hands' to issue a challenge to those who had allegedly offended them, so long as the two sides were evenly matched in status and physique. Castile moved more quickly than the Crown of Aragon to limit this freedom, it is true. Alfonso XI (1312–50) affirmed that the king would have to approve all such duels, 'for so great is the power of the king that he holds all business and all privileges in his own hand, and he does not derive his power from men but from God'. Isabel tried to outlaw duelling altogether in 1480, on pain of forfeiture of one's property, though allowing a felon, if legitimately challenged and failing to turn up to court within a month to clear his name, to be hunted down by his challenger. In the Crown of Aragon the right to private vengeance was more sturdily maintained by the parliaments throughout the sixteenth century.

But the influence of the church, which clearly outlawed the duel at the Council of Trent (1563), may have been the decisive factor in its ultimate demise. All Valencians must remember that they are brothers, decreed King Peter IV (1336–87), as he tried to limit the feud, 'brought to a new life by the one father, creator and redeemer, through one mother, the church'. The ritual of peace-keeping assumed great significance, in Spain as in other parts of Europe, in that popular expression of late medieval piety, the confraternity. That of Nuestra Señora de la Antigua (Zamora) ruled in 1566 that if one member offended another, 'the aggressor is to ask pardon from the entire council and the injured one, and to be friends'.[40] Duels were 'a plague and a pest gnawing at the heart of the commonwealth', thought the chronicler and priest Escolano in 1610. And saint-hood was often associated with the peace movement, as in the case of the great fifteenth-century Valencian Dominican, Vicente Ferrer, or the sixteenth-century Andalusian, John of God, graphically represented in his famous hospital for the poor in Granada reconciling the warring factions. The Jesuit preacher Pedro de León (1578–1616) has left us a vivid account of the reconciliations between enemies which he effected in the course of his missions through the countryside of Andalusia. Some were persuaded through the confessional, others, 'as they came out after the sermon, would throw their arms round those they had offended: "it is no time to do anything else; the fathers tell us that if we do not forgive each other, God will not forgive us"'.[41]

Whatever the immediate success of such missions, they could not always out-weigh the claims of honour. 'Since I am not a saint but a sinner, I trust more to the mercy of God than to my own works,' affirmed the Seville nobleman and memoir-writer Don Alonso Enríquez de Guzmán (1518–43). Though aware that vengeance was prohibited by 'our holy Catholic faith', Don Alonso believed that God was more likely to forgive the 'heat of passion' than the underhandedness of malice.[42] In actual fact, he demonstrated in the course of his autobiography the crucial role of intermediaries as a factor limiting the violence. Typically a celibate clergy – like Vicente Ferrer or Pedro de León – could fulfil this role very well, of 'imposing' a reconciliation by virtue of their moral authority, without public loss of face by either of the contending parties. But Don Alonso seems to have relied more on powerful patrons, men of whose friendship he stood in need or whose enmity he could ill afford to provoke. The important thing was to stand one's ground, to show that one had the courage to stand up to an opponent, then to defer to the 'moral authority' of a great man – whose influence could be almost visibly measured in terms of the gratitude of his reconciled following. Thus, Don Alonso fell into dependence on the marquis of Ayamonte – 'I sent him presents and he did favours for me.' But the relationship was somewhat delicate, since Ayamonte was suspected of favouring the other side. The business of reconciling feuds was a complex strategy and, if it went wrong, was liable to spread dissatisfaction even further. It was perhaps this latent tension at the heart of so many relationships, rather than the outright violence of the duel or the ambush, that shaped the ambivalent attitudes of so many towards the intervention of the state in their quarrels.

That intervention built itself up gradually. Since it might be counterproductive to take sides, a favourite recourse when trouble threatened was to impose a 'truce'. In Jerez in 1436 the justices tried to pacify two quarrelling aldermen, asking them formally, 'for the service of God and of the king our lord, and for the well-being, peace and quiet of this city, and out of respect for the justices, that they might deign to forgive each other'. But when one refused outright, he was confined to his house and a truce of two months imposed anyway.[43] These truces were a safeguard against violence, because any breach caused an aggravated offence – an attack not on the person of one's opponent but now on the public good. 'Anyone who kills, wounds or takes another captive during a time of truce,' ran the old Castilian law, still reissued in 1640, 'let him die the death of a traitor.'

But the Valencian parliament of 1552 complained that the Crown had begun compelling all parties which issued challenges to come before the courts and sign these letters of safeguard – of 'peace and truce'. But these were supposed to be voluntary agreements, unless there was some 'urgent or compelling cause', which too often there was not.[44]

Conciliation was a fundamental aspect of the administration of justice in those days. Writing around 1620 to his brother-in-law, governor of Milan, the duke of Sessa pleaded for clemency for a certain prisoner. His aim, he affirmed, was not to interfere with the law – 'for that would be to presume overmuch on your friendship and kinship with me'. But he drew the governor's attention to the honourable standing of the accused's family: 'when the punishment of a culprit will spread to many who are not guilty, but who are related to him by blood, it is most convenient that the judge remit much of the penalty'.[45] In practical terms it was often necessary to pardon the bandits of the Crown of Aragon in order to get them to come down from the hills. Thus Rocaguinarda, and Latrás earlier, were offered amnesties on condition of service in the army, a proceeding which had at least the advantage of removing them from the network of local friendships and enmities in which they flourished. A variant on this system was the offer of release of prisoners to their kinsmen who gave information relating to even more horrific crimes. Thus, the Audiencia of Valencia promised freedom for any two prisoners under sentence of death for help in tracking down the killers of the Admiral of Aragon in 1627. There was, after all, a general feeling that crimes were particular offences against specific individuals, and that the commonwealth would not be the loser if the parties were able to reach an accommodation between themselves. The Cortes of 1584, for example, made a 'charitable donation' to a lady of Toledo in order for her husband to negotiate a pardon from the family of a man he had murdered. And the parents of the great playwright Pedro Calderón de la Barca (1600–81) had had to pay out 600 ducats in order to secure his pardon after a brawl in which he was involved in his student days at Salamanca, in which a man died.[46]

Such attitudes were becoming less common in the early modern period, as the state sought to acquire for itself a special role as guardian of the peace. Castillo de Bobadilla agreed that there was a difference between offences which were mainly directed against a private party and which could therefore be pardoned by the latter, and those which represented a more general affront to public welfare. But he counselled the *corregidor* to ignore the distinction and to pursue all wrong-doing, even where the injured party was reluctant to press charges. His contemporary, the jurist Cerdán de Tallada, meanwhile deplored the custom in Valencia which left it to the discretion of the victim as to whether he prosecuted an attacker in a street brawl through the courts or not. He urged the magistrate to take action *ex officio* in all cases.[47] The developing concept of the 'public weal' was a slow construction, built up in an empirical and often untidy way from the Middle Ages onwards. We have alluded already to the special retribution reserved for someone who attacked another during a period of truce. The Furs of Valencia still proclaimed the death penalty in 1580, in similar fashion, for the treacherous act of wounding a man 'on Good Friday or other days of great devotion'. And a fourteenth-century Castilian law, reissued in the code of 1640, put the highways – 'like that which leads to Santiago, or goes from one town to its neighbour, or runs to a market or fair' – under the protection of the king, so that an offence committed on these attracted a fine in addition to whatever punishment was incurred by the act itself.

This gradual carving out of privileged space – special days, sacred places – gradually familiarised the citizen with the notion of a common good superior to his own private grievances against an opponent. Perhaps the most significant feature of this educative process was the increasing restrictions placed on the use of weapons. There had long been limitations on their handling inside city walls and during hours of darkness as precautionary measures. Thus it was the task of the local constable to see that the church bell was tolled every night for an hour – at nine in winter, ten in summer, according to Castillo de Bobadilla – in order to give country folk returning from the fields and travellers due notice of the 'curfew' which was approaching. During curfew the constable had increased rights of disarming passers-by, even those bearing traditional weapons like a sword if the circumstances were deemed suspicious (such as that the man was not carrying a lantern). Castillo de Bobadilla devoted much space to discussing the problem of who could be allowed to bear arms unchallenged. Muleteers clearly needed cutting weapons, and though any group of three armed individuals might be held to constitute a threat to public order, the constable would be well-advised not to question them if they were standing in front of the house of one of their number, taking the air. One senses here the slow evolution of the idea that bearing arms was a privilege, not an automatic right. Travellers were allowed to carry guns, but magistrates were insisting that these must be unloaded at the entrance to their town. Castillo de Bobadilla's list of those who could normally carry weapons of all kinds, whether by day or night, in built-up areas as well as in the country-side, was fairly restrictive: knights of the Military Orders (but not ordinary nobles) and public officials. Hence, perhaps, the increasing popularity in the seventeenth century of posts in the local militia or revenue collection (tax-farmers claimed a royal privilege of 1574 allowing them to go armed even at night, as a precaution against smugglers) or Inquisition.[48]

The development of the gun was making the new restrictions all the more necessary. Particular concern was shown at the flintlock mechanism (*pedreñal*), which meant that from the later sixteenth century ordinary citizens could carry on their persons a deadly weapon, no longer requiring the length of match needed to ignite the cumbersome arquebus of old. Already in 1563 the government decreed that the use of a firearm constituted an aggravation of any assault, entailing confiscation of all one's property. Laws dealing with guns speak of them as a 'treacherous' (*alevoso*) or 'cowardly' weapon, particularly the flintlocks going on sale now with a barrel shorter than four 'palms' (about 84 centimetres), which could be concealed under the cloak. The Valencian authorities originally banned guns under three 'palms' in length, but then found it necessary after 1584 to outlaw flintlocks altogether, given the particularly disturbed conditions in the province. These laws were extremely unpopular. The Valencian estates alleged that travellers needed to protect themselves, and suggested that the crime rate had actually increased since the ban. Anyway, said the Cortes of 1626, flintlocks were 'often carried by our young people, without the least intention of causing bodily harm'. This was perhaps the key point: were the restrictions enforceable? Castillo de Bobadilla spoke of seeing short-barrelled *pedreñales* openly on sale in the streets of Madrid. From a contrary viewpoint, the Valencian Cortes of 1626 complained that the judges were not respecting the relaxation introduced in 1621, which permitted bona fide travellers to carry guns over four palms in length through the countryside. The king returned a non-committal reply. What one senses here and elsewhere is a desire on the part of the government to have a free hand to intervene with full rigour when and where disturbances or banditry were rife. Overall, it is clear that it was winning this war of attrition – very gradually building up a mentality of good citizenship in which the risk of carrying weapons was seen to outweigh the advantages of self-defence.[49]

But ultimately the efficacy of this policy depended on the functioning of the courts. The cosmographer Pedro de Medina described in 1548 the sight that greeted him as he crossed La Mancha from his native Andalusia. Just north of Ciudad Real, 'I saw beside the road, here and there, bodies of men shot to death with arrows, a great multitude of them'; and on a hill-top a charnel house, where their bones were thrown when the flesh rotted – 'one of the fiercest deaths meted out to delinquents in a Christian country'.[50] These were the culprits tried and executed by the famous *Santa Hermandad* (Holy Brotherhood), set up by Ferdinand and Isabel as a league of towns to police a disturbed countryside. With a special royal commission, municipal *alcaldes* enjoyed summary jurisdiction over criminals who acted or took refuge outside their community, and could mete out one hundred lashes for petty theft, proceed to cut off ears or feet for anything graver, and put to death by a firing squad of crossbow-men for thefts over 5,000 *maravedís* (equivalent to half a year's wages for an agricultural labourer at the time). 'From this derives great security of property in the countryside,' commented Pedro de Medina, 'and men pass along the highways day and night with great peace and safety.' The contrast with the bandit-ridden Crown of Aragon could hardly have been greater.

But it was above all the famous *corregidor* – the 'corrector', sent out to preside over the *regidores* – who may be chiefly credited with the transformation of Castile from one of the most factious to one of the most law-abiding societies in early modern Europe. The chronicler of John II (1406–54) wrote that, 'because in the cities and towns of his realm there were many feuds, from which stemmed many deaths of people and robberies and arson and other great mischiefs . . . for this reason he would often send out his *corregidores*'.[51] The officers might enjoy a certain initial popularity, and we find their equivalent in Valencia at this time – commissioners dispatched with the full authority of the king, sometimes at the request of the local aldermen, in order to restore justice. But these authoritarian outsiders were not welcomed as a permanent institution. Thus the Andalusian town of Ubeda wrote to the king in 1412 that they did not need a *corregidor*, 'for the citizens and *regidores* here are all principal noblemen . . . and in order to put a stop to the disturbances and scandals which there had been, the town council ordered the inhabitants not to go about armed and not to form gangs, and told innkeepers to report the names of anyone coming in to lodge with them'.[52]

It was under the Catholic Kings (1474–1516) that what had been intermittent commissions became permanent features of the Castilian landscape. Their number increased to sixty-eight officers by the middle of the seventeenth century, delegated initially for two years at a time but usually staying five or six, spread out over the main cities of Castile. Their peace-keeping functions extended to cover all matters of government: thus in 1608 they were asked to report to Madrid on the state of the harvest in their area. After an initial reluctance to have them, which surfaced in the revolt of the Comuneros (1520–1), the towns seem to have settled down to regarding them as a useful part of the civilising process. The Cortes of 1579–82, though concerned that 'sometimes we have seen these offices given away as a reward for services . . . and by way of favour', nevertheless accepted that most *corregidores* were 'men of ability' (*personas calificadas*). Its main concern – like that of its predecessor of 1576–8 – was to ensure that the king got to know the names of all 'the gentlemen and virtuous persons in these kingdoms' who, because of their provincial obscurity, were never considered for appointment. Also, it was worried that the investigation into their conduct (*residencia*) which *corregidores* were supposed to undergo at the end of their term was perfunctory: 'they usually have men of standing (in the community) who are their friends and supporters, who speak up for them and protect them'.[53]

The ideal *corregidor* was supposed to conform to the portrait painted by Castillo de Bobadilla in 1597. He should be an outsider to the community in which he administered justice, for people tended to have less respect for an official whose private life was known to them, while 'many who know his failings will reproach him with these'. On the other hand, the Valencian jurist Cerdán de Tallada, in whose province all magistrates had by law to be natives, thought this was less of a disadvantage than might appear, for 'we cannot be confident that an outsider will not very quickly make enemies and friends, and have his own interests'. A balance had to be struck, concluded Castillo de Bobadilla, between allowing the *corregidor* to get acquainted with the people he was governing and ensuring that he did not put down local roots. 'For we see that friendships often spring up between ruler and ruled, who become good comrades, playing cards and attending festivities together.' The ideal *corregidor* would avoid such compromising relationships. He did not have to be a professional – a man of the law; normally he would have a university-trained deputy, an *alcalde mayor*, for that. Rather, it was useful if he was capable of inspiring respect through his birth and breeding. Noble birth acted as a spur to virtue, though it required strengthening through study, which 'corrects the vices of intemperance, rashness, injustice, imprudence and pusillanimity'. Julius Caesar and Alfonso the Wise, the thirteenth-century king of Castile, were the models to imitate here.[54]

Above the *corregidores* were the chancery courts. Their rise was one of the significant features of Habsburg power in both Castile and the Crown of Aragon. The Chancillería building in Granada, completed in 1587, carried on its façade the proud legend that it had been built so that its architectural magnificence 'might not be out of keeping with the weightiness of the business herein transacted'. Legend has it that the staircase was paid for out of a fine on a nobleman who had refused to take off his hat to the king's judges. Whether or not you can keep your hat on in my presence, Philip II was alleged to have told him, you certainly cannot do so in the presence of the law represented by my judges. As the Granadan chronicler Bermúdez de Pedraza put it, a writ of the Chancillería was 'a graven image of the king, sometimes more highly esteemed than in other kingdoms is the person of the monarch'.[55]

Studies of colonial Latin America have made us aware of how human these emblems of the majesty of the law actually were. Sent in to Mexico or Quito as representatives of the king of Spain, they often ended up acquiring property in the locality or marrying into the landowning families, and could scarcely be relied upon to enforce the more unpopular edicts of the sovereign. The Castilian *oidores*, as these chancery judges were known, were perhaps more mobile, but suffered from a similar tendency to put down roots. Graduates of the law schools, commented the humanist Diego Hurtado de Mendoza around 1570, they had been the backbone of the administration of the Catholic Kings. 'A middling sort of people,' they were expected to lead a life of 'modesty, reserve, truthfulness, simplicity, all free of scandal; not to pay social calls, not to accept gifts, not to have any close friends; not to dress or spend in a lavish way. . .' In brief, they were to set an example, in their deportment, which was at odds with the wild life-style of the nobility.[56] Perhaps it was hardly surprising that the noble families somewhat turned their backs on them in the early days. There was also unease at the pettifogging, hair-splitting activities of the lawyer. The Basque chronicler Garibay, born in 1533, tells us how, 'when I was getting ready to study law . . . my uncle . . . so persuaded my father that this field was so dangerous for the soul' that he abandoned the idea. Another member of the gentry, Cristóbal Crespí de Valldaura (1599–1672), recalled how his mother had advised him against a legal career, 'because she held it to be dangerous for one's salvation'. But ultimately the hardships of life as a widow 'forced her to change her mind', so that her son went on to become a high-court judge and eventually vice-chancellor of the Council of Aragon.[57]

By the time Castillo de Bobadilla was writing (1597), however, the Castilian nobility had overcome such prejudices against the men of the long robe. In the Crown of Aragon the caste-like differences, as Gilabert suggested in 1616, survived longer. But in 1644 the viceroy of Valencia could report that the nobles were now anxious to have more members in the Audiencia, 'now that there are so many men of letters in their ranks'.[58] The problem by this time was rather the suspiciously close links, of marriage and friendship, which were uniting the judges with local elites. Already in 1579–82 the Cortes had sounded a note of alarm which grew stronger with the years: 'since the *oidores* are left so long in the same tribunal, they often go on to acquire relatives and friends in the area'. And the *jurados* (lesser town councillors) of Seville, possibly because as former merchants they had been exposed to favouritism, asked that judges there be moved on after three years to prevent them acquiring 'clients' (*allegados*).[59]

Some 70 corregidors, perhaps 150 magistrates of the high courts and councils of Madrid: on their broad shoulders reposed the government of Castile.[60] But beneath them was an army of bureaucrats – bailiffs, clerks, police constables – whose unpopularity is reflected in the outbursts of the sixteenth-century Cortes. The *alguacil* was an enormously responsible peace-officer, more akin to a sheriff in the Old West than to a modern policeman. He would need great self-discipline, wrote Castillo de Bobadilla, and must be immune to the temptations he would surely face of anger, bribery or arrogance. For this reason the Valencian Cortes of 1604 wanted him to be of noble status. But Antoni Clara, who was denounced by the Valencians in 1625 for opening fire on a man 'without any cause or justifica-tion whatsoever', remained extremely unpopular, even though he (or possibly his son) purchased the status of noble from the Crown in 1645 for the hefty sum of 10,000 *reales*.[61] Though there were supposed to be only fourteen *alguaciles* in the kingdom, answerable directly to the viceroy, the Cortes of Valencia complained constantly about the growth in number. Their ideal was self-policing. Thus, they demanded in 1626 and 1645 that the governor of Xàtiva should not have a standing police force, 'but that when he needs men for any duty, he should summon them there and then'. On the other hand, the Cortes also sought to reduce the liability of towns to escort prisoners, and those of 1585 secured the exemption of the city guilds from having to form a posse to chase bandits more than four or five leagues (say, 25–30 kilometres).

The best-known example of the posse in action is the Catalan *sometent* – a general call-out of citizens to chase outlaws. In reply to the viceroy's suggestion that it be used, however, Philip II showed himself reluctant in 1565: 'It is a great burden, which people will much resent and they will in the end not turn up . . . and the first day they catch one of the wanted men, all his side will join together and harry the town.'[62] The *sometents* were tried anyway, on a piecemeal basis, usually lasting about a month in disturbed areas. But the government also drafted in troops, in Catalonia and Aragon from the 1560s, sometimes paid out of the treasury, sometimes (after much haggling) subsidised by the local communities. In Valencia in 1615, the town council of Alzira, threatened by a high court judge, 'who says that he will bring in soldiers at our expense', resolved that its own *justicia* would raise twenty-five men to sweep the territory. There was major protest on the whole subject in the Cortes of 1626, where the forces under the command of Antoni Clara and others were denounced as 'idle vagrants and ruffians [who], under the name of soldiers . . . have committed great crimes and offences, including some killings . . . and demand food and lodging in a high-handed manner'.[63] Olivares, desperate to placate the Valencians so that they would vote subsidies for the war, promised that only the Crown could in future authorise such commissions. But the Cortes of 1645 were soon complaining that this restriction was not being observed.

There were other measures that could be adopted, but all seemed to lead to an increase in the arbitrary power of government. Around 1580 the Council of Aragon debated and rejected a proposal that the kin of wanted men should be removed from their homes – 'it is so repugnant to our notions of fairness and in conflict with the laws of that kingdom [Valencia]'. But in 1586 it threatened the galleys for anyone, family member or friend, who gave succour to an outlaw – 'even though he did this just once and without evil intent, since the public good comes before that of the individual'. And the saintly Juan de Ribera, as viceroy of

Valencia, published the draconian decree of 1603 for the disturbed Alicante territory, that if any wanted man was seen in his native village, all his family to the second degree (parents and siblings) would be expelled from the place forthwith, 'without any other proof being needed'.[64]

Such measures were, no doubt, a confession of weakness. In Catalonia, Valencia and Aragon a running feud began to develop in the later years of the sixteenth century between the authorities and the estates over the medieval privileges which safeguarded the liberty of the subject, restricting the use of torture and the length of time suspects could be held without trial. In Castile, where royal authority was stronger, Castillo de Bobadilla wrote of the problem of well-born troublemakers – 'dissolute characters, seditious and causes of scandal' – who had not actually broken the law or could not be dealt with in open court. 'Let the magistrate draw up secret indictments against them and send these to the government . . . telling them, for the sake of public order, to leave town and show themselves at court.' In 1662 the viceroy of Valencia submitted a list of a score of prominent citizens – including the Admiral of Aragon and two canons of the cathedral – whom he wanted removed in this way. But when he followed this up with a second list a month later, the Council of Aragon recoiled from 'ordering so many people out all at once'.[65] In this faction-ridden province, the decision was taken in 1693 to interrogate suspects, after the defeat of the peasant revolt (the Second Germanía), in secret – 'given the delays and inconvenience which might arise in villages so infested with factions, feuds and vendettas, if it was generally known what one person said about another'.[66]

One of the causes of disorder in Catalonia, commented Guicciardini in 1512, was that many of the feudal lords 'have villages and castles over which the king exercises no authority, and in these places all the criminals take refuge'. In Castile, the situation may not have been so very different, to judge by the opinion of the Chancillería of Granada as late as 1687, that seigneurs often allowed criminals 'to walk around free on their estates, though responsible for atrocious crimes'.[67] In fact, a long campaign from the middle of the sixteenth century would gradually change this situation. One finds early echos of it in the use of troops by the Chancillería of Granada throughout the Alpujarras in the 1560s, and in 1586 the Valencian seigneurs were threatened with loss of their jurisdictions unless they showed themselves active against banditry. It is true that the Cortes of 1604 rescinded this decree of 1586, but in return the feudal lords agreed that anyone sentenced as a 'thief or a highway robber' would not find shelter with them but would be returned forthwith to his place of trial.

The authorities tried to get the localities to form 'unions' – agreements signed for generally four years at a time in Catalonia, allowing the men of one area to pursue outlaws into another, and to club together to compensate anyone who suffered loss as a result of bandit activity anywhere in the Union. The viceroys of Catalonia had to keep up a relentless pressure in order to secure these agreements, writing in 1565 to the steward of the viscount of Cabrera i Bas that he should join, since his territories were 'rugged terrain, ideal for such rogues and bandits, and much favoured by them'. The fundamental problem, in Catalonia as in Castile, was that all communities wanted to keep jurisdiction in their own hands and showed a fierce mistrust of their neighbours. Nor were they keen to commit themselves to reimbursing arson damage in the countryside, as the Union contracts required. But the Crown was reducing the possibility of non-cooperation, sequestrating the barony of Baga in 1564 for allegedly being a safe-haven for bandits, or ordering the abbot of Ripoll to cut down the trees on the roads through his estate so that travellers could not be waylaid so easily.[68]

What tended to happen in the seventeenth century was that a partnership developed between seigneurs and the Crown, each relying for help on the other. Thus the marquis of Ariza, faced by the return of amnestied outlaws to his villages of Calpe and Altea, where they were given refuge by the inhabitants 'partly out of friendship, partly out of fear or kinship', asked the Audiencia in 1636 to send in an *alguacil* with troops. On the other hand, the patrons of these outlaws prevailed with the royal judges the following year – much to the annoyance of the marquis – to have the commission withdrawn. Indeed, given the relative weakness of feudal authority in Spain, to which we referred in Chapter 5, these ties of patronage between village potentates and the royal authorities might well undermine seigneurial control. Thus the duke of Infantado complained in 1648 that the royal commissioner sent in to settle the feuds in the ducal fief of Ayora was himself involved on the side of one of the factions.[69] And when the steward of the duke of Gandia tried to investigate feuding in the town of Pego on his master's estates, he was met with a hail of bullets from behind the walls and an appeal by the citizens to the Audiencia that the duke was oppressing them. It required a royal judge to restore order. Nevertheless, as late as 1690 the viceroy of Valencia was writing that the turbulent Antonio Palacios, farmer of the seigneurial revenues of the barony of Alcalalí, could only be captured by the forces of the duke of Gandia, who had his estates near this remote, mountainous village.[70] Rather than a clear confrontation between seigneurial and royal jurisdictions, there was thus a network of multiple ties of dependence and influence.

Judging by the amount of space he devotes to it, it was the immunity of the Church rather than of the seigneurs which preoccupied Castillo de Bobadilla. The great jurist acknowledged the special role of the clergy: they were engaged alongside magistrates in the common task of building a Christian commonwealth, and their sacred status entitled them to the privilege of governing themselves. Very tentatively – 'I lay myself always under correction by Holy Mother Church' – Castillo de Bobadilla suggested that clerical tribunals were subject in certain matters to supervision by the royal courts. In civil matters – marriage cases were a recurring problem – a layman might sue out an injunction (*recurso de fuerza*) ordering the bishop or his vicar general to amend his proceedings, though leaving the definitive judgement in his hands. As regards 'criminous clerks', an old source of contention throughout Europe since the days of Thomas Beckett, the Council of Trent (1563) had ruled that such individuals would only enjoy immunity from state prosecution if they wore the tonsure and a soutane or its equivalent, and held some benefice. But in practice much confusion continued to reign. Even priests were supposed to be handed over to the royal courts if accused of 'atrocious crimes', but the archbishop of Valencia wrote to the king in 1649 that manslaughter was regrettably so common in his diocese that it could not be classed, without further enquiry, under this heading. In Catalonia, given the ferocity of banditry there, the authorities had managed to secure the so-called Papal Brief (*Breve*), allowing a mixed panel of ecclesiastical and royal judges to arbitrate on this matter, and it was a prime aim of the Valencians in the seventeenth century to secure an equivalent concession. In 1622 the viceroy was complaining that many unsavoury individuals were being given the tonsure only to acquire immunity for their bad behaviour, 'as the way they dress and live goes to show'.[71] The problem with the church courts, as Castillo de Bobadilla pointed out, was the laxity of the sentences they bestowed. Reluctant to shed blood, their greatest penalty – in cases other than heresy, of course – was a perpetual life sentence, at a time when the Crown sought to impress the people with the savage spectacle of public execution. Hence, 'secular magistrates, for the peace and quiet of the commonwealth . . . delay and resist handing over criminous clerks to their ecclesiastical colleagues'.

A further problem was sanctuary – the right of even a layman to claim immunity by running into the sacred space of a church. The Furs limited sanctuary in Valencia to the main church in each town, and excluded it in cases of murder with intent or highway robbery. But the Spanish ambassador in Rome was still trying to get this limitation extended to the hinterland of Alicante, which had only been incorporated into the Valencian kingdom in 1305, after the Fur in question was decreed.[72] The ramshackle nature of these privileges meant that judges were often tempted to drive a coach and horses through them. But for many people a bad privilege was better than no protection at all against arbitrary government. The chronicler Bermúdez de Pedraza reports how the crowd clamoured for the 'freedom of the Church' when the Chancillería hanged a priest in Granada in 1556. 'You did not hang a man, you hanged Christ,' a Jesuit preacher thundered from the pulpit, as the judges gathered for mass in the cathedral, and the archbishop proceeded to lay an interdict on the city. The three judges mainly responsible backed down and agreed to accept any penance imposed by the prelate; but our source grimly notes that they and their children all came to a bad end.[73] Interdicts – the prohibition of the sacraments in a particular town – recurred through the seventeenth century in relation to such matters (in Valencia, for example, in 1620 and 1680). More usually, it was personal excommunication which an over-eager magistrate had to face. Castillo de Bobadilla noted the inevitability of conflict – the royal judge determined to uphold the rigour of the law the more resistance he encountered, the bishops and vicars general responding with sanctions. The government will not be much help, Castillo advised the *corregidor*: rather, do what you have to do, then ask for absolution and perform the penance required, 'for if justice was done, you will hold your head up, not hang it in shame'.[74]

Two concepts of public order were here in conflict, and they were only part of a wider struggle between traditionalists and the new proponents of strong government. Rebutting criticism of the Fueros of Aragon which seemed too favourable to the criminal, the chronicler Argensola wrote (1604): 'Some peoples love punishment so much that they give a free hand to the judge, so that no offence may escape retribution . . . Others feel that a man not limited by law is a wild beast, and that they would rather have many culprits go free than that one innocent man should suffer.'[75] Castillo de Bobadilla set out the alternative expectations of the Castilian judge: that the safety of the commonwealth was the supreme law, as in ancient Rome, and the *corregidor* might well execute summary justice against offenders. However, he did recommend caution, noting that only the king or his specially delegated commissioner could safely set aside due process. In practice, the very vivid picture of justice in operation in Toledo in 1613, contained in the picaresque memoir of Diego Duque de Estrada, suggests that much latitude had to be left to individual magistrates. Here torture was applied in a manslaughter case to a man who claimed to be noble; detention without trial was applied not only to him but to the kin of the victim, in order to nip any feud in the bud; the culprit's escape from custody seemed very close to succeeding until the justice of Ecija took a personal dislike to him and decided to return him for trial in Toledo. Finally, one has a picture of the sheer horror of the Toledo gaol, where suspects languished for up to seven years, awaiting trial or review of their sentence, and the arbitrary action of the government in 1614 ordering all prisoners awaiting appeal to be transferred immediately to the galleys in view of the need for oarsmen. When Duque de Estrada joined a riot, he was sentenced summarily to death, and only escaped through the intervention of his patron at court.[76]

The great Valencian jurist, Cerdán de Tallada, insisted that the letter of the law had to be interpreted according to the spirit – in a 'Christian' and not a 'Pharisaical' manner. But here lay the rub: the Crown of Aragon had its very specific privileges – Habeas Corpus, limitation or prohibition of torture – which were repeatedly denounced by the authorities as making their task of peace enforcement impossible. In reply to a protest by the noble estate of Valencia against detention without trial, the government invoked 'the difficulty there has been in getting evidence together'; but the Valencians resolved that this was not a satisfactory answer, for it could apply to 'any case at all in future', so that 'we can only conclude that the minds of the magistrates are not well disposed towards the members of this house'. In this same year (1616), a major confrontation erupted over the humiliating treatment of one aristocratic prisoner, so that the estate resolved to exclude four members of the Audiencia from ever sitting in its ranks. The debate was over more than law and order: it was an attempt to define the limits of government itself. At least that was how it appeared to the diarist and priest Joan Porcar. No friend to the irresponsible and violent nobility of his native Valencia, he yet could not refrain from setting down in his journal the way people were talking about the end of an era, the demise of a feudal nobility: 'People say that . . . the upholders of the freedom of the land are all dead now.'[77]

It was becoming clear, in fact, that the government was finding quite a few supporters for its hard-line attitude within the ranks of the governed. The 'Unions' of Aragonese towns to pursue bandits represented a voluntary suspension of the Fueros in some instances for the greater good of public order, and Zaragoza set forth a spirited defence of its invasion of local immunities in the same cause (1588). In 1653 one of the rising stars in the Valencian political firmament, the first count of Cervellón, defended – in a session of the estates, no less – the high-handed actions of the government against outlaws. 'When one could see that the law was being applied in a way which kept the peace,' he affirmed, 'one would have to have a very cogent reason before criticising the ministers of the Crown.' Anyway, such magistrates stood in relation to the subject like a father to his children, 'and if they are found wanting, one should rather accept this as a chastisement from the hand of God'.[78] One senses a shift in attitudes towards good citizenship. The Valencian Cortes of 1626 had already tried to limit the sacrosanct right of duelling, allowing any ambush or any attack of a weaker party by a more numerous gang to be prosecuted ex officio by the state, without waiting for a complaint from the victim. In 1716 and 1757 the Bourbons tightened up the old Castilian prohibition of the duel, applying it to Spain as a whole and sanctioning infractions now with the death penalty. Spaniards no longer needed to show their valour, ran the decree, 'in such an ugly, criminal and abominable way'.[79]

Tracing the change in social attitudes which underlay this legislation is not always easy, and more will be said on the subject when we come to religion and family control. But clearly the advance of a new urban and bureaucratic elite was significant. The Jesuit Luis de la Palma recalled in his Life of his father (1595) how this merchant of Toledo would teach his sons to fence but rarely wore a sword himself because of his short temper. 'The more valiant a man is,' he would say, 'the more patience and forbearance must he display.' It was equanimity (*apacibilidad*) which Cristóbal Crespí counselled to his younger brother in 1627 as the latter set out to join the army of Flanders: 'It is right to give vent to a grievance, but let it be in due time . . . Not to feel resentment shows a want of feeling, but to display forbearance is a mark of wisdom.'[80] Castillo de Bobadilla's prescription for the ideal *corregidor*, that he should be of good lineage as well as of good character, lettered as well as self-disciplined, was holding up a new model of aristocratic leadership.

Of course, the bureaucracy would meet the nobility half-way. When Don Luis de Gudiel, former judge of the Chancillería of Granada, was sent back to that city in 1636 to press the local elites for donatives to the Crown, the chronicler refers to the heart-attacks his mission caused. But then we see Don Luis admitted to the chivalric order of Calatrava during his stay, in a splendid cere-mony at which the high-court judges rubbed shoulders with 'the flower of the knighthood of Granada'. The patronage ties between both no doubt facilitated the new judicial absolutism. Thus we find the duke of Sessa writing to one of the Granadan magistrates, Don Juan Chumacero, around 1618 thanking him for a favourable decision in a lawsuit: 'Though truly it would not be proper to invoke friendship if one were not also in the right, yet it often requires effort to establish that right.'[81] The Chumacero connection stretched back through his mother's family, the Carrillos, to Cordoba, where Sessa was influential. Whether the duke's promise of 1618 to have him promoted actually played any role in his subsequent ministerial career, as member of the Council of Castile from 1626, then president from 1643, is unclear. Chumacero had a reputation, at least in later life, as something of a puritan. The essayist Luis Zapata (1532–98?) described one Granadan judge as turning his back on all such compromising friendships. At his death they found 'three or four chests full of letters from princes and great lords, which he had not looked at nor read nor answered'. And Castillo de Bobadilla recalled that he as a *corregidor* had been in receipt of numerous begging letters, which he had carried around in his pocket for days without opening. But he advised a magistrate to refrain always from discourtesy. If a petition can be granted 'without hurting the public weal', then it was perfectly legitimate to show oneself attentive to it. After all, Holy Mother Church 'invokes and requests the help of the saints, like favourites who have special access to God'.[82] No doubt this cultural model helped to shape a certain expectation of the bureaucratic system, even though its practical application in individual cases would be hard to demonstrate. In this way, over time it would help reconcile the old nobility, who had lived by a different code, to the constraints of legalism.

Part of the education in the new ways was, of course, judicial terrorism. In Seville over the thirty-eight years that the Jesuit Pedro de León served as prison chaplain (1578–1616) there were 570 death sentences issued (and 309 executions carried out), mostly for murder but also for robbery.[83] In Valencia one finds an equally steady stream of men going to the scaffold, the common criminals usually garrotted (as an act of mercy) before their bodies were strung up in the market square, the relatively few nobles being decapitated in front of the cathedral. Particular examples were made of any who had resisted authority: bandits, for example, might be dragged through the streets – unless the rains had turned them to mud – before being hanged and then quartered.[84] But this spectacle was perhaps a confession of weakness: running parallel to it was the strategy of amnesty and pardon for those with influence or for those who could not be caught.

The idea of mercy was, after all, built into the judicial system through the pervasive influence of the church. 'God have mercy on his soul', commented Mossèn Porcar on a bandit executed in 1612; and the popular ballads of seventeenth-century Castile displayed a certain compassion for the outlaw, though only after he had paid the penalty for his misdeeds.[85] The most visible expression of this sense of a common, fallen humanity are the various confraternities dedicated in one form or another to the succour of the criminal. Thus on Saint Mathias's Day (24 February) the Valencian brotherhood of Our Lady of the Forsaken would gather up the remains of those executed during the preceding year, whose corpses had been left to rot on gallows a couple of kilometres outside the city gates. The bones were brought back, 'in solemn procession', for interment in the grounds of the General Hospital. In Granada the Confraternity of Mercy, composed of the greatest families in the city, would accompany condemned men to the scaffold and gather the remains of those quartered for burial in its chapel. The most famous of all, that of the Holy Charity in Seville, knelt in prayer while the execution took place, then at three in the afternoon, in memory of the Crucifixion, took down the corpse.[86]

One of the significant changes taking place in the early modern period was a greater attention to the soul of the condemned man. As part of its campaign of evangelisation, the Counter-Reformation church sought to use ritual in a more 'rational' way, as part of the reform of character. Thus Don Miguel Mañara, as director of the Holy Charity in the later seventeenth century, got it to pay for friars to accompany a condemned man in his cell continuously during the interval between sentence and execution. Among jurists too one notices a greater attention to reform of the criminal. Castillo de Bobadilla reflected on the way in which Canon Law had pioneered the idea of prison as a place of correction, where men, 'like brute beasts, tied down and restrained, might become peaceful'. But the secular law still used gaol mainly for those awaiting trial and for debtors. The galleys, increasingly fashionable from the middle of the sixteenth century, were hardly an adequate substitute. The zealous reformer Francisco Martínez de Mata, a kind of lay preacher who went around in Franciscan robes, spent seven years tending to galley slaves in the 1640s, before he began writing the treatises on the causes of crime – poverty and economic decline – for which he is best remembered. In a memorial of 1648, he noted that the galleys were supposed to be a merciful alternative to the death penalty. But the condemned were being left there to rot: 'The aim of the punishment is that the criminal should be reformed. Well, if you leave him there for life, when does reform come in?' And life in the galleys was not anyway conducive to improvement: 'There is not a word of good advice given and no sacraments are administered, so that the Devil takes hold of the soul . . .'[87]

The Jesuit Pedro de León's mission to the prisoners of Seville, Martínez de Mata's experiences of the galley slaves of Malaga, were pointers to the future. But it was not really until the eighteenth century that the slow business of penal reform would come into its own. The abolition of the galleys in 1748 and of torture in 1814, the shifting of the gallows away from the centres of towns, were all signs of a new willingness, in Spain as in the rest of Europe, to ask fundamental questions about the nature of crime and punishment. 'Houses of Correction' were set up throughout the peninsula in the later eighteenth century, accompanied by a more systematic reclusion of vagrants, as part of a campaign to tackle more effectively the causes of anti-social behaviour. Castillo de Bobadilla had already written of the need to do something of the kind. 'It would be a better form of government,' he wrote, 'to accustom citizens to be virtuous through helpful and repeated interventions, so that they may easily and enthusiastically obey good laws, for otherwise laws are only a heavy burden on weak shoulders.'[88] This process of moral reform would require a more general change, though, in social values, not least in the way families were formed and the way the young were educated.

9

THE POLICING OF THE FAMILY

In Spain, as in the rest of traditional Europe, the individual was enveloped by the corporate structure of the society. Of these corporate institutions one of the most powerful was the family. Castillo de Bobadilla noted that the government of the commonwealth (*política*) had its counterpart in economics (*económica*), 'which deals with the management of the household, for a well-run family is the very portrait of the commonwealth'. The distinguished Portuguese military expert and writer, Don Francisco Manuel de Mello, put the same point across in his treatise of 1651 on the topic: 'a man who knows how to run his house properly would know how to run the state, for it is true that the city is a large family and the family a city in miniature'.[1]

Inculcating self-discipline was of increasing concern to writers during the early modern period, and those who discussed the well-ordered commonwealth found it useful to devote at least some of their attention to the family. Some of the leading Spanish humanists – Luis Vives, Fray Luis de León – devoted entire books to aspects of the topic. But in their case, as in others of the Renaissance period, advice on family matters tended to be addressed directly to women, whereas for men it figured usually as one part of a wider treatise on good citizenship. Alternatively, as in the case of the famous Cordoban Jesuit Tomás Sánchez, whose 'Ten Books of Controversy on the Holy Sacrament of Matrimony' (1592) became a cornerstone of marriage law throughout Catholic Europe, the clergy wrote in Latin for confessors. Admittedly, things were changing in this respect, and the Jesuits – like Sánchez's contemporary Gaspar Astete – played a key role in Spain as elsewhere in bringing the family forward as a topic of discussion in books and preaching. By the eighteenth century – certainly rather later, one may feel, than in Protestant Europe – the household was seen as a major source of moral formation of the individual, and the Jesuit Matías Sánchez's treatise of 1740 could now carry the significant title: 'The Father of a Family Briefly Instructed in his Many Obligations'.

Many of the sources on which we depend for an insight into this rather private, therefore rather hidden aspect of past life are legal in nature – testaments and marriage contracts, litigation over inheritance, records of the moral policing exercised by ecclesiastical tribunals. Historians are sometimes made aware by discrepancies in this material – if the anthropologist had not already forewarned them – that in an essentially oral and small-scale society these documents are not always what they seem, and that the real business is going on in face-to-face discussion outside the notary's study or the court. People of the time tell us so, in the precious autobiographies which have come to light. It is probably true that the confessional in Catholic countries provided an alternative means of unburdening the soul, so that the range of written material is not as great as, say, in Puritan England. Nevertheless, similar promptings could be at work, as in the case of the Valencian priest Juan Martín Cordero (born in 1531), who wrote his life to show his family 'the great obligation I have to be grateful to Our Lord for the innumerable favours I have received from his blessed hand'. His near-contemporary, the historian Esteban de Garibay (born 1533), wrote his memoirs for his three sons who were being reared in Castile, far from their Basque homeland, as a stimulus to their self-improvement, 'for this brief life of man, full of misery and upsets, has to be a continual battle on this earth'. The Catalan peasant Sebastià Casanovas (1710–56?) had a rather similar philosophy. Battling all his life against misfortune, he resolved to set down for his offspring an account of the struggle. 'Most of it I have written by night,' he told them, 'when I got back from work.' His escape, and that of the family farm, from disaster, 'I attribute to the spirits of my ancestors, who were looking down and took a hand on behalf of the house.'[2]

At the social level of Casanovas, the more usual source is likely to be a household book – a journal of accounts, in which the author would note down the hiring of a servant or the satisfaction of a debt or the payment of a dowry, adding a comment on the harvest, or some public or private event.[3] Those which have survived have sometimes followed circuitous routes before reaching a wider public – leaving the family of origin after the failure of direct heirs, lucky to be preserved in some convent library, until it too was broken up in the liberal revolutions of the nineteenth century. Some only survive in copies made by the busy monks, in which private material may tend to have been edited out to the benefit of comments on public events. The instability of families – a factor particularly of Castilian life, to which we shall return – affected one of the most valuable sources of all: the letter. Don Luis de Requesens, on the eve of his departure for Flanders as governor, drew up his testament (1573). In view of the confusion and dispersal of his papers, he asked his brother to go through his letters and burn those which were of no permanent interest (that is, not relating to administration), with two significant exceptions: correspondence from King Philip, and from his mother, Doña Estefanía. The latter, in fact, provides unparalleled insight into the infancy of a nobleman in this period. Curiously, some of the best material of this kind has come down to us through the judicial archives, where letters between lovers or between parents and children were submitted as evidence of parentage and the like. How far these missives reflect the attitudes of the people, when so many were illiterate, is another question. The English traveller Joseph Townsend found the professional letter-writer busy at his trade in the 1780s: 'When the market square is not taken over by the preachers, the scribes take up their positions with their tables, near which they sit with ink, quill and paper to draw up and read out letters of all kinds.'[4]

In the very mobile society that was early modern Spain – mobile through the existence of frontier and empire – solidarities existed which provided a framework for individual lives. In the first place, there was the *patria*. The Castilian law code of the thirteenth century, the *Siete Partidas*, spoke of the *natura* (the blood) which unites men, and of the *naturaleza* (the common homeland) which 'makes them like one through long usage of true love'. When two men from the same town find themselves in a strange place, 'they enjoy each other's company and help each other in the things which are needful'.[5] The correspondence of Spanish emigrants to the Indies with their folk back home during the sixteenth century makes the point vividly enough. 'Certainly my spirit has long desired to see someone from home here in this land,' wrote the deputy governor of one Mexican town to his nephew in Extremadura in 1577.[6] The Granadan chronicler Bermúdez de Pedraza noted that there was a harmony of humours between a person and the physical environment where he had grown up: 'whence it happens that a sick man will recover his health and cheerfulness not only in his own land but with the sight of a man who comes from there'.[7]

Pride in ancestry, as we noted in an earlier chapter on the aristocracy, was an important feature of this sense of belonging. Something like a clan network stretched across the face of the empire. It was embodied in the concept of the *solar*, a difficult term to translate, but equivalent to the idea of a 'base' and often a tower or a domain associated with a particular family. From the towers of the Basque Country, Aragon and the Pyrenean region generally, the men of the Reconquista had fanned out over the peninsula during the Middle Ages, sometimes establishing new *solares* for themselves as they acquired land from the Moor and founding new branches of a clan. The Spanish lineages were thus pyramid-like in structure; each branch was headed by a *pariente mayor* (a 'chief kinsman'), who might not necessarily be the most powerful man within it. Thus the duke of Alburquerque was a junior member of the Cueva clan, whose headship resided in the marquis of Bedmar. The clan functioned as a network of patronage and honour, so that when the duke returned from his viceroyalty of Mexico in 1662 another junior kinsman from Granada, the lord of Las Uleylas, organised a great poetic 'joust' in celebration.[8]

The most visible expression of the lineage was surely the burial vault; the patron of one of these was effectively a *pariente mayor*, and when a new branch had outgrown its stem in terms of its wealth or power, it would signal its presence by establishing a new vault, and thereby a new *solar*. Thus, when the famous Beltrán de la Cueva, third son of a family of Ubeda, rose to fortune in the troubled politics of the fifteenth century, becoming duke of Alburquerque, he established a new mausoleum for that branch of the clan in his lordship of Cuéllar. 'All else in this world is passing,' proclaimed the bishop and chapter of Jaén as they authorised the lords of Garcíez to found a new chapel for their lineage in the cathedral in 1412, but 'these places of burial remain for ever more as testimony to those for whom they were set up.' The chronicler Argote de Molina described one in these precincts in 1588, draped with the 'blazons and banners and coats of arms' of its owner.[9]

Tombs and burial chapels were costly. In the Dominican convent of Palencia Antonio Ponz could still admire in 1787 the 'sumptuous sculpture, with kneeling figures', of the marquis of Poza (died 1557) and his wife, and opposite, 'another, more grandiose tomb in black marble, which seems to be by the celebrated Leoni, with kneeling figures' of the succeeding marquis (died 1604) and his spouse. He lamented that nowadays, through 'meanness or want of piety . . . the most that people will do is to place a sad stone with its epitaph over the grave'.[10] Spanish funerary sculpture, in fact, seems to have followed the trend in Europe generally, though perhaps at its own pace. The explosion of artistic investment during the Renaissance period, celebrating the virtues of the founder, seems to have been choked off by a new spirituality which found such hubris rather distasteful. When Don Bernardo de Valdés, member of the aristocratic confraternity of the Holy Charity of Seville, died in 1655, he left an endowment for its chapel on condition that he was buried there under his coat of arms. The reforming Chief Brother, Miguel Mañara, suggested – as the chapel neared completion in 1674 – that God would be better pleased if the money, 'which was blindly to be used for the commemoration of a dead man whom the worms had eaten', was devoted instead to the cult of Christ. It was agreed that Valdés would have, instead of his elaborate tombs and coat of arms, a simple plaque with the inscription: 'Here lie the ashes of our well loved brother.'[11] This Counter-Reformation spirituality, with its interiorisation of piety, emerges well in the request of Don Luis de Requesens (1573) for burial under a simple slab of marble, with just his name and date of death, 'so that those who read it and knew me in this life may remember to say a prayer to God for my soul'.

Death represented, indeed, a prime opportunity for the solidarity of friends and helpers to express itself. The diarist Jeroni Soria recalled the constant tolling of bells and the cries of the heralds through the streets of sixteenth-century Valencia for prayers at the deaths of the great ones of the land – a practice still followed for ordinary citizens in the little communities of the region down to the early twentieth century.[12] Funerals were dramatic affairs – the weeping women, described by the traveller Lalaing in 1501–3, the knight dragging the standard of his dead comrade through the dust while a throng dashed his shield ritually to the ground . . . The processions perhaps reached a peak during the Baroque: those of the duchess of Uceda in Madrid 1611, or of the marquesa of Armuña in Granada in 1633, where 'one could hardly get through the streets for the crush of people', attracted attention by their splendour. Mourning dress identified the circle of friends. Thus when the vice-chancellor of the Crown of Aragon, Don Simón Frígola, died in 1599, 'all those of his house wore hoods, such as notaries, lawyers, doctors, barbers, apothecaries and the like'.[13] While the corpse itself might be interred on the day following death, elaborate gatherings of the clan would take place to express solidarity with the bereaved for some time after that.

Garibay recalled how, after the death of his father in 1556, 'his kinsmen and friends demonstrated their great emotion, and they came up from all the surrounding towns, each in his own way, on different days of this month (March) and the following one of April'.[14]

Both the state and the church were nervous, each for its own reason, about these demonstrations. Ferdinand and Isabel tried to restrict gatherings of the clan, worried about the vendetta, and sixteenth-century bishops legislated against the *caridades* or distribution of food at funerals. Major decrees of Philip II in 1565, implementing the Council of Trent, limited to a dozen those kinsmen or friends who could hold candles at the funeral procession and restricted mourning dress to those of the household. These laws seem to have varied in their effect from region to region. They did not apply, for example, in the Crown of Aragon. In general, the older established communities of Old Castile and the north appear to have kept their semi-pagan customs longer than the Reconquest areas of Valencia and Andalusia, where an evangelical church shaped popular practice from a much earlier date. Thus the Valencian diarist Bernardo Catalá, in his travels through the mountainous borderland of León and Asturias in 1606, noted: 'it is the custom in these lands to leave few masses when they die, and they give food to all the laity who go to the funeral, to each one a pound of bread, together with three or four draughts of wine, and in some villages, cheese'.[15] By contrast, the law of 1565 tried to foster the spiritual solidarity of the godly: one could have as many members of one's spiritual confraternities at one's funeral as desired. The Council of Trent, taking its stand against Protestant individualism, emphasised that salvation was a collective phenomenon in part, and a sinner would do well to seek the help of the prayers of the 'saints'. As well as the confraternities, which came increasingly to constitute a kind of alternative network of friends and which we shall explore in the following chapter, the dying man or woman would rely on masses for the soul – 2,588 were ordered on average by each town councillor of Madrid in the early seventeenth century in his will. *Capellanías*, or chantries, became increasingly popular as perpetual endowments of masses for the dead. The historian of Seville, Diego Ortiz de Zúñiga, described their great number in the cathedral of that city in 1677, 'and on the eve and day of the commemoration of All Souls [2 November], so great a quantity of candles and monuments and effigies are placed over the graves that the whole temple is turned into a thick forest of torches and lights'.[16] The cult of the dead, in other words, absorbed much of the energy and resources of Spaniards of the Golden Age. A traditional solidarity survived quite well the attempts of church and state to prune it back, adapting new forms of piety to old constraints of the family. It was really only in the later eighteenth century that one notices a marked change here – a decline in the numbers of masses for the soul and a greater emphasis on the inner preparation of the individual soul *before* death.

If the cult of the dead helped reinforce the memory of a shared ancestry and a common identity, the test of solidarity would come in the world of the living. There is a certain contrast in testaments between the concern for property, identified generally with the household, and the sense of kinship, which might extend more widely. Thus the duke of Frías in 1612 asked his wife 'most earnestly that in everything relating to the upbringing and administration of my offspring, and in all else of importance, she consult with and take the advice of the senior knights and gentlemen of my lineage and house of Velasco, for they will be those who with most love and commitment will look to its grandeur and enhancement'. At a lower social level, the cloth trader Martín Fernández Cubero wrote from Mexico to a nephew in Castile in 1572, explaining that he was no longer able to run his business through advancing age and ill-health. 'If a man doesn't have someone to take his affairs to heart and look after his property, everything goes badly,' he explained; 'I need a relative here, and I would make something of him.'[17] Bernardo Catalá had continual dealings with some – not all – of his kin, particularly with his mother's brother, Francisco Juan Catalá, who had been his tutor, and with his maternal cousin, the powerful Don Juan Vivas de Cañamas, Spanish ambassador to Genoa from 1600. Bernardo agreed to look after the Cañamas estates while their owner was away in Italy; but when another cousin, Serafín Juan Catalá, died in 1601, he noted in his diary that he would have to refuse the wardship of the children, because he was too busy. Reluctantly, though, he agreed to become guardian of the offspring of Uncle Francisco Juan, after the latter died later in 1601. The chief consideration seems to have been that he was reversionary heir to this uncle's estate.[18] The cycle of broken families, so typical of the Old Regime, opened enormous possibilities of collaboration between kin, but also great opportunities of conflict over inheritance.

Nothing perhaps contributed more to the fashioning of family structure than the system of inheritance. It was in the nineteenth century, faced with rapid changes to the inheritance laws in the name of greater egalitarianism, that sociologists in various European countries began exploring the effects of these on the way society itself developed. The name of Le Play is well known in the French context, but hardly less meritorious was the work done for Spain by Joaquín Costa (1846–1911). Costa's great concern was to reform the economic and political life of his country, and he attributed much of the poverty and instability to be found above all in Castile to the splitting up of the family farm at the death of the father. By contrast, in the old Crown of Aragon the law had favoured a single heir. 'He is not the heir just to enjoy life and do what he likes, but rather to ensure the continuity of the physical and moral evolution of the family; he is a kind of serf tied to the reputation of the name he bears, a servant of his aged parents and of his unmarried aunts and uncles, whom he has to look after, and of his brothers and sisters, whom he has to place in life and provide with a dowry.' By following this model, the Pyrenean family had helped shape 'those characters at once inflexible, austere, upright, thrifty and hard-working, and those habits of individual *self-government*, which explain the admirable political history of Aragon'.[19] Costa was here tending to overlook the less admirable aspects of Aragonese indiscipline – the banditry which characterised the region in the early modern period – in favour of the long history of freedom associated with it.

As was suggested above in Chapter 2, the inheritance systems of medieval Spain tended to reflect the opportunities of the frontier, with a prevalence of subdivision and egalitarianism among heirs – except, indeed, in the old-established Pyrenean regions, like Aragon, Navarre or Old Catalonia. The closure of the frontier had led gradually to attempts to restrict succession to one child by allowing a parent, if he or she so wished, to give him or her a *mejora*, an 'advantage' out of the fifth of the estate which might be left freely for masses or legacies, together with a third of the remaining four-fifths, which traditionally had to be split up equally in *legítimas* ('mandatory shares') to each boy or girl. In practice, the great majority of Castilians continued to adhere to the principle of equality, which poses interesting questions about how a social elite was able to form and to perpetuate itself. As we described in an earlier chapter, the aristocracy had increasing recourse to the *mayorazgo* or entail. At a lower social level, village elites seem to have used *capellanías* or chantry benefices. Thus, when Doña Bernarda Chavarría of the Granadan community of Orgiva – a wealthy *labradora* or 'peasant', as she called herself – founded an endowment of fifteen masses every year for her soul, she set aside a house and fields worth 22,000 *reales* for this purpose, specifying that the priest should at each generation be her 'nearest kinsman' (1742). When the priest Miguel Tello drew up his will in 1682, he divided land worth 50,000 *reales* among his four nephews, but set aside a house and fields worth 19,800 for a chantry of twenty masses to be said every year for his soul. It was the accumulation of these small benefices which marked out the rural elites of early modern Spain.[20]

The egalitarianism of Castilian inheritance remained, nevertheless, a significant factor. One safety-valve, of course, was the demography of the period. As Paloma Fernández Pérez reminds us in her study of the merchants of Cadiz in the eighteenth century, mortality rates at the time were high and a fifth of the testators in her sample had no surviving offspring, and another two-fifths had only one or two. The merchants might also try to offload their surplus children into the ample bosom of the Catholic Church, as nuns or friars. They would use the *mejora* in some cases, often apparently as a kind of advance on the inheritance, for a son embarking on his first trading voyage to America or on an apprenticeship. And there were the exhortations – persuasive, even if they may have lacked legal force – to heirs to leave their portions with the estate for a time, until the business partners could adjust the accounts and pay each what he or she was owed.[21]

The former silk merchant and now municipal councillor (*jurado*) of Granada, Don Jerónimo de Aranda Sotomayor, tried to reconcile conflicting claims when he came to draw up his testament in 1704. He had had ten children, of whom only three were left alive. His son Luis had received 33,000 *reales* at his marriage, his daughter Josefa had got 50,000 at hers; now he was resolved to leave his house and furniture – but not the stores of raw silk – to his other daughter Angela, who had come back to live with her parents after the annulment of an unhappy marriage, looking after her father and mother 'with great care and love and obedience'. So she was granted a *mejora*, which would not need to be specifically valued, 'given the union, affection and love which the said Don Luis, Doña Josefa and Doña Angela bear one another . . . and the obedience they have always shown me . . . thanks to which God has greatly favoured them'. When it came to dividing up the property, the old man appealed to his son, 'that he favour his sisters, letting them choose the best property, the ones easiest to administer or to collect, so that they can get by, since they are women with no knowledge of the world . . .'. In return, they would repay such kindness by leaving Luis or his children as their heirs (Josefa was widowed, with no children of her own).[22] In fact, the records of litigation in the chancery court of Granada bear witness to the frequent souring of such relationships – kept alive, perhaps, during the lifetime of the siblings, but subject to all kinds of strain and misapprehensions even then and certainly when the next generation began to assert its claims.

The discussion of inheritance needs to focus more on the ongoing relationship between the parties, on the possibilities opened up by cooperation or foreclosed by conflict, rather than on a simple accounting of the material assets available for distribution at the death of the parents. In the first place, even the peasant farm was heavily involved with the market, for it needed money to pay its taxes and to provide for the recurring cycle of domestic festivities associated with birth, marriage and death. One of our best sources of information here are the memoirs of the Catalan peasant Sebastià Casanovas (1710–56?). Essentially the owner of this *masia* of four or five hectares depended on being able to lease other fields in order to get by. Leasing, in turn, depended on a host of other factors, principally on one's reputation for reliability. Sebastià's father could get no one to entrust him with fields on lease unless he brought his own plough animals, but because he was so heavily in debt already no one would rent him the mules he needed.

The debts of the Casanovas family stemmed from more than one cause, but one of the most significant factors was commitments to junior family members. Though under the Pyrenean stem-family system one son would take over the farm, he had to see to the endowment of his brothers and sisters. Sebastià was bitter against his paternal grandmother for having used her dowry to give too much away. With one of his first cousins, who claimed part of the grandmother's estate, 'with tears in my eyes I begged him for pity's sake not to harm his own flesh and blood in this way'. But the reality was that the younger children of the Casanovas household generally married, setting up for themselves in crafts or as leaseholders, and exacting the maximum *legítimas* to which the law or the favour of a particular parent entitled them. In spite of Sebastià's quarrels with his kin over inheritance, though, he could not afford to ignore them. The family remained for him a source of inspiration in spite of all its debts and mismanagement. Though his friends advised him to strike out on his own and abandon the little homestead, 'so great was my heart-break at seeing how the place was going to rack and ruin and that the name of my ancestors would be lost, that it would make me weep just to think of it'.[23]

References have been made several times already to the importance of marriage and the dowry in the whole strategy of inheritance, and it is time we examined this aspect more closely. It was noted in Chapter 2 that frontier customs favoured the wife's right to one half of the homestead, which she may often have helped to found. Though the closure of the frontier led to a reshaping of inheritance law from the later Middle Ages, women continued to control much property – as heiresses in their own right, as recipients of dowry from their parents, as claimants on that dowry when widowed, together with one half of any 'gains' (*gananciales*) made during the marriage. 'The common custom of mankind,' thought the social reformer López Bravo in 1627, explaining these rights, 'held it to be absolutely unfair that women, being more fragile and leisured, and less apt for work and earning a living, should be left disinherited and poverty-stricken.'[24]

The rise of the dowry in this period in Europe generally has been connected to the greater emphasis on conservation of the patrimony in the male line, with the corresponding submission of the woman, as daughter and bride, to an increasingly patriarchal society. No doubt there was something of this in Spanish developments too. But one needs to remember that the dowry was part of a system of female inheritance – inheritance in the form of liquid assets (cash, jewels, furnishings) which might have to be mobilised through the mortgaging of the patrimony. Inevitably the dowry reflected an urbanising economy, where money was more abundant and where it was used to promote the social mobility of families. López Bravo deplored the fact that many parents, 'in order to place their daughters with illustrious and opulent spouses, leave their offspring penniless and disinherited'. And the Junta of Reform around the same time (1621) declared: 'It has become so much the usage in our Spain for parents to give all their property to one daughter in order to marry her advantageously that they leave the others without any dowry.'[25] In response to its concern, a law was adopted in 1623 refurbishing earlier restrictions of 1534 and 1573 on the dowry in proportion to the income of the brides' parents. But like the previous measures, it quickly proved to be a dead letter. The Portuguese writer on the family, Francisco Manuel de Mello, pointed out the terrible moral cost, in the wreckage of individual lives, of the need for dowries. Girls of good family but small means were often 'condemned to lose perforce their freedom and take an estate in life which they do not desire and must take on sufferance' – that is, they would have to become nuns. 'For this ill there is almost no cure, for it would be necessary first to set the commonwealth as a whole to rights.'[26]

What seems to have happened in many cases was that – because girls were seen to be 'unprotected', as López Bravo and Don Jerónimo de Aranda Sotomayor claimed – much of the patrimony was actually placed on their head, at least below the level of the lineage-conscious aristocracy. A daughter of an eighteenth-century merchant of Cadiz tended to be married when she was twenty or twenty-one years of age, with her father bringing his new son-in-law into the household for a few years as a business partner, while 'exporting' his own sons into positions else-where.[27] An illustration of this way of life can be found in the memoirs of Raimundo de Lantery. In 1695 he married off his seventeen- or eighteen-year-old daughter Clara to José Antonio de Iriberri, a friend of Clara's brother and a man of about twenty-three or twenty-four. Although Iriberri had never actually met Clara, Lantery tells us, 'having made enquiries about who he was and where he was from, I agreed to it, because all my friends advised me to make the match'. The ceremony was a simple one, a semi-private exchange of vows, as allowed by the church. Iriberri embarked for the Indies in 1696, after the birth of their first child, carrying 'knick-knacks' (*niñerías*) which his father-in-law gave him to trade with, 'with no accounts drawn up, since he was part of the household, and his wife and child remained at my expense'. When Iriberri returned in 1699, the marriage was formalised in church through the public blessing and *velación* of the couple – the placing of the veil on the head of the woman and shoulders of the man – which marked at this time the departure of bride and groom into a home of their own, accompanied by the transfer of dowry. In this case the dowry seems to have taken the form of a consignment of goods from Lantery to Iriberri, with which to trade in the Indies. Later that year Iriberri was dead, of yellow fever in Veracruz. His widow returned, now with two infants, to live with her father, until the latter found her another protector, his clerk, Don José Ponce de León. After consulting his confessor, friends, brother and wife, Lantery broached the subject to Clara: 'She replied that she had no other desire but to do the will of her father.' On 11 April 1700, therefore, arrayed in mourning still for her first husband, she married again.[28]

The dowry was often the very foundation of a new family in material terms, a bedrock of resources on which it could fall back in hard times. The Cortes of sixteenth-century Castile voiced their concern that married women controlled so many assets, yet were regarded as judicial minors. Thus, they were frequently asked to sign contracts alongside their husband, but if the deal turned out badly, it would be assumed by an investigating magistrate that their signature was invalid, extorted by force or deceit.[29] Women were entitled to *gananciales* – one half of the assets of the household 'acquired' during the marriage – over and above the return of their dowry, when their husband died. Merchants were sometimes concerned to get their wives to commute this by the terms of the marriage contract to a legacy, in order to prevent the inevitable break-up of the business at their death should the widow insist on her full claims.[30] Of course, while the husband was alive, it was he who actually administered his wife's estate, though even here Manuel de Mello refers to the recent growth (1651) of the custom among aristocrats of specifying an annuity for the wife – her 'pin money' or *alfileres* – which was under her entire control.

Marriage negotiations played a vital role, therefore, in ensuring the future success of a family, and involved an elaborate mobilisation of the energies and resources of the clan as a whole. When Esteban de Garibay, Basque gentleman and chronicler, lost his first wife around 1574, a nun of Toledo began to find him a replacement – her fifteen-year-old sister, Doña Luisa de Montoya. She acted thus, Garibay tells us, 'because not only did she and her relatives know me from my youth, but her parents and mine had had dealings for a very long period of over forty years'. Garibay was hesitant: to marry a girl from Toledo would tie him down there and prevent him returning to the Basque Country. But after long consultations with friars and friends, he agreed with her brother and uncle to conclude the match – on condition of a large dowry, which involved the brother sacrificing some of his own claims on his parental inheritance. The same day Garibay sat down to write his first letter to his new bride, 'congratulating her on a union which is to the service of God and our own repose'.[31]

Essentially the conduct of marriage negotiations was a delicate business, involving as it did the weighing up on each side of a variety of factors: geographical location of the family, wealth, honour, influence exerted by intermediaries. A vivid insight into the whole process is provided by the letters of the Manso de Velasco family (1752–4), a noble family from the Rioja region. One of its members had become viceroy of Peru and count of Superunda, thanks in part to the patronage of his fellow Riojan, the famous marquis of Ensenada, chief minister of Spain between 1743 and 1754. Superunda's nephew, Don Félix José Manso, began to contemplate a second marriage in 1752 in order to procure a male heir. We find him contacting a canon of nearby Burgos to find out 'if in Burgos there is anything suitable, assuming that the lady would be of quality and bearing, and that she would have some property'. But his enthusiasm seems to have cooled when the worthy priest replied that in old Burgos 'you will only find much honour, but nothing in the way of material assets'. Another intermediary, Canon Mortela of Calahorra close by, who had stood as godfather to Don Félix's younger brother, now took a hand, promising to use his contacts in Madrid and Zaragoza. He asked Félix to give him a list of his rents so that he could show it to the father of one possible candidate, but he warned that the girl herself might not be appealing: 'They tell me that even if she got the whole of Viana as her portion, she would not get a husband, since she is so ugly and sickly and so very blear-eyed.' Anyway, Don Félix, with daughters of his own, must realise that it would be hard to find a woman prepared to take on the responsibility of rearing them, nor was the canon sure that many women would want to leave their homes in Madrid or Zaragoza for the isolation of La Rioja.[32]

Rather than a simple transfer of dowry and a bride, therefore, marriage involved the mobilisation of a network of intermediaries and reinforced the clan structure of Spanish society. Given that so much property was pledged to and with women, their alliances were critical to the re-establishment of family status at each new generation. When Don Félix Manso's younger brother Diego came to marry, he had set his sights on an heiress, the marquesa of Bermudo, of Ciudad Rodrigo, then aged seventeen or eighteen. Once again intermediaries were called upon, with the clergy utilising their particularly well-established networks of information. The eight months of discussion had to be conducted discreetly, with the bride's father reluctant to meet Don Diego openly, for that would send out a public signal of his commitment to the marriage. Instead, he wanted to be sure that this cadet of a minor Riojan house was a suitable match for his daughter. The youth was presently gazetted as a naval captain: would his patron Ensenada ensure his promotion? Alternatively, would he be allowed to retire from the service (the young marquesa seems to have begged for this, reluctant to be left alone at home)? Above all, would the boy's uncle, the count of Superunda, viceroy of Peru, guarantee the boy's future by buying land immediately for him? The negotiations stalled when Ensenada fell from power in 1754; but his successor at the War Office, Don Sebastián Eslava, was beholden to Superunda for finding husbands for two of his nieces in Peru and tried to help out.[33]

In general, it would seem that marriage was arranged where possible within a known circle of friends, given that it would effectively commit two family networks to a continuing interaction and cooperation over time. The essayist Francisco Manuel de Mello commented on the delicacy of relations with the parents, brothers and sisters of the spouse: 'so great is the love we owe to such near kin that, because it can never be paid, it may turn to loathing'.[34] Would there be a tendency, therefore, to restrict the range of marriage partners to the group of those related anyway by blood? The Spanish government became concerned in the Age of the Enlightenment with the amount of money flowing out to Rome in order to purchase dispensations from the so-called prohibited degrees of kinship – descendants of a common great-great-grandfather, whom canon law barred from marrying one another. In response to enquiries from the Council of Castile in 1783, one bishop noted that such close unions were particularly frequent in the smaller villages of his diocese: 'the women of a particular *pueblo* usually practise just one handicraft or skill from the time they are girls . . . and this means that outsiders are not useful in the community'. The Bishop of Almería reported that there were some 200 marriages a year within the prohibited degrees in his diocese of 95,204 people, and thought it must have something to do with the Reconquest, when Christian settlers had shunned contact with those of suspect ancestry, a phenomenon aggravated by 'the rivalry which usually exists between one village and its neighbour'.[35]

The government estimated in 1762 that there were between 10,000 and 11,000 dispensations issued for Spain as a whole every year – roughly equivalent to one marriage in nine. The phenomenon seems to have been particularly marked among certain sections of the elite – one in four marriages among the oligarchy of Cartagena, for example, between 1750 and 1850 – and in villages.[36] The investigations which preceded the issue of dispensations are stored in the episcopal archives – quite substantial documents, which are impressive testimony in their own way to the sense of genealogical memory kept alive in peasant communities. But they are a difficult source to exploit, at least on their own, for the alleged need for the dispensation had to fit one of the 'good causes' recognised by canon law: that the village was too small or the girl's family too poor for her to find a suitable partner of the same honourable standing, or alternatively (if the relationship was that of first cousin) that she had been 'dishonoured' by her fiancé's too frequent visits to the house, especially at dusk. In some cases it is evident that there were strategic property considerations at stake – especially when an heiress was married off to a paternal kinsman in order to keep alive the name of the family. But more often the dispensations seem to reflect merely the tight circle of friendships within which the family moved, reflecting its choice of a bride who would consolidate existing links of neighbourhood. They symbolise a certain tension between ecclesiastical and secular views of the purpose of marriage, typical of western Christendom generally since the central Middle Ages. The emphasis of the church on the individual and its concerns about the exclusive loyalties associated with the kin group find an echo in Spanish literature. Echoing Saint Augustine, the sixteenth-century Dominican theologian Pedro de Ledesma justified the church's basic reluctance to see cousins marry each other: 'The reason is in order for amity to be extended and propagated to more people' – to foster social harmony and avoid the old perils of the kin feud.[37]

'The intrinsic aim of marriage,' wrote the Franciscan moralist Antonio Arbiol in his treatise of 1715, 'is the conjoining of souls.' Echoing other theologians, he stressed the sacred nature of the union between a man and a woman, an unbreakable bond whose prime purpose was to strengthen each on the path to eternal life. 'No one after God must a woman love or esteem more than her husband, nor a husband more than his wife.'[38] Even the good Don Quixote noted that one would want to choose a companion carefully before embarking on a long journey: 'So, why should one not do the same for a journey which will last a lifetime, down to the abode of death, especially if the companion will be with us in bed, at the table and everywhere, as a wife will be with her husband.'[39] There was a risk of conflict here, between the emotional and spiritual needs of the individual man and woman, safeguarded in the main by the church, and the strategic interests of the family as a whole.

The risk might be minimised, of course, by the rather strict seclusion of women in Mediterranean countries, so that – as Clara Lantery told her father – the young people had 'no other will' but that of their parents. Fray Miquel Agustín, in his influential handbook of 1617 for the running of the Catalan peasant household, devoted a lengthy section to the role of the unmarried daughters. They should stay upstairs, out of the way of the labourers, except at meal times or when invited down by their elders. They should always keep their feet covered with shoes and stockings, and fix their eyes on the ground. 'Whenever they go out of the house, they will stay close beside their mother . . . They will wear their shawl a little down over their face . . .' In church, they would take care to avoid the glances of men, especially as attention wandered during the sermon. A century later, Antonio Arbiol was warning about the dangers of the *velada*, the gathering of neighbours 'in the long nights of winter', when boys and girls often met in one another's houses.[40] He wanted girls to avoid 'plays, strolls, visits and card games', which occupied the time of their 'empty-headed' sisters.

Such ideals took little account of the reality of life for many women. These figure largely in the chronicles of Spanish cities of the Golden Age as market vendors and bakers and servants in inns – a wide variety of trades where they were constantly in touch with the public. In 1548 Pedro de Medina noticed the contrast as he moved north from his native Andalusia into the Old Christian lands of

Castile, that the women got 'tougher' (*recias*). In some parts they worked in the fields, reaping grain (at most Andalusian women would pick olives) and travelling to market to sell their produce. In the market square of Bilbao, he remarked that one would usually find over one hundred maidens selling food, 'all of them bareheaded . . . and their heads close-shaven', until they found a husband, when they would adopt the coif, which everywhere marked out the married woman.[41] Campomanes in 1775 also remarked on this contrast between the 'idle' women of Andalusia and their active sisters further north. The elite were, indeed, more sheltered everywhere, but literature and litigation offer much insight into how contacts were actually made between the sexes at this level. In one of her short stories, María de Zayas (1590–1661?) describes the meeting of the sixteen-year-old Jacinta with the twenty-four-year-old Félix, just returned from the wars in Flanders to his home town of Baeza. She visited him in the company of her friend, Félix's sister, 'in which visit Don Félix let me know by his eyes and his words the love he bore me'. She reciprocated: 'I encouraged him as he walked up and down my street by day and night, strumming a guitar', and they met, as Andalusian couples traditionally did, at the *reja*, the downstairs window with its grille, while the family slept above.[42] The records of the diocesan courts of Andalusia, called upon to arbitrate in these cases of love which crossed family interest, often contain precious letters from this period. 'The sun would have first to fail before I give him up', 'I shall not give him up, though they tear me into a thousand pieces': the language of all classes is wildly romantic, no doubt doctored by professional scribes, but cautioning the historian against neglect of the personal element in traditional marriages.

The thirteenth-century Castilian law code, the *Siete Partidas*, had stated quite clearly that 'parents may not marry off their children unless they are present or give their consent', though warning against love matches made by young people, 'from which sometimes arise very great feuds, and the death of men and bloodshed'. But the frontier situation seems to have favoured elopement, with local customs allowing fugitives to defy the wrath of their kin and establish themselves in the new communities founded during the Reconquest.[43] Above all, canon law, developing in effectiveness from the twelfth century everywhere in Western Europe, began to apply the basic idea of the church that marriage was a sacrament, a means of salvation for two souls, in which considerations of kinship or property should not intervene. Thus, the bishop or his vicar general would receive petitions from youths claiming that the parents of his beloved were impeding the course of true love, and by the mechanism of the *saca* (the 'taking out') a royal constable would be instructed to remove the girl and 'explore her wishes' regarding matrimony. Since marriage itself was made, in the eyes of the church, by the exchange of vows between two individuals, it was sometimes assumed that a 'promise to marry in the future' (*palabra de futuro*) was equivalent to the marriage vow itself (*palabra de presente*). The informality of the wedding ceremony in Spain – as more generally in Mediterranean lands – has to be borne in mind. It was conducted in many cases in the house of the bride, with the procession to church for the solemn blessing (*velación* or veiling), only taking place when the dowry was handed over and the bride was ready to leave the parental home – perhaps months or years after the wedding itself.

Sometimes the betrothal itself was allowed to drag on in much the same way. Thus the Jesuit missionary Pedro de León observed in parts of the mountainous regions of Granada in the later sixteenth century the behaviour of the Christian settlers who had supplanted the Moriscos. They would stay 'two, three, four and more years betrothed without getting married, and they were burdened with children and in a state of mortal sin'.[44] By the suit known as *demanda de palabra* a girl could 'demand' enforcement of a promise of marriage. The jurisprudence of the Spanish diocesan courts – perhaps with an eye on the risk of feud rather than on the strict letter of canon law – would allow circumstantial evidence (typically that the boy and girl had been seen together too much in each other's company) to establish the case, whereupon a constable would swing into action again, gaoling the young man until he consented to go through with the marriage.

In these cases much depended on the initiative of the parties themselves; one finds little enough of the attempt to regulate morality from above, typical of the Puritan Reformation in northern Europe. There were, indeed, traditional sanctions against sexual relationships which upset the social order. Thus the Valencian guilds, like their counterparts in Germany, adopted measures in this regard, which were designed to protect the integrity of a home which was also the place of work. Thus the shoemakers in 1421 resolved to expel masters who had concubines, while the woollen weavers more modestly excluded such from guild office in 1472.[45] Such measures were directed fundamentally against married men: so the *jurats* of Valencia decreed in 1446 that the yellow hood, which marked the shame of concubines, would not be applied if both parties were free to marry.

Such laxity came under threat at the time of the Counter-Reformation. The Council of Trent specifically enjoined bishops to enquire into public sin, expelling from the community any woman living in concubinage who had ignored three warnings. But attempts to apply these regulations were not notably successful. The cathedral chapter of Granada protested that the Tridentine ruling would cause 'very great inconveniences' by publishing liaisons best left discreet; and the Cortes of Valencia pointed out in 1626 that the shaming of a married woman in this way would inflict 'infamy' on her husband, sons and relatives, 'broadcasting with these demonstrations what was not known, and giving rise to a lot of vendettas and killings'. Castillo de Bobadilla thought that there needed to be grave public scandal if the corregidor was to act in support of the bishop in these cases, and that the unmarried, where there was no adultery involved, should be warned but rarely prosecuted.[46] In practice, the pursuit of public sin seems to have proceeded by fits and starts. Archbishop Ribera, as viceroy of Valencia between 1602 and 1604, displayed a keenness, as one might expect of the man, to round up concubines, giving them a warning for the first offence, then a public admonition, and finally gaol (even for nobles). Fray Antonio de Tapia, low-born and zealous bishop of Cordoba from 1649, began a similar drive there. The

Inquisition for its part began to take an increasing interest in Castile from the middle of the sixteenth century in fornication, though in a curiously indirect way, as befitted a tribunal which was supposed to limit itself to heresy. Thus, it could not punish men for illicit sexual relations, but it would whip and shame them for boasting that it was no grave sin to lie with an unmarried woman if she consented.[47]

It had been a feature of late medieval reform to deal with marginal groups by separating them from the body politic and placing them in their own ghetto, subject to close surveillance. Thus from the middle of the fourteenth century the 'loose woman' tended to be herded into one of those official brothels whose size and policing attracted the attention of foreign travellers in Renaissance Spain. That of Valencia consisted around 1500 of three or four streets, walled off from the rest of the city, with taverns and rooms for 200–300 women. It was in terms of 'moral hygiene' that these institutions were defended, even by some of the clergy, like the Valencian priest and historian Escolano. Thus no girls were allowed in except of their own free will – the justices were to interrogate them about this every month according to the Cordoban regulations of 1545, for example, which also ensured that they paid a fixed tariff for food and lodging in order to avoid their falling into the clutches of pimps. There were also fixed tariffs for customers, who must be unmarried men.[48]

This 'ghettoisation' of the marginal was already breaking down in respect of Moors and Jews, as we shall see in the next chapter, and it was probably inevitable that the moral reprobates would also be reintegrated into the wider society by an increasingly evangelical church. Various regulations provided that the inmates of these *mancebías* (brothels) attend mass once a week, that they be offered dowries at municipal expense in order to marry, and that they attend sermons in Holy Week in order to persuade them to repent. Concern about venereal disease also played a role, with monthly visits by surgeons prescribed by several towns, extended to weekly inspections in all of them by the terms of a royal decree of 1571. A home for ex-prostitutes who could be persuaded to leave the brothel, was set up in Valencia in 1600, with a subsidy from the city hall, and even Escolano, despite his defence of the *mancebía* itself, thought the new foundation was pleasing to God and had helped avert the plague of that year from his native city. In Madrid a 'house of correction' was set up for fallen women in 1608 – 'where they gather girls who don't want to go into service and who are living in sin', as the chronicler Cabrera de Córdova put it. With heads shaved and clothed in sackcloth, the inmates were set to spin and meditate in silence on the error of their ways.[49] It was only a matter of time before the government bowed to pressure for moral reform and closed down the municipal brothels throughout Spain (1623).

A major part of this new policy of rigour must be attributed to the Jesuits, founded in 1540 to bring the word of God to the laity, and some of the most active preachers in the brothels, prisons and remote villages of Spain. But their campaign also had its limits. Pedro de León, whom we have come across before, has left a precious record of how the evangelist had to take account of the susceptibilities of lay society. When he went to preach a Lenten mission in Cazorla in 1589, he found a nobleman there who had been living with his mistress for twenty-four years past, 'and he had many children by her'. Father León eventually persuaded the gentleman to marry, but only on condition the marriage was kept secret for his kinsmen would oppose it. In spite of the recent regulations of the Council of Trent (1563) that the banns must be published on three successive holy days before the assembled congregation in the parish church, León and the governor's wife got the local parish priest to conduct the ceremony on the spot, without telling anyone, promising to have the bishop ratify it afterwards. In September 1590 Father León had a similar success in another part of Andalusia, getting a nobleman to marry his Moorish slave by whom he had offspring.[50]

The Council of Trent refused to go along with Protestant reformers and strengthen parental control over marriage. At most, it consented to abolish clandestine marriages – that is, insisting on the presence of a priest and two witnesses at an exchange of vows, and publishing the banns beforehand, unless the bishop saw fit to dispense with these for good cause. But on the main issues – the absolute freedom of the bride and groom, the binding nature of the promise to marry – the Catholic Church refused to budge. The Cortes of Castile voiced their particular concern with the betrothal, still often clandestine even if the marriage itself was not. 'Many honourable girls of good family are taken in by promises of marriage which are made to them and many youngsters married off to persons of lower rank, to the dishonour of their parents and lineages, because of the binding nature of these promises, which, being only young, they give lightly to each other.'[51] Though Philip II repeatedly promised to write to the pope on the matter, nothing was actually done.

Spanish theologians made an important contribution to the development of canon law, notably the Cordoban Jesuit Tomás Sánchez, whose great work of 1592 on marriage ran through many editions in Catholic Europe down to the eighteenth century. To some extent these men seem to be reflecting the constraints of their own society – that is, the honour-conscious Spanish lineage. But mostly their work was clearly guided by their perception of the 'natural law', as expressed in the wisdom of the Roman legislators and the tradition of the church. So Sánchez praised the freedom of the individual to make his or her own choice of partner, while upholding the need of the state to guarantee social order. Children, on pain of mortal sin, should bear in mind the common good, thus accepting a match if it would help to reconcile warring kin groups. The supreme rule was *caritas*, that 'good fellowship' which led the church also to set its face in principle against marriage within an existing kin group. On the question of sanctions against a disobedient child, though, Sánchez was less clear. The Castilian law of 1505 had only allowed disinheritance in the case of a marriage which was 'clandestine'; but it was not clear what, if anything, could be done about children who used the lawful instruments of the *saca* and the *demanda* to thwart parental wishes. There was always the possibility of leaving the child without a dowry, and with the legal minimum – *legítima* – when one came to die (and in the

Crown of Aragon the *legítima* was often pretty small). But the Dominican theologian Pedro de Ledesma cautioned fathers and mothers against nourishing anger in their hearts against wayward offspring: 'Confessors and learned men must advise parents not to use the full rigour of the law . . . unless there has been very great disrespect shown to them.'[52]

'The church has left no one in any doubt how displeasing to God parental oppression can be,' commented a later Jesuit writer, Matías Sánchez (1740), adding that these were often bad judges of what constituted a dishonourable match, 'because they get so angry'. Luther and Calvin, with their horror of celibacy and exaltation of the married state, 'favour excessively the jurisdiction and authority of the parent'. But, if the diocesan courts decided there was good cause, children could not be disinherited for following their own inclinations and even marrying 'a person of lower condition' – though they would often 'sin very gravely' in upsetting their families in this way. 'The whole difficulty,' concluded the worthy Jesuit, 'is to maintain a balance.'[53]

How are we to understand the long duration of this apparent conflict between moral principle and family interest? One of the few lay writers on the subject, Francisco Manuel de Mello, recognised that 'unsatisfactory marriages, which upset parents' were frequent enough in his own day (1651). But most of these cases, he thought, involved errors of judgement and wounded pride, 'few of them, real pain'.[54] As one studies the records of the diocesan courts, one is struck by a certain ambiguity surrounding the whole notion of *mésalliance* in a society, where the kin group was such an open, rambling network of members occupying very different social and economic positions. Respectable ancestry and the opportunity of patronage could be offset against lack of wealth.

An illustration of this comes with the 'unequal marriage' in Granada in 1542 between Leonor, grand-daughter of the secretary of the Catholic Kings, Hernando de Zafra, as well as grand-niece on her mother's side of the chief minister of Charles V, Francisco de los Cobos. Leonor was sixteen when she began to be courted by her brother's friend, Diego de Pisa, younger son of a Granadan judge. As the eldest daughter, Leonor was reserved by her parents for a match with 'some titled gentleman of these realms', using Uncle Francisco's great influence, and certainly not for a penniless younger son like Diego. The trouble was that Diego had a powerful patron, the marquis of Mondéjar, who held court in the Alhambra as captain general of Granada, and who pressed the suit on Los Cobos. Leonor's mother (who, as one of the powerful clan of Los Cobos, did the talking in place of her husband) was suitably evasive. But time was not on her side, as the young lovers began to exchange letters through the servants and arrange trysts. Diego wrote to Leonor, in one of those touching letters which still lie, oddly out of place, in the legal archives, that if they were caught out, she was not to worry: 'These storms usually last for a week or so.' In the event, they were surprised together, along with their incriminating correspondence, which led the distraught mother, after consultation with Uncle Francisco, to save what could be saved of the family honour by having Diego wed Leonor in a simple, lonely ceremony. She ordered all the doors and windows of the house locked, recalled one witness, 'so that none of the servants could look out to see what was going on'. Friends arranged a reconciliation within a year. But it was a fragile peace, which broke down when Francisco de los Cobos died in 1547 and Diego sued for a dowry, since he had not got the promotion he was hoping for from a relationship with this politically powerful family.[55]

In this case the canon law, by upholding the concept of the freedom of individuals to marry, served as a kind of lightning-conductor. When Leonor's brother challenged Diego in the street – telling him that 'he had behaved very badly in being his friend and hatching betrayal in his house, whereupon the two reached for their swords and lunged at each other' – trouble was ultimately averted by the moral authority of the church in these disputes over matrimony. Equally, of course, there might be occasions when the canon law would prove counterproductive. One such incident concerned Don Fadrique de Toledo, eldest son and heir of the great duke of Alba. In 1567, as a callow youth, he made a promise of marriage to Doña Magdalena de Guzmán, daughter of a royal judge and a lady-in-waiting at court. When Alba arranged for the young man to marry a cousin instead in 1578, Doña Magdalena appealed to the king. Philip II referred the case to a special junta, giving his own opinion that Fadrique was obliged to respect his promise, 'both in conscience and as a gentleman'. But he did not hold out much hope that a *demanda de palabra* suit before the diocesan court would give much satisfaction – 'because of the delays there will be, with appeals to Rome and other circumstances that usually arise in these cases, so that not only will her youth be spent but her life will be over'. Pressure brought to bear on Alba, currently out of favour at court anyway, had to be dropped at the beginning of 1580 when he was needed to lead the army for the invasion of Portugal that year. Magdalena made a last appeal to the king: 'I shall strive all my life to uphold my honour and the truth of my case.' But she found it prudent in the end to drop her suit – in return for a handsome dowry to marry a descendant of the conqueror of Mexico, Hernán Cortés.[56]

In practice, therefore, the letter of canon law seems to have been adapted to take account of social reality. Litigation over betrothals or promises of marriage depended generally on circumstantial evidence, leaving considerable leeway for the diocesan court to make up its own mind. As one canon lawyer put it in 1594, a man who seduced a woman of notably lower class than himself could be presumed not to have given her a valid – that is, an intentional – commitment to marry her. Yet the letter of the law remained, inviting exploitation at unscrupulous hands. This was what worried Joaquín Amorós, whose lengthy treatise of 1777 was devoted to explaining why the law had to be reformed. 'Any woman can come forward with a suit to the vicar general,' he wrote, 'presenting a summary statement from witnesses, most of them of doubtful character', alleging betrothal to someone. The poor fellow would 'generally' be arrested and detained until he agreed to marry. The suits of *demanda* and *saca* had been sprouting 'like weeds' in the diocesan courts in recent years.[57]

The language was fairly similar in the preamble to the great government decree of 1776, which marked one of the several attacks on the power of the church then being mounted by the Enlightened statesmen of Spain. 'So frequent has the abuse of children entering into unequal marriages become,' thundered the edict, that all men and women under twenty-five must obtain the consent of their parents to marry. The law was tightened in 1803, and another measure of 1796 exempted those facing a betrothal suit from being gaoled.[58] It is possible that the old system was becoming disfunctional as social mores changed during the eighteenth century, given the greater informality in the *paseos* (promenades), now gracing many a Spanish town, and in the evening gatherings (*tertulias*), where men and women would meet. Joaquín Amorós thought the social hierarchy itself was imperilled by excessive upward mobility of families in this new age of enterprise, and he pointed to the danger of money undermining respect for lineage. But there was also a concern with the lower classes, now more prone to marry improvidently as more employment became available and the economy expanded. The journeyman fails to consult his father or employer before setting up a home, lamented the count of Campomanes, later president of the Council of Castile. 'He is saddled with offspring before he has a shop of his own or has passed his master's examination, and his family is a wretched affair, lacking education or discipline.'[59]

The emphasis on the household as a form of education was an old enough concept, but one which took on increasing importance in the early modern period. Whereas 'politics' was the art of citizenship, wrote the Augustinian theologian Camos in 1592, the 'economy' reposed on the *oikos*, the management of the household, where the elderly were taken care of and the young reared for responsibilities in the outside world. The union of man and woman, therefore, was a cornerstone of the social order – 'the most important and the most perfect union that there can be among human beings'.[60] What kind of household predominated, therefore, in Spain? The censuses tend to suggest that, as in the rest of Western Europe, it was mostly nuclear, with the father and mother and their children, excluding other relatives. The church, interestingly enough, seems to have favoured this model – possibly on the basis of the experience of its confessors with personal unhappiness in more extended units. Writing in Aragon in 1715, where the temptation to keep the family together for economic reasons was very strong, the theologian Arbiol commented: 'A loaf of bread in peace and quiet is better than wealth and ease when you are always upset and quarrelling.'[61]

But if families did tend to live apart, they cooperated very closely, and often one needs to get beyond the censuses in order to perceive this underlying reality. The domestic architecture of Andalusian villages, for example, reflects an age-old pattern of division of the parental dwelling between two or more siblings, whose own offspring may still be neighbours. Party walls are run up and torn down, new doors opened into the patio or street, windows blocked off, according to the needs of each generation. Though the space available would clearly vary with the economic situation of the owner, there may have been a certain lack of privacy in Spanish houses. Joly observed, for example, that even in the bigger ones one passed directly from the common living room (*sala*) to the bedrooms (the suitably named *alcobas*, or alcoves) – 'though you don't go into them unless you want to sleep, for they are dark and lack chimneys or any window, and they have no wardrobe or cabinet'.[62] Much remains to be studied about the distribution of domestic space, but we have one interesting description from the pen of the merchant Lantery of the house he leased in 1680 in Cadiz (admittedly a town where building land was always peculiarly scarce). His family in these years seems to have consisted of himself, his wife and four young children, together with his brother and nephew (who helped in the business), three black slaves (a mother and her two daughters), and two old ladies, one a godmother of the children and another 'whom I took in out of charity'. Given that the house was built around its inner patio, with no windows on to the street, this female company seems to have played a key role in the life of Lantery's wife. The brother and nephew may have lodged in the company offices on the ground floor, and the slaves (who refused to leave Cadiz when Lantery sent his family back to Savoy in 1685 and had to be sold off) may have had rooms in the kitchen area. Otherwise, the domestic space, though large, hardly provided much intimacy, with its 'dining room', off which led one *alcoba*, and its living room, off which led another. Lantery would, no doubt, receive male company in his 'office' (*despacho*) at the head of the stairs, while his wife entertained her female friends on the *estrado*, the typical platform with its cushions on which Spanish women squatted in one corner of the *sala*, leaving men to sit on chairs elsewhere.[63]

Though the women of a respectable household were, in this way, sheltered from the street, they had frequent communication with the outside world through the ubiquitous *criado* – 'reared one', or servant. The Spanish word (used also of a foster-child at the time) reflects an inherent ambiguity about the status of this personage – who sometimes turns out to be an illegitimate son or daughter of the household head in the litigation over inheritance. Diego de Torres Villarroel, author of a classic autobiography (1743), recounted how his great-grandfather, a penniless immigrant, started up in business in Salamanca. Taken in by a pharmacist, he was set to 'draw water from the well, wash the pots, grind roots in the mortar, and now and again rock the cradle', until, when his master died, he took over the shop and married the widow, 'as was the custom'.[64] Joly noted that Spaniards had many servants, but they were not necessarily to be found within the household itself. Rather, half-a-dozen youths would turn up at their master's door in the morning, ready 'to accompany him about town until the midday meal'. The lines of communication between the house and the neighbourhood were, thus, multiple and strong. In Ecija in 1612 one man was objected to as a witness in a court case involving Don Fernando de Aguilar, because 'he had dealings with a black woman who nursed some of Don Fernando's children . . . and he is in the service of a kinsman of the said Don Fernando, for which reason he has regular entry into Don Fernando's house'.[65]

The Jesuit Gaspar Astete was aware of the difficulty, especially for a woman on her own, of running such an establishment. Nevertheless, he believed that the widow should strive to be 'a masterful woman' and (foreshadowing Bernarda Alba) keep order in her own household, though she might have to call upon the authority of her kinsmen.[66] In general, the running of a home was regarded as a partnership between the husband and wife, the one attending to the outside world and the other to domestic affairs. Lucinda, daughter of wealthy Andalusian peasants, described her day to Don Quixote: 'I saw to the dispatch of the servants; the accounts of what was sown and harvested passed through my hands . . .' And Fray Miquel Agustín's Catalan housewife was to look after the poultry and dairy products and vegetable garden, as well as baking and carding wool. She would be first up in the morning and last to go to bed. She would not, however, handle money, but 'at night-time she would give her husband an account of anything new affecting the running of the property that day'.[67]

From this economic role there was fashioned an ideal portrait of the mutual trust and harmony which should reign between the two administrators of the patrimony. 'The argument and opinion of the discreet wife carry more weight than any other in a man's ears,' thought Fray Luis de León; the 'love and friendship' between both constitute the 'closest tie' of all. This may have been rather idealistic, given the age gap often found between spouses: a good six years in the case of the eighteenth-century Cadiz merchants, with the husband as much as sixteen years older in a quarter of cases surveyed later in the century.[68] Nevertheless, Manuel de Mello stressed the emotional bonding which must develop if the arranged marriage was to work: affection, if not 'passion' would develop as the perceptive husband noticed that his wife was probably better at 'taking things in' (*perceber*) and 'thinking them through' (*discorrer*). Criticising Don Francisco Manrique in 1527 for neglecting his wife, the humanist Antonio de Guevara defined sharply the Renaissance ideal: that when a man married, he must show his maturity by abandoning the pastimes of youth, for 'the man who pays no heed to his wife merits that others pay no heed to him in turn'.[69]

Spanish art, it is true, seems to have been slower than that of northern Europe in portraying the intimacy of family life. The well-known portraits by Velázquez of Diego del Corral, Councillor of Castile, and his wife Antonia de Ipeñarrieta with their son Luis – like many of the altarpieces of the period – tend to reflect dynastic continuity rather than domesticity. Antonia was a widow anyway, and it is possible that Diego's features were painted over those of her husband after her remarriage in 1627. It is, rather, in the religious art that one tends to find the moral exemplar of the home – in the 'Holy Family with the Sleeping Child' and 'Holy Family in the Carpenter's Workshop' by the Valencian Jerónimo Jacinto Espinosa (1600–67), and in similar canvases by Murillo (1617–82). Saint Joseph had been becoming a prominent figure in Christian devotion in Renaissance Europe generally, but in Spain his depiction as a relatively youthful father for the boy Jesus seems to have been precocious.[70]

The fundamental aim of this moralisation of the family was to ensure that the young were raised as proper Christians and citizens. Good upbringing, commented the theologian Camos in 1592, is more important than good laws, 'for if men were properly trained when they were children and youths, there would be fewer offences to punish through the courts when they grow up'. It was a point echoed later in the Enlightenment by the statesman Campomanes: 'The way to make people behave is to instil in them virtuous customs . . . from their childhood, at home, at school and as apprentices.'[71] Though the church was keen to foster this approach, there was perhaps a certain ambivalence about its teaching on a fundamental problem: the number of the offspring. A couple should think carefully before having more children than they could care for, suggested Tomás Sánchez in 1592. But, addressing the question more directly, his fellow Jesuit Matías Sánchez noted in 1740 that the only lawful way for a Christian to achieve this end was to abstain from sexual intercourse. It would be less sinful to abandon an unwanted child in a foundling home than to interfere with pregnancy – which by the eighteenth century seems to have been becoming a feature of life in Spain as elsewhere in Europe. In a veiled allusion to contraception, the Franciscan Antonio Arbiol lamented that couples 'lack a proper idea of Divine Providence, in whose hands it must be left to feed every creature'.[72]

There was not, in fact, a large number of children in the average family, given the interruption of marriage by death and high infant mortality. Thus, in one parish in seventeenth-century Medina del Campo, despite a consistently high birth rate, 40 per cent of the households had no children living with them, and 25 per cent had only one. The great census of 1787 indicates that just over a half of the Spanish population was under twenty-five years of age, and over a third under sixteen. As we suggested in Chapter 2 when looking at demography, many of these were the products of broken homes – some illegitimate, especially in the towns, many more orphans. Something like a fifth of marriages in seventeenth-century Spain were remarriages for one or both partners, and many homes contained stepchildren.[73]

One of the most significant problems facing ecclesiastical reformers as they sought to found a more 'godly' household was the existence of so many illegitimate offspring. The Venetian ambassador Morosini commented in 1581 that the illegitimate child enjoyed a higher status in Spain than in other countries. The third duke of Alcalá brought one bastard, Fernando, with him on official missions, from which the young man rose to the Council of War, while another, Pelayo, went on to become archbishop and viceroy of Mexico in 1673.[74] An earlier generation of the same family had produced one of the outstanding figures of the Counter-Reformation, Juan de Ribera (1532–1611), illegitimate son of the first duke of Alcalá – and, as we have seen, a hammer of moral delinquents as archbishop of Valencia. Though the inheritance rights of the illegitimate were constricted, they crop up in the chancery courts in cases where a direct line of succession has come to an end, claiming entails in preference to collateral kin. At least 65 of the 600 or so noble families in the kingdom of Valencia asked the king for legitimation of offspring for purposes of inheritance in the Cortes of 1626.

It would seem, nevertheless, that the status and expectations of the illegitimate were gradually in decline over the early modern period. Manuel de Mello noted in his treatise of 1651 that they would have to be reared away from home if a man's legitimate spouse objected to their presence, though he urged that they never be neglected. Many would fall into poverty, saddled with a proud name but few resources: 'The Indies and the church usually furnish a good welcome to this kind of person.'[75] Among the ordinary people illegitimate children could expect even less succour, because of the lack of resources. Concerned to check the prejudice against them, writers of the Enlightenment sometimes painted tragic pictures of their plight. Thus Cabarrús described the unmarried peasant mother around 1792, driven out of her village by 'the thoughtless rigour of my family and of those who knew me', unable to find a job as a maid in the big city because of her pregnancy, eventually sinking to prostitution.[76]

It would seem that illegitmate children were often registered as foundlings, as Father Porcar recorded in his journal in 1619, when his superior, the parish priest of Saint Martin (Valencia) wanted to register the name of the father of an infant presented 'secretly' for baptism. The vicar general of the diocese, 'with his customary prudence, in view of the great problems which might arise from writing down the names of the parents of infants brought in secretly, advised that names should not be entered, but that the old custom be kept of calling the baby a "child of Saint Martin"'.[77] We know from other sources that unclaimed children born in villages were liable to be carted off, because there was no money to pay for their rearing, and to end up as foundlings at the door of some church or household in the neighbouring city. This makes it difficult to establish illegitimacy ratios with any exactness, but we estimated in Chapter 2 that 2–3 per cent of the newly born in the countryside and 10 per cent or more in cities might have to grow up without recognised parents.

One of the great features of the early modern period was, indeed, the increased provision for foundlings. There were charitable confraternities set up for this purpose in Toledo in 1504, Valencia in 1537, Valladolid in 1540. That of Seville was founded in 1558 to remedy 'the frequent distress of finding in its streets and squares and at the gates of its temples innumerable newborn children', who were often killed by the cold or by scavenging dogs. In spite of its efforts, though, perhaps only a quarter of the inmates taken into the foundling home would survive the first months of life.[78] The Enlightenment saw further strides in Spain as in the rest of Europe to implement a more 'humanitarian' and more socially efficient policy towards the illegitimate, admitting them to guilds and trying to reform the foundling homes. But the general trend of the early modern period was rather towards discriminating against those 'born outside the family'. As the humanist educator López de Montoya put it, fornication was not only a sin but inflicted 'injury' on the offspring of such liaisons, 'who can usually not be reared in a fitting manner'. While Spain was a frontier land, manpower was valued and its origins not too rigorously scrutinised. In a more ordered society the presence of the illegitimate was troublesome. As the political writer Fernández Navarrete suggested in 1626, it seemed unwise to entrust those of uncertain parentage with positions of responsibility in the commonwealth, 'since they have no property to lose nor honour to stain'.[79]

The emphasis was, therefore, increasingly on the proper rearing of future citizens within a formally constituted household. In spite of – or because of – the shortness of life, enormous fuss was made of children in early modern Spain, and their births and their tragically early deaths were the occasion of great ceremony. Bernardo Catalá's diary pays considerable attention to these events. He describes his anxiety at the difficult birth of his daughter Ana in 1600, placing a relic of the True Cross, which he always carried about with him, on his wife's abdomen while she was in labour. And Estefanía de Requesens told her mother how her husband had encouraged her for half an hour as she sat in labour on the birthing-chair in 1538.[80] Birth was, though, mainly an occasion for the solidarity of the womenfolk to express itself: 'neighbours, relatives and friends gather round to help a woman in labour – the event suspends any quarrels or spiteful gossip there might be'. And then when it came to the baptism, a wider gathering of the clan would take place – something which preoccupied the Catholic Kings on the score of public order, as they legislated in 1493 against the customs of north-western Spain of having large numbers of kinsmen assemble, with feasting for more than one day.[81]

Esteban de Garibay described the excitement and discussion which went on over the choice of names and godparents for the newly born, for a child embodied the hopes of a dynasty and served to consolidate ties between the household and a wider world. Thus, a week after the birth of his eldest son in 1581, he was visiting his 'great protector' and fellow Basque Doña Ana Manrique, who, on being informed that the child had not yet been baptised (because the kin could not agree on a name, in part), 'told me that he was to be called Luis, and that the godfather would be her son Don Luis de Vargas Manrique'. Choosing godparents could be difficult. Estefanía de Requesens wrote to her mother in 1535 that the norm at court was three godmothers and two godfathers for a girl, but that she and her husband had decided to choose lowly people of virtue, in order to avoid having to pick and choose from among their own circle of friends, divided as these were by 'passions'.[82] The Council of Trent (1563) reduced godparents to one of each sex in order to emphasise the spiritual rather than the social function of this tie. But still in 1607 Bernardo Catalá noted how important the gathering of the kin was in León, where baptism was delayed for a week in order to facilitate it (the pious Catalá had his children baptised within a day of birth). As late as 1675 the merchant Lantery was prepared to delay the baptism of his new offspring for several months, until the return of the chosen godfather from Honduras – 'which caused my heart, and that of its mother, to miss several beats', in case the babe died in the interval and was consigned to Limbo.[83] Godparents often remained close friends of the family. The duke of Sessa reminded Lerma around 1618 – rather inappropriately, perhaps, on the eve of the great minister's fall from power – that he had stood as sponsor at the baptism of the count of Cabra, Sessa's son and heir, so that 'since he is so much your child, you should be interested in his welfare'.[84]

But clearly it was the relationship between parents and children that increasingly interested early modern writers. Fray Luis de León was at pains to encourage the 'Perfect Married Woman', aristocrat or not, to nourish the new-born with her own milk: nurture in the womb only lasts nine months, but the formative period of suckling twenty-four. 'Will the mother not be well paid for her efforts when she holds him naked on her lap,' he commented, 'when he plays with her breast . . . when he looks at her with a smile, when he gurgles?' And a little before the humanist Pedro de Luxán had emphasised the rewards for the caring mother, 'when she sees her infant break into a laugh, or make a face as though to cry, or ask for his gruel, or run his hand over her breast and even pull at her coif, running his hands over his parents' chins and saying a thousand funny little things'.[85] Some aristocratic mothers did breast-feed their offspring. Garibay was 'often told' by his parents that 'I was suckled by my mother until she felt she was pregnant with my brother the priest', whereupon he was handed over to a wet-nurse. His wife suckled in turn their own son Luis, 'until at fourteen months, feeling herself pregnant, she gave him over to wet-nurses'. The norm seems to have been about eighteen months on the breast; but when Luis de Garibay was weaned at this age in July 1583, he lost his appetite and his face swelled up with fever, so that he had to be put back on the breast again for a few more months.[86]

Estefanía de Requesens's correspondence with her mother in the 1530s is one of our best sources of information on the early years of life. She did not give the breast, but brought the wet-nurses into her own (rather cramped) apartment in the royal palace. Though both she and the wet-nurse would fondle the infant Juan, she wrote that it was only the nurse who could get him to stop crying: but 'he and I are also good friends, and he speaks to me more than to anyone else, I would say'. The lesser aristocracy seem to have given their children out to be suckled, though usually within the same town or neighbourhood, keeping a close enough eye on their welfare. Thus, Bernardo Catalá recorded in his diary how he had his second son, Benito, brought home from the wet-nurse's house on 9 December 1600 because he had contracted smallpox (*viruelas*) – he had been born on 20 April 1599.[87]

Infant deaths, however common, were felt keenly by the parents, though in a religious age, it was some consolation to feel that the little one was 'with the angels', as Bernardo Catalá put it when his infant daughter 'Estefanita' died of smallpox (or perhaps measles). An elaborate network of protection had to be woven round these fragile lives, involving recourse to astrology in part (Garibay and others took care to determine the exact date of each child's birth in order to prognosticate the influences affecting its future life), but mostly to medicine and religion. When Luis de Garibay sickened in 1583, just after he had been weaned at eighteen months, he was dressed solemnly in a little habit of a Dominican monk, in honour of Saint Vincent Ferrer, who interceded for him and restored him to health (as the grateful parent duly recorded). When new fevers struck him in October 1584, he was taken to the Dominican convent in Toledo, and there, before the altar of Saint Vincent Ferrer, he was again robed as a Dominican friar. In June 1585, attacked once more by tertian fevers, the three-year-old was bled by the doctors (three 'ounces' of blood), while the mother, 'in a very tearful state', had to leave the room. 'I made a vow,' recalled the father, 'on bended knee at the bedside of the child, that I would go on pilgrimage' – once again, to the Dominican convent, but now to the great one in Valencia, where Saint Vincent Ferrer had taken his own vows.[88]

Those youngsters who survived were subjected to an upbringing of some moral rigour. After supper, Pedro de Luxán's ideal father would have 'everyone gather round the fireplace' and get one of the boys to read, while the mother and daughters occupied themselves with their needlework. The servants, meanwhile, would be sent to confession at the major festivals of the church year. The Toledan merchant Gonzalo de la Palma would ask his sons for 'an exact account of the sermon they had heard at mass on holy days'.[89] The family was regarded as a nursery of future citizens of a Christian commonwealth. Father Arbiol advised that fathers 'must be . . . zealous evangelists for the whole of their household', and in free times after meals must instruct both children and *criados* in the ways of God. The Jesuit Matías Sánchez gave his readers an interesting personal insight into his own experience in this regard: 'It moves me now to recall the tears I would see in the eyes of my family when they would get me to read to them the *Lives of the Saints*.'[90]

In Protestant countries the moral authority of the father may have tended to grow as he assumed many of the roles of spiritual director for his little community. In Spain the 'holy' was often located outside the household. Bernardo Catalá describes how he and his wife would separately draw by lot the name of one of the twelve Apostles, who would serve as their individual spiritual 'counsellor' for the year ahead. In 1604 the simple domestic ceremony was interrupted by a protest from the wife, 'saying that since Otger [their son] was now nearly six years old and could say his prayers, would I be so good as to let him draw a name for himself . . . . Seeing that my wife was so determined, I said that if she would promise to get Don Otger to say his prayer to the saint every day, I would let him draw. She said she would, and that when the lad could not, she would say it for him.' As it turned out, Otger drew Saint James that year, like his mother, while his father went under the patronage of Saint Andrew.[91] These spiritual divisions within the home were reinforced by solidarity with confraternities. Occasionally Bernardo and his wife would enter the same one, but mostly they seem to have gone different ways in this regard.

Schooling began to occupy a major place in the life of the young during the Renaissance. One of the great educators of Renaissance Spain, Pedro López de Montoya, wrote in his treatise of 1595 that the proper upbringing of the nobility must include training in letters, for these were a means of self-defence more suited to rational man than weapons.[92] It was an attitude which one finds again in Castillo de Bobadilla, and which indeed can be traced back to the fifteenth century and the new chivalry proposed by Fernando del Pulgar. Pulgar's 'Noble Men' (*Claros Varones*) exercised self-restraint and used reason. Reinforcing the argument of the Council of Trent (1563) that schooling should be more readily available for the creation of a truly Christian commonwealth, the Cortes of Castile in 1577 affirmed: 'Good religious teaching and training is very appropriate at all times and at every age, but principally in a man's tender years, for since he is naturally inclined towards evil, if he is not set upright and placed on the path of virtue before vices take hold of him, it will be very hard for him to mend his ways later.'[93] Renaissance optimisim about man had clearly given way here to Counter-Reformation pessimism, but both attitudes stressed the importance of schooling in the formation of character.

Traditional forms of upbringing for the nobility had involved the departure of youths from the 'softness' of the parental home as they entered their teens, to be placed as pages or *criados* ('foster-children') in the household of some great personage, baron, king or prelate. The bishops seem to have maintained this role for some time after Renaissance ideas began to lay emphasis on learning rather than mere courtliness. The first archbishop of Granada after its reconquest (1492), Hernando de Talavera, kept 250 *criados*, we are told, and 'his household was a seminary where the younger sons of the great lords of Spain were brought up, as well as other orphans . . .'. One of the leading prelates of the Counter-Reformation, Juan de Ribera of Valencia, had regularly a score or more of noble youths in his palace in the years between 1568 and 1611, for whom he purchased copies of the Classics, especially Cicero.[94] What was missing in this educational system, perhaps, was some sense of universality or systematisation. The chronicler of Archbishop Talavera grouped together 'younger sons of great lords' and 'other orphans', because, as he put it, 'they are both poor in their different ways'. More favoured sixteenth-century nobles, who did not have to seek a career in law or the church, might follow their fathers to the wars, like the great duke of Alba (1507–82), who was on campaign from the age of six. The eldest son might withdraw from schooling early, like the third duke of Alcalá (1583–1637), who was married off at fourteen in order to ensure the continuity of the estate. As his Jesuit tutor commented, 'he passed from first letters to the marriage bed and the arms of Venus . . . leaving the delights of literature and the sweet governance of his mother for the field of politics and the troubles of married life'.[95] The actual effects of this educational pattern might be investigated further: both Alba and Alcalá were cultivated men, though the record of Alcalá's litigation with a mistress later in life suggests a rather undisciplined and overbearing character, at variance with the Counter-Reformation ideal.

The slow rise of the 'school' in the Renaissance, in place of the private tutor may have had something to do with this concept of discipline. Certainly the best masters were to be found there, suggested López de Montoya, as he advised aristocratic parents to use the 'public school', hitherto associated more with clerks and paupers. The sixteenth century saw some notable experiments in Spain as in the rest of Western Europe – the foundation of the *Casas de Doctrina* ('Houses of

Religious Instruction') by Juan de Avila from 1554 onwards for orphans, the *Escuelas Pías* (Escolapians) founded by the Catalan José de Calasanz slightly later (though they first took root in Italy and only spread in Spain during the eighteenth century, giving an artisan's son, like Goya, his chance of an education), and, of course, the Jesuits.[96] Drawing on the lessons of the Renaissance, these schools emphasised the formation of character as a main purpose of education, to be achieved through awakening the pupil's curiosity and ambition rather than through flogging.

The Jesuit schools merit particular study. In his life of the founder, Ignatius of Loyola (1491–1556), Ribadeneira set out the extraordinary effect they were having: 'the pacification of youth who were once obstreperous and rebellious, the peaceful way they now live at home, their obedience towards their parents, their modest behaviour towards their peers . . .'. Some people ask us, commented Ribadeneira, why, unlike earlier friars who had taught in universities, we bother with grammar schools for youngsters, hitherto left to hired hands – 'a new and unusual calling, even out of keeping with the gravity of religious life'. The answer was partly the need to combat Protestant heresy, but also to reform morals, for the loss of a good conscience, 'greed and an insatiable desire for money', were, as Saint Paul suggested, the slippery slope which led to a challenge to Faith itself. By 1572 Ribadeneira could point to a record of unusual success: the Jesuit schools were growing in number and changing social attitudes. After God's providence, one might explain this through their emphasis on instilling virtue in the pupil, through morning prayers, evening examination of conscience and frequent confession, and paying particular attention to any 'weaknesses' (*siniestros*) in the character of individuals, as well as the more general 'vices and waywardness . . . which are typical and almost inevitable at that age'.[97]

This kind of supervision was costly in terms of manpower. 'In other schools one master has different orders of pupils, lesser, medium and upper . . . But the Society [of Jesus] has its pupils separated out into their different classes, each with its own particular master appointed for that purpose.' The pioneering use of the word 'class' in this text of 1572 foreshadows a new terminology which would eventually be applied to the social hierarchy itself. Jesuit schooling was disciplinarian, with censorship of the Classics, but it drew heavily on Renaissance ideas of encouragement of the pupil and on fostering a sense of self-discipline. Thus, great use was made of 'new forms of instruction and new kinds of lectures and debates', with more emphasis on prize-giving than on the rod. The participation of Jesuit pupils in school plays was, of course, to become famous. There was also a pioneering use of prefects – *síndicos* or *decuriones* – and what we might now call 'student fraternities', which grew out of the religious confraternity and which became a badge of distinction for the aspiring pupil. The members of these clubs, 'through the offices and positions given to them, and through the rules and regulations they draw up, have a forestaste of later life and start to become a kind of citizen'. In 1625 the Jesuits were entrusted with the Imperial College in Madrid, a new experiment in fashioning an educated elite, since the pupils would no longer be younger sons eager for a career in the church or bureaucracy, but elder sons of the nobility, needing a general grounding in history, mathematics and science. The Jesuit Order, ran the foundation statutes, 'is the one which most successfully fosters the education of the young, combining instruction in letters with virtue and good character'.[98]

Most young Spaniards, of course, never went to school at all, and few even of the nobility passed through the hands of the Jesuits. Nevertheless, their model – borrowed from some of the main stream of Renaissance thought – spread its influence widely. The training for citizenship by means of self-discipline was to be a powerful factor in the moulding of a new social hierarchy, whose 'classes' were based increasingly on individual achievement. The noble must get used from an early age to a regular rhythm of work during the day, advised Diego Gurrea, tutor to the dukes of Cardona, in his educational handbook of 1627. Allowing more room for sport in the education of the young than the Jesuits seem to have done, Gurrea nevertheless pointed to the challenge facing a feudal aristocracy, of learning to control its passions. Physical exercise must never be pushed to the limit where a man lost his temper or sense of proportion: the hunter must not become as brutish as his prey.[99] This transformation of social attitudes was, of course, gradual. The seed might be implanted in the family and the school, but its fuller realisation depended on wider influences in the society at large, and it is to one of the most significant of these – religion – that we must now turn.

10

THE COMMUNITY OF
THE FAITHFUL

The great Jesuit historian Juan de Mariana (1536–1624) wrote that the contemplation of nature and of human frailty would convince all men of the existence of God. But if men were left to themselves, 'would there not shortly be as many religious opinions scattered across the world, as many sacred rituals, as wide a variety of ecclesiastical organisations as there are differences of opinion among men?' Acceptance of such a plurality would lead to wars between and within nations. 'There is nothing . . . which is so contrary to peace as having many religions in the same commonwealth . . . Nothing has greater force when it comes to stirring up the populace than the mask of religion.'[1] Spain had formed herself, of course, out of many centuries of religious struggle. At the western edge of Christendom, she had been engaged since the Muslim invasion of 711 in the Reconquest of the national territory, a confused affair which had at times assumed the features of a crusade. The completion of the reconquest with the overthrow of the last Muslim kingdom, Granada, in 1492 ushered in a new age of cultural and religious imperialism. 'Faith' was listed by the cosmographer Pedro de Medina, along with wine, wool, the overseas discoveries and good government, in his treatise of 1548 exploring the 'Great Things of Spain'. 'The reason for our triumph throughout the world is our faith, without which it is impossible to appease God . . .' And a century later the geographer Rodrigo Méndez Silva could write in much the same terms, that Spain, honoured by the preaching of the Apostle Saint James, guardian of his shrine and defender of Christendom, is the land 'which most firmly upholds and venerates' the Christian tradition.[2]

There is, no doubt, a certain irony in all this, for within a few years Méndez Silva would be arrested and penanced by the Inquisition for Judaic practices (1662), a reminder, if any were needed, of the complex amalgamation of cultures that was Spain. The exceptional 'authority and severity' of this tribunal in the Hispanic world, thought the Venetian ambassador Donà in 1573, was 'because the number of New Christians, of Jewish and Moorish origin, is everywhere so great', and, given that they had been mostly forced into the church, 'Spain would run a great risk of being infected and losing its religion'.[3] It was in the struggle with the Jews that the Inquisition was born. *Sefarad* (Spain) was home to one of the most numerous and distinguished branches of that people, the Sephardic Jews.

Men of eminence in the towns, in learning as well as trade, they were the crucial bridge between Islam and Christendom in the Middle Ages. Long centuries of coexistence came gradually to an end for a variety of reasons, which have perhaps as much to do with European as with purely Spanish developments – the rise of the preaching friars, with their evangelical zeal, the fear induced by the Black Death, the messianic fervour whipped up among a new kind of proletariat as towns grew. These movements culminated in the Iberian peninsula with the great wave of pogroms in 1391, followed by intermittent violence thereafter, in which Jews seem frequently to have been made the scapegoat of conflict between a series of weak kings and their overmighty subjects.[4] Mass conversions of Jews to Christianity merely created the figure of the *Converso*, the New Christian, against whose alleged deviousness further popular hostility was whipped up, culminating in the riots of Toledo and the adoption by that city of a statute demanding *limpieza de sangre* ('purity of blood', or Old Christian ancestry) for its officers in 1449.

The foundation of the Inquisition by Ferdinand and Isabel in 1478 can be seen as part of the task of restoring public order after a century of civil conflict. Henceforth it would be the sovereign, through state-appointed inquisitors (a wresting of power here from the bishops), who would decide who was or was not a good Christian. The measure was rounded out in 1492 by requiring the rest of the Jewish population either to accept baptism or leave the country (up to 200,000 may have left). The numerous remaining New Christians posed a challenge – unique in Europe at the time – which was as much social and political as religious. In the first place there was great opposition to the establishment of the Inquisition in many quarters. The trading cities of the Crown of Aragon protested against a tribunal which had its seat in Castile claiming to exercise jurisdiction over them, and were worried about too rigorous an enquiry into the faith driving away trade. Without trade, affirmed Valencia, 'one cannot live happily or prosperously in cities, and the commonwealth itself cannot be maintained'.[5] In the event, after the murder of Inquisitor Pedro de Arbués in Zaragoza cathedral in 1485, opposition crumbled in the face of royal determination.

Mariana would later echo some of the disquiet felt by the Converso and humanist Pulgar ('a man of sharp and elegant wit'), and others: that the Inquisition was too rigorous, that its secrecy prevented the preparation of a proper defence, that the *sambenitos* (the penitential tunics which those condemned by the court had to wear for a time) were hung up in perpetuity in the local church, so that 'children would pay for the sins of their fathers . . .'. Most serious of all, in Mariana's words, 'through those secret enquiries, the freedom to talk and listen to one another was taken away, since there were people specially appointed in the cities, towns and villages to report what was going on'.[6] In the words of ambassador Donà in 1573, 'such is the fear that everyone has of this tribunal that no one talks about or enquires into its proceedings very much, for fear of becoming himself in any way an object of suspicion'. Nevertheless, both Donà and Mariana seem to have concluded that the exceptional nature of the threat to Spain required these sacrifices.

The most visible expression of the problem was no doubt to be found in the frontier with Islam. Essentially the reconquest of much of Spain, notably of Granada in 1492, had been achieved through negotiations with individual Moorish cities and their rulers, who had obtained the safeguard of their lands and religion, and extensive rights of self-government, in return for recognition of Christian suzerainty. It would be misleading to talk of tolerance, but coexistence there certainly was. Like the Jews, the Moors began to suffer increasing pressure during the later Middle Ages – popular pogroms, like the sack of their quarter of Valencia city in 1455, and the accumulation of restrictive legislation, such as the ban on the muezzin calling to prayer from the minaret (though mosques themselves remained open), the prohibition on work during Christian holy days, the adoption of rules by some guilds excluding non-Christians . . .[7] Though the Treaty of Granada proclaimed toleration, this quickly broke down. The reasons would seem to be a mixture of evangelical and social pressure from at least some sections of the victorious camp. Even the gentle Hernando de Talavera, archbishop of Granada (1492–1507), though happy to use Moorish song and dance in the Corpus Christi processions and rejecting the use of force, was a keen evangelist, preaching through the hill country, and also trying to get the local people to accept 'Christian customs, sitting in chairs and eating our food'. He would also get them to dress 'in the Castilian way', and distribute benches and tables to the poor, 'so that they would not eat on the floor'.[8] Immigration of Christians in search of land and work created familiar problems of social conflict. Though the Moors had been guaranteed the right to property, it became increasingly difficult to maintain this once the notarial registers began to be kept in the language of the conquerors (virtually everywhere in Granada from the 1520s). It was hard for an Arabic-speaking peasantry to secure a fair hearing in court against usurers and land-grabbers. Diego Hurtado de Mendoza commented on the effects of the official enquiry into title to land in Granada conducted by the government after 1559: 'The New Christians, lacking a tongue and with no friends, found sentence given against them, their farms taken away or divided up, though they were theirs, purchased by them or inherited from their forefathers.'[9]

This pressure is reflected in the statistics of demography. Between 1492 and 1568 the Moors seem to have fallen to about half of the population of the kingdom of Granada, while those of Valencia fell between the thirteenth-century reconquest there and the mid-fourteenth century to about one-third. It was in this unstable environment that conflict erupted – popular disturbances, Muslim resistance, royal intervention. The flash-point in Granada was the very basic question of mixed marriages. Islam exerted an attraction on the humbler people of Christian Europe during the Middle Ages and beyond – a refuge for the oppressed, where they could rise to positions of authority. Fray Diego de Haedo found Algiers in 1612 virtually in the hands of these 'Renegades', as they were known – about 6,000 of them, holding 'almost all the power, dominion, government and wealth'.[10] When the Christians entered Granada after 1492, they were particularly keen to win these people back, which often meant breaking up families. Tensions here erupted in the first Moorish rising of 1499–1501, which gave the Catholic Kings the excuse to tear up the treaty of 1492 and offer all Muslims living in the Crown of Castile the choice of baptism or exile. Solemn promises by the Crown to the worried seigneurs of Valencia in the Cortes of 1510, that the Moorish peasants there would not be converted by force, eventually collapsed in the revolt of the Germanías (1519–22). The rebel armies combined godly zeal with anti-seigneurial venom by invading the *aljamas* (Muslim communities) and offering their inhabitants the choice of baptism or death. After the suppression of the revolt, the Crown found it prudent to accept this development and to proclaim the end of Islam throughout the Crown of Aragon.

The problem was now one of assimilating the new converts. At first there was confidence that much could be achieved by preaching and teaching, and, symptomatic of the optimism of this period, the *concordias* of 1526 and 1528 promised the Moriscos (as the converts were known) that the Inquisition would not be too rigorous in enquiring into the relics of Islamic practice among them, at least for a term of forty years during which they must be instructed in Christianity. But looking back on a wasted opportunity, one observer around 1570 commented: 'I do not know why it is that we are so blind . . . that we go off to convert the infidels of Japan, China and other remote parts . . . rather as if someone had his house full of snakes and scorpions, yet took no care to clean it but went to hunt for lions or ostriches in Africa.'[11] Certainly there were constant complaints that the mission to the Arabic peoples of the peninsula never attracted the enthusiasm accompanying Spanish imperialism overseas, and, as late as 1604, there were proposals for instructing preachers in Arabic so that they could perform more effectively. But Fray Jaime Bleda, a Valencian Dominican and the leading spokesman for the 'final solution' of getting rid of the Moriscos altogether, believed that preaching was not the heart of the problem. Based on his own experience as rector of Valencian parishes in the 1580s and 1590s, he gave his opinion that this people rejected Christianity not out of 'ignorance' but out of 'malice'.[12]

By the time Bleda was active the Morisco question had anyway changed, as Renaissance optimism gave way to Counter-Reformation pessimism about the nature of man. In the 1560s the forty years of grace conceded by the *concordias* for the Moriscos to learn about Christianity came to an end, coinciding with the Council of Trent and the advent of the more combative monarchy of Philip II. Old measures prohibiting the Arabic language and customs were resurrected in 1566, despite the appeal of Francisco Núñez Muley, spokesman of the Granadans, that Egyptian Christians spoke Arabic and that the dress and music of Granada were regional, not religious, and names a way of identifying families rather than proclaiming Islam.[13] Even the acerbic Bleda was later to criticise this policy – maintained by the secular authorities – as mistaken: if the members of the Junta for Morisco affairs in Madrid only knew, he commented, that 'the greatest *alfaquíes* (jurists and teachers) are quite happy to dress in the Christian way'. In fact, what is clear is the great difficulty contemporaries had in distinguishing between ritual and belief, between the social customs of the Moors and their separate culture. It is significant that it was the *alfaquí*, the man of law, who became the religious leader of the Moriscos after open adherence to Islam became impossible, maintaining a set of rules relating to every aspect of daily life.

The various tensions in Granada were exacerbated by the decrees of 1566 on language and customs, erupting in the great Second Revolt of the Alpujarras (1568–70), whose costly suppression led to the dispersal of the Granadans throughout Castile. Thereafter the Morisco problem became essentially a Valencian and, to a lesser extent, Aragonese one, with the *aljamas* there trying to maintain their identity, with some support from the feudal aristocracy, against the enveloping tide of an ecclesiastical and royal bureaucracy. In this last phase of Moorish Spain the Inquisition acquired increasing importance, but so too did the parish. The parish structure was very imperfect, to be sure, but it generated a new routine of religious observance, reflected still in the registers of baptisms, marriages and burials from the last quarter of the sixteenth century, which throw interesting and, indeed, unusual light on the demography of a non-Christian population. Attempts to set up parishes in Muslim areas had begun in Valencia in 1535, but made only slow headway, given the costs involved: the destruction or rebuilding of the mosque, the endowment of a resident priest. It was found that the *habices* – rents from fields, houses or the like, used to support the mosque – were too small to pay for the more elaborate worship of Christians. The traditional Christian resource, the tithe of crops (which Moors were obliged to pay after their conversion), went mostly to bishops and cathedral chapters or to the seigneurs and the Crown, with only a small share – the first fruits or *primicias* – reserved for the parish. The initial endowment of the Morisco parishes with 30 Valencian pounds a year – less than a chantry priest could earn, as was pointed out at the time – had to be augmented to 100 pounds in 1572. But the negotiations with cathedral chapters and seigneurs which were required in order to provide the money dragged on, and still in the early seventeenth century only 74 out of the proposed 129 Morisco parishes in Valencia had reached this figure.

Lacking adequate funding, the parishes, nevertheless, came to constitute a rudimentary framework within which the Morisco people had now to live out their lives. Stricter control was thus kept over the various stages of the life-cycle. Midwives were supposed to be Old Christians, and Bleda thought it would be difficult for the inhabitants of the relatively compact *aljamas* to keep births secret – even if the holy oils were washed off as soon as the infant was brought home, where a separate naming ceremony would take place. Marriages were conducted by the priest, but the latter generally did not stay long enough in a particular village to become familiar with names and relationships, and Bleda may be right to suggest – based on his own eight years as a parish priest – that the canonical norms on dispensations of consanguinity, bigamy or divorce simply could not be enforced. As the bishop of Orihuela suggested in 1595, for the Moriscos the real marriage was the contract drawn up by the *alfaquí*. The few examples which have come to light indicate the survival of Islamic bridewealth (the endowment of the bride by the groom) rather than European dowry, and suggest how a separate culture continued to flourish at the very basic level of the family. Muslim rituals of death – turning of the dying person to face east, burial in virgin soil – were combated from the 1570s by increasingly strict injunctions that the priest must be called to the bedside of sick Moriscos, and must witness the laying of the corpse in the grave.

The priests were aware, commented Bleda, that 'the Moriscos were not playing fair, but since the poor fellows had to live among them, and on the scant income they got from them, they did not dare open their mouths'. Similarly, the constables responsible for enforcing edicts against Muslim practices were subject to great pressures within the small communities where they operated. During the fasting month of Ramadan, 'sometimes they would go into the houses to eat with them, when they saw the inhabitants, as the first star appeared in the sky, close their doors and make ready the first meal of the day'. Butchers, who by law had to be Christian, were also to be found slitting the throats of animals in the ritual way of Islam in order to find customers.[14] There was, of course, the risk of intervention by the Inquisition. Bleda suggests that most Moriscos escaped with a warning and with some public penance, but paid little real heed to the censures of that tribunal. This was especially the case after 1571, when the Morisco leaders of Valencia managed to negotiate a concession from the Crown that, in return for an annual subsidy from the *aljamas*, the Inquisition would in no circumstances confiscate property. This had been a long-standing demand of the Valencian seigneurs, on whose estates the Moriscos mostly lived and who were anxious to avoid damage to the rural economy.

Certainly the Inquisition over the years managed to destroy much of the formal apparatus of Islam. But the *alfaquís*, through their knowledge of the rites and their activity in circumcision, marriage contracts, preparation of the dead for burial, and the like, managed to keep alive a flourishing underground religion. It was among them that a quite extensive clandestine literature circulated, writings in either Arabic or *aljamía* (Castilian in Arabic characters). This last echo of the glorious literary heritage of Al Andalus had shed its former interest in secular themes, and now concentrated mostly on religion – a conservative adherence to the works of the past, though curiously deviating into folk culture, with apocryphal lives of Mohammed and verses designed to ward off sickness or the evil eye.[15] 'In each house, in every corner, we have found even primers for children, with the commands of Mohammed written in verse,' wrote Aznar Cardona in 1610. And certainly one prominent feature of this clandestine literature was its polemical nature – its utter rejection of Christianity.[16]

One of the Morisco leaders of Valencia, Don Cosme Abenamir – who had been offered a post as familiar of the Inquisition around 1560 in an attempt to win over men who were regarded as reliable and influential – was arrested in January 1568. Under interrogation, he confessed that though he had gone to confession 'now and again', yet 'in his heart he was never [a Christian]'. His mother had brought him up to believe that Christ and Mohammed were both prophets, and had taught him the *zalá*, the ritual prayer said five times a day, as well as to observe the fast of Ramadan. He had no books in Arabic, though – other than his own book of accounts – and could remember little of the Koran. A protégé of the powerful duke of Segorbe, Don Cosme seems to have been one of those who negotiated the royal concession of 1571, exempting Moriscos from confiscation of property for heresy, and he also obtained that year a pardon for himself. When the duke, his protector, died in 1575, Don Cosme's position became vulnerable once more, and he was rearrested for continuing to live as a Muslim.[17]

This case suggests some of the informal protection which the Moriscos enjoyed. One of the surprising features to emerge from Bleda's account of his own determined campaign against this people from the 1580s, is how little interest or support he managed to get from his ecclesiastical colleagues. Even that great Counter-Reformation prelate, Archbishop Ribera of Valencia, seems to have been somewhat hesitant, believing that the Moriscos were not going to become true Christians, but reluctant to proceed with too much rigour because of the social and political implications. Anyway, all measures had to pass through a government junta in Madrid, 'than whom no one knew less about the Morisco question'. Here was dominant the 'abominable sect of the *políticos*' – an early example of the borrowing of a word coined to apply to the moderates in the French Wars of Religion in the 1590s, who believed that toleration was a greater virtue than the religious fanaticism which tore the commonwealth apart.[18] One of the members of the Junta in the 1580s was Don Jerónimo de Corella, heir to the count of Cocentaina, on whose estates lived the wealthy Morisco Gaspar Masot – '*mi amigo*', as Don Jerónimo addressed him when he borrowed money, and among whose books at his death in 1602 was to be found an Arabic manuscript with lives of Muslim heros and popular devotions.[19]

The reason why the government eventually began to shift its attitude on the Morisco question and adopt a policy of rigour is complex. The seigneurs themselves were, no doubt, coming increasingly under the sway of the Counter-Reformation. The trial of Don Sancho de Cardona, Admiral of Aragon, in 1569 for obstructing the work of evangelisation on his estates marked something of a turning-point – the end of the old, free-wheeling seigneurs who had been a law unto themselves. One notes from the 1580s an increase in litigation between the *aljamas* and their feudal lords over rents, as the economic situation began to deteriorate – even Gaspar Masot towards the end of his life was engaged in this kind of confrontation. The Old Christian population in Valencia had advanced by 45 per cent to 65,016 households between 1565 and 1609, whereas the Moriscos had increased by 70 per cent over the same interval to 31,715.[20] This marked a reversal of earlier trends which had seen the minority everywhere on the retreat, and generated increasing fear and suspicion on the part of the majority, as it lost confidence in itself. San Luis Beltrán was already stirring fear by his prophecies from the 1570s that the recurring bad harvests were a mark of God's anger with Spain for tolerating heretics in its midst, and that worse was to follow. The anti-Morisco zealot Bleda got his first hearing in official circles as translator of the documents for the canonisation process of this influential seer, who had interestingly started out as an apostle to the American Indians.

No doubt, it would have required more than a handful of zealots to force the hand of the government. The old argument that the Moriscos were a 'fifth column', a potential ally of Spain's enemy, the Ottoman Turk, was no longer so relevant as it had been, since the great victory of Lepanto (1571) and the gradual retreat of that power into prolonged confrontation with Persia. Nevertheless, the situation in the Barbary States was worrying, with continuing corsair raids against the shipping and coastal villages of the peninsula, and a civil war in Morocco between 1603 and 1610, which the Spanish candidate was losing.[21] Plots and rumours of plots – of a Morisco uprising in alliance with the French or the English – abounded around 1600. How seriously to take all this is unclear. Clearly, there was much Morisco unrest, and prophecies circulated in manuscript among this people foretelling the triumph of the Turk and keeping alive a sense of resistance.[22] Rather like the hunt for scapegoats at all times and all places, the evidence of unrest fuelled Christian fears, and led to the fatal denouement of 1609–14 – the decision to uproot 275,000 men, women and children, herd them to the ports and transport them by ship to North Africa. The scale of the upheaval was not perhaps so very great at the level of the Spanish population as a whole – though close to one in twenty-five must have been Morisco at the time; but in the case of Aragon, and especially Valencia (one in every three persons affected) it was traumatic. Arguments continue about the economic effects, but certainly the event brought down the curtain on the cultural pluralism typical of medieval Iberia, and ushered in a more integrated kind of society.

The activity of the Inquisition peaked around 1580–1600 and then began a period of steady decline. A new concern with economics shaped the work of the *arbitristas*, as attempts were made to halt Spanish decline, and greater pragmatism was visible in relations with foreign countries. Thus, following the treaty of 1604 which brought to an end hostilities with Protestant England, the Inquisition was told not to investigate sailors of that nation in Spanish ports, 'so that the reign of commerce which will flow from the peace may not turn out sterile, as would happen if the subjects of His Majesty, the King of England . . . were to be arrested and molested on grounds of religion'. Foreign residents from Protestant countries had still to take care in the seventeenth century, especially in time of war; but generally, if they maintained a discreet behaviour and gave no cause for scandal, the Inquisition would not open windows into their souls. By 1787 when the Wiltshire rector, Joseph Townsend, could praise one of the Inquisitors of Granada whom he met as a man of 'much learning and notable humanity', the archbishop jokingly commented: 'The Inquisitors of the present day were become more gentle than their fathers . . . but they have not yet forgot the taste of blood.'[23]

Overall, cases of heresy – Jews, Moriscos, Protestants (almost all foreigners) – accounted for only about 40 per cent of Inquisition business between 1540 and 1700, as the tribunal became more concerned instead with policing the faith and morals of the majority Old Christian population. Their so-called 'lesser offences' reveal how tenuous was the hold of official Catholicism on the bulk of the peasantry. In Galicia, reported the Inquisitors in 1585, those who deny the bodily presence of Christ in the Eucharist are very numerous, but err 'more through ignorance than malice'. Many deny the Virgin Birth, 'out of sheer dull-wittedness rather than a desire to offend'; nevertheless, 'they give great scandal and make it hard for the church to get its message across'.[24] These so-called 'propositions' or 'blasphemies', together with 'superstitions' (belief in magic or witchcraft) either attracted a warning, or 'abjuration' of slight or grave suspicion of heresy. Thus, one Galician peasant who had denied that Mary could have given birth to Christ without losing her virginity was sentenced to attend high mass with a gag in his mouth, followed by 200 lashes and a prohibition on his coming nearer than six leagues (about 30 kilometres) to his village for the next five years.

The severity of these punishments seems to have depended on family background, with more indulgence shown towards the nobility and those of Old Christian ancestry. Formal heretics were 'reconciled' to the church, losing their property and being gaoled for a period, and perhaps appearing at one of the formal *autos de fe* in penitential garb (the *sambenito*), which would then be hung up in the local church, to the eternal shame of one's family. The *autos de fe* were increasingly costly spectacles – great processions and preachings, which might last a day or more – and many tribunals found it hard to afford them with much frequency. They were followed by the separate execution of those who had lapsed into heresy a second time and were 'relaxed' to the secular authorities for burning (being garrotted first if they showed any repentance). Only 3 or 4 per cent of trials ended with a death sentence, and about half of these were against those who had escaped abroad anyway.[25]

By the seventeenth century the Inquisition was becoming a great, privileged corporation, symbol of an orthodoxy which was no longer really in question. The tours of their jurisdictions by the Inquisitors in person began to fade from the later sixteenth century, as the tribunals became more sedentary and bureaucratic. From about 1620 in Galicia, the Inquisitors, who had hitherto been outsiders, came to be drawn from the families of local notables, while the lesser agents of the court – *comisarios* and familiars – equally reflected the aspirations for dignity and power of Galician gentry and wealthy peasants.[26] But, as the function of these dignitaries became less evident, complaints arose. The Cortes of Aragon in 1563 protested that there were too many officials, and that they enjoyed excessive privileges 'both in buying and selling food and other things, and in irrigation and other rights connected with their houses and fields'. The Cortes of Castile echoed this: Inquisitors enjoyed the right of purveyance – buying up supplies cheaply for their own households – but their officers abused it by reselling on the black market. Yet, if the municipal magistrate intervened, he was liable to be arrested and thrown in the Inquisition gaol, inmates of which were tarred for life with the suspicion of heresy.[27] *Concordias* of 1553 (Castile) and 1568 (Aragon) allowed the Inquisition jurisdiction over its own members in civil matters where they were the defendants, and in petty criminal offences, though graver crimes were to be referred to the royal courts. These 'Agreements' also sought to place an upper limit on the numbers of laymen who could be admitted as familiars, or spies, of the tribunal – no more than four in communities of 500 households, rising to a maximum of fifty in the biggest cities, Granada, Seville and Toledo.

The familiars actually played very little role in bringing suspects before the Holy Office; rather, they were positions conferring social status, particularly the valued certificate of 'purity of blood' (*limpieza de sangre*) – that one's family background had been investigated and no record found of heresy. 'A noble kingdom is one in which no vassal is considered of vile lineage, nor humiliated for his background . . . How can there be justice if some are despised and humiliated from generation to generation?' The words of the great sixteenth-century Spanish theologian and poet, Fray Luis de León, himself of Converso origin suggest the terrible damage done to the social fabric by the perpetuation of the shame of those penanced by the Holy Office – the innuendo and feuding which could grow up around it.[28] The *limpieza* statutes had spread from the town council of Cordoba in 1449 to the Jeronimite friars in 1495, who, following a scandal over the secret Judaism of prominent members, demanded that new entrants demonstrate that their great-grandparents had been Old Christians. Then the cathedral chapter of Seville in 1515 excluded those whose parents had been converted from the Hebrew faith, and the movement culminated with the bitterly contested statute for the cathedral of Toledo, approved by Philip II in 1556.[29] The measures were designed fundamentally against the Jews, since they, unlike the Moors, were an urban, professional class who competed for the top positions in church and state. They were patchy in their incidence: the more prestigious university colleges adopted them, the Military Orders, about a third of the cathedral chapters, individual convents . . . The Jesuits held out for a period, but, with their college in Cordoba, for example, suffering from 'an ill fame that only Jews go there', were eventually persuaded to adopt *limpieza* for entrants to their order in 1593.[30]

What was the religion of the Conversos? The great humanist Pulgar, who was one himself, suggested around 1485 that the Inquisition was fundamentally mistaken in its aims. Judaisers, 'in great ignorance and danger to their souls, kept neither the one nor the other law correctly, because they were not circumcised like Jews . . . and although they observed the Sabbath and some Jewish fasts, they did not observe all the Sabbaths nor all the fasts'.[31] In later days, Judaism seems to have survived only at the level of domestic ritual and family memory. 'And when I was six years old my parents told me that I am a Jew': the memoir of the younger brother of the great Spanish/Portuguese doctor Isaac ('Fernando') Cardoso, who was born around 1603–4, provides a brief glimpse into a world which had perforce to remain hidden. It was more usual to keep the fact of Jewishness hidden from children so young, for fear of indiscretion, and the Cardosos seem to have been given a fairly conventional Christian upbringing, though with a perhaps unusual space found for reading the Bible – in Latin.[32] Some Conversos eventually declared themselves openly Jews in the safety of Venice or Amsterdam – or in Brazil, after it was occupied by the Dutch between 1630 and 1654.

On the other hand, the great number of very orthodox Christians of Jewish family in Spain – the humanist Luis Vives, the poet Fray Luis de León, the saintly Teresa of Avila – has to be borne in mind. One would hardly guess from the outward circumstances of Vives's life that it was overshadowed by tragedy – the burning by the Inquisition in Valencia of his father for having lapsed into Judaism. Though the penance imposed on Saint Teresa's grandfather, a merchant of Toledo, for the same fault in 1485, was thrown in the face of her father when he tried to establish his nobility in Avila 1520, powerful friends there managed to swing the verdict of the court in favour of the family. The Cortes of 1551 complained that grandchildren of persons condemned by the Holy Office were not supposed to hold municipal office, 'but since such people are all wealthy, they obtain validation of their status from Your Majesty by favour'. And the deputy from Avila to the Cortes of 1618 was sure that investigations of genealogy were only an opportunity for lying and feuding, 'for the only nobility or *limpieza* in Spain nowadays is whether a man is well liked or not, or whether he has the means and adroitness with which to purchase it'.[33]

The role of religion in assuring political stability was taken as axiomatic. Beware of religious innovators, warned López Bravo, 'those who, dreaming up new ways of understanding or worshipping God, fill with sedition the fickle mind of the people'.[34] Certainly the link between Christianity and the state had become very close in the crusader kingdoms of Spain, culminating with the pope's concession to the Crown of the right to appoint to all major benefices in the recently conquered territory of Granada, extended to the presentation to bishoprics throughout Spain in 1523. Bishops were arms of the monarchy. On 26 October 1588 Philip II wrote to them in connection with the Enterprise of England: 'I would ask you affectionately that through preachers, confessors and other grave persons you would try to intimate to those who have votes in the town councils the obligation upon them to assist us at the present time . . . without anyone suspecting that I have written to you about this.' But divine guidance was notoriously slippery, and already in 1576 the *corregidor* of Murcia had reported that confessors were placing scruples in the minds of the councillors about the level of taxation – 'but knowing exactly what they said is impossible, since the advice was given in confession'.[35] Though the kind of open confrontation which the Puritans indulged in with the governments of Elizabeth or the early Stuarts was not visible in Spain, religion was still a two-edged sword. The lower clergy joined the Catalan revolt of 1640, chasing out Castilian bishops. And after the suppression of the revolt in 1652, the government ordered parish priests there 'on every holy day, at high mass where most people are present, from the pulpit or the foot of the altar, to proclaim to their flock how greatly they must attend to the service of His Majesty'.[36] When the papacy hesitated about recognising this Habsburg victory, delaying the confirmation of royal nominees for the vacant sees of Barcelona and Urgell, the Council of Aragon advocated a tough response. Vice-chancellor Crespí, a devout Catholic, agonised over the issue: the king was 'head of the church in everything other than matters of faith', and the pope could err 'as a man'; but one must never press things to a 'rupture', but rather play for time, trusting that God would restore the king's rights over his bishops 'in ways which human endeavour could not envisage'.[37]

It is true that by this time bishops were coming to play a less active political role, partly under the prompting of the Council of Trent, which had wanted them to reside in their sees rather than at the king's court. But at the local level they continued to wield enormous influence. 'The greatest calamities which have befallen our community,' wrote the chronicler of Segovia, 'have occurred when its bishops were not around or had died.'[38] And he, like Ortiz de Zúñiga for Seville, painted a vivid picture of the role of the prelate in pacifying feuds between warring families. Even the somewhat controversial Archbishop Aliaga of Valencia (1611–48), who had fallen foul of the *jurats* and the cathedral chapter over jurisdictional matters, was welcomed back from the Cortes of Monzón in 1626 to the loud peal of church bells, amid – as a diarist of the time put it – 'the joy we had at seeing our beloved father and shepherd return to his home and his city'.[39]

One has to remember the tremendous influence of the pulpit in an age when alternative forms of instruction and entertainment were relatively restricted. Juan Martín Cordero (born 1531) describes in his autobiography the public disputations by university students which attracted 'all the nobility and gentlemen' of Valencia to come and listen – a kind of testing of the oratorical skills on points of ethics or morality, which won the fourteen-year-old Cordero a prize of three silver spoons on one occasion.[40] At a lower level there was the popular preacher, like Fray Pere Esteve (1582–1658), a Franciscan who could stand for an hour in the market square of Valencia, holding spellbound a crowd of 'porters, message-boys, idlers and the like'. He spun homely yarns with a sharp political message – like the one about the little man pestered by flies, but happy enough that they were no bigger (partly referring, perhaps, to the French armies poised on the Valencian border with Catalonia in the 1640s).[41]

The most visible expression of the power of the church was its wealth. 'I have never been able to fathom,' commented Joly as he surveyed the little diocese of Osma, 'how the clergy can have so much property, given the infertility and poverty of Spain.' The churches, to be sure, were not as well-built or as handsome as those of France, but 'they are better than ours in their fine gilded altarpieces, their superb reliquaries, images and ornaments'. Of course, the French churches had recently been plundered during the Wars of Religion, and Spaniards who had grown wealthy in the Indies endowed theirs, 'in fulfilment of vows they made when threatened by the great perils and hazards of the sea'.[42] There was, indeed, increasing concern about the wealth of the church as the economy entered a period of decline. The reformer Lisón told the Cortes of 1621 that, on present trends, 'in a few years the greater part of landed property will belong to ecclesiastics'. This was something of an exaggeration, but by the time reliable statistics become available, in the cadastral survey of Ensenada (1750–54), the clergy accounted for about an eighth of the assessed revenues of the population of the Crown of Castile.[43] In the Crown of Aragon there were medieval laws against mortmain, but monarchs allowed the church to acquire land rather freely, on payment of a tax of a quarter of the value, and often dispensing individual applicants from the tax on grounds of poverty. The Cortes of Valencia in 1626 protested that convents 'have acquired and are acquiring much property of great value in the royal domain . . . so that they are becoming the masters of the biggest and best part of the whole'; and – rather nervously exempting church buildings from the ban, 'for this reverence is due to the place where the Most Holy Sacrament of the Eucharist is reserved' – they tried to stop monasteries invading any more city space.[44]

But it was perhaps the tithe – often close enough to the proverbial tenth of the harvest, though its incidence varied enormously from place to place and crop to crop – which aroused most controversy. One observer around 1600 wrote of the great burden falling on the peasant, who often had not enough left over, after he had paid his rent and other charges, for next year's sowing. When he defaulted, the authorities replied with excommunications, 'whence it happens that in a village of a hundred households there are usually a dozen excommunicated because of the tithe'. Those who failed to purge their fault within the year were supposed to be denounced to the Inquisition as 'suspect in faith'; but this seems to have been rare. One had to give scandal first – as did one man in Galicia who denounced the tithe as of human, not divine origin, and urged that it be limited to what was strictly necessary for the priest to live off and for the succour of the parish poor. For his pains he was ordered by the Inquisition to abjure of 'slight suspicion of heresy' in church before the assembled congregation, paying a fine of 800 ducats and being banished from the village.[45] But in an increasingly commercialised society, where the tithe was farmed out to businessmen for a lump sum and the proceeds ended up mostly with bishops, chapters, feudal lords and the Crown, the tithe became a subject of increasing controversy. The peppery Valencian jurist, Cerdán de Tallada, who had conducted an investigation of ecclesiastical revenues in 1593, argued that major reforms were needed here 'for the conservation of our religion'. There were too many clergy, the tithe was being abused, and monasteries too often presented to the peasant the face of a grasping landlord than of a spiritual guide. His Castilian contemporary, Castillo de Bobadilla, bore him out: 'There are some greedy prelates who are so lacking in charity that not only do they let the people in their care suffer extreme hardship and let the sheep they shear perish of hunger, but they will not even sell them the wheat they need for money', preferring to get a higher price on the urban market.[46]

However, Spain would not follow the Protestant road. The great Jesuit philosopher-historian, Mariana, argued that it was 'a very grave error' to seek to reduce the church to the poverty of Apostolic times, for wealth was necessary to its authority, and anyway more responsibly administered by it than by some greedy and ambitious courtier. Defending the endowments of the Jesuit colleges, Ribadeneira wrote in 1572 that thanks to them the fathers were better able to devote themselves to their principal task of education and evangelisation. And even a layman like the deputy from Burgos to the Cortes of 1593–5 thought that ecclesiastical wealth was an advantage to a community, since it gave employment and was recycled in the form of alms, building of temples and upward mobility for priestly nephews.[47] In fact, the Spanish state made good use of ecclesiastical assets. It is true that taxing the clergy provoked all kinds of political battles, after the government sought to get them to contribute to the *millones*, the new excises on food from the 1590s. In the Cortes of 1579–82 the always latent anti-clericalism surfaced when one of the Madrid deputies announced that his reading of the Bible told him that the clergy must pay taxes like any other citizen, and the pope did not need to be asked for his permission.[48]

But every six years frenzied negotiations in Madrid and Rome were needed in order to secure the papal warrant authorising the collection of the *millones* from priests. However, in other respects the state benefited greatly from its long association with the crusade against the infidel, collecting the 'third of the tithe', for example, and from 1567 also the entire tithe of the richest farm in the parish (the *excusado*). The popes had given the king as well the right to sell Bulls of Crusade. The sixteenth-century novel *Lazarillo de Tormes* satirised the trickery practised on the peasants in order to get them to buy these indulgences; but one village Luther in Galicia was given 200 lashes and banished by the Inquisition for two years for attacking the Bull as a swindle.[49] It, together with the *excusado* and the ecclesiastical donative or *subsidio*, brought in for the Crown as much as it received from the Indies every year. Additionally, bishoprics were saddled with pensions to nominees of the Crown – up to a third of their annual revenues under Philip II.

The diversion of so many ecclesiastical revenues to the Crown (and to the seigneurs) was matched by considerable inequality in the distribution of wealth within the church itself. While the Valencian Cortes of 1626 complained of the growing wealth of convents, they also pleaded on behalf of individual parish churches, which stood in great need of money. The Morisco parishes, as we saw earlier, proved often unable to get the cathedral chapters and the seigneurs to disgorge their shares of the tithe. While the local magistrates clearly played an important role in maintaining the church building itself, their funds were increasingly under strain thanks to royal taxation in the seventeenth century. Bernardo Catalá de Valeriola's diary would suggest that the gentry were reluctant to give up time and money to serve as churchwardens. Some of this may be due to uncertainty about the actual pastoral role of the parish, given that so many families and so many guilds had their own chapels and their own endowments for masses to their patron saint.

The clergy were not only pastors, but men and women set apart by their style of life, intermediaries with God through their holiness and prayer. Nuns, for example, did little of the 'practical' work – nursing, teaching – for which they became famed in the nineteenth century. Yet the reader of Saint Teresa of Avila (1515–82) senses the excitement with which this woman founded her enclosed communities – places where Christ would be honoured and from which a life of self-denial and prayer might persuade God to take pity on the heretic and sinner outside. 'Fleeing from intercourse with the world, eating coarse food, wearing very rough habits' were not particularly meritorious acts in themselves, suggested the Franciscan humanist Antonio de Guevara in 1529, but they were a way of reducing the temptation to sin. Laymen could live a godly life, but 'in truth, among a thousand, you will barely find one who can abstain from sin when the occasion presents itself'. And shortly before, the humanist Pulgar had written a moving letter to his twelve-year-old daughter who had chosen to become a nun. In giving up her freedom for the cloister, she was in fact more free than those she left behind in the world, including her sorrowing parents, who like the performers in the bull-ring must scurry hither and thither, driven breathless by the hope and fear of the moment.[50]

As well as the monks and nuns, there were the chantry priests, men who fulfilled no pastoral role but whose prayers kept open the bridge to the supernatural, across which divine favour flowed. In Viciana's chronicle of 1563–6 one notes the pride with which local communities reported the numbers of such holy men. Onda, with its 560 families, had its parish priest, but also 26 other *capellanes* or chantry priests. More usually in towns of this size there would be about a dozen such benefices, but up to 800 in the city of Valencia attached to its twelve parishes, in each of which (according to Escolano) 'they take pride in saying the offices and celebrating the masses with the utmost attention to detail, so that each parish looks as if it is a cathedral'. A great cycle of spirituality was, in fact, coming to an end about this time; together with the changing economic climate, it meant that Valencia had still only 771 benefices by the end of the Old Regime, and that other towns of the kingdom were complaining that the endowments were now too small to attract the full number of occupants.[51]

Only a limited number of these priests received licences from the bishop to confess sins or preach. Inevitably, therefore, a considerable responsibility fell upon the friars to help out in pastoral work. Seville told the Cortes of 1623 that there was a great need of Discalced Franciscans in the towns of its district to administer the sacraments and hear confession. Castillo de Bobadilla was somewhat angry that it was the municipal budget and not the tithe which had to pay for the summoning of preachers and confessors during Lent every year. 'The parish priests evade their obligation by saying that they are no good at preaching and that they do their duty by declaring the Gospel to the people on holy days, and that as regards confession, they do what they can. So that the town itself has to invite in a friar for both purposes', giving him and his companion food and lodging and 100 *reales* 'for books'.[52] Paralleling Castillo de Bobadilla's concern about the cost of this to small villages, more questions were beginning to be asked about whether Spain needed or could afford so many clerics. Fernández Navarrete, himself a priest, wrote in his great treatise of 1626 on the decline of his country, that though the ecclesiastical state was indeed most pleasing to God, Saint Paul had envisaged the Christian community as a body composed of different members with different functions, none of which must be allowed to grow out of proportion to the others. Many convents were founded to serve the vainglory of their patrons, and many chantry priests could hardly manage on the pittance they were paid, having to take 'menial jobs'. Indeed, from the last third of the sixteenth century the Cortes tried to apply some brake to the foundation of new convents, in a time when 'these realms have a smaller population and people are worse off'.[53]

According to the census of 1591 there were 33,087 parish and chantry priests, 20,697 monks and friars, and 20,369 nuns in Castile – equivalent to about 1.5 per cent of the population at the time.[54] There was some imbalance between regions. Of Catalonia its geographer Pere Gil (1551–1622) wrote proudly: 'Many Catalans become friars and priests, and, all things considered, there is no realm in Spain or Italy or France which, with the same number of households as Catalonia, has as many clergy as it.' But it was above all in the towns that the first estate was concentrated: 2,000 priests and friars in the city of Valencia – 'as well as the nuns, who are countless' – according to the chronicler Escolano, for a population of about 50,000 souls; and about 1,400 friars and nuns and 400–500 priests in Toledo, where the population was similar, in 1575.[55] Many of these, believed the Council of Castile in 1660, had little vocation, placed in religion by their parents, who transferred nominal ownership of their land to them in order to benefit from tax immunities. Secular priests had to have some property, as laid down by the Council of Trent, in order to avoid the proliferation of 'hedge priests' who had plagued the medieval church. But the level – at around 40 or 50 ducats a year – was less than the annual income of a wage-labourer. It was, however, the friars who were accused of recruiting too many of the poor, placed in convents by their parents after they had acquired a smattering of grammar, in order to 'free them from the cares of this world' – according to one government minister in 1683.[56] By contrast, nuns had to bring a dowry on entering a convent, and there were frequent complaints in the Cortes that the level was too high. On the other hand, the 2,000 ducats which the Madrid patricians gave their daughters when they took the veil was a fraction – about a tenth – of what they would have had to provide had they married.[57]

Obviously a mixture of motives – economic and cultural – shaped the thinking of families in this matter. Esteban de Garibay recounted how he had orientated his eldest son Luis, born in 1581, towards a clerical career. Set to primary school at age six, when 'he became fairly good at reading and writing, and at prayers and the catechism, I decided to have him receive the first tonsure so that I could get him some ecclesiastical funding for his further study'. Many people held the first tonsure – set apart as 'clerks', under the jurisdiction of the church courts and forbidden to marry – who had no intention of becoming ordained priests. Luis received his at age ten, and a couple of years later (1593) went to the Jesuit grammar school in Madrid. 'He keeps saying he wants to be a clergyman, and that's what I want, so that he may serve God in the priestly state, and be a protector for his brothers and sisters, since he is the eldest.'[58]

The clergy were inevitably a mixed bunch, given their sheer numbers and the diversity of motives which had brought them to where they were. The great poets and playwrights of the Golden Age who became priests, sometimes late in life – Lope de Vega, Góngora, Calderón – suggest at once the pervasive currents of spirituality of the time, and the contamination of the spiritual ideal by worldly concerns. The parish clergy seem often to have been local men – a fifth of the vicars and rectors in the diocese of Cuenca were appointed to their native village, and another quarter to within 30 kilometres of it.[59] These *curas* often stayed a long time in the same place, if not particularly zealous at preaching or guiding consciences, at least providing a framework for the Christian life which can still be glimpsed through their records, year after year, of the baptisms, marriages and burials of their flock. The chantry priest of Valencia, Mossèn Porcar, keeps us informed through his diary of the life of a community. He had grown up in the city and was thirty-five before he got his benefice in 1595. For Porcar religion was a round of devotions and processions which brought together a community he knew so well in its secular aspects as well. We find him chatting to fishwives in the spring of 1625 about the high price of lobster that season. From the fish-stalls (after morning mass) to the market and then across the river to the viceroy's palace, where throngs of litigants and curiosity-seekers gathered to await the arrival of the mail from Madrid, this seems to have been the daily itinerary which would provide him with the gossip which he would then write up in his diary. He had books in his house, and some interest in the topography and archaeology of his neighbourhood. He was, above all perhaps, a man of the people – concerned by pirate raids from North Africa rather than by remote wars against 'Lutherans' in northern Europe, bitter against nobles and prelates who sold out the people and voted taxes on food to pay for crusades abroad.

One thing that emerges clearly from his diary is how closely everyday life was bound up with religion – but a religion which took account of the natural harmony of the seasons rather than of official dogma. Work seems to have been interrupted for lunch when the sun was at its height (perhaps one or two of the clock), and people would begin to gather indoors for cards and conversation when bells rang out for vespers (at the fifth or sixth hour after high noon, corresponding to around seven o'clock nowadays). The curfew bell, summoning people to pause and say a prayer for the souls of the dead, rang at the eighth hour (say, nine or ten by today's clock). Clocks were coming in, but the governor of Llombai wrote still of that village in 1756, 'there is not even a clock to regulate the day and the night'.[60] Only the tolling of the bells at the canonical hours marked out time, somewhat like the call of the muezzin to prayer five times a day in Muslim countries. The contrast between hours of daylight and darkness was, of course, very striking, and the greatest festivities were signalled by the blaze of torches hung from every balcony or window – the *luminarias* – which momentarily turned night into day.

The visibility of the heavens in the normally long hours of darkness must have fostered the prevalent belief in their influence on the affairs of this world. Chroniclers like Bermúdez de Pedraza or Escolano, priests though they were, knew that the stars played a role in the fortunes of a city and the character of its inhabitants. Though the church had forbidden the belief that the fate of individuals was fixed by the stars (1583), one of the most popular almanacs of the time affirmed that men's destinies were indeed 'guided' by them.[61] Lope de Deza in his classic treatise of 1618 on agriculture was sure that the heavens announced good or bad years ahead for the farmer. The jurist López Bravo agreed that the farmer and also the doctor of medicine would want to consult the zodiac before acting; but those who predicted the fate of a particular individual or stirred up fear of famine by their prognostications were to be condemned.[62] Laws of 1410 and 1598 outlawed the foretelling of the future through crystal-gazing or watching the flight of birds or in other ways, on pain of death – 'and let the justices have this ordinance read in public, preceded by the ringing of a bell, once every month on market day'. Castillo de Bobadilla noted that there were cunning folk who were consulted 'about thefts, births and other matters not relating to agriculture or shipping or medicine'. Such 'sorcerers, diviners and seers' were to be punished by either the secular or the ecclesiastical courts. The black witch, the *bruja*, guilty of invoking the aid of Satan, would have to be left to the Inquisition, as would 'charmers' who meddled with the sacred, getting holy images 'to weep or perspire . . . in order to deceive the public and get money'.[63]

Spain, like Italy, was relatively free of the witch-craze sweeping early modern Europe. There were, indeed, panics from time to time – in Catalonia in 1622, for example, where the loss of crops through hailstones motivated a spate of accusations against persons, who were also blamed for the death of infants and of cattle. As the government recognised, once the ball started rolling, it had a momentum of its own: 'there is no town or village which has not started investigating whether it has any [witches] in its own district'. It was also concerned a few years later that these local investigations were linking up with feuds, 'as one side tries maliciously to get even and besmirch the other with this crime'. The caution of the central government was matched by that of the church hierarchy. The bishop of Solsona, in reply to a general enquiry by the ministers of Charles II on the situation in Catalonia in the later seventeenth century, gave his opinion that 'this matter of witches is a most difficult one'. He had had one witch-finder gaoled for wild accusations. Even when the accused persons confessed, little reliance could be placed on their testimony: 'they confess under threat of torture, and many die without being guilty'.[64] In fact, the Inquisition had the power of evoking some of these cases to itself, but the limits of its jurisdiction were not entirely clear. One 'white witch' in Toledo in 1594 was sentenced by the *corregidor* to whipping and perpetual banishment from town for making love-potions and curing a child with a parchment inscribed with crosses. The latter offence interested the Inquisition, which demanded her to be surrendered to it – fortunately for her, since her banishment was reduced to just six years, though she was required now to abjure formally of 'slight suspicion' of heresy at a private mass in its audience chamber. In Galicia such cases of witchcraft were generally treated in a similar way, as superstitions which smacked of heresy and required a formal protestation of innocence (that is, the so-called 'abjuration'), rather than as formal heresies or pacts with the Devil, which would require recantation, or 'reconciliation' with the church.[65]

The dividing-line between good and bad magic must anyway have been hard to draw in a society which paid great attention to the prophet and the visionary. The black slave girl, Catalina Muñoz, was sentenced by the Inquisition of Valencia to reconciliation in 1588, involving gaol for life and confiscation of her property, for having made a pact with the Devil in order to work miracles. For a time she had deceived much of the city, including Archbishop Ribera, into believing that her gifts were of divine origin.[66] The proximity of the supernatural was a major factor in orthodox belief. Some of the classics of medieval literature – the thirteenth-century *Cantigas de Santa María*, or the *Milagros de Nuestra Señora* by Gonzalo de Berceo, speak of the intervention of Our Lady and of her son on behalf of sinful man, setting aside the natural order in return for devotion to their cause. The miracle was what tended to remain in the popular memory after the ethical teaching of an evangelist had faded – as in the stories told about the fifteenth-century preacher, Saint Vincent Ferrer, which live on in the street theatre of Valencia and emphasise his communication with the divine through the wonders he worked.

The miracle, after all, provided some hope in a world lacking alternative means of protecting itself against the hazards of nature. Recording the birth of their first son in 1598 after numerous miscarriages, Bernardo Catalá de Valeriola noted how his anxious wife 'commended herself to the glorious Saint Raymond (de Penyafort?) and swallowed some earth from his tomb'. After the safe delivery, he burst out in a paean of praise to all the saints in heaven who had interceded for him with Christ, who thus 'would not punish my child as my sins deserve'.[67] The chronicler of Toledo in 1617 devoted many pages to the miracles performed on the sick, especially on those 'given up as hopeless by the doctors'. A cape from a statue of the Virgin, for example, would be placed over the patient, or children laid on the steps of the altar where her image was venerated.[68] The Dominican friar Gavaldá, who played such an active part in combating the plague of 1647 in Valencia, summed up the conventional wisdom: 'Much was owed to human prudence, but if it had not been helped along by greater powers, vigilance would have achieved little.'

The great enquiry conducted by Philip II's government into the way of life of the Castilian peasantry in 1575 throws much light on these forms of popular devotion. Faced by disease or famine, villages would commend themselves by a collective decision to a particular saint, chosen sometimes by lot from within a list of likely candidates, or by lighting several candles and choosing the name given to the one which burned longest. In thanksgiving the village would celebrate an annual *caridad* or fellowship ritual, involving communal feasting and distribution of food to the poor. Sometimes the exact cause of the original vow was forgotten, and only the festival remained.[69] Retorting to the Protestants, the Sevillian essayist Pedro de Luxán noted in 1550: 'It is no lack of breeding nor indeed of prudence for a man who is going to negotiate with the king to ask his chamberlain to put in a good word for him and attend when he is making his petition.' The saints as such had no power, but their merits were pleasing to God, and since they had themselves walked this earth, they felt love and pity for humankind. Thus, the Cortes of Valencia, pressing for the canonisation of several recently dead Valencians, spoke of how 'with their exemplary lives and holy deaths, they have shed lustre on this realm, and, what is more, having lived and died within it, they will intercede with his Divine Majesty that he may favour the said kingdom at every opportunity and in all its needs'.[70]

The political use of saints was important. Among the 'high secrets of government' outlined by the political theorist López Bravo in 1627, was the importance for the ruler of identifying himself with the devotions of his subjects. Though, unlike the masses, 'he is not taken in by the fables . . . which greed for fame or dominion invented in more barbarous times', nevertheless he would benefit from his association with the patriotism which they often conveyed.[71] But perhaps Spain failed to achieve the kind of cultural integration envisaged by López Bravo. The national saint of Castile, Saint James 'the Moorslayer', whose cult had presided over much of the Reconquest, had to take second place in the Crown of Aragon to that other patron of the crusade, Saint George, who had appeared to the Christian armies fighting outside Valencia in 1238. And it was the thirteenth-century canon lawyer, Saint Raymond of Penyafort, adviser to the old kings of Aragon, whom the ministers of the Crown of Aragon honoured as their patron in solemn procession through the streets of the Spanish capital. The commemoration of the victory of Lepanto over the Turk (7 October 1571), though the subject of a famous canvas by El Greco, was left largely in the hands of the church. Rather than celebrating the virtues of the monarch, therefore, it tended to become a religious fiesta. The Valencian priest Porcar noted in his diary in the early seventeenth century how it was being assimilated by the Dominicans to their own cult of the Holy Rosary (4 October). The contrast with England at this time could hardly be greater, where, as David Cressy notes, the celebration of the safe accession of Queen Elizabeth and the discovery of the Gunpowder Plot (17 and 5 November) were becoming great national holidays. 'Bells and bonfires' gave the ordinary Englishman a sense of belonging to a Protestant nation.

At most, the Spanish kings did try to latch on to existing cults – often local – and to promote them. The classic example is the way they adopted some of the popular devotions of Madrid, those of Saint Isidore and Our Lady of Atocha, referred to in an earlier chapter. And, of course, the cosmopolitanism of the Catholic Church facilitated the migration of the holy. Thus Bernardo Catalá de Valeriola, a Valencian in charge of the province of León, must have endeared himself to his subjects by stopping in 1606 at their local shrine to Our Lady of the Wayside to say a prayer for the recovery of his son from sickness. But, as against this, one has to set the potentially disruptive effects of religious patriotism. Thus, a riot broke out in Font d'En Carròs (Valencia) in 1601, when its feudal lord sought to remove a venerated image of Our Lady. Armed forces had to be sent in to punish the local aldermen.[72]

Visions and healing power could be associated with people who seemed to threaten rather than strengthen good order in church and state. The twenty-one-year-old Lucrecia de León, daughter of a Madrid notary, was tried by the Inquisition in 1590 for her 'dreams', which foretold the punishment to befall Spain for the extortions practised by the king, Philip II. She became widely popular after foretelling the defeat of the Armada, and attracted some powerful members of the elite into her circle. After a lengthy investigation the Inquisition decided, given among other things her character (she had an illegitimate child), that her dreams must be either invention or of diabolical rather than divine origin, and sentenced her in 1595 to abjure *de levi* (from slight suspicion of heresy), to a hundred lashes and to reclusion for a couple of years in a convent.[73] Thanks to the Inquisition, it was becoming more difficult for popular visionaries to establish a hold during this period. The trials suggest the enormous temptation to claim links with the supernatural, though. Thus, in 1523 one twenty-five-year-old woman, the wife of a carder, said that she had seen the Virgin Mary appear on a rock outside her house one night. The village women assembled, and one of their sick children was cured by kissing the spot. The parish priest advised the woman to keep quiet in case the vision was the work of the Devil, and the Inquisition soon intervened. Finding that the visionary was not particularly devout, and that her evidence was unpersuasive, it sentenced her to one hundred lashes.[74]

One of the most dangerous threats to Inquisition authority arose in Valencia between 1612 and 1619, over the folk saint Mossèn Francesc Jeroni Simó. Orphaned son of an immigrant French carpenter, he had got an education through the patronage of various people, obtaining a benefice in the rather dangerous parish church of Sant Andreu – dangerous because it was in the district of the fishermen (one of the few trades not regulated by guilds) and near the university, where student rags and riots were a recurring feature of life. Father Simó's early death at the age of thirty-three in 1612 sent shock-waves through a city reeling at this very time from a confrontation between the artisan assembly and the *jurats* over new taxes to stave off municipal bankruptcy. During the three days in which the body was exposed after death (25–27 April), many cures were reported of the blind, deaf and lame, and great crowds, including the viceroy, turned out for the funeral. Gifts poured in over the next few months from the guilds and the peasants in order to construct a shrine for the dead hero, with individual communities contributing their special product – whether it be limestone, silk, bricks or whatever – in grandiose and colourful processions headed by their musicians. Some of the clergy encouraged the devotion – notably the Jesuits and the stricter orders of Franciscans (Discalced and Capuchins) – together with many of the elite. On 9 September 1612 the new shrine in Sant Andreu was inaugurated, celebrated by three days of festivities and illuminations, with enormous processions thenceforward bringing the city to a halt as they wound their way through the market square every Friday morning for prayers at Simó's tomb. Following representations from the archbishop, Aliaga, the Inquisition tried to curb the excesses of this popular devotion, ordering (1614–5) that no more pictures were to be produced showing rays of light radiating from Simó's head, and that his body must be removed from the altar and no more masses said there, pending official investigations of his sanctity by Rome. Complicated manouevres then ensued, with the *jurats* and the noble estate trying to get these decrees suspended, warning of the risk of popular disturbances and using the influence of the duke of Lerma, whose grandchild, accidentally smothered by the wet-nurse, had been revived in 1614 by the application of a relic of Simó. It was Lerma's fall from power in 1618 which led the Inquisition to swing into action again, on 3 March 1619, banning any further public cult of the dead priest. A riot ensued: the secretary of the Holy Office had to take refuge in the sacristy of the cathedral after reading out the decree at mass, and the crowd stoned the windows of the archbishop's palace and broke down the gates of the Dominican convent (whose friars had led the campaign against the cult). The Inquisition had to agree to suspend the decrees for three weeks, while desperate efforts were made by the Crown to get the *jurats* and the nobility to use their influence to restore order. In the event, Simó's shrine was gradually dismantled, while the populace was assuaged by promises that the authorities would make every effort to pursue official canonisation proceedings in Rome. Pope Urban VIII's order of 1628, for the Catholic world as a whole, that canonisation proceedings were not to be started until fifty years after an alleged saint had died, marked a decisive removal of sainthood from the hands of the people into that of the hierarchy. And the control of the church over popular spirituality received a further boost when Miguel de Molinos, envoy of the Valencians to Rome to secure Simó's canonisation, was condemned in 1687 for Quietism – the notion that through inner surrender of the soul to God one can dispense with the discipline of the church.[75]

Though the Counter-Reformation Church began to make life difficult for folk saints, they were still to be found at the very end of the Old Regime. Fray Diego José de Cádiz (1743–1801), the son of a junior army officer, entered the Capuchins when he was fourteen. The English traveller Townsend saw him when he was at the peak of his popularity, just after Easter 1787: 'He would preach every night in the main square [of Cartagena] to more than ten thousand people . . . The good father is knowledgeable, eloquent and modest, and though the crowd attribute various miracles to him, he makes no claim to that distinction . . . He was escorted everywhere by a guard to prevent his habits being torn from him to make relics of them.' Old enemies would patch up their quarrels when they heard him speak, but the audience was less impressed by his invitation to denounce even close kin to the Inquisition if they were guilty of heresy. In fact, the Inquisition was more concerned about pamphlets which were circulating with miraculous prayers which Fray Diego had supposedly authorised against sickness or the evil eye. And the government, though later grateful for his propaganda on behalf of the war against godless France (1793–6), had to reprimand him for attacking its policy of 'enlightened self-interest' as regards the economy.[76]

A deep sense of community was one of the significant features of Spanish Catholicism. In his testament of 1573 Don Luis de Requesens stressed his own unworthiness and his hope for salvation in the mercy of Christ and – departing at this point from Puritan ideas – the merits of the saints, particularly those depicted on the altarpiece in his burial chapel in Barcelona, where chantry priests would celebrate mass every day for the repose of his soul, and where nine paupers, to be clothed every year on the eve of the commemoration of All Souls, were to be invited to come and pray for him. The classic expression of this solidarity was the confraternity, engaged in promoting good works and the collective salvation of its members. Bernardo Catalá de Valeriola tells us in his diary that from the time he was a child he had been enrolled by his parents in several of these, and he recorded the consolation he felt in 1592 at the 'infinite prayers' being offered up for his recovery from sickness by his fellows in the Confraternity of Saint Peter Martyr. Though often these associations created new ties of solidarity, occasionally they reinforced existing ones, as in 1591, when Bernardo joined his wife, mother and some servants of the family in the Confraternity of the Rosary, whose headquarters lay in the Basque Country, in the Dominican convent in Vitoria. Many indulgences were accorded to members, he noted, 'and many miracles have been attested for women in childbirth'.[77]

Confraternities were often class-specific. Thus, each trade had its own – a kind of social counterpart to the guild, providing an extensive range of charitable and spiritual benefits for its members. The feasting and conviviality associated with them became increasingly suspect to the religious reformers of the sixteenth century, and to economists at a later date. Fernández Navarrete believed there were too many of these brotherhoods: 'artisans spend half the year vying with one another in display rather than in devotion'.[78] The Jesuits pioneered new forms, the 'congregations', designed for the literate men and women who desired a deepening of their spiritual life. Bernardo Catalá de Valeriola joined that of Valencia in 1600, but his spiritual loyalties were perhaps already so widely dispersed that it is difficult to see much of its influence in his diary.

Religion shaped human relationships and provided the basic framework for living out one's life. Just as the hours of the day were marked by the bells for vespers or the souls of the deceased, so the seasons were graced by the red-letter days of ritual celebration. Lope de Deza noted that the ploughing of the fallow would usually be completed in New Castile by Saint John's Day (24 June), before the earth baked hard under the summer sun, while by Saint Andrew's Day (30 November) the autumn ploughing would have to be done, before the rains and snow made the soil unworkable again. Saint James's Day (25 July) generally marked the completion of the wheat harvest in New Castile, and the migrant reapers from Galicia, where his great shrine lay at Compostela, would have time to celebrate as they made ready for home.[79] Porcar gives a vivid insight into the frequency and importance of these fiestas throughout the year in his native Valencia. After the splendid processions of Holy Week 1617, culminating on Easter Day, 26 March, there was the commemoration of Saint Vincent Ferrer on 3 April, with the suspension of work that day and a week of celebration, including the famous miracle plays mounted in the streets. On 23 April came

Saint George's Day, patron of the knights of this crusader kingdom, and on 25 May Corpus Christi, followed by a week of street theatre and processions. Work was suspended in the heat of summer, between 9 and 12 August, to commemorate Saint Lawrence and a papal jubilee. And the autumn was marked by the usual celebrations commemorating Valencia's capture from the Moor (9 October), followed by a new public holiday that year, 19 October, declared by the magistrates to honour a local hero, the Dominican friar Luis Beltrán (died 1581 and beatified 1608, though not yet canonised as a saint).

The calendar was crowded with these red-letter days, in which the community came together, displaying its finery and hierarchy in processions, investing its ingenuity in the delicate and transient tableaux of flowers and wood which graced the streets, decking the houses in competitive displays of *luminarias* by night, mounting plays, bull-fights and the mock tournaments known as *cañas*. Fireworks and bonfires – of which the modern Fallas in Valencia are a remote echo – completed the celebrations. The pealing of the church bells added sound to the visual splendour. 'They mingle profanities with the divine ceremonies,' commented the Venetian ambassador Soranzo (1597–1602), 'to the great amazement of those who are not used to seeing it, maintaining here an old habit bequeathed to them by the Moriscos.' In their religious processions, 'they jumble up masks, women, animals', and with their hymns 'they mix in profane song, music and dancing, and even in church, right before the Blessed Sacrament, costumed figures break into dance'.[80]

Occasionally the profane seemed to take over. On the feast of Saint Nicholas (6 December), as in many parts of Europe, a 'boy bishop' was elected – by the cathedral schools often – exercising an authority which culminated, in the case of Granada, on the Day of the Holy Innocents (28 December), when the students took the seats of the canons in church and the archbishop, 'standing, with head uncovered', attended as a choir-master. The first archbishop of Granada, Talavera, 'was very fond of these ceremonies of humility', which the chronicler, Bermúdez de Pedraza, thought came ultimately from the Romans, 'who in certain of their feasts would elect and revere a slave as king'.[81] The rite of inversion no doubt provided a useful safety-valve in a hierarchical society, but there was increasing concern about what the Seville chronicler, Ortiz de Zúñiga, called 'the pranks which any gathering of young people is liable to get up to' – pranks like the plastering of the faces of those coming forward for 'confirmation' by the boy bishop with ash mixed with flour (in Toledo, for example), or the riots in Seville in 1641 when the students tried to commandeer the carriages of nobles to escort their 'bishop' to the cathedral.[82] One by one these festivities were cut back, forbidding the *obispillo* to parade through the streets of Seville on horseback after his election, for example (1512), and then prohibiting his enthronement inside the cathedral (1563), with similar steps being taken in the dioceses of Granada in 1526 and Tarragona in 1565.[83]

The most famous and enduring of these riotous festivities was carnival – the celebration of the good life before the rigours of the Lenten fast purified the soul at the beginning of each spring. In Valencia the students became active from the end of January every year, dressing up, ringing bells and generally engaging in a sort of rag through the streets. On 3 February 1627, however, the grim sight of the Observant Franciscans processing with chains, their heads covered with ashes and their mouths gagged with the cross-bones, begging God for an end to that winter's crippling drought, led the viceroy to ban carousing, and on Shrove Tuesday (16 February) to forbid the habitual pelting of passers-by with water-filled oranges.[84] The town council of Barcelona banned carnival on nine occasions between the mid-sixteenth and mid-seventeenth century, because of 'many fights, quarrels, woundings, deaths . . .'. And the authorities intervened increasingly in other Catalan towns as well to stop celebrations – as in Girona in 1638, forbidding the fiestas in honour of the canonisation of Saint Narcís, in view of the poor harvest, the risk of plague and the threat of a French invasion. From such celebrations, argued the viceroy's letter, 'irreparable evils and scandals usually flow, especially at the present time when hatreds have been so fanned between powerful families'.[85] Ironically, perhaps, in view of all the precautions, it was at Corpus Christi 1640, when the labourers began to gather in Barcelona for the wheat harvest, that tensions with the government culminated and the Catalans rose in revolt.

Fiestas, thought Castillo de Bobadilla, were often a waste of money and a threat to public order, but they were a necessary *desahogo* – a relief or safety-valve – for wilder spirits. It was, in fact, through controlling spectacle rather than abolishing it that the church sought to get its message across. Some official fiestas failed to take hold, though – like Archbishop Aliaga's cult of the Holy Grail, preserved in the cathedral of Valencia since 1437, but the object of public veneration through street processions only from 1623. It was the aim of ecclesiastics to wean the people away from their own, sometimes dubious folk saints to the contemplation of the Christian mysteries, but this was only liable to work where it coincided with some popular fervour. One of the most striking success stories in this regard is the celebration of Holy Week, so much part of Spanish folklore now that great numbers of tourists come to the country just to witness the elaborate street pageants. Ortiz de Zúñiga believed that those of Seville had grown up in the wake of Saint Vincent Ferrer's preaching mission there in 1408.

The Holy Week processions, organised by brotherhoods and accompanied by elaborate tableaux of Christ's passion, were an unusually vivid blend of the sacred and the profane. Joly described the flagellants who took part in those of Valladolid in 1604: hooded figures, stripped to the waist, flogged themselves 'to excess', under the blaze of torches and to the mournful notes of trumpets. Even nobles took part, 'and had to be assisted home on the shoulders of others, bleeding and half dead'.[86] Joly was unsure of the religious effect: some were, no doubt, moved to repentance by the spectacle, but there seemed to be much vainglory too – a criticism more strongly voiced by the English clergyman Townsend in 1787. Porcar described two flagellants striking an officer of the archbishop of Valencia, when he tried to confiscate their scourges apparently because they were too sharp.

More concern was voiced at the 'theatricality' of the event, at least as far as the spectators were concerned. For Holy Week 1617 these were forbidden to sit in comfort on chairs or cushions, or to dress up in 'bright colours'.

Rivalling Holy Week in splendour was Corpus Christi, instituted as an official holiday throughout Christendom by Pope John XXII in 1316 in honour of the real presence of Christ in the Eucharist. Escolano dated the great processions of Valencia back to 1374. Originally an opportunity for the guilds to display their finery, it came increasingly to be controlled by the authorities. The magistrates of Seville spent a tenth of their annual budget on mounting the elaborate festivities. The dragon and giants of old were now turned into representations of the Devil and of 'vices fleeing from the Blessed Sacrament', noted Ortiz de Zúñiga in 1677, who also commented on the declining participation of the trade guilds, their place occupied by religious brotherhoods. Instead of the old 'mystery plays', with their emphasis on 'farce', specially commissioned *autos sacramentales* took 'moral stories and allegories relating to the sacrament of the Eucharist' to the people by means of street theatre.[87] Some of the most precious of these come from the pen of Calderón in the third quarter of the seventeenth century, written for the public of Madrid. They describe in the form of allegory the meaningless of the hierarchy of this world; the true worth of the pauper and the prince can only be gauged in the next life. Like the wafer of bread venerated by the crowds, physical appearance was deceptive. It was a powerful message, at once subversive and yet ultimately conservative, in the way of all rituals of inversion.

In 1638, surveying the lapse of Granadan Christians to Islam after the Arab invasion of the eighth century, the chronicler Bermúdez de Pedraza suggested that the phenomenon was hardly surprising. Look now at the Alpujarras, he suggested. Resettled by Christians after the expulsion of the Moriscos in 1570, 'they are in many places, for lack of instructors . . . and because of an excess of hardships, so ignorant . . . that they barely retain any vestiges of Christianity'. Shortly before, the reformer Sancho de Moncada had left a legacy in his will of 1631 for catechisms, prints and 'knick-knacks' (*niñerías*) which might attract the children of his native Toledo to the Christian schools – 'for it is heart-breaking to see the want of instruction in the hill country round about'. In the Valle de Lecrín near Granada in 1590 the indefatigable Jesuit missionary Pedro de León commented: 'It had been more than twenty years since they had heard a sermon or a homily or the catechism. Most of these are small villages, where no preacher is brought in, not even for the Bull of Crusade . . .'[88] Thanks in part to the efforts of preachers like Father León, thanks to the gradual control of saints and fiestas by the authorities, thanks too to the relentless pursuit of popular 'superstitions' by the Inquisition from the later sixteenth century, it is clear that Spain by 1700 was more of a Christian community than it had been before. The parish framework, which had failed the Moriscos, was increasingly efficient by the middle of the seventeenth century, as one can see from the registers which survive, covering all aspects of the Christian life from the cradle to the grave. Before 1550 40 per cent of those interrogated by the Inquisition of Toledo could recite satisfactorily the basic Christian prayers – the Creed, the Pater Noster, the Ave Maria and the Salve Regina; by 1650, this had risen to 82 per cent.[89]

Yet, as this achievement became a reality, the definition of the 'godly commonwealth' itself was beginning to change, as more emphasis was put on good citizenship rather than on storming the heavens with prayer. 'Building bridges, making roads' is a 'pious work' as good as any other, commented Ponz at the end of the Old Regime, as he gave reference after reference to bishops setting up workshops, distributing spindles, wool and flax to the poor. He cited with approval the letter of the archbishop of Toledo to the priests of his diocese in 1779, urging them to take an interest in the material welfare of their parishioners.[90] His great friend Jovellanos, in his treatise of 1795 on economic reform, doubted whether the church needed so many friars (or chantry priests) as in the Middle Ages. The aim should be a well-educated pastoral clergy, acting as guides to their flock. And the enlightened statesman Campomanes, in his treatise of 1774 on manufactures, had suggested there were too many fiestas. In addition to the fifty-two Sundays of the year, there were forty-three other holidays, the most congested months being December and May with seven each, followed by August with five. In addition, there were other local saint's days and customary pilgrimages to their shrines – 'during which, in addition to the loss of work that day, many expenses are caused to a family, not to mention the frequent disorders and even homicides which occur'.[91]

In 1782 Jovellanos gave a vivid insight into the three four-day pilgrimages of his native Asturias. Since there were no theatres or bull-fights in the villages, the peasants indulged in these forays to a sacred location in the countryside, usually in the summer months. Near the shrine, 'they place the tents round about, their provisions, their barrels of cider and wine . . .'. Bonfires, music, dancing, feasting created a jovial atmosphere: 'these are usually the only opportunities courting couples have to see and talk to each other'. Meanwhile, their elders did business: 'each pilgrimage becomes a kind of fair, where cattle are sold, along with clothes and jewellery, accounting for virtually all the domestic trade of this region outside the weekly markets'. He thought misguided the censoriousness of some authorities – not least the church itself, which tried in the Synod of Oviedo (1769) to restrict the licentiousness of the pilgrimage. 'Music, dancing, carousing are in a sense bound up with the religion of ancient peoples.' And, after all, the *pueblo* needs the opportunity to let off steam from time to time – though the shrines, often at the boundaries of different communities, were flash-points of rivalry between them.[92] How sensible of the Catholic Church, thought his correspondent Ponz, to allow these cults to continue. Referring to the shrine of Our Lady near Talavera de la Reina, he remarked on the elaborate wreaths woven in her honour, which probably dated back to the cult of some earth goddess. 'Perhaps the difficulty of uprooting it caused the bishops to convert the custom into an offering to Our Lady, as the church has wisely done with other pagan rites.'[93]

The imaginative flair of Jovellanos and Ponz prefigured the insights of Romanticism. But the last stages of the Old Regime were marked rather by a desire to uproot popular customs and to create a more disciplined, more hard-working citizenry. Though in a sense the ministers of the Enlightenment were merely carrying forward the reforming programme of the Counter-Reformation – seeking to crack down on immorality and superstition and thereby safeguarding 'true religion' – they were ultimately on a collision course with the church. Floridablanca, as Secretary of State, issued a circular to the bishops in 1777 ordering them to have plans for church buildings submitted first to the Royal Academy of Art. Wood was to be avoided as far as possible in altarpieces, because of the fire hazard. Fire could be avoided, the prelates were lectured, 'if the number of candles could be reduced to the limit required by the aesthetic needs of the temple and dictated by serious-minded devotion'.[94] This kind of detailed regulation was rather typical of the mentality of Benevolent Despotism, and symbolised the fact that there was no longer room in the one commonwealth for two different ideas of the nature and function of the citizen.

Already in the 1650s Martínez de Mata had signalled the shift with his call for greater attention to the economy if the decline of Spain were to be arrested. 'The kind of devotion which consists of friars flogging themselves, nuns fasting and people coming out in processions' would not help the commonwealth. God had made this world of matter, with which mortal man would have to learn to work.[95] Government measures to liberalise the economy – to install the regime of enlightened self-interest – took a decisive step forwards when Campomanes freed the grain trade in 1765. It was the mentality underlying this abandonment of the notion of a just price which would later fuel Fray Diego de Cádiz's attack on the new economic thinkers. Meanwhile, it was accompanied – almost paradoxically it would seem – by a determination on the part of the government to act as moral counsellor to the people. Campomanes was to pay considerable attention to dress and cleanliness as part of the new artisan he envisaged in his great treatise of 1775 – a God-fearing but rational citizen, devoted to work rather than fiesta, avoiding taverns and gambling. It was little surprise, therefore, when the government introduced decrees in 1766 forbidding people to wear slouch hats (they must adopt the smart tricorne) or to wrap themselves up in the long, flowing Spanish cape. Through a combination of hunger and resentment at having their capes cut in half by the police with ruling measures and scissors, the people of Madrid erupted in March 1766 in one of the most serious outbreaks of rioting to shake the Old Regime. The trouble – which quickly spread to other Spanish cities – was eventually mastered. But the search for scapegoats led the enquiring minister, Campomanes, to pick on the Jesuits. Whether they had any hand in the riot or not – and the evidence was far from conclusive – their victimisation and expulsion from Spain in 1767 were surely inevitable developments in the long run. For though they represented much of what the reformers had been trying to achieve – a better-educated laity, a more moral citizenry – their organisation and continuing commitment to the old ways were ultimately incompatible with the new Spain which the Enlightenment was trying to create.

CONCLUSION

In one of his short stories which seek to capture the character of Castile, the writer Azorín (1874–1967) conjures up for us the small town of the high plateau as it might be glimpsed by an observer from the top of the cathedral tower around 1500. A cloud of dust on the approaches to the gates heralds the arrival of a lord and his troupe of pages and lackeys. The countryside is open range, grazed by flocks of sheep which will head south in winter on their great annual migrations. Near the river are numerous tanneries and a mill for fulling cloth. Inside the walls, the city is a labyrinth of streets, each echoing to the cries and songs of its particular craftsmen, who work away in the porches of their houses. Amid the clamour of bells, friars and nuns make their rounds, and a blind man begs for alms, intoning psalms and offering householders 'secret remedies . . . for all kinds of pain and mortal crises'. News is just beginning to filter in of great discoveries beyond the ocean, of the rediscovery of ancient worlds, of the new opportunities for those who can read and write. Meanwhile, a knight (to whom Don Quixote will later bear a family resemblance) sits in pensive melancholy in a great house overlooking the square.

Azorín shifts our gaze to the same scene in 1800. The woods round the town have been felled, and the pastures and herds have diminished; in their place are fields of wheat and market-gardens. On the road where the lord and his equipage once rode, now there is a stage-coach, hurtling along, trying to arrive at the same time every day of the week; 'of the old trades of leather and wool, almost all have disappeared' (victims of the new markets and routes). The blind man chants still his charms and prayers, but the friars and nuns are not so visible, and the news now is of a 'tremendous revolution', which has led a king and a queen to the guillotine, and of the promulgation of laws 'in which it is proclaimed that all human beings are free and equal'. Everywhere newspapers and books spread the expectation of change. Still, in the great house overlooking the square there sits in pensive melancholy a gentleman – clean-shaven now, a round-faced bourgeois rather than a wild-eyed cavalier.[1]

Azorín's story is concerned with the continuity of the human dilemma and the ultimate loneliness of the individual amid the bustle of change in the world around him. It is, however, the background noise – the relationship of the individual to his fellows – that ultimately interests the historian. How significant were the changes, how significant the continuity in Spain between 1500 and 1800? For the political historian there is the undoubted drama of the ascent to empire of one of the more marginal countries in Europe, and the long, melancholy retreat from the summits of power by a giant who was found, after all, to have feet of clay. Social history lacks some of the clarity of this analytical and chronological framework. But one could suggest that between 1500 and 1800, underneath the theatre of high politics, a certain 'Spain' was slowly and quietly taking shape – through the internal colonisation of a relatively empty, frontier land, and through the forging of a stable commonwealth. In view of the turmoil of Spanish history in the Middle Ages and in modern times, the latter achievement – so basic to all social development – merits particular emphasis.

The development was taking place against a background of crisis in Europe generally. The concept of the 'Seventeenth-Century Crisis' seems as slippery and as indispensable as that of feudalism. It reflects that caesura in European history between the optimism of the Renaissance and that of the Enlightenment. Those twisted, turbulent years between, say, 1550 and 1750, are overshadowed by hunger, bubonic plague, bonfires of witches and heretics, wars of religion. 'The Age of Iron' for Cervantes, the 'Age of Copper' for his contemporary Bermúdez de Pedraza (1638) is a paradox in the history of Spain as in that of Europe as a whole, for it seems to combine within it – not unlike the history of our own times – great fear and great progress, poverty and prosperity, regression to barbarism and the building of a more civilised world. Valencia, Barcelona, Madrid were probably more safe, more comfortable places in which to live in 1700 than in 1500. Despite the apparent loss of power by the bankrupt Habsburg monarchy during the seventeenth century and its sale of feudal jurisdictions to its nobility, there was to be no return to the anarchy of the fifteenth century. Rather, the steady growth of a well-policed society, with a certain degree of equality of all citizens before the law, was to attract the admiration of foreign observers.

The relationship between political structures and economic development has long interested historians, with greater emphasis now being put on the relative autonomy of the political process – in the sense that it is not seen as being determined by prior economic change.[2] Rather, the distribution of power critically affects the economy – for example, in the attention paid to safeguarding routes and markets, or in the fairness or otherwise of the way taxes are levied and allocated. One of the aspects of the seventeenth-century crisis in Spain as in the rest of Europe seems to have been a remodelling of the state. It would surely be misleading to speak of a retreat of the central authority and a surrender of power to local oligarchies, without pointing out that this surrender depended on a refashioning of the social hierarchy and of social attitudes, which meant that the oligarchies were more tightly integrated with the state than before. An analogy presents itself with modern times: just as governments today are beginning to find that their commitments to welfare and education have outrun their capacity to administer or fund them, and just as they are preparing to 'enfeoff' private groups with much of the responsibility (but under more supervision, paradoxically, than ever before), so the seventeenth-century monarchy in Spain and Europe found its military obligations growing so fast that they required a 'fiscal partnership' with mighty subjects – who were never allowed, though, to become 'over-mighty' again in the way their ancestors had been. One step backwards and two steps forwards seems to summarise seventeenth-century developments. They created an ordered but decentralised political commonwealth in Spain.

That community attracted, as we have noted, much foreign admiration, and it guaranteed the security of the citizen within which the internal colonisation of the country could be completed. But there was a price to be paid. In the age of empire, and despite access to the silver of Mexico and Peru, Spain remained a land of small-scale communities, like the one described by Azorín. Compared with England in the seventeenth century, one notes a marked absence of that fiscal and cultural integration, which was to lay the foundations of imperial success and social transformation. The philosopher John Locke summed up around 1690 the fundamental dilemma which was to afflict continental monarchies: that their concentration of power might guarantee political tranquillity for a time, but they could never achieve fiscal stability because they were not to be trusted when it came to property and taxes. Lisón's debate with Olivares in 1622 had been on just this question.

Spain might have continued for many generations with the forms of attenuated decentralisation – or regulated corporatism – built up in the seventeenth century. In his immortal tale, *The Three-Cornered Hat* (an indirect allusion to the riots of 1766 over the 'Europeanisation' of Spanish customs and dress), the writer Pedro Antonio de Alarcón (1833–91) described the small-town atmosphere of the kingdom of Granada, where he had grown up, as it must have been on the eve of the Napoleonic invasion of 1808. 'Once a week (or twice at most), the mail would arrive from Madrid in most of the important towns of the peninsula,' carrying the government gazette which would tell of 'whether there was one state more or one state less north of the Pyrenees.' For the Spaniard who could read, it hardly mattered: the wars of Napoleon were talked about 'as if they were about a hero from a novel of chivalry, or were about things that were happening on another planet'. People got on with their own lives – 'living in the old Spanish manner, which is to say taking their time, and holding fast to the ancient ways . . .'. David Ringrose has pointed out that the 'old Spanish manner' was, in fact, changing: a great growth of population and of economic production characterised the country in the last generations of the Old Regime, and he argues that this was transforming the society anyway, and would go on to do so during the nineteenth century.[3] From his analysis it would rather appear that the political upheavals which marked the advent of liberalism, overthrowing the absolute monarchy, the church and the aristocracy, were hardly necessary, since a 'bourgeoisie' was taking shape in any event as the guiding hand in the destinies of the nation.

Certainly there is an element of chance in the collapse of the old regime – the Napoleonic invasion of Spain in 1808, the bitter war of liberation which followed, the inability of the restored Bourbons in 1814 to master the fiscal crisis which ensued from the independence of the American colonies at this time. Josep Fontana has argued persuasively that the 'bankruptcy' of the old regime, if in part a historical accident, reflected a more enduring problem of the relationship between the government and its subjects. The inefficient superstructure of absolutism, with its parasitic noble and clerical elites, could only be tolerated for as long as the windfall profits from Mexican silver and South American entrepôt trade were available. Once they had gone, the battle for revenue between government and Spanish tax-payer would have to be fought out in earnest – with all the implications that brought, of tax-raising parliaments, release of entailed lands of feudal and clerical landlords, and freedom of debate.[4]

The mutual influence of economic and political developments is one of the areas of Spanish history currently attracting most research. But perhaps ultimately for the social historian it is the way our ancestors perceived reality that is the interesting thing. Their view was necessarily limited, but its very imperfections impose a sense of humility on the observer, who has a god-like vantage point from which to survey three centuries of development but must try to share some of the hopes and fears of people struggling for twenty-five years at a time. The ideology of the old regime – Catholicism, the family, chivalry – gave shape to many lives. The symptoms of change were surely there in the questions which people began asking, in Spain as in other parts of Europe, about the wisdom of some of these values, which in their day had helped create an impressive form of society. We may leave the last word to the Enlightened minister Campomanes. In his treatise of 1775 he addressed the problem of the corporate structure of the old regime, the emphasis on hereditary honour and privilege, rather than on individual application to productive work. When warfare was the great occupation and defence the prime concern of a people, one might understand this – as among the Moroccans still, who 'just look after their horses and plough strips of land one year here, another there'. But a modern nation 'does not count its might in an untrained horde, but in the general wealth of its people, which helps maintain well disciplined and well provided armies'. For this purpose trade and technology were as important as nobility of arms: 'in any of these professions one can acquire glory and fame; but in all of them . . . one has to respect the individual who strives best'.[5] Here already, a generation before it collapsed, one of its foremost servants was sounding the death-knell of the Spanish old regime.

NOTES

INTRODUCTION

1 Townsend 1791, I, 115–6.

1 AN INHOSPITABLE LAND

1 García Mercadal 1952–62, II, 750; *Relazioni di Ambasciatori Veneti*, vols VIII and IX.
2 Ungerer 1956, footnote 201.
3 Ponz, IX, 290–1.
4 García Mercadal 1952–62, I, 869.
5 Ponz, IX, iv–xxi.
6 Mariana cited in Carrera Pujal 1943, I, 350; Philip II in March 1941, I, 182.
7 Way 1962, 58.
8 *Actas de las Cortes*, 9, petition 63.
9 *Actas de las Cortes*, 7, 331–62.
10 Townsend 1791, I, 212–5 and 367–9; Ringrose 1970, 16.
11 Ponz, I, 5–6, and III, 150.
12 Escolano 1610–11, IV, 768.
13 Gondomar 1936–45, II, 135.
14 Joly 1603–4, 463.
15 Ponz, III, 200–3, and XII, 103–4; Viciana 1563–6, III, 48.
16 *Relaciones*, 78.
17 Salomon, 1964, 94.
18 Ponz, XIII, 121.
19 García Mercadal 1952–62, I, 1,479; Townsend 1791, I, 187–8; Catalá de Valeriola 1929, 114–5; *Actas de las Cortes*, 6, petition 76.
20 Gautier 1840, 331–2; Borrow 1842.
21 Escolano 1610–11, VI, 3.
22 López Piñero 1979, 220–1.
23 Rosselló 1988, II, 177–99.
24 Abad León 1985, I, 192–3.
25 López 1762–87, 356.
26 Cavanilles 1795–7, I, 1.

2 THE FEWNESS OF PEOPLE

1 *Relazioni*, IX, 673.
2 Campomanes 1774, 89 and 103–4.

3 García Cárcel *et al.* (eds) 1991, 69 (chapter by Antoni Simon Tarrés).
4 Pérez Moreda and Reher (eds) 1988, 40–1 (article by Jordi Nadal).
5 Marcos Martín 1978, 252.
6 Alvaro Castillo 1965, 719–33.
7 Castelló Traver 1978, 82 and 85 note 3.
8 Joly 1603–4, 538; *Relaciones*, 126–7 and 153.
9 Camps Arboix 1969, 77.
10 Domínguez Ortiz and Vincent 1978, 83.
11 Parker 1972, 28.
12 Thompson 1976, 103; Domínguez Ortiz 1963–70, I, 94–5.
13 *Relazioni*, VIII, 398.
14 Bennassar 1985, 532; Lynch, 1989, 308; Desdevises du Dezert 1899, I, 236–8.
15 Porcar 1934, paragraphs 2,650 and 2,734.
16 Cervantes 1605–14, I, chapter 51.
17 Carande 1943–67, I, 421–2.
18 García Cárcel *et al.* (eds) 1991, 69–70 (chapter by Antoni Simon Tarrés).
19 Altman 1989, 189.
20 Joly 1603–4, 519 and 536; Nadal and Giralt 1960, 81.
21 Poitrineau 1976, 109–33.
22 Nadal and Giralt 1960, 161; Poitrineau 1976, 123.
23 Gutiérrez Alonso 1989, 44–5; Reher 1990, 75; Pla Alberola 1987, 125–6.
24 Martínez de Mata 1650–60, 198.
25 Pérez Moreda and Reher 1988, 109–11 and 303.
26 Jovellanos 1782, 200–1; Benlloch 1756, 101.
27 Torró Abad 1992, 116–7; Dillard 1984, 47–9.
28 Vercher Lletí 1992, 54–65.
29 *La Familia* . . . 1987, 93 (article by Antoni Simon Tarrés).
30 Pérez García 1992, 71–101.
31 Fernández Cortizo 1982, 237–76.
32 Mejide Pardo 1960, 461–606.
33 Reher 1990, 249; Marcos Martín 1978, 268–71; Carbajo Isla 1987, 119–20.
34 Pérez Moreda and Reher (ed.) 1988, 301 (article by J.M. Pérez García); Pérez Aparicio (ed.) 1988, 219 (article by J.M. Pérez García); Reher 1990, 95–6.
35 Alvarez Santaló 1977, 510–11: Carbajo Isla 1987, 56.
36 Sancho de Moncada 1619, 137–8.
37 Péréz Moreda 1980, 188.
38 Porcar 1934, paragraph 2,974; Collantes de Terán 1977, 85; Díez del Corral 1987, 247–50.
39 Viciana 1563–6, III, f. 158v; Collantes de Terán 1977a, 83–4; Ponz, IX, 208.
40 Porcar 1934, chapters 1,269 and 1,928; Salavert and Navarro 1992, 16.
41 Herrera Puga 1971, 86.
42 Jovellanos 1782, 160–1; *Relaciones*, 71; Ponz, IX, viii–ix.
43 León 1981, 137–8; Salazar 1866, 83.
44 Joly 1603–4, 514; Díez del Corral 1987, 154–5.
45 *Actas de las Cortes*, 6, 359–60.
46 Sancho de Moncada 1619, 179; Asensio Salvadó 1954, 254.
47 Salvá Ballester 1988, chapter 4.
48 Vincent 1985, 163–78.
49 Cabarrús, in Ochoa (ed.) 1856–70, II, 578.
50 *Actas de las Cortes*, 26, 426.
51 Pérez Moreda 1980, 294–6.
52 Reher 1990, 153–4.

53 Carreres Zacarés 1935, II, 696, 753, 779, 818, 869 and 1,006.
54 Gavaldá 1651, chapter 33.
55 Ortiz de Zúñiga 1677, 708–9; Colmenares 1637, II, 363.
56 Amelang 1991, 78–9.
57 López Piñero 1979, 355.
58 Ballesteros Rodríguez 1982, 168–9.
59 Granero 1961, 214.
60 Peset 1974–5, 223.
61 Pérez Moreda 1980, 286–7 and 292.

3 THE LIMITS OF A PEASANT ECONOMY

1 Ringrose 1996.
2 *Cortes Valencianas*, 1645, petitions 327 and 328 of Braç Real; Jovellanos 1795, 172–4.
3 Vilar 1962, II, 326–8, and III, 292–9.
4 Burriel de Orueta 1971, 183–4.
5 Ximénez Patón 1628, f. 15v–16; Asso 1798, 77.
6 Alonso de Herrera 1513, lxxxviii–ix.
7 Viñas Mey 1947, 152.
8 Townsend 1791, I, 296.
9 García Sanz 1977, 113.
10 *Actas de las Cortes*, 40, 299; Fernández Navarrete 1626, 339.
11 Caxa de Leruela 1631, 202.
12 Borrow 1842, 105 and 217.
13 Ramírez y las Casas-Deza 1840–2, I, 20.
14 Yun Casalilla 1987, 119–20; García Sanz 1980, 95–127.
15 Ponz, X, 189–219.
16 Le Flem 1972, 28; García Sanz 1989, 184–90; Phillips 1997, 294.
17 Vassberg 1984, 172–6.
18 Yun Casalilla 1987, 291–303; García Sanz 1980, 95–127.
19 López-Salazar 1987, 28–9.
20 Klein 1920, 60–1; Caxa de Leruela 1631, 252.
21 Thompson and Yun Casalilla 1994, 22, 79–82 and 132; Goy and Le Roy Ladurie 1982, I, 295–461.
22 Vilar 1962, III, 322; Alonso de Herrera 1513, 37–46 and 244–5.
23 Deza 1618, 50–1; García Fernández 1963, 24–33.
24 García Fernández 1965, 692–718.
25 López Ontiveros 1974, 293.
26 Vilar 1962, III, 302.
27 Domínguez Ortiz 1987, 219.
28 Ardit 1993, I, 270.
29 Caxa de Leruela 1631, 149–50; Deza 1618, 34^v–6^v.
30 Ardit 1993, I, 185–6; Peris Albentosa 1989, 82–3 and 196.
31 *Relaciones*, 297.
32 *Actas de las Cortes*, 6, 359–62; Martínez de Mata 1650–60, 124–5.
33 Benlloch 1756, 101.
34 Jovellanos 1782, 213.
35 Cerdán de Tallada 1604, 172.
36 Madoz 1845–50, 39.
37 Grice-Hutchinson 1952, 118.
38 Mercado 1569, 60.
39 Hamilton 1934, 258–9.

40 Rodríguez Díaz 1975, 201–3 and 212–3.
41 Deza 1618, 24–7^v and 37–8^v; *Actas de las Cortes*, 13, 136–44.
42 Deza 1618, 37^v–8^v.
43 Fernández Navarrete 1626, 322–3.

4 TREASURE AND THE COST OF EMPIRE

1 Caxa de Leruela 1631, 10–11.
2 *Relaciones*, 416–7; Viciana 1563–6, III, 51^v; Cavanilles 1795–7, I, 74; Medina 1548, 170.
3 García Sanz 1977, 214–5; Ruiz Martín 1965, 267–76.
4 Santos Isern 1981, 237.
5 Ponz, I, 23–4; García Sanz 1977, 216–7; Fortea Pérez 1981, 337–52.
6 García Sanz 1977, 234; Le Flem 1976, 53; *Relazioni*, VIII, 256.
7 Thompson and Yun Casalilla 1994, 101–14 (article by Bilbao and Fernández de Pinedo); Phillips 1997, 291.
8 Sempere y Guarinos 1806, 55–66.
9 *Actas de las Cortes*, 35, 384–5.
10 Halperin Donghi 1980, 4; Rodríguez García 1959, 43; Santos Isern 1981, 86–7.
11 García Mercadal 1952–62, III, 1,477 and 1,634–6; Cavanilles 1795–7, I, 6–7; Ponz, X, 221–2 and 269–73.
12 Campomanes 1775, 91.
13 Garzón Pareja 1972, 420–1.
14 Piles Ros 1969, 76.
15 Iradiel Murugarren 1974, 75–7; Fortea Pérez 1981, 381, note 151; Villas Tinoco 1982, I, 184–9.
16 García Cárcel 1975, 51.
17 Tramoyeres Blasco 1889, 292–5 and 337–43.
18 Colmenares 1637, II, 296; Carande 1943–67, I, 183–6.
19 Fortea Pérez 1981, 257, 281–8 and 352–8; Castillo Pintado 1967, xiv (preface by Viñas Mey).
20 Vilar 1962, II, 321–3.
21 Hamilton 1934, 152–67.
22 Carrera Pujal 1943, I, 277–8; Al-Hussein 1986, II, 13–266.
23 Salomon 1964, 101.
24 Hamilton 1934, 34–5.
25 *Relazioni*, VIII, 454–5.
26 Gondomar 1936–45, IV, 94–8; Grice-Hutchinson 1952, 97–8.
27 Domínguez Ortiz 1976, 98–9; Vilar 1962, II, 373–5 and 433–5.
28 Carreres Zacarés 1957, 10.
29 Domínguez Ortiz 1976, 398–9.
30 Mercado 1569, 134–5 and 152–3.
31 Fernández Navarrete 1626, 65; Mercado 1569, 208–10.
32 González Palencia 1932, 45–51.
33 Ibid., 106–7.
34 López Cordón 1978, 71–119.
35 Campomanes 1774, 76–7 and 118–24.
36 Jovellanos 1795, 148–9; Ponz, XVI, 258–9, and XVII, 84.
37 González Palencia 1940, 58.
38 Mercado 1569, 171–2; *Relazioni*, IX, 437.
39 Herrera García 1980, 223 and 251.
40 Lynch 1989, 359.

41 Bakewell 1971, 138–43 and 206–7.
42 Morineau 1985, 563; Lynch 1989, 358.
43 Lynch 1989, 154–5.
44 Cabrera de Córdova 1857, 292 and 535.
45 Fernández Navarrete 1626, 85.
46 Gondomar 1936–45, II, 142–6.
47 Domínguez Ortiz 1963–70, I, 85.
48 Israel 1982, 215–7 and 344–5; Casey 1979, 97–8.
49 Martínez de Mata 1650–60, 196; Gondomar 1936–45, I, 136–7.
50 García Martínez 1968, 42–4; Salvador 1972, 130; Castillo Pintado 1967, 23.
51 López Piñero 1979, 197–212; Carande 1943–67, I, 444.
52 Lynch 1964–9, I, 166, and II, 189; García Fuentes 1980, 203.
53 Carrera Pujal 1943, I, 441–2.
54 Phillips 1986, 78–9.
55 Sánchez Albornoz 1959, 106–7.
56 Abad León 1985, I, 186 and 227–8; *Relazioni*, IX, 569–70.
57 Goodman 1988, 77.
58 Abad León 1985, I, 278; Ortiz de Zúñiga 1677, 528.
59 *Actas de las Cortes*, 10, 242.
60 Domínguez Ortiz 1960, 319.
61 Ulloa 1977, 523.
62 Fortea Pérez 1986, *passim*; Thompson and Yun Casalilla 1994, 171–3 and 192–5 (articles by F. Ruiz Martín and J. Gelabert).
63 Domínguez Ortiz 1960, 74.
64 *Actas de las Cortes*, 6, 365–6.
65 Ibid., 38, 129–86.
66 Abad León 1985, I, 174.
67 Artola 1982, 233 and 246; Molas 1973, 105–6.
68 Garzón Pareja 1980–1, I, 476–8.
69 Lynch 1991–2, II, 274–6; Garzón Pareja 1980–1, I, 335–6; Boyajian 1983, 159.
70 Abad León 1985, I, 218.
71 Yun Casalilla 1987, 374–7.
72 García Mercadal 1952–62, III, 1,643.
73 Fernández Navarrete 1626, 180; *Relazioni*, IX, 73–4 and 568.

5 FEUDAL LORDS AND VILLAGE POTENTATES

1 Ladero Quesada 1982, I, 228–30; Cerdà 1988, I, 231–2; Artola 1978, 55.
2 Viciana 1563–4, III, 158; Domínguez Ortiz and Aguilar Pinal 1976, 87–8.
3 Castillo de Bobadilla 1597, II, 625–9.
4 *Cortes Valencianas*, 1604, petition 22 of Braç Real; Escolano 1610–11, IV, 672.
5 Thompson and Yun Casalilla 1994, 196–7; Nader 1990, 3.
6 Caxa de Leruela 1631, 77–86; *Actas de las Cortes*, 28, 157.
7 *La Sociedad Castellana en la Baja Edad Media*, 1969, 261.
8 Ramírez y las Casas-Deza 1840–2, I, 187–96.
9 Argote de Molina 1588, 500.
10 Estepa Giménez 1987, 40; Nader 1990, 106–8.
11 Soria Mesa 1997, 76–82 and 92.
12 Domínguez Ortiz 1976, 430; Lemeunier 1993, 355–86; Ardit 1993, I, 83.
13 Colmenares 1637, II, 347; Haliczer 1981, 82–90; Castillo de Bobadilla 1597, I, 442.
14 Viciana 1563–4, III, 150–1.
15 *Cortes Valencianas*, 1626, petition 4 of Braços Eclesiàstic and Militar.

16 Nader 1990, 174–5.
17 Castillo de Bobadilla 1597, I, 457, 473–8 and 483.
18 Arias Abellán 1984, 182–3; Moxó 1973, 62 and 254–7.
19 Benítez Sánchez-Blanco 1982, 123–4.
20 Moxó 1965, 221.
21 Estepa Giménez 1987, 142–4 and 240–7.
22 García Sanz 1977, 368–70.
23 Vicens Vives 1972, II, 212–6.
24 Casey 1979, 101–26.
25 A. Franco Silvela in *El Pasado Histórico de Castilla y León*, I, 145–6.
26 Pineda 1589, IV, 190; Castillo de Bobadilla 1597, I, 469.
27 Estepa Giménez 1987, 92–8; Torres López 1932, 554–5.
28 Momblanch 1959, 62–4.
29 Mora Cañada 1986, 109–10.
30 Castillo de Bobadilla 1597, I, 482.
31 Archivo de Protocolos de Granada, Office of Manuel de Quesada y Huerta 1787–92, ff. 24–9ᵛ.
32 Archivo del Reino de Valencia, Clero, *legajo* 750, *visita* of 1593–4; Palomeque Torres 1947, 91–7.
33 Yun Casalilla 1987, 77–80; Collantes de Terán 1977, 331–6.
34 Escolano 1610–11, X, 1,793.
35 Císcar Pallarés 1977, 255–6; Ardit 1993, I, 200–1.
36 Císcar Pallarés 1975, 159.
37 Furió 1982, 149.
38 Salomon 1973, 266.
39 Morant 1984, 131–2; Peris Albentosa 1989, 140–1.
40 Mora Cañada 1986, 187–8.
41 López-Salazar 1981, 354–407.
42 Cerdán de Tallada 1604, 174.
43 Yun Casalilla 1987, 107; Nader 1990, 199.
44 *Actas de las Cortes*, 5 *adicional*, petition 5; cf. *Actas*, 7, petition 68 of 1585.
45 Benlloch 1756, 88, 105 and 138.
46 Ibid., 139–40 and 147–8.
47 Gutiérrez Nieto 1973, 156–8.
48 Soria Mesa 1997, 222–3.
49 Momblanch y Gonzálbez 1959, 64–5.
50 Olmos Tamarit and López Quiles 1985, *passim*.
51 Arjona Castro and Estrada Carrillo 1977, 128–31.
52 Catalá Sanz 1995, 276–80.
53 Amezúa 1934–41 *Lope de Vega en sus Cartas*, IV, 284–5.
54 Castillo de Bobadilla 1597, I, 445–54; Cerdán de Tallada 1604, 174.
55 *Actas de las Cortes*, 28, 538.
56 Salomon 1965, 429 and 722–3.
57 Matilla Tascón 1983, 178; Alba 1927, 314–5; Chabas 1874, II, 123.
58 Momblanch y Gonzálbez 1957, 40.
59 Cabrera de Córdova 1857, 519 (1 June 1613); Yun Casalilla 1987, 107.
60 Domínguez Ortiz 1964, 183.
61 Dantí 1994, 52–5, and 1995, 15–28; Kamen 1993b, 210–30.
62 Jago 1979, 87.
63 *La Segona Germania* 1994, 133–60.
64 *Relazioni*, IX, 49; Castillo de Bobadilla 1597, I, 473.
65 Colás Latorre and Salas Auséns 1982, 98–122.

66 Leonardo de Argensola 1604, 41.
67 *La Segona Germania* 1994, 158–9.
68 García Martínez 1991, chapter IV, and 1993, *passim.*
69 Jovellanos 1782, 206–8; Olaechea and Ferrer Benimeli 1978, II, 132–6.
70 Moxó 1965, 221; 'Compendio genealógico . . .', Infantado mss. in Real Academia de Historia 9–7078.
71 Guggisberg and Windler 1995, 149–50.
72 Morant 1984, 211.
73 Ardit 1993, II, 170–1.
74 Ruiz Torres 1981, 231–48.

6 PATRICIANS AND PAUPERS: THE URBAN COMMONWEALTH

1 González 1958, 159–60.
2 Gelabert, in Thompson and Yun Casalilla (eds) 1994, 182–3.
3 Valdeavellano 1969, 188–9.
4 Bermúdez de Pedraza 1638, 199–200.
5 Bermúdez de Pedraza 1608, 146–7; Escolano 1610–11, IV, 848.
6 Guevara 1539, 59; González Palencia 1932, 77–87.
7 Ponz, IX, 205–11, and I, 19.
8 Torres Balbás, n.d., I, 428; Díez del Corral 1987, 147.
9 Ponz, IV, 19–20.
10 Henríquez Jorquera 1934, I, 227–8 and 263–4.
11 Castillo de Bobadilla 1597, II, 86; Bermúdez de Pedraza 1638, 32.
12 Sanchis Guarner 1972, 319–21; Martz 1983, 101–3; Ponz, XI, 206.
13 Ortiz de Zúñiga 1677, 473–6; Mesonero Romanos 1861, 170–1.
14 López Bravo 1627, 250–4 and 258–9; Gutiérrez de los Ríos 1600, 77 and 253–4.
15 Madramany 1788, 410; Argote de Molina 1588, 611.
16 Castillo de Bobadilla 1597, II, 122–7; Escolano 1610–11, V, 1,081–4.
17 Martín de Marco 1990, 154–6; Moreno de Guerra 1929, 77; *La Sociedad Castellana en la Baja Edad Media* 1969, 255–6. (I owe this reference to Fernando del Ser.)
18 Ruiz 1981, 189.
19 Danvila 1889, 398; Lorenzo Toledo, in Lorenzo Sanz 1986, I, 424.
20 Gerbet 1979, 441–53.
21 Torras Ribé 1983; Belenguer 1976, 36–8.
22 Lorenzo Sanz 1986, I, 286–94; Carande 1990, II, 66–7; Ladero Quesada 1973, 81.
23 Domínguez Ortiz and Aguilar Piñal 1976, 86 and 146; Gutiérrez Alonso 1989, 306–9.
24 Felipo Orts 1996, 19–20.
25 Casey 1979, 170.
26 Castillo de Bobadilla 1597, II, 95–6 and 121–2.
27 Contreras 1991, 183–4; Chacón Jiménez 1979, 467.
28 Castillo de Bobadilla 1597, II, 193.
29 Amelang 1986, 48.
30 Ortiz de Zúñiga 1677, 467–8.
31 Ródenas Villar 1990, 140.
32 Pike 1972, 21–52; Herrera García 1980, 137; Hernández 1995, 8; Cortés Peña and Vincent 1986, 292.
33 Ortiz de Zúñiga 1677, 419 and 463.
34 Christian 1981, 9; Colmenares 1637, II, 180.
35 Domínguez Ortiz 1946, 75–6; Sentaurens 1975, 321–90.
36 Gelabert González 1982, 203; Garcia Espuche and Guàrdia Bassols, 1986, 51–2.

37 Domínguez Ortiz 1988, 10.
38 Pérez de Herrera 1598, 101–2; *Actas de las Cortes*, 7, 657.
39 Martínez de Mata 1650–60, 164.
40 Domínguez Ortiz 1973, 92; Manuel de Mello 1645, 37–8.
41 Callahan 1980, 140.
42 Gavaldá 1651, chapter xxiii; López Bravo 1627, 237–8; Pérez de Herrera 1598, 100–1.
43 Moreno Casado 1948, 12; Salavert 1992, 58–9; Narbona Vizcaíno 1992, 66–7.
44 Pérez de Herrera 1598, 98–9 and 126; *Actas de las Cortes*, 6, petition 90 of 1582.
45 Tramoyeres Blasco 1889, 150–1 and 226–7; Campomanes 1775, 251.
46 Bonnassie 1975, 130–8.
47 Campomanes 1775, 215.
48 Catalá de Valeriola 1929, 11; Porcar 1934, paragraphs 1,319 and 2,859.
49 Palma 1595, 37; Blanco White 1821, 3rd letter.
50 Pérez de Herrera 1598, 24–5 and 136–40; Castillo de Bobadilla 1597, I, 380–1.
51 Escolano 1610–11, V, 1,051.
52 Calero Palacios 1979, 390–8; Pérez de Herrera 1598, 96–7.
53 Sentaurens 1975, 349.
54 Martz 1983, 114.
55 *Actas de las Cortes*, 7, 657.
56 Martz 1983, 119–30.
57 Flynn 1989, 104–5.
58 Domínguez Ortiz 1988, 12.
59 Pérez de Herrera 1598, 59; Flynn 1989, 99–102.
60 Flynn 1989, 105–7; Martz 1983, 142.
61 Granero 1961, 326–7 and 444–5.
62 Caxa de Leruela 1631, 30–1.
63 Castro 1987, 192–206.
64 Henríquez de Jorquera 1934, I, 160; Viciana 1563–4, III, 142, 161 and 165[v];
   Domínguez Ortiz 1973, 215–6.
65 Castillo de Bobadilla 1597, II, 19; *Nueva Recopilación*, 5/11/19; Carande 1989–90, II,
   109 and 112–13.
66 Domínguez Ortiz 1973, 191–3.
67 Castro 1987, 228–32.
68 Guiral 1986, 249–50; Ladero Quesada 1976, 86–8.
69 Castillo de Bobadilla 1597, II, 39–40.
70 Martínez Ruiz 1984, 237–44.
71 Castillo de Bobadilla 1597, II, 134, 574 and 604.
72 Maravall 1963, 132; Haliczer 1981, 177–9; Pérez 1970, 545–67.
73 Gutiérrez Nieto 1973, 283.
74 *Epístolas Familiares*, 2 January 1521.
75 García Cárcel 1975.
76 Castillo de Bobadilla 1597, II, 95–6 and 108–10; *Actas de las Cortes*, 5 adicional, 225;
   Jago 1985.
77 Fray Antonio de Jesús 1688, 86–92.
78 Domínguez Ortiz 1973.
79 Rodríguez Díaz 1973(a) and 1973(b).

7 THE CONSOLIDATION OF AN ARISTOCRACY

1 Esquerdo 1963, 19; Guardiola 1591, 53[v].
2 Viciana 1563–4, f. xxi.
3 Madramany 1790, 94; Pérez y López 1781, 157.

4 Pulgar 1486, letter 14.

5 Pérez y López 1781, 39; Madramany 1790, 100–1.

6 Viciana 1563–4, I, 82–3 and II, 14; Argote de Molina 1588, 21.

7 Archivo de la Real Chancillería de Granada, 301/109/43, 301/103/41 and 301/115/8.

8 *Actas de las Cortes*, 13, 63–83.

9 Gómez-Menor Fuentes 1970, 25–37; Bilinkoff 1989, 64–7.

10 Catalá de Valeriola 1929, 106–7.

11 Archivo de la Real Chancillería de Granada 301/109/43.

12 Catalá de Valeriola 1929, 126–7.

13 Peñalosa, in Salomon 1965, 771.

14 Archivo de la Real Chancillería de Granada 3/122/6, and 301/61/13.

15 Cited by J.I. Gutiérrez Nieto, in Elliott and García Sanz (eds) 1990, 436–7.

16 González Alonso 1981, 75; *Actas de las Cortes*, 13, 63; *Nueva Recopilación*, 2/11/33.

17 Fernández Alvarez 1989, I, 75; Montojo Montojo, 1983, 83.

18 Atienza Hernández 1987, 17 and 41.

19 Viciana 1563–4, II, 15 and 19^v, and III, 34; Salomon 1965, 771.

20 Argote de Molina 1588, 471–3 and 494–5.

21 Meneses García 1973, I, 87–8; Cerdán de Tallada 1604, 240.

22 Matilla Tascón 1983, 121.

23 Cerdán de Tallada 1604, 240; López Bravo 1627, 178.

24 Hernández 1995, 162–3.

25 Gerbet 1989, 94; Layna Serrano 1942, II and III.

26 García Cárcel 1985, I, 199; *Cortes Valencianas*, petition 4 of Braç Real 1510 and petition 3 of Braç Militar 1542.

27 Jovellanos 1795, 105–6; Cerdán de Tallada 1604, 244; *Relazioni*, IX, 51.

28 Matilla Tascón 1983, 22–3.

29 Catalá Sanz 1995, 302.

30 Fayard 1979, 316–28; Gerbet 1979, 83–4; Manuel de Mello 1651, 154–5.

31 Simon Tarrés 1991, 44.

32 Pineda 1589, IV, 77.

33 Archivo de la Corona de Aragón, Consejo de Aragón, *legajos* 882 (22 September 1640), 723 (1643) and 709 (20 April 1644) for count of Real; 654 (6 October 1617 and 7 July 1622), and Archivo del Reino de Valencia, Procesos de Madrid, P/751 (1623), for Carlet.

34 Morant 1984, 83–92; Serra i Puig 1988, 295–6; Yun Casalilla in Sarasa Sánchez and Serrano Martín (eds) 1993, II, 19–23.

35 Kessell and others (eds) 1992, 121–3; Atienza Hernández, in Chacón Jiménez (ed.) 1991, 42–3.

36 *Relazioni*, VIII, 20 and IX, 51.

37 Cabrera de Córdova 1857, 79–80 and 268–9.

38 Mérimée 1907, lx.

39 Atienza Hernández 1984, 49–81.

40 Porcar 1934, paragraph 2,072.

41 Fernández Navarrete 1626, *discurso* xxvi.

42 *Actas de las Cortes*, 5 adicional, petitions 15 and 38 of 1578; 9, petition 55 of 1588; 11, petition 45 of 1590.

43 Fernández Navarrete 1626, *discurso* xxxv, 294; Amelang 1986, 95–6; *Cortes Valencianas*, Fur 47 of 1537, and item 22 of *oferta* (subsidy) of 1552.

44 Pérez de Herrasti 1750, 46; Joly 1603–4, 565.

45 Guevara 1539, 61.

46 Ximénez Patón 1628, 107^v-8.

47 Brown and Elliott 1980, 36; Kamen 1983, 65; Carrera Pujal 1943, I, 337.

48 Salazar 1866, 60–1; Enríquez de Guzmán 1886, 14.
49 Méchoulan 1973, 47ff.
50 Menéndez Pidal 1959, 81–2.
51 Fayard 1979, 281–3; Kagan 1974, 93–8.
52 Rodríguez Díaz 1975.
53 Abad León 1985; cf. Keniston 1958, and Lovett 1977.
54 Benítez Sánchez-Blanco 1995, 4.
55 Matilla Tascón 1983, 121–2; González Moreno 1969.
56 González Palencia and Mele 1941–3, II, 246 and 284–9.
57 Elliott and García Sanz 1990, 480; Benítez Sánchez-Blanco 1982, 158.
58 Domínguez Ortiz 1969, 120; Atienza Hernández 1984, 49–81.
59 Fernández Navarrete 1626, *discurso* xxvi.
60 Matilla Tascón 1983, 178.
61 *Actas de las Cortes*, 39, 154, and 38, 129–86.
62 Vilar 1971, 263–94; Lera García 1988, 909–62.
63 Jago 1979, 82–3 and 87.
64 *Relazioni*, IX, 59; Domínguez Ortiz 1969.
65 Cooper 1980–1; Bayon 1967.
66 Manuel de Mello 1645, 125.
67 Thompson 1976, 154–6; ACA CA 570/12/46.
68 Manuel de Mello 1645, 86–7.
69 Amelang 1986, 118–24.
70 Robres Lluch 1960, 334–9.
71 Catalá de Valeriola 1929, 156.
72 Martí Grajales 1927, 75–84.
73 Catalá de Valeriola 1929, 124 and 139.
74 Almarche Vázquez 1919, 190–251.
75 Catalá de Valeriola 1929, 149.

8 OBEDIENCE TO THE LAW

1 Sempere y Guarinos 1805, 97.
2 Pulgar 1971, f. v–vi.
3 Pineda 1589, V, 137; Bernáldez, in Fernández Alvarez, I, 1989, 287–8.
4 *Relazioni*, VIII, 144; Joly 1603–4, 604.
5 Camos 1592, 205; Castillo de Bobadilla 1597, II, 261.
6 Casanovas 1978, 69–77.
7 Castañeda Alcover 1949, 451–71.
8 Castillo de Bobadilla 1597, I, 73, 132 and 282–6.
9 ACA CA leg. 713, reports of Don Martín de Funes, 1635–6.
10 Lope de Deza 1608, 37–8^v and 117^v–20.
11 Castillo de Bobadilla 1597, I, 443 and II, 631; González Palencia 1932, 250.
12 Benlloch 1756, 134–5.
13 *Actas de las Cortes* 6 (1579–82), petition 53.
14 *Actas de las Cortes* 8 (1586–8), petition 54.
15 Catalá 1994, 105–20; *Cortes Valencianas*, petition 246 of Braç Real 1645.
16 Colás Latorre and Salas Auséns 1982, 126–50 and 597–610.
17 Crespí de Valldaura, f. 4^v–5 and 65^v.
18 Leonardo de Argensola 1604, 56–7.
19 Castillo de Bobadilla 1597, II, 104 and 219.
20 Soria 1960, 128–30; Sanchis Guarner 1972, 211.
21 Carreres Zacarés 1930, 11; Castillo de Bobadilla 1597, II, 197.

22 Escolano 1610–11, IV, 863–4; Domínguez Ortiz 1969, 24–5.
23 Moreno de Guerra 1929, 64–6.
24 Reglà 1955, 25 and 187–8.
25 Leonardo de Argensola 1604, 61.
26 ACA CA leg. 882, consulta, 13 May 1641; Cabrera de Córdova 1857, 148.
27 Reglà 1955, 35; Torres 1993, 28.
28 Castillo de Bobadilla 1597, II, 19, 197 and 200–1.
29 Moreno de Guerra 1929, 86–7; *Nueva Recopilación*, 8/14/6 and 8/15/6.
30 López Bravo 1627, 264–8.
31 Reglà 1956, 20.
32 Zapata 1859, 469; Reglà 1955, 107–8.
33 Colás Latorre and Salas Auséns 1982, 230–76.
34 Reglà 1956, 20.
35 Torres 1993, 60–1, 174, 184–212 and 343–56.
36 Cervantes 1605–14, II, chapter 60.
37 Lantery 1949, 212; Barrionuevo 1968, I, 195 and II, 165; Tomás y Valiente 1969, 264.
38 Reglà 1956, 47; Casey 1979, 217.
39 Lantery 1949, 86.
40 Flynn 1989, 40–3; Tarazona 1580, Fur of Peter II of Valencia (IV of Aragon).
41 Herrera Puga 1981, 82–8; Escolano 1610–11, IV, 862.
42 Enríquez de Guzmán 1886, 74–5.
43 Moreno de Guerra 1929, 27–9.
44 *Cortes Valencianas*, petition 1 of Braços Militar and Real (1552); Carreres Zacarés 1930, 37–8; *Nueva Recopilación*, 8/8/3–6.
45 Amezúa 1935–41, IV, 313.
46 Fernández Alvarez 1989, II, 1014–5; *Actas de las Cortes* 7 (1583–5), 413; Porcar 1934, paragraphs 3106 and 3116.
47 Cerdán de Tallada 1604, 206–7; Castillo de Bobadilla 1597, II, 288.
48 Castillo de Bobadilla 1597, I, 161–78.
49 García Martínez 1991, 139; *Cortes Valencianas*, Fur 68 of 1585, Contrafur 20 of 1626, and petitions 85 and 369 of Braç Real (1645).
50 Medina 1548, 114–5; Lunenfeld 1970.
51 González Alonso 1970, 40.
52 Argote de Molina 1588, 618–9; Carreres Zacarés 1930, 79 and 112–3.
53 González Alonso 1970, note 382; *Actas de las Cortes*, 6 (1579–82), petitions 27 and 28; 5 adicional (1576–8), petition 3; Lunenfeld 1987, 171–95.
54 Castillo de Bobadilla 1597, I, 118 and II, 220; Cerdán de Tallada 1604, 44–5.
55 Bermúdez de Pedraza 1638, 5ᵛ.
56 Mendoza 1627, 8.
57 Garibay 1854, 263; Crespí de Valldaura, f. 195.
58 ACA CA leg. 623, consulta, 9 March 1644.
59 González Palencia 1932, 179–81; *Actas de las Cortes*, 6 (1579–82), petition 24.
60 Kagan 1974, 83.
61 ACA CA leg. 658, consulta, 2 May 1645; AMV MC session of 6 October 1625.
62 Reglà 1955, 127–8.
63 Casey 1979, 219; *Cortes Valencianas*, Fur 17 of 1626; Colás Latorre 1976, 88–9.
64 AMV Colección Churat, 1634/1/42; *Cortes Valencianas*, Contrafur 1 of 1604.
65 ACA CA 582/45/2 and 5, consultas, April/May 1662.
66 ACA CA 579/53/4, viceroy to king, 2 June 1693.
67 Reglà 1955, 107–8; Domínguez Ortiz 1989, 584.
68 Reglà 1955, 150–62; Colás Latorre and Salas Auséns 1982, 281–303.

69 ACA CA leg. 583/2, duke of Infantado to king, 21 February 1648; legs 878 and 713, petitions of marquis of Ariza, 8 October 1636 and 13 July 1637.
70 ARV R 593, viceroy to king, 27 June 1690; ACA CA leg. 725, viceroy to king, 23 June 1647.
71 ACA CA leg. 725, Archbishop to king, 13 August 1647; leg. 707, viceroy to king, 11 May 1622.
72 ACA CA leg. 594, duke of Pastrana (ambassador in Rome) to king, 11 June 1624.
73 Bermúdez de Pedraza 1638, 228–9.
74 Castillo de Bobadilla 1597, I, 634.
75 Leonardo de Argensola 1604, 66–7.
76 Duque de Estrada 1860, 60–84.
77 Porcar 1934, paragraph 1,246; ARV R 528, f. 486.
78 ACA CA leg. 580/44/3, 'Relación del 26 de agosto 1653'; Colás Latorre and Salas Auséns 1982, 447–9 and 612.
79 *Novísima Recopilación* 11/20/2; *Cortes Valencianas* Furs 28 and 102 of 1626.
80 Ochoa 1856–70, II, 63–5; Palma 1595, 13.
81 Amezúa 1935–41, IV, 196; Elliott 1986, 436; Henríquez de Jorquera 1934, II, 771–3 and 790–1.
82 Castillo de Bobadilla 1597, II, 208–11; Zapata 1859, 483–4.
83 Herrera Puga 1971, 83.
84 Porcar 1934, paragraphs 1,308, 1,583, 2,066 and 2,374.
85 García de Enterría 1973, 324–6.
86 Granero 1961, 492–4; Escolano 1610–11, V, 1117–8; Henríquez de Jorquera 1934, I, 258.
87 Martínez de Mata 1971, 420–3; Castillo de Bobadilla 1597, II, 266.
88 Castillo de Bobadilla 1597, I, 387; Pike 1983, 52–5.

9 THE POLICING OF THE FAMILY

1 Manuel de Mello 1651, 132; Castillo de Bobadilla 1597, I, 12.
2 Casanovas 1978, 70–1; Garibay 1854, 1–3; Martí Grajales 1927, 128–68.
3 Simon Tarrés 1991.
4 Matilla Tascón 1983, 26; García Mercadal 1952–62, III, 1,563.
5 *Siete Partidas*, 4/27/4.
6 Lockhart and Otte 1976, 247–52.
7 Bermúdez de Pedraza 1608, 146.
8 Gallego Morell 1950, 32–3; Fernández de Bethencourt 1900–20, X, 31–61.
9 Argote de Molina 1588, 612–4 and 652.
10 Ponz 1771–93, XI, 177–80.
11 Granero 1961, 413–4.
12 Altamira 1905, 22–3.
13 Porcar 1934, paragraph 136.
14 Garibay 1854, 257–60; Foster 1960, 148–50.
15 Catalá de Valeriola 1929, 147.
16 Ortiz de Zúñiga 1677, 441; Hernández 1995, 160, note 25.
17 Lockhart and Otte 1976, 128–31; Matilla Tascón 1983, 117.
18 Catalá de Valeriola 1929, 100–1.
19 Costa 1882, 447.
20 Casey 1988, 183–200.
21 Fernández Pérez 1997, chapter 5.
22 APG *escribanía* of Juan Bautista de Palacio, ff.352–7ᵛ.
23 Casanovas 1978, 84.

24 López Bravo 1627, 290–2.

25 González Palencia 1932, 237–9.

26 Manuel de Mello 1651, 154–5.

27 Fernández Pérez 1997, 162–82.

28 Lantery 1949, 291–2, 299–300 and 361–3.

29 *Actas de las Cortes*, 7 (1583–5), petition 25; 6 (1579–82), petition 36; *Novísima Recopilación* 5/3/9; Moret and Silvela 1863, 118–9.

30 Fernández Pérez 1997, 105–6.

31 Garibay 1854, 349–51.

32 Ochagavía 1958–9, XIV, 25–44.

33 Ochagavía 1958–9, XIII, 131–54.

34 Manuel de Mello 1651, 158.

35 Sierra 1964, 151 note 11; Llorente 1809, 2.

36 González 1973, 12–13; Sánchez Baena and Chaín Navarro in Chacón Jiménez (ed.) 1992, 199–201.

37 Ledesma 1601, 150; Camos 1592, II,70; *Siete Partidas*, 4/6/preamble.

38 Arbiol 1715, 3 and 54.

39 Cervantes 1605–14, II, chapter 19.

40 Arbiol 1715, 516–7; Agustín 1617, 27–31.

41 Medina 1548, 110 and 173.

42 Zayas 1637–47, 50–1.

43 MacKay 1977, 38–9; Dillard 1984, 80.

44 Herrera Puga 1971, 454.

45 Tramoyeres Blasco 1889, 363–4.

46 Castillo de Bobadilla 1597, I, 497 and 511; *Cortes Valencianas*, petition 6 of Braços Militar and Real (1626), and cf. Fur 39 of 1626; Tejeda y Ramiro, 1849–55, V, 397–400.

47 Dedieu in Bennassar (ed.) 1979, 318–27; Domínguez Ortiz 1973, 80; Robres Lluch 1960, 351; Mantecón Movillán 1997, 125–6.

48 Escolano 1610–11, V, 1,125–8; CODOIN, CXII, 115–49; Graullera Sanz 1980, 75–98.

49 Perry 1990, 141–3; Cabrera de Córdova 1857, 342–3.

50 León 1981, 89–93 and 110–11.

51 *Actas de las Cortes*, 6 (1579–82), petition 19; 9 (1586–8), petition 43; 11 (1588–90), petition 21.

52 Ledesma 1601, 110.

53 Sánchez 1740, 128–36.

54 Manuel de Mello 1651, 157.

55 Casey in Redondo (ed.) 1985, 57–68.

56 Fernández Martín 1980, 559–638; CODOIN, VII (1845) and VIII (1846).

57 Perry 1990, 59; Amorós 1777, 173 and 179–85.

58 *Novísima Recopilación*, 10/2/8 and 9.

59 Campomanes 1775, 276.

60 Camos 1592, II, 57.

61 Arbiol 1715, 95–6.

62 Joly 1603–4, 514.

63 Lantery 1949, 119 and 180–1; Fernández Pérez 1997, 227–8.

64 Torres Villarroel 1743, 5.

65 ARCG 3/548/11; Joly 1603–4, 567–70.

66 Astete 1603, 54.

67 Agustín 1617, 19; Cervantes 1605–14, I, chapter 28.

68 Fernández Pérez 1997, 105–6.

69 Guevara 1940, 144–8; Manuel de Mello 1651, 89–97; León 1583, 132–3.

70 Amades 1969, III, 897; Brown 1991.

71 Camos 1592, I, 25; Campomanes 1775, 189.
72 Arbiol 1715, 462; Sánchez 1740, 43 and 52–3.
73 Marcos Martín 1978, 52.
74 González Moreno 1969, 92–3.
75 Manuel de Mello 1651, 119–20.
76 Ochoa 1856–70, II, 562.
77 Porcar 1934, paragraph 1,710.
78 Alvarez Santaló 1977, 495; Alvarez Santaló 1980, 44; Morales 1960, I, 447.
79 Fernández Navarrete 1626, 365; Hernández Rodríguez 1947, 262.
80 Catalá de Valeriola 1929, 87; March 1941, II, 54–5.
81 Ochoa 1856–70, II, 561; *Nueva Recopilación*, 5/1/12 and 13.
82 Garibay 1854, 612–4; March 1941, II, 259–61.
83 Lantery 1949, 35; Catalá de Valeriola 1929, 150.
84 Amezúa 1935–41, IV, 170–1.
85 León 1583, 140; Luxán 1550, 133.
86 Garibay 1854, 261 and 615.
87 Catalá de Valeriola 1929, 90; March 1941, II, 310–12.
88 Garibay 1854, 615–7.
89 Palma 1595, 16–17; Luxán 1550, 154.
90 Sánchez 1740, 88; Arbiol 1715, 338.
91 Catalá de Valeriola 1929, 122.
92 Hernández Rodríguez 1947, 404–5.
93 *Actas de las Cortes*, 5 *adicional* (1576–7), 540–1.
94 Robres Lluch 1960, 334; Bermúdez de Pedraza 1638, 187[v].
95 González Moreno 1969, 59; Maltby 1983, 12–13.
96 Kagan 1974, chapters 1 and 2; Redondo (1996), part III.
97 Ribadeneira 1572, 185–6.
98 Simón Díaz 1952–9, I, 66.
99 Gurrea 1627, 72.

10 THE COMMUNITY OF THE FAITHFUL

1 Mariana 1599, 149 and 154.
2 Medina 1548, 46; Méndez Silva 1645, 3[v]–4.
3 *Relazioni* VIII, 371.
4 MacKay 1972, 55–67.
5 Belenguer 1976, 158–66; Monter 1990, 3–28.
6 Mariana 1601, 156–7.
7 Myerson 1991, 44, 128 and 230.
8 Bermúdez de Pedraza 1638, 187.
9 Caro Baroja 1957, 147.
10 Bennassar 1989; Haedo 1612, 9[v]–10.
11 Janer 1857, 266–8.
12 Bleda 1618, 882.
13 Englander 1990, 301–3.
14 Bleda 1618, 882 and 942; Halperin Donghi 1980, 115.
15 Harvey 1958; García Arenal 1978, 110–13; García Ballester 1984.
16 Cardaillac 1977, 58.
17 Boronat 1901, I, 549–69.
18 Bleda 1618, 1,027.
19 Momblanch y Gonzálbez 1959, 50–5.
20 Lapeyre 1959, 30.

21 Bennassar 1989, 401–8; Hess 1978.

22 Cardaillac 1977, 49.

23 Townsend 1791, III, 82–4; Contreras 1982, 621–3.

24 Contreras 1982, 455–7; García Cárcel 1980, 217–94.

25 Kamen 1985, 189–97.

26 Contreras 1982, 179–297.

27 *Actas de las Cortes* 26 (1607–10), draft petition 61; 6 (1579–82), petition 35; 11 (1588–90), petition 15; Carrasco Urgoiti 1969, 25–31.

28 Silverman, in Perry and Cruz (eds) 1991, 167; López Bravo 1627, 185.

29 Sicroff 1960, 85, 90 and 135–8.

30 Domínguez Ortiz 1971, 103.

31 Roth 1995, 240–1.

32 Yerushalmi 1981, 64–5.

33 Domínguez Ortiz 1971, 93 and 242–3.

34 López Bravo 1627, 104–5.

35 *Actas de las Cortes* 5 *adicional* (1576–7), 345–6; 11 (1588–90), 455–60.

36 Reglà 1956, 23.

37 Crespí de Valldaura, 59^v–60^v.

38 Colmenares 1637, II, 159.

39 Porcar 1934, paragraph 2,799.

40 Martí Grajales 1927, 129–30.

41 Fuster 1968, 213–25.

42 Joly 1603–4, 546–53.

43 Domínguez Ortiz 1963–70, II, 131; Vassberg 1984, 112.

44 *Cortes Valencianas*, petition 1 of Braços Militar and Real of 1626, and petition 75 of Braç Real.

45 Contreras 1982, 680; Domínguez Ortiz 1963–70, II, 142–3, note 50.

46 Domínguez Ortiz 1963–70, II, 36; Cerdán de Tallada 1604, chapter 9.

47 *Actas de las Cortes* 13 (1593–5), 55–60; Ribadeneira 1572, 190; Mariana 1599, 152.

48 *Actas de las Cortes* 6 (1579–82), 392; Domínguez Ortiz 1984, 143–7.

49 Contreras 1982, 674.

50 Pulgar 1486, letter 23; Guevara 1539, letter 30.

51 Escolano 1610–11, V, 891; Pons Fuster 1991, 52; Viciana 1563–6, III, 149^v.

52 Castillo de Bobadilla 1597, II, 586; *Actas de las Cortes* 39 (1623), 27–9.

53 Domínguez Ortiz 1963–70, II, 72–3; Fernández Navarrete 1626, 348–57.

54 Rodríguez Sánchez, in García Cárcel and others 1991, 228.

55 Christian 1981a, 9; Reglà 1955, 26.

56 Domínguez Ortiz 1963–70, II, 79, note 34, and 228–9.

57 Hernández 1995, 194.

58 Garibay 1854, 626.

59 Nalle 1992, 96–103.

60 Benlloch 1756, 99.

61 López Piñero 1979, 194–5.

62 López Bravo 1627, 158–9.

63 Castillo de Bobadilla 1597, I, 514; *Novísima Recopilación*, 12/4/2.

64 Reglà 1956, 81–2.

65 Contreras 1982, 568–9; Lea 1905, IV, 190.

66 Ehlers 1997, 101–16.

67 Catalá de Valeriola 1929, 49–50.

68 Pisa 1617, 63 ff.

69 Christian 1981a, 47–66.

70 *Cortes Valencianas*, Fur 250 of 1604; Luxán 1550, 157.

71 López Bravo 1627, 205.
72 Martí Grajales 1927, 77.
73 Kagan 1990.
74 Christian 1981b, 159–84.
75 Felipo Orts, Pons Fuster and Callado Estela 1997, 149–210.
76 López-Cordón 1978, 71–119; García Mercadal 1952–62, III, 1,064.
77 Catalá de Valeriola 1929, 10–15; Matilla Tascón 1983, 11–13.
78 Fernández Navarrete 1626, 106.
79 Mejide Pardo 1960, 461–606.
80 *Relazioni*, IX, 76.
81 Bermúdez de Pedraza 1638, 185ᵛ.
82 Granero 1961, 146–7; Ortiz de Zúñiga 1677, 460–1; Díez del Corral 1987, 298.
83 Kamen 1993, 99–100.
84 Porcar 1934, paragraphs 2,967 and 2,716; Foster 1960, 172–7.
85 Reglà 1955, 34; Kamen 1993, 177–8.
86 Joly 1603–4, 556.
87 Ortiz de Zúñiga 1677, 443–4; Sentaurens 1984, II, 613–76; Kamen 1993, 182–6.
88 Herrera Puga 1981, 103; Matilla Tascón 1983, 159; Bermúdez de Pedraza 1638, 95ᵛ.
89 Dedieu, in Cruz and Perry (eds.) 1992, 15.
90 Ponz 1771–93, III, 225–6, and IX, 30–4.
91 Campomanes 1774, 51–2; Jovellanos 1795, 92–6.
92 Jovellanos 1782, 227–33.
93 Ponz 1771–93, VII, 29–30.
94 Ibid., VII, 8–12.
95 Martínez de Mata 1971, 347.

CONCLUSION

1 Azorín, 'Una ciudad y un balcón', in his collected essays, *Castilla*.
2 Brenner 1976, 30–74.
3 Ringrose 1996.
4 Fontana 1971.
5 Campomanes 1775, 197 and 332.

BIBLIOGRAPHY

Abbreviations

ACA CA   Archivo de la Corona de Aragón, Consejo de Aragón.
AMV MC   Archivo Municipal de Valencia, Manuals de Consells.
APG JBP   Archivo de Protocolos de Granada, Escribanía de Juan Bautista de Palacio.
            MQH   Manuel Quesada y Huerta.
ARCG   Archivo de la Real Chancillería de Granada.
ARV   Archivo del Reino de Valencia.
CODOIN   Colección de Documentos Inéditos para la Historia de España.
leg.   legajo (bundle of documents).
MHE   Memorial Histórico Español.
RAH   Real Academia de Historia.

Texts

Abad León, Felipe 1985, *El Marqués de Ensenada*, 2 vols, Madrid.

Actas de las Cortes de Castilla, 58 vols, down to 1651.

Actes du Ier Colloque sur le Pays Valencien à l'Epoque Moderne, Pau 1980.

Agustín, Fr. Miquel, 1617, *Libro de los Secretos de Agricultura* (Castilian edition, Barcelona 1722).

Alba, Duque de, 1927, 'Relaciones de la nobleza con sus pueblos', *Boletín de la Real Academia de Historia* 91, 259–318.

Alcalá, Angel (ed.), 1987, *The Spanish Inquisition and the Inquisitorial Mind*, Highland Lakes, NJ.

Alcalá-Galiano, Antonio, 1886, *Memorias*, 2 vols, Madrid.

Alcalá-Zamora, José N. (ed.), 1994, *La Vida Cotidiana en la España de Velázquez*, Madrid.

Al-Hussein, F.H., 1986, 'Las Ferias de Medina', in Lorenzo Sanz (ed.), *Historia de Medina del Campo*, II, 13–266.

Almarche Vázquez, Francisco, 1919, *Historiografía Valenciana*, Valencia.

Alonso de Herrera, Gabriel, 1513, *Obra de Agricultura*, ed. J.U. Martínez Carreras, Madrid 1970.

Altamira y Crevea, Rafael, 1905, *Derecho Consuetudinario y Economía Popular en la Provincia de Alicante*, Madrid.

Altman, Ida, 1989, *Emigrants and Society: Extremadura and Spanish America in the Sixteenth Century*, Berkeley.

Alvarez Santaló, León Carlos, 1977, 'La casa de expósitos de Sevilla en el siglo XVII', *Cuadernos de Historia*, VII, 491–532.

—— 1980, *Marginación Social y Mentalidad en la Andalucía Occidental: Expósitos en Sevilla 1613–1910*, Seville.

Amades, Joan, 1969, *Folklore de Catalunya, III (Costums i Creences)*, Barcelona.

Amelang, James S., 1986, *Honored Citizens of Barcelona. Patrician Culture and Class Relations 1490–1714*, Princeton.

—— 1991, *A Journal of the Plague Year: The Diary of the Barcelona Tanner Miquel Parets, 1651*, Oxford.

Amezúa, Agustín G. de, 1934–41, *Lope de Vega en sus Cartas*, 4 vols, Madrid.

—— 1950, *La Vida Privada Española en el Protocolo Notarial*, Madrid.

Amorós, Joaquín, 1777, *Discurso en que se manifiesta la necesidad y utilidad del consentimiento paterno para el casamiento de los hijos*, Madrid.

Anes, Gonzalo, 1970, *Las Crisis Agrarias en la España Moderna*, Madrid.

—— 1975, *El Antiguo Régimen: Los Borbones, Historia de España Alfaguara, IV*, Madrid.

Aracil, R. and García Bonafé, M., 1974, *Industrialització al País Valencià: El Cas d'Alcoi*, Valencia.

Arbiol, Fr. Antonio, 1715, *La Familia Regulada con Doctrina de la Sagrada Escritura*, Zaragoza.

Arco, Ricardo del, 1950, 'La vida privada en la obra de Cervantes', *Revista de Archivos, Bibliotecas y Museos*, 56, 577–616.

Ardit, Manuel, 1977, *Revolución Liberal y Revuelta Campesina: Un Ensayo sobre la Desintegración del Régimen Feudal en el País Valenciano 1793–1840*, Barcelona.

—— 1993, *Els Homes i la Terra del País Valencià*, 2 vols, Barcelona.

Argote de Molina, Gonzalo, 1588, *Nobleza de Andalucía*, ed. Enrique de Toral, Jaén 1957.

Arias Abellán, Jesús, 1984, *Propiedad y Uso de la Tierra en el Marquesado del Cenete*, Granada.

Arias de Saavedra, Inmaculada, 1987, *Las Sociedades Económicas de Amigos del País del Reino de Jaén*, Granada.

—— 1988, *La Real Maestranza de Caballería de Granada en el Siglo XVIII*, Granada.

Arjona Castro, A. and Estrada Carrillo, V., 1977, *Historia de la Villa de Luque*, Cordoba.

Artola, Miguel, 1978, *Antiguo Régimen y Revolución Liberal*, Barcelona.

—— 1982, *La Hacienda del Antiguo Régimen*, Madrid.

Asensio Salvadó, Eduardo, 1954, 'El arbitrista Jerónimo Ibáñez de Salt', *Estudios de Historia Moderna*, IV, 227–72.

Asso, Ignacio de, 1798, *Historia de la Economía Política de Aragón*, Zaragoza.

Astete, Gaspar, SJ, 1603, *Tratado del Govierno de la Familia*, Burgos.

Atienza Hernández, Ignacio, 1987, *Aristocracia, Poder y Riqueza en la España Moderna: La Casa de Osuna, Siglos XV–XIX*, Madrid.

—— 1984, 'La "quiebra" de la nobleza castellana en el siglo XVII', *Hispania*, 44, 218–36.

Bakewell, Peter, 1971, *Silver Mining and Society in Colonial Mexico: Zacatecas 1546–1700*, Cambridge.

Ballesteros Rodríguez, Juan, 1982, *La Peste en Córdoba*, Cordoba.

Barrionuevo, Jerónimo de 1654–8, *Avisos*, ed. A. Paz y Meliá, 2 vols, Madrid 1968.

Bayon, Damien, 1967, *L'Architecture en Castille au XVIᵉ Siècle*, Paris.

Belenguer Cebrià, Ernesto, 1976, *València en la Crisi del Segle XV*, Barcelona.

Benítez Sánchez-Blanco, Rafael 1982, *Moriscos y Cristianos en el Condado de Casares*, Cordoba.

—— 1995 '"El cargo de menos importancia . . .": la provisión del virreinato de Valencia', *Homenaje a Antonio de Bethencourt Massieu*, Las Palmas, I, 189–209.

Benlloch, Francisco, 1756, *Descripción de el Marquesado de Lombay*, Valencia 1975.

Bennassar, Bartolomé, 1967, *Valladolid au Siècle d'Or*, Paris.

—— 1975, *L'Homme Espagnol*, Eng. trans. as *The Spanish Character: Attitudes and Mentalities from the Sixteenth to the Nineteenth Centuries*, Berkeley 1979.

—— 1979, *L'Inquisition Espagnole (XV–XIXᵉ siècle)*, Paris.

—— 1982, *Un Siècle d'Or Espagnol (vers 1525–vers 1648)*, Paris.

—— 1985 (ed.), *Histoire des Espagnols (VIᵉ–XXᵉ siècle)*, Paris; paperback edition 1992.

—— 1989 (with L. Bennassar), *Les Chrétiens d'Allah*, Paris.

Berger, Philippe, 1987, *Libro y Lectura en la Valencia del Renacimiento*, 2 vols, Valencia.

Bermúdez de Pedraza, Francisco, 1608, *Antigüedad y Excelencias de Granada*, Granada.

—— 1638, *Historia Eclesiástica . . . de Granada*, Granada.

Bernabé Gil, David, 1990, *Monarquía y Patriciado Urbano en Orihuela 1445–1707*, Alicante.

Bernardo Ares, J.M. and Martínez Ruiz, E. (eds), 1996, *El Municipio en la España Moderna*, Cordoba.

Bilinkoff, Jodi, 1989, *The Avila of Saint Teresa: Religious Reform in a Sixteenth-Century City*, Ithaca.

Bishko, Charles J., 1980, *Studies in Medieval Spanish Frontier History*, London.

Blanco White, José, 1822, *Cartas de España*, ed. V. Llorens and A. Garnica, Madrid 1977.

Bleda, Jaime, 1618, *Crónica de los Moros de España*, Valencia.

Bonnassie, Pierre, 1975, *La Organización del Trabajo en Barcelona a Fines del Siglo XV*, Barcelona.

Bonnassie, P. and others, 1980, *Structures Féodales et Féodalisme dans l'Occident Méditerranéen (Xᵉ–XIIIᵉ Siècle)*, Rome; Spanish translation Barcelona 1984.

Boronat, Pascual, 1901, *Los Moriscos Españoles y su Expulsión*, 2 vols, Valencia.

Borrero Fernández, Mercedes, 1983, *El Mundo Rural Sevillano en el Siglo XV*, Seville.

Borrow, George, 1842, *The Bible in Spain*, ed. T. Walker, London 1985.

Botero, Giovanni, 1589, *The Reason of State*, ed. D.P. Wiley, London 1956.

Boyajian, James C., 1983, *Portuguese Bankers at the Court of Spain 1626–50*, New Brunswick, NJ.

Braham, Allan (ed.), 1981, *El Greco to Goya: The Taste for Spanish Paintings in Britain and Ireland*, London.

Brenner, Robert, 1976, 'Agrarian class structure and economic development in pre-industrial Europe', *Past and Present*, 70, 30–74.

Brines Blasco, J. and others, 1995, *Formación y Disolución de los Grandes Patrimonios Castellonenses en el Antiguo Régimen*, Castelló.

Brown, Jonathan, 1991, *The Golden Age of Painting in Spain*, New Haven.

Brown, J. and Elliott, J.H., 1980, *A Palace for a King: The Buen Retiro and the Court of Philip IV*, New Haven.

Brumont, Francis, 1984, *Campos y Campesinos de Castilla la Vieja en tiempos de Felipe II*, Madrid.

Burriel de Orueta, Eugenio, 1971, *La Huerta de Valencia*, Valencia.

Cabrera de Córdova, Luis, 1857, *Relaciones de las Cosas Sucedidas en la Corte de España desde 1599 hasta 1614*, Madrid.

Cabrera Muñoz, Emilio, 1977, *El Condado de Belalcázar 1444–1518*, Cordoba.

—— 1982, 'Orígenes del señorío de Espejo . . . 1297–1319', in Ladero Quesada (ed.), *Estudios en Memoria de . . . Salvador de Moxó*, I, pp. 211–31.

Cabrera, Emilio and Moros, Andrés, 1991, *Fuenteovejuna: La Violencia Antiseñorial en el Siglo XV*, Barcelona.

Cabrillana, Nicolás, 1989, *Almería Morisca*, Granada.

Cahner, Max (ed.), 1978, *Epistolari del Renaixement: La Cort de Carles V a través d'Estefania de Requesens*, Valencia.

Calderón de la Barca, Pedro, 1642, *The Mayor of Zalamea*.

Calero Palacios, Maria C., 1979, *La Enseñanza y Educación en Granada bajo los Reyes Austrias*, Granada.

Callahan, William J., 1972, *Honor, Commerce and Industry in Eighteenth-Century Spain*, Boston.

—— 1980, *La Santa y Real Hermandad del Refugio . . . 1618–32*, Madrid.

Camos, Marco Antonio, 1592, *Microcosmia y Govierno Universal del Hombre Cristiano*, Barcelona.

Campomanes, Pedro Rodríguez, Conde de, 1774–5, *Industria y Educación Popular: Discursos*, ed. John Reeder, Madrid 1975.

Camps i Arboix, Joaquim de, 1959, *La Masia Catalana*, Barcelona.

—— 1969, *Història de l'Agricultura Catalana*, Barcelona.

Canet Aparici, Teresa, 1986, *La Audiencia Valenciana en la Epoca Foral*, Valencia.

Capella, M. and Matilla, A., 1957, *Los Cinco Gremios Mayores de Madrid*, Madrid.

Carande, Ramón, 1943–67, *Carlos V y sus Banqueros*, 3 vols, new edn Madrid 1987.

—— 1989–90, *Estudios de Historia*, 2 vols, Barcelona.

Carbajo Isla, María F., 1987, *La Población de Madrid desde finales del siglo XVI hasta mediados del siglo XIX*, Madrid.

Cardaillac, Louis, 1977, *Morisques et Chrétiens: un affrontement polémique 1492–1640*, Paris.

—— (ed.) 1983, *Les Morisques et leur Temps*, Paris.

—— (ed.) 1990, *Les Morisques et l'Inquisition*, Paris.

Carlos III y la Ilustración, 1988, 2 vols, Madrid.

Caro Baroja, Julio, 1957, *Los Moriscos del Reino de Granada*, Madrid.

—— 1978, *Las Formas Complejas de la Vida Religiosa: Religión, Sociedad y Carácter en la España de los siglos XVI y XVII*, Madrid.

—— 1981, *Los Pueblos de España*, 3rd edn, 2 vols, Madrid.

—— 1990, *Ensayo sobre la Literatura de Cordel*, Madrid.

Caro López, C., 1983, 'Casas y alquileres en el antiguo Madrid', *Anales del Instituto de Estudios Madrileños*, 20, 97–153.

Carrasco Urgoiti, María S., 1969, *El Problema Morisco en Aragón al Comienzo del Reinado de Felipe II*, Madrid.

Carrera Pujal, J., 1943, *Historia de la Economía Española*, I, Barcelona.

Carrère, Claude, 1966, 'La vie privée du marchand barcelonais dans la première moitié du XVe siècle', *Anuario de Estudios Medievales*, III, 263–92.

Carreres Zacarés, Salvador, 1930, *Notes per a la Història dels Bandos de València*, Valencia.

—— 1935, *Libre de Memòries de Diversos Sucesos e Fets Memorables . . . de València 1308–1644*, 2 vols, Valencia.

—— 1957, *La Taula de Cambis de Valencia 1408–1719*, Valencia.

Casanovas i Canut, Sebastià, 1978, *Memòries d'un Pagés del Segle XVIII*, ed. Jordi Geli and Maria Angels Anglada, Barcelona.

Cascales, Francisco, 1621, *Discursos Históricos de la Muy Noble y Muy Leal Ciudad de Murcia*, facsimile of 1775 edn, Murcia 1980.

Casey, James, 1979, *The Kingdom of Valencia in the Seventeenth Century*, Cambridge.

—— 1988, 'Matrimonio y patrimonio en un pueblo alpujarreño: Orgiva 1600–1800', in *Sierra Nevada y su Entorno*, Granada, pp. 183–200.

Castañeda, Vicente, 1949, 'Las instrucciones de Felipe II al conde de Benavente para la governación del reino de Valencia en 1566', *Boletín de la Real Academia de Historia*, 124, 451–71.

Castelló Traver, Josep E., 1978, *El País Valenciano en el Censo de Floridablanca (1787)*, Valencia.

Castillo de Bobadilla, Jerónimo, 1597, *Política para Corregidores y Señores de Vasallos*, 2 vols, Madrid.

Castillo Pintado, Alvaro, 1965, 'Richesse et population dans la deuxième moitié du XVIe siècle', *Annales ESC*, 20, 719–33.

—— 1969, *Tráfico Marítimo y Comercio de Importación en Valencia a Comienzos del Siglo XVII*, Madrid.

Castro, Americo, 1971, *The Spaniards: An Introduction to their History*, Berkeley.

Castro, Concepción de, 1987, *El Pan de Madrid: El Abasto de las Ciudades Españoles del Antiguo Régimen*, Madrid.

Catalá Sanz, Jorge A., 1994, 'Violencia nobiliaria y orden público en Valencia durante el reinado de Felipe III', *Estudis*, 20, 105–20.

—— 1995, *Rentas y Patrimonios de la Nobleza Valencia en el Siglo XVIII*, Madrid.

Catalá de Valeriola, Bernardo, 1929, *Autobiografía y Justas Poéticas*, ed. S. Carreres Zacarés, Valencia.

Cavanilles, Antonio Joseph, 1795–7, *Observaciones sobre la Historia Natural . . . de Valencia*, ed. J.M. Casas Torres, 2 vols, Zaragoza 1958.

Cavillac, Michel, 1983, *Gueux et Marchands dans le Guzmán de Alfarache (1599–1604)*, Bordeaux.

Caxa de Leruela, Miguel, 1631, *Restauración de la Antigua Abundancia de España*, ed. J.P. Le Flem, Madrid.

Cerdà, Manuel (ed.), 1988, *Historia del Pueblo Valenciano*, 3 vols, Valencia.

Cerdán de Tallada, Tomás, 1604, *Veriloquium en Reglas de Estado*, Valencia.

Chabas, Roque, 1874, *Historia de la Ciudad de Denia*, 2 vols, Denia.

Chacón Jiménez, Francisco, 1979, *Murcia en la Centuria del Quinientos*, Murcia.

—— 1986, *Los Murcianos del Siglo XVII: Evolución, Familia y Trabajo*, Murcia.

—— (ed.), 1990, *Historia Social de la Familia en España*, Alicante.

—— (ed.), 1991, *Familia, Grupos Sociales y Mujer en España (Siglos XV–XIX)*, Murcia.

Chacón Jiménez, F. and Hernández Franco, J. (eds.), 1992, *Poder, Familia y Consanguinidad en la España del Antiguo Régimen*, Barcelona.

Chacón Jiménez, F. and others, 1997, *Historia de la Familia: Nuevas Perspectivas sobre la Sociedad Europea*, 5 vols, Murcia.

Chauchadis, Claude, 1984, *Honneur, Morale et Société dans l'Espagne de Philippe II*, Paris.

Chaunu, Pierre, 1973, *L'Espagne de Charles Quint*, 2 vols, Paris.

—— 1977, *Séville et l'Amérique (XVIe–XVIIe Siècle)*, Paris.

Chevalier, Maxime, 1976, *Lectura y Lectores en la España del Siglo XVI y XVII*, Madrid.

Christian, W.A., 1981a, *Apparitions in Late Medieval and Renaissance Spain*, Princeton.

—— 1981b, *Local Religion in Sixteenth-Century Spain*, Princeton.

Císcar Pallarés, Eugenio, 1975, 'El endeudamiento del campesinado valenciano', *Estudis* 4, 147–62.

—— 1977, *Tierra y Señorío en el País Valenciano 1570–1620*, Valencia.

Clavero, Bartolomé 1974, *Mayorazgo y Propiedad Feudal en Castilla (1369–1863)*, Madrid.

CODOIN vols 7 and 8, 'Matrimonio del marqués de Coria 1578–80'.

CODOIN vol. 112, 'Acuerdos del ayuntamiento de Córdoba relativos a la mancebía'.

Colás Latorre, G. and Salas Auséns, J.A., 1976, 'El fenómeno social del bandolerismo en el reino de Aragón durante el siglo XVI', *Estudios del Departamento de Historia Moderna*, Zaragoza, pp. 79–146.

—— 1982, *Aragón en el Siglo XVI: Alteraciones Sociales y Conflictos Políticos*, Zaragoza.

Collantes de Terán, Antonio, 1977a, *Sevilla en la Baja Edad Media*, Seville.

—— 1977b, 'Nuevas poblaciones del siglo XV en el reino de Sevilla', *Cuadernos de Historia*, 7.

Colmeiro, Manuel, 1863, *Historia de la Economía Política en España*, ed. G. Anes, 2 vols, Madrid.

Colmenares, Diego de, 1637, *Historia de la Insigne Ciudad de Segovia*, 2 vols, Segovia.

Contreras, Jaime, 1982, *El Santo Oficio de la Inquisición de Galicia*, Madrid.

—— 1992, *Sotos contra Riquelmes: Regidores, Inquisidores y Criptojudíós*, Madrid.

Cooper, Edward, 1980–1, *Castillos Señoriales de Castilla de los Siglos XV y XVI*, 2 vols, Madrid.

Cortés Peña, A. and Vincent, B., 1986, *Historia de Granada. III: La Epoca Moderna, Siglos XVI, XVII y XVIII*, Granada.

Cortes Valencianas 1484–1645, 6 vols of the laws, facsimile edn Valencia 1972–84.

Costa, Joaquín, 1882, 'La libertad de testar y las legítimas', *Revista General de Legislación y Jurisprudencia*, 60, 422–50.

—— 1885–1902, *Derecho Consuetudinario y Economía Popular en España*, 2 vols, Barcelona.

—— 1898–1915, *Colectivismo Agrario en España*, 2 vols, Zaragoza.

Crespí de Valldaura, Cristóbal, 'Diario del Señor Vicecanciller Crespí 1652–71', ms. of Biblioteca Nacional, Madrid.

Cressy, David, 1989, *Bonfire and Bells: National Memory and the Protestant Calendar in Elizabethan and Stuart England*, London.

Cruz, Jesús, 1996, *Gentlemen, Bourgeois and Revolutionaries: Political Change and Cultural Persistence among the Spanish Dominant Groups (1750–1850)*, Cambridge.

Cruz, A.J. and Perry, M.E. (eds), 1992, *Culture and Control in Counter-Reformation Spain*, Minneapolis.

Dantí, Jaume, 1990, *Aixecaments Populars als Països Catalans 1687–93*, Barcelona.

Danvila, Manuel, 1889, 'Nuevos datos para escribir la historia de las cortes', *Boletín de la Real Academia de Historia*, XV, 385–433 and 497–542.

Dedieu, Jean-Pierre, 1989, *L'Administration de la Foi: L'Inquisition de Tolède XVIe–XVIIIe siècles*, Madrid.

Defourneaux, Marcelin, 1970, *Daily Life in Spain in the Golden Age*, London.

Desdevises du Dezert, G., 1899, *L'Espagne de l'Ancien Régime*, 2 vols, Paris.

Deza, Lope de, 1618, *Govierno Polytico de Agricultura*, Madrid.

Díez del Corral, Rosario, 1987, *Arquitectura y Mecenazgo: La Imagen de Toledo en el Renacimiento*, Madrid.

Dillard, Heath, 1984, *Daughters of the Reconquest: Women in Castilian Town Society 1100–1300*, Cambridge.

Domínguez Ortiz, Antonio, 1946, *Orto y Ocaso de Sevilla*, Seville.

—— 1960, *Política y Hacienda de Felipe IV*, Madrid.

—— 1963, 'Guerra económica y comercio extranjero en el reinado de Felipe IV', *Hispania*, 23, 71–110.

—— 1963–70, *La Sociedad Española en el Siglo XVII*, 2 vols, Madrid.

—— 1964, 'Ventas y exenciones de lugares durante el reinado de Felipe IV', *Anuario de Historia del Derecho Español*, pp. 99–124.

—— 1969, *Crisis y Decadencia de la España de los Austrias*, Barcelona.

—— 1971, *Los Judeoconversos en España y América*, Madrid.

—— 1973, *Alteraciones Andaluzas*, Madrid.

—— 1976, *Sociedad y Estado en el Siglo XVIII Español*, Barcelona.

Domínguez Ortiz, Antonio, 1984, *Política Fiscal y Cambio Social*, Madrid.

—— 1987, *Estudios de Historia Económica y Social de España*, Granada.

—— 1988, 'Repercusiones en Sevilla de los motines de 1766', *Archivo Hispalense*, 217, 3–13.

Domínguez Ortiz. A. and Aguilar Piñal, F., 1976, *Historia de Sevilla, IV: El Barroco y la Ilustración*, Seville.

Domínguez Ortiz, A. and others, 1989, *Historia de España Menéndez Pidal, XXIII: La Población, La Economía, La Sociedad*, 3rd edn Madrid 1996.

Dubert García, Isidoro, 1987, *Los Comportamientos de la Familia Urbana en la Galicia del Antiguo Régimen*, Santiago de Compostela.

Duque de Estrada, Diego, 1860, *Comentarios del Desengañado*, MHE, XII, Madrid.

Duran, Emilia, 1982, *Les Germanies als Països Catalans*, Barcelona.

Edwards, John, 1982, *Christian Cordoba: The City and its Region in the Late Middle Ages*, Cambridge.

—— 1996, *Religion and Society in Spain, c.1492*, London.

Ehlers, B.A., 1997, 'La esclava y el patriarca', *Estudis*, 23, 101–16.

Eiras Roel, A. and others, 1981, *La Historia Social de Galicia en sus Fuentes de Protocolos*, Santiago de Compostela.

Elliott, John H., 1963a, *The Revolt of the Catalans: A Study in the Decline of Spain 1598–1640*, Cambridge.

—— 1963b, *Imperial Spain 1469–1716*, London.

—— 1989, *Spain and its World 1500–1700*, New Haven.

Elliott, J.H. and García Sanz, A. (eds), 1990, *La España del Conde Duque de Olivares*, Valladolid.

Englander, D. and others, 1990, *Culture and Belief in Europe 1450–1600: An Anthology of Sources*, Oxford.

Enríquez de Guzmán, Alonso, 1534, *Vida*, CODOIN, vol. 85, Madrid 1886.

Equipo Madrid de Estudios Históricos 1988, *Carlos III, Madrid y la Ilustración*, Madrid.

Escolano, Gaspar 1610–11, *Década Primera de la Historia de Valencia*, facsimile edn, 6 vols, Valencia 1972.

Esquerdo, Onofre, *c.*1686, *Nobiliario Valenciano*, ed. J. Martínez Ortiz, Valencia 1963.

Estepa Giménez, Jesús, 1987, *El Marquesado de Priego en la Disolución del Régimen Señorial Andaluz*, Cordoba.

Estudios 1976, *Estudios del Departamento de Historia Moderna de Zaragoza*.

La Familia en la España Mediterránea (Siglos XV–XIX), Barcelona 1987.

Fayard, Janine, 1979, *Les Membres du Conseil de Castille à l'Epoque Moderne (1621–1746)*, Geneva.

Felipo Orts, Amparo, 1996, *Insaculación y Elites de Poder en la Ciudad de Valencia*, Valencia.

Felipo Orts, A., Pons Fuster, F. and Callado Estela, E., 1997, 'Francisco Jerónimo Simó . . .', *Estudis*, 23, 117–210.

Fernández, Roberto (ed.), 1985, *España en el Siglo XVIII: Homenaje a Pierre Vilar*, Barcelona.

Fernández Alvarez, Manuel, 1989, *La Sociedad Española en el Siglo de Oro*, 2nd edn, 2 vols, Madrid.

Fernández de Bethencourt, F., 1897–1920, *Historia Genealógica y Heráldica de la Monarquía Española*, 10 vols, Madrid.

Fernández Cortizo, Camilo, 1982, 'A una misma mesa y manteles: la familia de Tierra de Montes en el siglo XVIII', *Cuadernos de Estudios Gallegos*, 23, 237–76.

Fernández Martín, Luis, 1980, 'La marquesa del Valle: una vida dramática en la corte de los Austrias', *Hispania*, 40, 559–638.

Fernández Navarrete, Pedro, 1626, *Conservación de Monarquías*, ed. M.D. Gordon, Madrid 1982.

Fernández Pérez, Paloma, 1997, *El Rostro Familiar de la Metrópoli: Redes de Parentesco y Lazos Mercantiles en Cádiz 1700–1812*, Madrid.

Flynn, Maureen 1989, *Sacred Charity: Confraternities and Social Welfare in Spain 1400–1700*, London.

Fontana, Josep, 1971, *La Quiebra de la Monarquía Absoluta 1814–20*, Barcelona.

Fortea Pérez, Jose I., 1981, *Córdoba en el Siglo XVI*, Cordoba.

—— 1986, *Fiscalidad en Córdoba 1513–1619*, Cordoba.

—— (ed.) 1997, *Imágenes de la Diversidad: El Mundo Urbano en la Corona de Castilla (Siglos XVI–XVIII)*, Santander.

Fortea Pérez, J.I. and C.M. Cremades Griñán (eds), 1993, *Política y Hacienda en el Antiguo Régimen*, Murcia.

Foster, George M., 1960, *Culture and Conquest: America's Spanish Heritage*, New York.

Franco Silva, Alfonso, 1983, 'El linaje Sandoval y el señorío de Lerma en el siglo XV', in *El Pasado Histórico de Castilla y León*, I.

Freedman, Paul, 1991, *The Origins of Peasant Servitude in Medieval Catalonia*, Cambridge.

Furió, Antoni, 1982, *Camperols del País Valencià: Sueca, una Comunitat Rural a la Tardor de l'Edat Mitjana*, Valencia.

Fuster, Joan, 1968, *Heretgies, Revoltes i Sermons*, Barcelona.

—— 1976, *La Decadència al País Valencià*, Barcelona.

Gallego Morell, Antonio, 1950, *Francisco y Juan de Trillo y Fugueroa*, Granada.

García Arenal, Mercedes, 1978, *Inquisición y Moriscos: Los Procesos del Tribunal de Cuenca*, Madrid.

García-Baquero, Antonio, 1986, *Andalucía y la Carrera de Indias 1492–1824*, Seville.

García Ballester, Luis, 1984, *Los Moriscos y la Medecina*, Barcelona.

García Cárcel, Ricardo, 1975, *Las Germanías de Valencia*, Barcelona.

—— 1976, *Orígenes de la Inquisición Española: El Tribunal de Valencia 1478–1530*, Barcelona.

—— 1980, *Herejía y Sociedad en el Siglo XVI: La Inquisición en Valencia 1530–1609*, Barcelona.

—— 1985, *Historia de Cataluña, Siglos XVI–XVII*, 2 vols, Barcelona.

García Cárcel, R. and others, 1991, *Manual de Historia de España*, vol. III: Siglos XVI–XVII, Madrid.

García de Cortázar, J.A. and others, 1985, *Organización Social del Espacio en la España Medieval*, Barcelona.

García de Enterría, María C., 1973, *Sociedad y Poesía de Cordel en el Barroco*, Madrid.

Garcia Espuche, A. and Guàrdia Bassols, M., 1986, *Espai i Societat a la Barcelona Pre-industrial*, Barcelona.

García Fernández, Jesús, 1963, *Aspectos del Paisaje Agrario de Castilla la Vieja*, Valladolid.

—— 1965, 'Champs ouverts et champs clôturés en Vieille-Castille', *Annales ESC*, 20, 692–718.

—— 1975, *Organización del Espacio y Economía Rural en la España Atlántica*, Madrid.

García Fuentes, L., 1980, *El Comercio Español con América 1650–1700*, Seville.

García González, Francisco, 1995, *Familia, Propiedad y Reproducción Social en el Antiguo Régimen: La Comarca de la Sierra de Alcaraz en el Siglo XVIII*, Murcia.

García Martínez, Sebastián, 1968, *Els Fonaments del País Valencià Modern*, Valencia.

—— 1991, *Valencia bajo Carlos II*, Villena.

—— 1993, *Francesc García*, Teulada.

García Mercadal, Fernando, 1930, *La Casa Popular en España*, ed. A. Bonet Correa, Barcelona 1981.

García Mercadal, Juan, 1952–62, *Viajes de Extranjeros por España y Portugal, Siglos XVI–XVIII*, 3 vols, Madrid.

García Sanz, Angel, 1977, *Desarrollo y Crisis del Antiguo Régimen en Castilla la Vieja: Economía y Sociedad en Tierras de Segovia 1500–1814*, Madrid.

—— 1980, 'Bienes y derechos comunales', *Hispania*, 40, 95–127.

—— 1989, 'El sector agrario durante el siglo XVII', *Historia de España Menéndez Pidal*, XXIII, 161–235.

Garibay, Esteban de, 1854, *Los Siete Libros de la Progenie y Parentela de . . .*, MHE, VII.

Garrad, Keith, 1957, 'The Causes of the Second Rebellion of the Alpujarras (1568–71)', PhD thesis, University of Cambridge.

Garzón Pareja, Manuel, 1972, *La Industria Sedera en España: El Arte de la Seda de Granada*, Granada.

—— 1980–1, *Historia de Granada*, 2 vols, Granada.

Gautier, Théophile, 1843, *Voyage en Espagne*, Paris 1981.

Gavaldá, Fr. Francisco, 1651, *Memoria . . . de Valencia . . . en Tiempo de Peste*, Valencia.

Gelabert González, Juan E., 1982, *Santiago y la Tierra de Santiago de 1500 a 1640*, Corunna.

Gentil da Silva, José, 1965, *En Espagne; Développement Economique, Subsistance, Déclin*, Paris.

Gerbet, Marie-Claude, 1979, *La Noblesse dans le Royaume de Castille: Etude sur ses Structures Sociales en Extrémadure 1454–1516*, Paris.

Gil Olcina, Antonio, 1979, *La Propiedad Señorial en Tierras Valencianas*, Valencia.

Gil Pujol, Xavier, 1997, 'Una cultura cortesana provincial. Patria, comunicación y lenguaje en la Monarquía Hispánica de los Austrias', in P. Fernández Albaladejo (ed.), *Monarquía, Imperio y Pueblos en la España Moderna*, Alicante, pp. 225–57.

Gimeno Sanfeliu, María J., 1990, *La Oligarquía Urbana de Castelló en el Siglo XVIII*, Castelló.

Gómez-Menor Fuentes, José, 1970, *El Linaje Familiar de Santa Teresa*, Toledo.

Gondomar, 1936–45, *Correspondencia Oficial de Don Diego Sarmiento de Acuña, Conde de Gondomar*, 4 vols, Madrid.

González, Fernando, 1973, 'La agencia oficial de Preces en Roma', *Revista Española de Derecho Canónico*, XXIX.

González, Nazario, SJ 1958, *Burgos, La Ciudad Marginal de Castilla*, Burgos.

González Alonso, Benjamín, 1970, *El Corregidor Castellano 1348–1808*, Madrid.

—— 1981, *Sobre el Estado y la Administración de la Corona de Castilla en el Antiguo Régimen*, Madrid.

González Moreno, Joaquín, 1969, *Don Fernando Enríquez de Ribera*, Seville.

González Palencia, Angel (ed.), 1932, *La Junta de Reformación*, Madrid.

—— 1940, *La Primera Guía de la España Imperial*, Madrid.

González Palencia, A. and Mele, E., 1941–3, *Vida y Obras de Don Diego Hurtado de Mendoza*, 3 vols, Madrid.

Goodman, David, 1988, *Power and Penury: Government, Technology and Science in Philip II's Spain*, Cambridge.

Goy, J. and Le Roy Ladurie, E. 1982, *Prestations Paysannes . . . et Mouvement de la Production Agricole à l'Epoque Préindustrielle*, 2 vols, Paris.

Granero, Jesús M., SJ 1961, *Don Miguel Mañara (Un Caballero Sevillano del Siglo XVII)*, Seville.

Graullera Sanz, Vicente, 1978, *La Esclavitud en Valencia en los Siglos XVI y XVII*, Valencia.

—— 1980, 'Un grupo social marginado: las mujeres públicas (el burdel de Valencia en los ss. XVI–XVII)', in *Actes du I*er *Colloque sur le Pays Valencien*, pp. 75–98.

Grice-Hutchinson, Marjorie 1952, *The School of Salamanca: Readings in Spanish Monetary Theory 1544–1605*, Oxford.

Guardiola, Fr. Juan Benito, 1591, *Tratado de la Nobleza*, Madrid.

Guerrero Mayllo, Ana, 1993, *Familia y Vida Cotidiana de una Elite de Poder: Los Regidores Madrileños en Tiempos de Felipe II*, Madrid.

Guevara, Antonio de, 1539, *Menosprecio de Corte*, re-edited Buenos Aires 1947.

—— 1539–41, *Epístolas Familiares*, 2 vols, Valladolid; re-edited Buenos Aires 1946.

Guggisberg, Hans R. and Windler, Christian (eds), 1995, *Instituciones y Relaciones Sociales en un Municipio de Señorío: Estudios sobre la Cuestión del Poder en Osuna 1750–1808*, Seville.

Guilarte, Alfonso M., 1962, *El Régimen Señorial en el Siglo XVI*, Madrid.

Guillamón Alvarez, Javier, 1981, *Honor y Honra en la España del Siglo XVIII*, Madrid.

Guiral-Hadziiossif, Jacqueline, 1986, *Valence, Port Méditerranéen au XV*e *Siècle*, Paris.

Gurrea, Diego, 1627, *Arte de Enseñar Hijos de Príncipes y Señores*, Lleida.

Gutiérrez Alonso, Adriano, 1989, *Estudio sobre la Decadencia de Castilla: La Ciudad de Valladolid en el Siglo XVII*, Valladolid.

Gutiérrez Nieto, Juan I., 1973, *Las Comunidades como Movimiento Antiseñorial*, Barcelona.

—— 1983, 'De la expansión a la decadencia económica de Castilla y León . . . El arbitrismo agrarista', *El Pasado Histórico de Castilla y León*, II.

Gutiérrez de los Ríos, Gaspar, 1600, *Noticia General para la Estimación de las Artes*, Madrid.

Haedo, Fr. Diego de, 1612, *Topographía e Historia General de Argel*, Valladolid.

Haliczer, Stephen, 1981, *The Comuneros of Castile: The Forging of a Revolution 1475–1521*, Madison, Wisconsin.

—— (ed.) 1987, *Inquisition and Society in Early Modern Europe*, London.

—— 1990, *Inquisition and Society in the Kingdom of Valencia 1478–1834*, Berkeley.

Halperin Donghi, Tulio, 1980, *Un Conflicto Nacional: Moriscos y Cristianos Viejos en Valencia*, Valencia.

Hamilton, Earl J., 1934, *American Treasure and the Price Revolution in Spain 1501–1650*, Cambridge, MA.

Harvey, L.P., 1958, 'The Literary Culture of the Moriscos 1492–1609', D.Phil., Oxford University.

Henningsen, Gustav, 1980, *The Witches' Advocate: Basque Witchcraft and the Inquisition*, Reno, Nevada.

Henningsen, G. and Tedeschi, J. (eds), 1986, *The Inquisition in Early Modern Europe*, Dekalb, Illinois.

Henríquez de Jorquera, Francisco, 1934, *Anales de Granada 1588–1646*, ed. A. Marín Ocete, revised by P. Gan and L. Moreno, 2 vols, Granada 1987.

Hernández, Mauro, 1995, *A la Sombra de la Corona: Poder Local y Oligarquía Urbana (Madrid 1606–1808)*, Madrid.

Hernández Franco, Juan, 1996, *Cultura y Limpieza de Sangre en la España Moderna*, Murcia.

Hernández Rodríguez, Emilio, 1947, *Las Ideas Pedagógicas del Doctor Pedro López de Montoya*, Madrid.

Herr, Richard, 1958, *The Eighteenth-Century Revolution in Spain*, Princeton.

—— 1989, *Rural Change and Royal Finances in Spain at the End of the Old Regime*, Berkeley.

Herrera García, Antonio, 1980, *El Aljarafe Sevillano durante el Antiguo Régimen*, Seville.

Herrera Puga, Pedro, SJ 1971, *Sociedad y Delincuencia en el Siglo de Oro*, Madrid.

Hess, Andrew C., 1978, *The Forgotten Frontier: A History of the Sixteenth-Century Ibero-African Frontier*, Chicago.

Highfield, J.R.L., 1965, 'The Catholic Kings and the Titled Nobility of Castile', in Highfield and others, *Europe in the Late Middle Ages*, London.

Infante-Galán, Juan, 1970, *Los Céspedes y su Señorío de Carrión 1253–1874*, Seville.

Iradiel Murugarren, Paulino, 1974, *Evolución de la Industria Textil Castellana en los Siglos XIII–XVI*, Salamanca.

Israel, Jonathan, 1982, *The Dutch Republic and the Hispanic World 1606–61*, Oxford.

—— 1990, *Empires and Entrepôts: The Dutch, the Spanish Monarchy and the Jews 1585–1713*, London.

Jago, Charles, 1973, 'The Influence of Debt on the Relations between Crown and Aristocracy in Seventeenth-Century Castile', *Economic History Review*, 26, 216–36.

—— 1979, 'The "Crisis of the Aristocracy" in Seventeenth-Century Castile', *Past and Present*, 84, 60–90.

Janer, Florencio, 1857, *Condición Social de los Moriscos de España*, Madrid.

Jesús, Fr. Antonio de, 1688, *Epítome de la Admirable Vida del Ilustre Varón Don Luis de Paz*, Granada.

Jiménez Salas, María, 1958, *Historia de la Asistencia Social en España en la Edad Moderna*, Madrid.

Joly, Barthélemy, 1603–4, 'Voyage en Espagne', *Revue Hispanique*, 20, 460–618.

Jovellanos, Gaspar Melchor de, 1782, 'Cartas del Viaje de Asturias', Obras Escogidas, vol. III, ed. A. del Río, Madrid 1956.

—— 1795, *Informe sobre la Ley Agraria*, ed. J.C. Acerete, Barcelona 1968.

Juliá, S., Ringrose, D. and Segura, C., 1995, *Madrid: Historia de una Capital*, Madrid.

Kagan, Richard L., 1974, *Students and Society in Early Modern Spain*, Baltimore.

—— 1981, *Lawsuits and Litigants in Castile 1500–1700*, Chapel Hill, NC.

—— 1990, *Lucrecia's Dreams: Politics and Prophecy in Sixteenth-Century Spain*, Berkeley.

Kamen, Henry, 1980, *Spain in the Later Seventeenth Century 1665–1700*, London.

—— 1983, *Spain 1469–1714: A Society of Conflict*, London.

—— 1985, *Inquisition and Society in Spain in the Sixteenth and Seventeenth Centuries*, London.

—— 1993a, *The Phoenix and the Flame: Catalonia and the Counter-Reformation*, New Haven.

—— 1993b, *Crisis and Change in Early Modern Spain*, London.

Kany, Charles E., 1932, *Life and Manners in Madrid 1750–1800*, republished New York 1970.

Kedourie, Elie (ed.), 1992, *Spain and the Jews. The Sephardic Experience: 1492 and After*, London.

Keniston, Hayward, 1958, *Francisco de los Cobos, Secretary to the Emperor Charles V*, Pittsburgh.

Kessell, J.L. and others (eds), 1992, *Letters from the New World: Selected Correspondence of Don Diego de Vargas to his Family 1675–1706*, Alburquerque.

Klein, Julius 1920, *The Mesta: A Study in Spanish Economic History 1273–1836*, Cambridge, MA.

Lacoste, Georges de, 1911, *Essai sur les Mejoras*, Paris.

Ladero Quesada, Miguel Angel, 1973, *Andalucía en el Siglo XV*, Madrid.

—— 1976, *Historia de Sevilla, II: La Ciudad Medieval (1248–1492)*, Seville.

—— (ed.) 1977, *Andalucía de la Edad Media a la Moderna*, Madrid.

—— (ed.) 1982, *Estudios en Memoria del Profesor Don Salvador de Moxó*, 2 vols, Madrid.

Lambert-Gorges, Martine (ed.), 1989, *Hidalgos et Hidalguía dans l'Espagne des XVIᵉ–XVIIIᵉ Siècles*, Paris.

—— (ed.) 1993, *Les Elites Locales et l'Etat dans l'Espagne Moderne, XVIe–XIXe Siècles*, Paris.

Lambert-Gorges, M. and Postigo, E., 1985, *Basques et Navarrais dans l'Ordre de Santiago 1580–1620*, Paris.

Lantery, Raimundo de, 1949, *Memorias . . . 1673–1700*, ed. A. Picardo y Gómez, Cadiz.

La Parra López, Santiago, 1992, *Los Borja y los Moriscos*, Valencia.

Lapeyre, Henri, 1955, *Une Famille de Marchands; Les Ruiz*, Paris.

—— 1959, *Géographie de l'Espagne Morisque*, Paris.

Larquié, Claude, 1976, 'Barrios y parroquias urbanas: el ejemplo de Madrid en el siglo XVII', *Anales del Instituto de Estudios Madrileños*, 12, 33–63.

—— 1978, 'Une approche quantitative de la pauvreté: les Madrilènes et la mort au XVIIe siècle', *Annales de Démographie Historique*, 175–96.

Larraz, José, 1963, *La Epoca del Mercantilismo en Castilla 1500–1700*, Madrid.

Layna Serrano, Francisco, 1942, *Historia de Guadalajara y sus Mendozas en los Siglos XV y XVI*, 4 vols, Madrid.

La Vida de Lazarillo de Tormes, 1554, English translation in Penguin Classics as *Two Spanish Picaresque Novels*.

Lea, Henry C., 1905, *A History of the Inquisition of Spain*, republished in 4 vols, New York 1966.

Ledesma, Pedro de, 1601, *Primera Parte de la Summa*, Salamanca.

Le Flem, Jean-Paul, 1972, 'Las cuentas de la Mesta 1510–1709', *Moneda y Crédito*, 121, 23–104.

—— 1976, 'Vraies et fausses splendeurs de l'industrie textile ségovienne (vers 1460–vers 1650)', in M. Spallanzani (ed.), *Produzione, Commercio e Consumo dei Panni di Lana nei Secoli XII–XVIII*, Florence 1976, pp. 525–36.

Lemeunier, Guy, 1993, 'El régimen señorial en cuestión . . . Murcia, siglos XVI–XVIII', in Sarasa Sánchez and Serrano Martín, II, 355–86.

León, Fr. Luis de, 1583, *La Perfecta Casada*, republished Madrid 1938.

León, Pedro de, SJ 1981, *Grandeza y Miseria en Andalucía . . . 1578–1616*, ed. P. Herrera Puga, SJ, Granada.

Leonardo de Argensola, Lupercio, 1604, *Información de los Sucesos del Reino de Aragón en los Años de 1590 y 1591*, ed. Xavier Gil Pujol, Zaragoza 1991.

Lera García, Rafael, 1988, 'Venta de oficos de la Inquisición de Granada 1629–44', *Hispania*, 48, 909–62.

Liehr, Reinhart, 1981, *Sozialgeschichte Spanischer Adelskorporationen: die Maestranzas de Caballería 1670–1808*, Wiesbaden.

Liñán y Verdugo, Antonio, 1620, *Guía y Avisos de Forasteros que Vienen a la Corte*, republished Madrid 1923.

Llorente, Juan Antonio, 1809, *Colección Diplomática de Varios Papeles . . . sobre Dispensas Matrimoniales*, Madrid.

Lockhart, James and Otte, Enrique (eds), 1976, *Letters and People of the Spanish Indies: The Sixteenth Century*, Cambridge.

Loftis, John (ed.), 1979, *The Memoirs of Anne, Lady Halkett and Ann, Lady Fanshawe*, Oxford.

Lohmann Villena, Guillermo 1968, *Les Espinosa: Une Famille d'Hommes d'Affaires en Espagne et aux Indes à l'Epoque de la Colonisation*, Paris.

López, Tomás, 1762–87, 'Relaciones geográficas, topográficas e históricas del Reino de Valencia', ed. V. Castañeda, *Revista de Archivos, Bibliotecas y Museos*, 1919 and 1922.

López Bravo, Mateo, 1616–27 – see Méchoulan, Henry.

López-Cordón, María Victoria, 1978, 'Predicación e inducción política en el siglo XVIII: Fray Diego José de Cádiz', *Hispania*, 38, 71–119.

López García, José Miguel, 1990, *La Transición del Feudalismo al Capitalismo en un Señorio Monástico Castellano; El Abadengo de la Santa Espina 1147–1835*, Valladolid.

López Ontiveros, Antonio, 1974, *Emigración, Propiedad y Paisaje Agrario en la Campiña de Córdoba*, Barcelona.

López Piñero, José María, 1979, *Ciencia y Técnica en la Sociedad Española de los Siglos XVI y XVII*, Barcelona.

López-Salazar, Jerónimo, 1981, 'Una empresa agraria capitalista en la Castilla del siglo XVII', *Hispania*, 41, 354–407.

—— 1986, *Estructuras Agrarias y Sociedad Rural en La Mancha, Siglos XVI–XVII*, Ciudad Real.

—— 1987, *Mesta, Pastos y Conflictos en el Campo de Calatrava, Siglo XVI*, Madrid.

Lorenzo Cadarso, P., 1996, *Los Conflictos Populares en Castilla, Siglos XVI–XVII*, Madrid.

Lorenzo Sanz, E. (ed.) 1986, *Historia de Medina del Campo y su Tierra*, 3 vols, Valladolid.

Lovett, A.W., 1977, *Philip II and Mateo Vázquez de Leca: The Government of Spain 1572–92*, Geneva.

Lunenfeld, Marvin, 1970, *The Council of the Santa Hermandad*, Coral Gables, Florida.

—— 1987, *Keepers of the City: The Corregidores of Isabella I of Castile 1474–1504*, Cambridge.

Luxán, Pedro de, 1550, *Coloquios Matrimoniales*, republished Madrid 1943.

Lynch, John, 1964–9, *Spain under the Habsburgs 1516–1700*, revised edition, 2 vols, Oxford 1991–2.

—— 1989, *Bourbon Spain 1700–1808*, Oxford.

Macanaz, Melchor de, 1713, 'Relación del antiguo gobierno de Aragón, Cataluña y Valencia', ms. of Biblioteca Universitaria, Valencia.

MacKay, Angus, 1972, 'Popular Movements and Pogroms in Fifteenth-Century Castile', *Past and Present*, 55, 33–67.

—— 1977, *Spain in the Middle Ages: From Frontier to Empire 1000–1500*, London.

Madoz, Pascual, 1845–50, *Diccionario Geográfico-estadístico-histórico de España y sus Posesiones de Ultramar*, 4 vols (Castile-La Mancha, Granada and Cordoba), facsimile reprint, Valladolid 1987.

Madramany y Calatayud, Mariano, 1788, *Tratado de la Nobleza de Aragón y Valencia*, Valencia.

—— 1790, *Discurso sobre la Nobleza de las Armas y las Letras*, Madrid.

Madrazo Madrazo, S., 1984, *El Sistema de Transportes en España 1750–1850*, 2 vols, Madrid.

Maiso González, Jesús, 1982, *La Peste Aragonesa de 1648 a 1652*, Zaragoza.

Maiso González, J. and Blasco Rodríguez, R.M., 1984, *Las Estructuras de Zaragoza en el Primer Tercio del Siglo XVIII*, Zaragoza.

Maltby, William S. 1983, *Alba: A Biography of Fernando Alvarez de Toledo, Third Duke of Alba 1507–82*, Berkeley.

Mantecón Movillán, Tomás A., 1997, *Conflictividad y Disciplinamiento Social en la Cantabria Rural del Antiguo Régimen*, Santander.

Manuel de Mello, Francisco, 1645, *Historia de los Movimientos y Separación de Cataluña*, republished Barcelona 1969.

—— 1651, *Carta de Guia de Casados*, ed. Edgar Prestage, Oporto 1923.

Marañón, Gregorio, 1960, *Los Tres Vélez*, Madrid.

Maravall, José Antonio, 1963, *Las Comunidades de Castilla: Una Primera Revolución Moderna*, Madrid.

—— 1975, *La Cultura del Barroco*, Eng. trans., Manchester 1986.

—— 1979, *Poder, Honor y Elites en el Siglo XVII*, Madrid.

—— 1982, *Utopía y Reformismo en la España de los Austrias*, Madrid.

—— 1986, *La Literatura Picaresca desde la Perspectiva Social*, Madrid.

March, José M., 1941, *Niñez y Juventud de Felipe II*, 2 vols, Madrid.

Marcos Martín, Alberto, 1978, *Auge y Declive de un Núcleo Mercantil y Financiero de Castilla la Vieja: Evolución Demográfica de Medina del Campo durante los Siglos XVI y XVII*, Valladolid.

—— 1992, *De Esclavos a Señores*, Valladolid.

Mariana, Juan de, 1599–1601, *Selected writings*, in M. Ballesteros-Gaibrois (ed.), *Juan de Mariana: Pensador y Político*, Ediciones Fe 1939.

Martí Grajales, Francisco, 1927, *Ensayo de un Diccionario . . . de los Poetas que Florecieron en el Reino de Valencia hasta el año 1700*, Madrid.

Martin, Roland, and others, 1978, *Forum et Plaza Mayor dans le Monde Hispanique*, Paris.

Martín de Marco, José A., 1990, *La Institución de Caballeros Hijosdalgo de los Doce Linajes de la Ciudad de Soria*, Soria.

Martínez de Mata, Francisco, 1650–60, *Memoriales y Discursos*, ed. G. Anes, Madrid 1971.

Martínez Ruiz, J.I., 1984, 'Donativos y empréstitos sevillanos a la hacienda real, siglos XVI–XVII', *Revista de Historia Económica*, 2, 233–44.

Martz, Linda, 1983, *Poverty and Welfare in Habsburg Spain: The Example of Toledo*, Cambridge.

—— 1994, 'Pure Blood Statutes in Sixteenth-Century Toledo', *Sefarad*, 54, 83–107.

Mateu Ibars, Josefina, 1963, *Los Virreyes de Valencia*, Valencia.

Matilla Tascón, Antonio (ed.), 1983, *Testamentos de 43 Personajes del Madrid de los Austrias*, Madrid.

Méchoulan, Henry, 1973, *Raison et Altérité chez Fadrique Furió Ceriol, Philosophe Politique du XVIᵉ Siècle*, Paris.

—— 1977, *Mateo López Bravo: Un Socialista Español del Siglo XVII*, Madrid.

Medina, Pedro de, 1548, *Libro de Grandezas y Cosas Memorables de España*, in A. González Palencia (ed.), *Obras de Pedro de Medina*, Madrid 1944.

Mejide Pardo, Antonio, 1960, 'La emigración gallega intrapeninsular en el siglo XVIII', *Estudios de Historia Social de España*, 4, 461–606.

Méndez Silva, Rodrigo, 1645, *Población General de España*, Madrid.

Mendoza, Diego Hurtado de, 1627, *Guerra de Granada*, republished Barcelona 1842.

Menéndez Pidal, Gonzalo, 1951, *Los Caminos en la Historia de España*, Madrid.

Menéndez Pidal, Ramón, 1959, *Los Españoles en la Historia*, Madrid.

Meneses García, Emilio (ed.) 1973, *Correspondencia del Conde de Tendilla*, 2 vols, Madrid.

Mercader, Gaspar, 1600, *El Prado de Valencia*, ed. H. Mérimée, Toulouse 1907.

Mercado, Tomás de, 1569, *La Economía en la Andalucía del Descubrimiento*, ed. Antonio Acosta, Seville 1985.

Mesonero Romanos, Ramón, 1861, *El Antiguo Madrid*, facsimile edn Madrid 1986.

Meyerson, Mark D., 1991, *The Muslims of Valencia in the Age of Fernando and Isabel*, Berkeley.

Mickun, Nira, 1983, *La Mesta au XVIIIe Siècle*, Budapest.

Millán, Jesús, 1984, *Rentistas y Campesinos: Desarrollo Agrario y Tradicionalismo Político en el Sur del País Valenciano 1680–1840*, Alicante.

Molas Ribalta, Pere, 1970, *Los Gremios Barceloneses del Siglo XVIII*, Madrid.

—— 1973, *Societat i Poder Polític a Mataró 1718–1808*, Mataró.

—— 1975, *Economia i Societat al Segle XVIII*, Barcelona.

—— 1977, *Comerç i Estructura Social a Catalunya i València als Segles XVII I XVIII*, Barcelona.

—— (ed.) 1980, *Historia Social de la Administración Española: Estudios sobre los Siglos XVII y XVIII*, Barcelona.

Molinié-Bertrand, Annie, 1985, *Au Siècle d'Or. L'Espagne et ses Hommes: La Population du Royaume de Castille au XVIe Siècle*, Paris.

Momblanch, Francisco de P., 1957, *La Segunda Germanía del Reino de Valencia*, Alicante.

—— 1959, *Historia de la Villa de Muro*, Alicante.

Moncada, Sancho, de 1619, *Restauración Política de España*, ed. J.Vilar, Madrid 1974.

Montemayor, Julian, 1996, *Tolède entre Fortune et Déclin 1530–1640*, Limoges.

Monter, William, 1990, *Frontiers of Heresy: The Spanish Inquisition from the Basque Lands to Sicily*, Cambridge.

Montojo Montojo, Vicente, 1993, *El Siglo de Oro en Cartagena 1480–1640*, Murcia.

Mora Cañada, Adela, 1986, *Monjes y Campesinos: El Señorío de la Valldigna en la Edad Moderna*, Alicante.

Morales, Juan Luis, 1960, *El Niño en la Cultura Española*, 4 vols, Madrid.

Morales Padrón, Francisco, 1977, *Historia de Sevilla: La Ciudad del Quinientos*, Seville.

Morant, Isabel, 1978, *Economía y Sociedad en un Señorío del País Valenciano: El Ducado de Gandía (Siglos XVIII-XIX)*, Gandia.

—— 1984, *El Declive del Señorío: Los Dominios del Ducado de Gandía 1705–1837*, Valencia.

Moreno Casado, Juan, 1948, *Las Ordenanzas Gremiales de Granada en el Siglo XVI*, Granada.

Moreno de Guerra, Juan, 1929, *Bandos en Jerez*, Madrid.

Moreno de Vargas, Bernabé, 1621, *Discursos de la Nobleza de España*, republished Madrid 1971.

Moret, S. and Silvela, L., 1863, *La Familia Foral y la Familia Castellana*, Madrid.

Morineau, Michel, 1985, *Incroyables Gazettes et Fabuleux Métaux: Les Retours des Trésors Américains . . . XVIe–XVIIIe Siècles*, Paris.

Moxó, Salvador de, 1963, *La Alcabala*, Madrid.

—— 1965, *La Disolución del Régimen Señorial*, Madrid.

—— 1971, 'La venta de alcabalas en los reinados de Carlos I y Felipe II', *Anuario de Historia del Derecho Español*, 41, 487–553.

—— 1973a, *Los Antiguos Señoríos de Toledo*, Toledo.

—— 1973b, 'Los señoríos: cuestiones metodológicas que plantea su estudio', *Anuario de Historia del Derecho Español*, 43, 271–309.

Nadal, Jordi, 1966, *La Población Española, Siglos XVI a XX*, Barcelona.

Nadal, J. and Giralt, E., 1960, *La Population Catalane de 1553 a 1714*, Paris.

Nader, Helen, 1979, *The Mendoza Family in the Spanish Renaissance 1350 to 1550*, New Brunswick, NJ.

—— 1990, *Liberty in Absolutist Spain: The Habsburg Sale of Towns 1516–1700*, Baltimore.

Nalle, Sara T., 1992, *God in La Mancha: Religious Reform and the People of Cuenca 1500–1650*, Baltimore.

Narbona Vizcaíno, Rafael, 1992, *Pueblo, Poder y Sexo: Valencia Medieval 1306–1420*, Valencia.

Novísima Recopilacion de las Leyes de España 1805–7, facsimile reprint, 6 vols, Madrid 1976.

Nueva Recopilación de las Leyes destos Reynos 1640, facsimile reprint, 4 vols, Valladolid 1982.

Ochagavía, Diego, 1958–9, 'Matrimonios en el siglo XVIII', *Berceo*, 13, 131–54, and 14, pp. 25–44.

Ochoa, Eugenio de (ed.), 1856–70, *Epistolario Español*, 2 vols, Madrid.

Olaechea, R. and Ferrer Benimeli, J.A., 1978, *El Conde de Aranda*, 2 vols, Zaragoza.

Olmos Tamarit, V. and López Quiles, A. 1987, *Administradors i Administrats: Introducció a l'Economia i a la Societat de la Catarroja del Sis-Cents (1652–8)*, Catarroja.

Ortiz de Zúñiga, Diego, 1677, *Anales Eclesiásticos y Seculares de . . . Sevilla*, Madrid.

Owens, John B., 1980, *Rebelión, Monarquía y Oligarquía Murciana en la Epoca de Carlos V,* Murcia.

Palma, Luis de la, 1595, 'Vida de su Padre', in C.M. Abad, SJ (ed.) *Obras Completas,* Biblioteca de Autores Españoles, vol. 144, Madrid 1961.

Palomeque Torres, A. 1947, 'Pueblas y gobierno del señorío de Valdepusa', *Cuadernos de Historia de España,* 8, 72–139.

Palop Ramos, J.M., 1977, *Hambre y Lucha Antifeudal: Las Crisis de Subsistencia en Valencia (Siglo XVIII),* Madrid.

Parker, Geoffrey, 1972, *The Army of Flanders and the Spanish Road 1567–1659,* Cambridge.

El Pasado Histórico de Castilla y León: Actas del Primer Congreso de Historia de Castilla y León, 3 vols, Burgos 1983.

Pastor, Reyna (ed.), 1990, *Relaciones de Poder, de Producción y Parentesco en la Edad Media y Moderna,* Madrid.

Pelorson, Jean-Marc, 1980, *Les Letrados: Juristes Castillans sous Philippe III,* Poitiers.

Perez, Joseph, 1970, *La Révolution des Comunidades de Castille 1520–1,* Bordeaux.

—— 1988, *Isabelle et Ferdinand, Rois Catholiques d'Espagne,* Paris.

Pérez Aparicio, Carme (ed.), 1988, *Estudios sobre la Población del País Valenciano,* 2 vols, Valencia.

Pérez Estévez, Rosa María, 1976, *El Problema de los Vagos en la España del Siglo XVIII,* Madrid.

Pérez García, José Manuel, 1992, 'Rural Family Life in La Huerta de Valencia during the Eighteenth Century', *Continuity and Change,* 7, 71–101.

Pérez García, Pablo, 1990, *La Comparsa de los Malhechores 1479–1518,* Valencia.

Pérez de Herrasti, Juan Francisco de P., 1750, *Historia de la Casa de Herrasti,* Granada.

Pérez de Heredia, Ignacio, 1985, *Dos Sínodos Segorbinos de la Primera Mitad del Siglo XVII,* Rome.

Pérez de Herrera, Cristóbal, 1598, *Amparo de Pobres,* ed. M. Cavillac, Madrid 1975.

Pérez y López, Antonio Xavier, 1781, *Discurso sobre la Honra y Deshonra Legal,* Madrid.

Pérez Moreda, Vicente, 1980, *Las Crisis de Mortalidad en la España Interior, Siglos XVI–XIX,* Madrid.

Pérez Moreda, V. and Reher, D.S. (eds) 1988, *Demografía Histórica en España,* Madrid.

Pérez Picazo, María Teresa and Lemeunier, Guy, 1984, *El Proceso de Modernización de la Región Murciana, Siglos XVI–XIX,* Murcia.

Peris Albentosa, Tomás, 1989, *Propiedad y Cambio Social: Alzira 1465–1768,* Valencia.

Perry, Mary E., 1980, *Crime and Society in Early Modern Seville,* Hanover, New Hampshire.

—— 1990, *Gender and Disorder in Early Modern Seville,* Princeton.

Perry, M.E. and Cruz, A.J. (eds), 1991, *Cultural Encounters: The Impact of the Inquisition in Spain and the New World,* Berkeley.

Peset, Mariano and Peset, José Luis, 1972, *Muerte en España: Política y Sociedad entre la Peste y el Cólera,* Madrid.

Peset, Mariano and others, 1974–5, 'La demografiá de la peste de Valencia de 1647–1648', *Asclepio,* 26–7, 197–231.

Phillips, Carla R., 1979, *Ciudad Real 1500–1750: Growth, Crisis and Readjustment in the Spanish Economy,* Cambridge, MA.

—— 1986, *Six Galleons for the King of Spain: Imperial Defense in the Early Seventeenth Century,* Baltimore.

Phillips, C.R. and Phillips, W.D. 1997, *Spain's Golden Fleece: Wool Production and the Wool Trade from the Middle Ages to the Nineteenth Century,* Baltimore.

Pike, Ruth, 1966, *The Genoese in Seville and the Opening of the New World*, Ithaca, New York.

—— 1972, *Aristocrats and Traders: Sevillian Society in the Sixteenth Century*, Ithaca, New York.

—— 1983, *Penal Servitude in Early Modern Spain*, Madison, Wisconsin.

Piles Ros, Leopoldo, 1969, *Apuntes para la Historia Económico-social de Valencia durante el Siglo XV*, Valencia.

Pineda, Fr. Juan de, 1589, *Diálogos Familiares de la Agricultura Cristiana*, ed. J. Meseguer Fernández, OFM, 5 vols, Madrid 1963–4.

Pisa, Francisco de, 1617, *Apuntamientos para la Segunda Parte de la Descripción de . . . Toledo*, ed. J. Gómez-Menor, Toledo 1976.

Pitt-Rivers, Julian, 1954, *The People of the Sierra*, London.

Pla Alberola, Primitivo, 1983, *La Población del Marquesado de Guadalest en el Siglo XVII*, Alicante.

Poitrineau, A., 1976, 'La inmigración francesa en el Reino de Valencia (siglos XV–XIX)', *Moneda y Crédito*, 137, 103–33.

Pons Alos, Vicente, 1982, *El Fondo Crespí de Valldaura en el Archivo Condal de Orgaz (1249–1548)*, Valencia.

Pons Fuster, Francisco, 1981, *Aspectos Económico-sociales del Condado de Oliva 1500–1750*, Valencia.

—— 1991, *Místicos, Beatos y Alumbrados: Ribera y la Espiritualidad Valenciana del Siglo XVII*, Valencia.

Ponsot, Pierre, 1985, 'Les comptes d'une hacienda oléicole andalouse au XVIIIe siècle', in J.B. Amalric and P. Ponsot (eds), *L'Exploitation des Grands Domaines dans l'Espagne d'Ancien Régime*, Paris.

—— 1986, *Atlas de Historia Económica de la Baja Andalucía*, Seville.

Ponz, Antonio, 1771–93, *Viage de España*, 18 vols, facsimile edn Madrid n.d.

Porcar, Joan, 1934, *Coses Evengudes en la Ciutat y Regne de València . . . 1589–1629*, ed. V. Castañeda Alcover, 2 vols, Madrid; new abridged edn Valencia 1983.

Postigo Castellanos, Elena, 1988, *Honor y Privilegio en la Corona de Castilla: El Consejo de las Ordenes y los Caballeros de Hábito en el Siglo XVII*, Valladolid.

Pulgar, Fernando del, 1486, *Libro de los Claros Varones de Castilla*, facsimile edn, Madrid 1971; edited, with introduction in English, by R.B. Tate, Oxford 1971.

Quintanilla Raso, María C., 1979, *Nobleza y Señoríos en el Reino de Córdoba: La Casa de Aguilar (Siglos XIV y XV)*, Cordoba.

Ramírez y Las Casas-Deza, Luis M., 1840–2, *Corografía Histórico-estadística de la Provincia y Obispado de Córdoba*, 2 vols, ed. A. López Ontiveros, Cordoba 1986.

Redondo, Augustin, 1976, *Antonio de Guevara (1480?–1545) et l'Espagne de son Temps*, Geneva.

—— (ed.) 1985, *Amours Légitimes, Amours Illégitimes en Espagne (XVIe–XVIIe Siècles)*, Paris.

—— (ed.) 1987, *Autour des Parentés en Espagne aux XVIe et XVIIe Siècles*, Paris.

—— (ed.) 1996, *La Formation de l'Enfant en Espagne aux XVIe et XVIIe Siècles*, Paris.

Redondo, Gullermo, 1982, *Las Corporaciones de Artesanos de Zaragoza en el Siglo XVII*, Zaragoza.

Reglà, Joan 1955, *Felip II i Catalunya*, Barcelona.

—— 1956, *Els Virreis de Catalunya*, Barcelona.

—— 1962, *El Bandolerisme Català del Barroc*, Barcelona.

Reher, David S., 1990, *Town and Country in Pre-industrial Spain: Cuenca 1550–1870*, Cambridge.

—— 1997, *Perspectives on the Family in Spain, Past and Present*, Oxford.

Relaciones de los Pueblos de España Ordenadas por Felipe II: Ciudad Real, ed. Carmelo Viñas and Ramón Paz, Madrid 1971.

Relazioni di Ambasciatori Veneti al Senato, ed. Luigi Firpo, vol. VIII (1497–1598) and IX (1602–31), Turin 1978–81.

Revah, I.S., 1971, 'La controverse sur les statuts de pureté de sang', *Bulletin Hispanique,* 75, 263–306.

Ribadeneira, Pedro de, SJ, 1572, *Vida de Ignacio de Loyola,* republished Madrid 1946.

Ringrose, David 1970, *Transportation and Economic Stagnation in Spain 1750–1850,* Durham, NC.

—— 1983, *Madrid and the Spanish Economy 1560–1850,* Berkeley.

—— 1996, *Spain, Europe and the 'Spanish Miracle' 1700–1900,* Cambridge.

Robres Lluch, Ramón, 1960, *San Juan de Ribera,* Barcelona.

Ródenas Vilar, Rafael, 1990, *Vida Cotidiana y Negocio en la Segovia del Siglo de Oro: El Mercader Juan de Cúellar,* Valladolid.

Rodríguez Díaz, Laura 1973, 'The Spanish Riots of 1766', *Past and Present,* 59, 117–46.

—— 1975, *Reforma e Ilustración en la España del Siglo XVIII: Pedro Rodríguez de Campomanes,* Madrid.

Rodríguez García, Santiago, 1959, *El Arte de las Sedas Valencianas en el Siglo XVIII,* Valencia.

Rodríguez-Salgado, M.J., 1991, 'The Court of Philip II of Spain', in R.G. Asch and A.M. Birke (eds), *Princes, Patronage and the Nobility,* Oxford, pp. 207–44.

Rodríguez Sánchez, Angel, 1977, *Cáceres: Población y Comportamientos Demográficos en el Siglo XVI,* Caceres.

Rosselló, V.M., Brines, J. and Guía, L. (eds), 1988, *Homenatge al Doctor Sebastià Garcia Martínez,* 3 vols, Valencia.

Roth, Norman, 1995, *Conversos, the Inquisition and the Expulsion of the Jews from Spain,* Madison, Wisconsin.

Royo Martínez, José, 1988, *Un Señorío Valenciano de la Orden del Hospital: La Encomienda de Torrent,* Valencia.

Ruiz, Teófilo, 1981, *Sociedad y Poder en Castilla: Burgos en la Baja Edad Media,* Madrid.

—— 1994, *Crisis and Continuity: Land and Town in Late Medieval Castile,* Philadelphia.

Ruiz Hernando, Juan Antonio 1982, *Historia del Urbanismo en la Ciudad de Segovia del Siglo XII al XIX,* 2 vols, Segovia.

Ruiz Martín, Felipe, 1965, 'La empresa capitalista en la industria textil castellana', *III° Conférence Internationale d'Histoire Economique,* Paris, pp. 267–76.

—— 1990a, *Pequeño Capitalismo, Gran Capitalismo: Simón Ruiz y sus Negocios en Florencia,* Barcelona.

—— 1990b, *Las Finanzas de la Monarquía Hispánica en Tiempos de Felipe IV,* Madrid.

Ruiz Torres, Pedro, 1981, *Señores y Propietarios: Cambio Social en el Sur del País Valenciano 1650–1850,* Valencia.

Saavedra, Pegerto, 1985, *Economía, Política y Sociedad en Galicia: La Provincia de Mondoñedo 1480–1830,* Madrid.

Sáez, Emilio (ed.), 1985, *La Ciudad Hispánica durante los Siglos XIII al XVI,* 2 vols, Madrid.

Salavert, Vicent and Graullera, Vicent, 1990, *Professió, Ciència i Societat a la València del Segle XVI,* Barcelona.

Salavert, Vicent and Navarro, Jorge, 1992, *La Sanitat Municipal a València, Segles XIII–XX,* Valencia.

Salazar, Eugenio de 1866, *Cartas . . . escritas a muy particulares amigos suyos,* published by Sociedad de Bibliófilos Españoles, Madrid.

Sales, Núria 1962, *Història dels Mossos d'Esquadra*, Barcelona.

—— 1984, *Senyors Bandolers, Miquelets i Botiflers: Estudis sobre la Catalunya dels Segles XVI al XVIII*, Barcelona.

Salomon, Noël 1964, *La Campagne de Nouvelle Castille à la Fin du XVIe Siècle d'après les Relaciones Topográficas*, Paris; Spanish edition Barcelona 1973.

—— 1965, *Recherches sur le Thème Paysan dans la Comedia au Temps de Lope de Vega*, Barcelona.

Salvá Ballester, Adolf, 1988, *De la Marina a la Muntanya*, ed. R. Alemany, Alicante.

Salvador, Emilia 1972, *La Economía Valenciana en el Siglo XVI: Comercio de Importación*, Valencia.

Sánchez, Matías SJ, 1740, *El Padre de Familias Brevemente Instruido en sus Muchas Obligaciones*, 2nd edn Madrid 1792.

Sánchez, Tomás SJ, 1592, *De Sancto Matrimonii Sacramento*, 2nd edn, 3 vols, Madrid 1604–5; and extracts in J.P. Migne (ed.), *Theologiae Cursus Completus*, vol. 25, Paris 1860.

Sánchez Albornoz, Nicolás, 1959, 'Un testigo del comercio indiano: Tomás de Mercado y Nueva España', *Revista de Historia de América*, 47, 95–142.

Sánchez-Montes, Francisco, 1989, *La Población Granadina del Siglo XVII*, Granada.

Sanchis Guarner, Manuel, 1972, *La Ciutat de València: Síntesi d'Història i de Geografia Urbana*, 5th edn, Valencia 1989.

Sancho de Sopranis, Hipólito, 1960, *Juegos de Toros y Cañas en Jerez de la Frontera*, Jerez.

Sancho de Sopranis, H. and J. de la Lastra Terry, 1965, *Historia de Jerez de la Frontera*, vol. II: *El Siglo de Oro*, Jerez.

Santos Isern, Vicente M., 1981, *Cara y Cruz de la Sedería Valenciana (Siglos XVIII–XIX)*, Valencia.

Sarasa Sánchez, E. and Serrano Martín, E. (eds) 1993, *Señorío y Feudalismo en la Península Ibérica (Siglos XII-XIX)*, 4 vols, Zaragoza.

Saugnieux, Joël (ed.) 1988, *Foi et Lumières dans l'Espagne du XVIIIᵉ Siècle*, Lyon.

La Segona Germania. Col.loqui Internacional, Valencia 1994.

Sempere y Guarinos, Juan, 1805, *Historia de los Vínculos y Mayorazgos*, Madrid.

—— 1806, *Memoria sobre las Causas de la Decadencia de la Seda en el Reyno de Granada*, Granada.

Sentaurens, Jean, 1975, 'Séville dans la seconde moitié du XVIe siècle', *Bulletin Hispanique*, 77, 321–90.

—— 1984, *Séville et le Théâtre, de la Fin du Moyen Age à la Fin du XVIIIᵉ Siècle*, 2 vols, Bordeaux.

Serra i Puig, Eva 1988, *Pagesos i Senyors a la Catalunya del Segle XVII: Baronia de Sentmenat 1590–1729*, Barcelona.

Serrano y Sanz, M. (ed.), 1905, *Autobiografías y Memorias*, Madrid.

Sherwood, Joan, 1988, *Poverty in Eighteenth-Century Spain: The Women and Children of the Inclusa*, Toronto.

Sicroff, Albert, 1960, *Les Controverses des Statuts de 'Pureté de Sang' en Espagne du XVᵉ au XVIIIᵉ Siècle*, Paris.

Sierra, Luis, SJ, 1964, *La Reacción del Episcopado Español ante los Decretos de Matrimonios del Ministro Urquijo de 1799 a 1813*, Bilbao.

Las Siete Partidas del Rey Don Alfonso el Sabio, facsimile edn, 3 vols, Madrid 1972.

Simón Díaz, José, 1952–9, *Historia del Colegio Imperial de Madrid*, 2 vols, Madrid.

Simon Tarrés, Antoni, 1987, 'La familia catalana del antiguo régimen', in *La Familia en la España Mediterránea, 65–92*.

—— 1991, *Cavallers i Ciutadans a la Catalunya del Cinc-Cents*, Barcelona.

288

La Sociedad Castellana en la Baja Edad Media, Madrid 1969.

Soria, Jeroni, 1960, *Dietari*, ed. F. de P. Momblanch, Valencia.

Soria Mesa, Enrique, 1995, *La Venta de Señoríos en el Reino de Granada bajo los Austrias*, Granada.

—— 1997, *Señores y Oligarcas: Los Señoríos del Reino de Granada en la Edad Moderna*, Granada.

Soubeyroux, Jacques 1978, *Paupérisme et Rapports Sociaux à Madrid au XVIIIe Siècle*, 2 vols, Paris.

Tarazona, Pere Hieroni, 1581, *Institucions dels Furs y Privilegis*, Valencia.

Tejeda y Ramiro, Juan (ed.), 1849–55, *Colección de Cánones y de Todos los Concilios de la Iglesia Española*, 5 vols, Madrid.

Santa Teresa de Jesús, 1562, *La Vida de . . .*, republished Madrid 1943.

—— 1573, *Libro de las Fundaciones*, republished Buenos Aires 1951.

Terrades, Ignasi, 1984, *El Món Històric de les Masies*, Barcelona.

Thompson, I.A.A., 1976, *War and Government in Habsburg Spain 1560–1620*, London.

—— 1992, *War and Society in Habsburg Spain*, London.

Thompson, I.A.A. and Yun Casalilla, B. (eds), 1994, *The Castilian Crisis of the Seventeenth Century*, Cambridge.

Tomás y Valiente, Francisco, 1969, *El Derecho Penal de la Monarquía Absoluta (Siglos XVI, XVII y XVIII)*, Madrid.

—— 1982, *Gobierno e Instituciones en la España del Antiguo Regímen*, Madrid.

Torras i Ribé, Josep M. 1976, *Evolució Social i Econòmica d'una Família Catalana de l'Antic Règim: Els Padró d'Igualada 1642–1862*, Barcelona.

—— 1983, *Els Municipis Catalans de l'Antic Règim 1453–1808*, Barcelona.

Torres, Xavier 1993, *Nyerros i Cadells: Bàndols i Bandolerisme a la Catalunya Moderna (1590–1640)*, Barcelona.

Torres Balbás, Leopoldo and Terrasse, Henri (n.d.), *Ciudades Hispano-Musulmanas*, 2 vols, Madrid.

Torres López, M., 1932, 'El origen del señorío solariego de Benamejí', *Boletín de la Universidad de Granada*, 545–76.

Torres Villarroel, Diego de, 1743, *Vida*, ed. Guy Mercadier, Madrid 1972.

Torró Abad, Josep, 1992, *La Formació d'un Espai Feudal: Alcoi de 1245 a 1305*, Valencia.

Torró Gil, Lluís, 1994, *Abans de la Industria: Alcoi als Inicis del Sis-Cents*, Alicante.

Townsend, Joseph, 1791, *A Journey through Spain in the Years 1786 and 1787*, 3 vols, London; Spanish translation in García Mercadal, vol. III.

Tramoyeres Blasco, Luis, 1889, *Instituciones Gremiales: Su Origen y Organización en Valencia*, Valencia.

Trillo de San José, Carmen, 1992, 'La implantación castellana en la Alpujarra: análisis de una política señorial en el Reino de Granada', *Hispania*, 52, 397–432.

Ulloa, Modesto, 1977, *La Hacienda Real de Castilla en el Reinado de Felipe II*, 2nd edn, Madrid.

Ungerer, Gustav, 1956, *Anglo-Spanish Relations in Tudor Literature*, reprinted New York 1972.

Val Valdivieso, María I. del, 1986, 'Medina del Campo en la época de los Reyes Católicos', in E. Lorenzo Sanz (ed.), *Historia de Medina del Campo*, I, 231–314.

Valdeavellano, Luis G. de 1969, *Orígenes de la Burguesía en la España Medieval*, Madrid.

Valdeón Baruque, Julio, 1975, *Los Conflictos Sociales en el Reino de Castilla en los Siglos XIV y XV*, Madrid.

Valverde de Arrieta, Juan 1578, *Despertador, que trata de la grande fertilidad, riqueza, baratos, armas y cavallos que España solía tener*, Madrid.

Vassberg, David, 1984, *Land and Society in Golden Age Castile*, Cambridge.

—— 1996, *The Village and the Outside World in Golden Age Castile*, Cambridge.

Vázquez de Prada, Valentín 1978, *Historia Económica y Social de España*, vol. III: *Los Siglos XVI y XVII*, Madrid.

Vega, Lope de, 1604–18, *Fuenteovejuna*.

—— 1614, *Peribáñez y el Comendador de Ocaña*, ed. Teresa Ferrer, Barcelona 1990.

Vercher i Lletí, Salvador 1992, *Casa, Família i Comunitat Veïnal a l'Horta de València: Catarroja durant el Regnat de Ferran el Catòlic (1479–1516)*, Catarroja (Valencia).

Vicens Vives, Jaime, 1955, *Manual de Historia Económica de España*, revised edn (with J. Nadal), Barcelona 1959; English edn Princeton 1969.

—— (ed.) 1972, *Historia de España y América: Social y Económica*, 5 vols, Barcelona.

Vich, Alvaro y Diego de, 1921, *Dietario Valenciano (1619 a 1632)*, ed. F. Almarche Vázquez, Valencia.

Viciana, Martín de, 1563–66, *Crónica de la Inclita y Coronada Ciudad de Valencia*, ed. S. García Martínez, 5 vols, Valencia 1972–83.

Viciano Navarro, Pau, 1989, *Catarroja: Una Senyoria de l'Horta de València en l'Epoca Tardo-medieval*, Catarroja (Valencia).

Vigil, Mariló, 1986, *La Vida de las Mujeres en los Siglos XVI y XVII*, Madrid.

Vilar, Jean, 1971, 'Formes et tendances de l'opposition sous Olivares: Lisón y Viedma, defensor de la patria', *Mélanges de la Casa de Velázquez*, 7, 263–94.

Vilar, Juan Bautista, 1981, *Orihuela: Una Ciudad Valenciana en la España Moderna*, 3 vols, Murcia.

Vilar, Pierre, 1962, *La Catalogne dans l'Espagne Moderne*, 3 vols; Catalan edition, 4 vols, Barcelona 1964–8.

—— 1964, *Crecimiento y Desarrollo. Economía e Historia. Reflexiones sobre el Caso Español*, Barcelona.

—— 1982, *Hidalgos, Amotinados y Guerrilleros: Pueblo y Poderes en la Historia de España*, Barcelona.

Villas Tinoco, Siro, 1982, *Los Gremios Malagueños (1700–46)*, 2 vols, Malaga.

Viñas y Mey, Carmelo 1941, *El Problema de la Tierra en la España de los Siglos XVI–XVII*, Madrid.

Vincent, Bernard, 1985, *Andalucía en la Edad Moderna: Economía y Sociedad*, Granada.

—— 1987, *Minorías y Marginados en la España del Siglo XVI*, Granada.

Vives, Juan Luis 1524, *Instrucción de la Mujer Cristiana*, re-edited Buenos Aires 1943.

Way, Ruth (assisted by Margaret Simmons), 1962, *A Geography of Spain and Portugal*, London.

Windler, Christian, 1992, *Lokale Eliten, seigneurialer Adel und Reformabsolutismus in Spanien 1760–1808: das Beispiel Niederandalusien*, Stuttgart.

Weisser, Michael, 1976, *The Peasants of the Montes*, Chicago.

Ximénez Patón, Bartolomé, 1628, *Historia de la Antigua y Continuada Nobleza de la Ciudad de Jaén*, facsimile edn Jaén 1983.

—— 1638, *Discurso en Favor del Santo y Loable Estatuto de la Limpieza*, Granada.

Yerushalmi, Yosef Hayim, 1981, *From Spanish Court to Italian Ghetto*, London.

Yun Casalilla, Bartolomé, 1987, *Sobre la Transición al Capitalismo en Castilla. Economía y Sociedad en Tierra de Campos 1500–1830*, Valladolid.

Zabalza Seguín, Ana, 1994, *Aldeas y Campesinos en la Navarra Prepirenaica 1550–1817*, Pamplona.

Zapata, Luis, 1859, *Miscelánea*, MHE, vol. 11, Madrid.

Zayas, María de, 1637–47, *Novelas Completas*, ed. María Martínez del Portal, Barcelona 1973.

INDEX